The Embedded Project Cookbook

A Step-by-Step Guide for Microcontroller Projects

John T. Taylor
Wayne T. Taylor

Apress®

The Embedded Project Cookbook: A Step-by-Step Guide for Microcontroller Projects

John T. Taylor
Covington, GA, USA

Wayne T. Taylor
Golden, CO, USA

ISBN-13 (pbk): 979-8-8688-0326-0
https://doi.org/10.1007/979-8-8688-0327-7

ISBN-13 (electronic): 979-8-8688-0327-7

Copyright © 2024 by The Editor(s) (if applicable) and The Author(s), under exclusive license to APress Media, LLC, part of Springer Nature

This work is subject to copyright. All rights are reserved by the Publisher, whether the whole or part of the material is concerned, specifically the rights of translation, reprinting, reuse of illustrations, recitation, broadcasting, reproduction on microfilms or in any other physical way, and transmission or information storage and retrieval, electronic adaptation, computer software, or by similar or dissimilar methodology now known or hereafter developed.

Trademarked names, logos, and images may appear in this book. Rather than use a trademark symbol with every occurrence of a trademarked name, logo, or image we use the names, logos, and images only in an editorial fashion and to the benefit of the trademark owner, with no intention of infringement of the trademark.

The use in this publication of trade names, trademarks, service marks, and similar terms, even if they are not identified as such, is not to be taken as an expression of opinion as to whether or not they are subject to proprietary rights.

While the advice and information in this book are believed to be true and accurate at the date of publication, neither the authors nor the editors nor the publisher can accept any legal responsibility for any errors or omissions that may be made. The publisher makes no warranty, express or implied, with respect to the material contained herein.

> Managing Director, Apress Media LLC: Welmoed Spahr
> Acquisitions Editor: Melissa Duffy
> Development Editor: James Markham
> Editorial Project Manager: Gryffin Winkler

Cover designed by eStudioCalamar

Cover image designed by Tom Christensen from Pixabay

Distributed to the book trade worldwide by Springer Science+Business Media New York, 1 New York Plaza, Suite 4600, New York, NY 10004-1562, USA. Phone 1-800-SPRINGER, fax (201) 348-4505, e-mail orders-ny@springer-sbm.com, or visit www.springeronline.com. Apress Media, LLC is a California LLC and the sole member (owner) is Springer Science + Business Media Finance Inc (SSBM Finance Inc). SSBM Finance Inc is a **Delaware** corporation.

For information on translations, please e-mail booktranslations@springernature.com; for reprint, paperback, or audio rights, please e-mail bookpermissions@springernature.com.

Apress titles may be purchased in bulk for academic, corporate, or promotional use. eBook versions and licenses are also available for most titles. For more information, reference our Print and eBook Bulk Sales web page at http://www.apress.com/bulk-sales.

Any source code or other supplementary material referenced by the author in this book is available to readers on GitHub. For more detailed information, please visit https://www.apress.com/gp/services/source-code.

If disposing of this product, please recycle the paper

To Sally, Bailey, Kelly, and Todd.

—*J.T.*

Table of Contents

About the Authors xiii

About the Technical Reviewer xv

Preface xvii

Chapter 1: Introduction 1
    Software Development Processes 2
    Software Development Life Cycle 5
    Outputs and Artifacts 7
    What You'll Need to Know 8
    Coding in C and C++ 9
    What Toys You Will Need 9
    Regulated Industries 10
    What Is Not Covered 11
    Conclusion 12

Chapter 2: Requirements 13
    Formal Requirements 14
    Functional vs. Nonfunctional 16
    Sources for Requirements 16
    Challenges in Collecting Requirements 18
    Exiting the Requirements Step 19
    GM6000 19
    Summary 22

TABLE OF CONTENTS

Chapter 3: Analysis 25

System Engineering 26
GM6000 System Architecture 26
Software Architecture 28
Moving from Inputs to Outputs 30
Hardware Interfaces 31
Performance Constraints 32
Programming Languages 34
Subsystems 35
Subsystem Interfaces 40
Process Model 42
Functional Simulator 45
Cybersecurity 48
Memory Allocation 49
Inter-thread and Inter-process Communication 50
File and Directory Organization 51
Localization and Internationalization 52
Requirement Traceability 54
Summary 56

Chapter 4: Software Development Plan 59

Project-Independent Processes and Standards 60
Project-Specific Processes and Standards 61
Additional Guidelines 62
Care and Feeding of Your SDP 62
SDP for the GM6000 63
Housekeeping 64

TABLE OF CONTENTS

Roles and Responsibilities 64
Software Items 65
Documentation Outputs 66
Requirements 68
Software Development Life Cycle Processes 69
Cybersecurity 70
Tools 71
Software Configuration Management (SCM) 71
Testing 73
Deliverables 74
Summary 75

Chapter 5: Preparation 77
GitHub Projects 78
GitHub Wiki 79
Continuous Integration Requirements 82
Jenkins 84
Summary 86

Chapter 6: Foundation 89
SCM Repositories 90
Source Code Organization 90
Build System and Scripts 92
Skeleton Applications 94
CI "Build-All" Script 94
Software Detailed Design 95
Summary 98

TABLE OF CONTENTS

Chapter 7: Building Applications with the Main Pattern **101**

About the Main Pattern 102

    Operating System Abstraction Layer 103

    Hardware Abstraction Layer 104

More About Main 105

Implementing Main 106

    Application Variant 110

Marketing Abstraction Layer 112

Ajax Main and Eros Main 113

Build Scripts 115

Preprocessor 119

Simulator 119

The Fine Print 120

Summary 121

Chapter 8: Continuous Integration Builds **123**

Example Build-All Scripts for GM6000 125

    The CI Server 125

    Directory Organization 125

    Naming Conventions 126

    Windows build_all Script 129

    Linux build_all Script 133

Summary 135

Chapter 9: Requirements Revisited **137**

Analysis 138

Requirements vs. Design Statements 139

    Design Statement for Control Algorithm 140

Design Statement for User Interface 142
Missing Formal Requirements 144
Requirements Tracing 146
Summary 149

Chapter 10: Tasks 153

1) Requirements 154
2) Detailed Design 155
3) Source Code and Unit Tests 155
4) Code Review 156
5) Merge 156
The Definition of Done 156
Task Granularity 158
Tasks, Tickets, and Agile 160
Summary 162

Chapter 11: Just-in-Time Detailed Design 165

Examples 168
    Subsystem Design 168
    I2C Driver Design 173
    Button Driver Design 174
    Fuzzy Logic Controller Design 175
    Graphics Library 177
    Screen Manager Design 178
Design Reviews 182
    Review Artifacts 182
Summary 184

TABLE OF CONTENTS

Chapter 12: Coding, Unit Tests, and Pull Requests 187
Check-In Strategies 189
Pull Requests 189
Granularity 191
Examples 191
    I2C Driver 191
    Screen Manager 196
Summary 200

Chapter 13: Integration Testing 203
Smoke Tests 208
    Simulator 208
Summary 210

Chapter 14: Board Support Package 213
Compiler Toolchain 214
Encapsulating the Datasheet 215
Encapsulating the Board Schematic 216
BSPs in Practice 217
    Structure 218
    Dos and Don'ts 220
Bootloader 222
Summary 223

Chapter 15: Drivers 225
Binding Times 226
Public Interface 227
Hardware Abstract Layer (HAL) 231
    Facade 231

TABLE OF CONTENTS

    Separation of Concerns 238

    Polymorphism 256

  Dos and Don'ts 263

  Summary 265

Chapter 16: Release 267

  About Builds and Releases 270

  Tightening Up the Change Control Process 273

  Software Bill of Materials (SBOM) 274

  Anomalies List 276

  Release Notes 276

  Deployment 277

    Over-the-Air (OTA) Updates 278

  QMS Deliverables 280

  Archiving Build Tools 282

  Summary 283

Appendix A: Getting Started with the Source Code 285

Appendix B: Running the Example Code 313

Appendix C: Introduction to the Data Model Architecture 349

Appendix D: LHeader and LConfig Patterns 353

Appendix E: CPL C++ Framework 363

Appendix F: NQBP2 Build System 411

Appendix G: RATT 437

Appendix H: GM6000 Requirements 449

Appendix I: GM6000 System Architecture 467

xi

TABLE OF CONTENTS

Appendix J: GM6000 Software Architecture **473**

Appendix K: GM6000 Software Development Plan **507**

Appendix L: GM6000 Software Detailed Design (Initial Draft) **533**

Appendix M: GM6000 Software Detailed Design (Final Draft) **545**

Appendix N: GM6000 Fuzzy Logic Temperature Control **611**

Appendix O: Software C/C++ Embedded Coding Standard **621**

Appendix P: GM6000 Software Requirements Trace Matrix **645**

Appendix Q: GM6000 Software Bill of Materials **659**

Appendix R: GM6000 Software Release Notes **665**

Index **671**

About the Authors

John Taylor has been an embedded developer for over 30 years. He has worked as a firmware engineer, technical lead, system engineer, software architect, and software development manager for companies such as Ingersoll Rand, Carrier, Allen-Bradley, Hitachi Telecom, Emerson, AMD, and several startup companies. He has developed firmware for products that include HVAC control systems, telecom SONET nodes, IoT devices, microcode for communication chips, and medical devices. He is the co-author of five US patents and holds a bachelor's degree in mathematics and computer science.

Wayne Taylor has been a technical writer for 27 years. He has worked with companies such as IBM, Novell, Compaq, HP, EMC, SanDisk, and Western Digital. He has documented compilers, LAN driver development, storage system deployment and maintenance, and dozens of low-level and system management APIs. He also has ten years of experience as a software development manager. He is the co-author of two US patents and holds master's degrees in English and human factors.

About the Technical Reviewer

Jeff Gable is an embedded software consultant for the medical device industry, where he helps medical device startups develop bullet-proof software to take their prototypes through FDA submission and into production. Combining his expertise in embedded software, FDA design controls, and practical Agile methodologies, Jeff helps existing software teams be more effective and efficient or handles the entire software development and documentation effort for a new device.

Jeff has spent his entire career doing safety-critical product development in small, cross-disciplinary teams. After stints in aerospace, automotive, and medical, he founded Gable Technology, Inc. in 2019 to focus on medical device startups. He also co-hosts the Agile Embedded podcast, where he discusses how device developers don't have to choose between time-to-market and quality.

In his spare time, Jeff enjoys rock climbing, woodworking, and spending time with his wife and two small children.

Preface

My personal motivation for writing this cookbook is so that I never have to start an embedded project from scratch again. I am tired of reinventing the wheel every time I move to a new project, or new team, or new company. I have started over many times, and every time I find myself doing all the same things over again. This, then, is a cookbook for all the "same things" I do—all the same things that I inevitably have to do. In a sense, these are my recipes for success.

On my next "new project," I plan to literally copy and paste from the code and documentation templates I have created for this book. And for those bits that are so different that a literal copy and paste won't work, I plan to use this cookbook as a "reference design" for generating the new content. For example, suppose for my next project I need a hash table (i.e., a dictionary) that does not use dynamic memory allocation. My options would be

1. Reuse or copy an existing module from this framework.

2. Adapt an existing module to meet my specific requirements.

3. Design and write the code from scratch.

For me, the perfect world choice is option one—copy, paste into a new file, and then "save as" with a new file name. Option two would be to use the material in this book as a reference design. Start with one of the code or documentation templates and adapt it to the needs of the new project. And option three would be the last resort. Been there; done that; don't want to do it ever again.

PREFACE

Even though nothing is ever a perfect world choice, I know from experience that I can reuse some of this code wholesale with hardly any changes. In fact, the entire impetus behind my early GitHub projects was to have a reusable repository of source code that was not owned by someone else that I could freely use as needed—both professionally and personally. And because you bought this book, I'm providing you with a BSD license to all the source code so you can use and reuse just as freely. And, in addition to the raw, reusable blocks of source code, I also have the building blocks for the framework, which is the automated test tools and simulators required for building and releasing embedded projects. In some ways, I think of this cookbook as the user manual for all my GitHub toys.

Beyond the obvious advantage of not having to rewrite code, there is also the advantage of having example documents and other materials that I can use when mentoring or training other engineers. In the past, when I've been trying to explain these concepts to new team members, it involved a lot of hand waving and hastily drawn boxes and arrows on the whiteboard. But now I have tangible examples of what I'm talking about at my fingertips. It's yet another thing I don't have to start from scratch. The next time I need to train or explain any of the best practices contained in this cookbook, I plan to say, "And if you want a better example of what I'm talking about, I know a really great book on this topic...."

—John Taylor, Covington, Georgia, March 2024

CHAPTER 1

Introduction

The purpose of this cookbook is to enable the reader to never have to develop a microcontroller software project from scratch. By a *project*, I mean everything that is involved in releasing a commercially viable product that meets industry standards for quality. A project, therefore, includes noncode artifacts such as software processes, software documentation, continuous integration, design reviews and code reviews, etc. Of course, source code is included in this as well. And it is production-quality source code; it incorporates essential middleware such as an OS abstraction layer (OSAL), containers that don't use dynamic memory, inter-thread communication modules, a command-line console, and support for a functional simulator.

The book is organized in the approximate chronological order of a software development life cycle. In fact, it begins with a discussion of the software development process and the software development life cycle. However, the individual chapters are largely independent and can stand alone. Or, said another way, you are encouraged to navigate the chapters in whatever order seems most interesting to you.

> **Note** The focus of this cookbook is on software development—not the processes or deliverables of other disciplines. Other disciplines that participate in the process are typically only discussed in the context of their providing inputs for project artifacts or their consuming of project artifacts.

CHAPTER 1   INTRODUCTION

Software Development Processes

Software development processes are different everywhere. No two organizations create software the same way, and in some organizations and companies, no two teams do it the same way. Additionally, processes that are intended to improve quality are not uniformly implemented: neither by companies in the same industry segment, nor, sometimes, by members of the same team. Consequently, there is no one-size-fits-all model or solution for professional software development. And yet, everybody ends up doing the same things.

For example, Figure 1-1 shows a straightforward model for developing a bit of software for an embedded system.

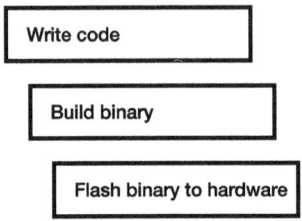

Figure 1-1. *A simple development model for embedded software*

At your discretion, you could add additional steps, or your organization might require additional processes. So the model might be expanded to something like what is shown in Figure 1-2.

CHAPTER 1   INTRODUCTION

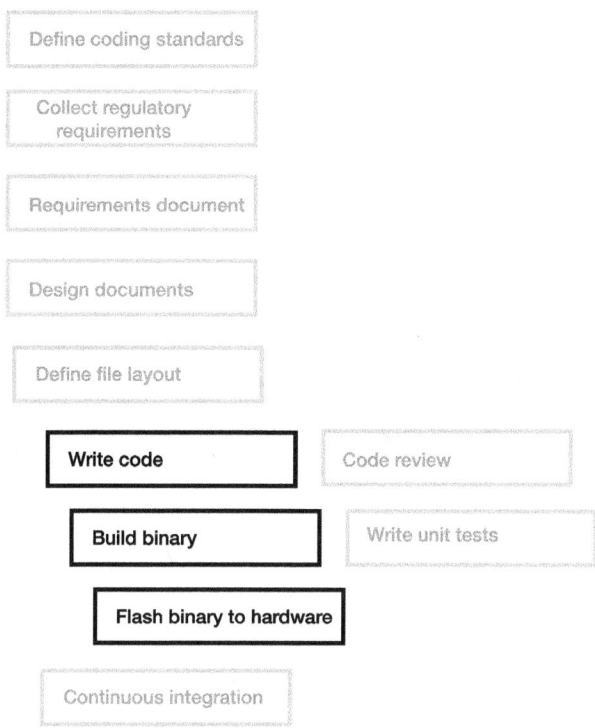

Figure 1-2. *Additional steps and processes for a simple development model*

The more additional processes and steps you add, the more sophisticated your development process becomes, and—if you add the right additional processes—the better the results. Figure 1-3 illustrates this continuum.

CHAPTER 1   INTRODUCTION

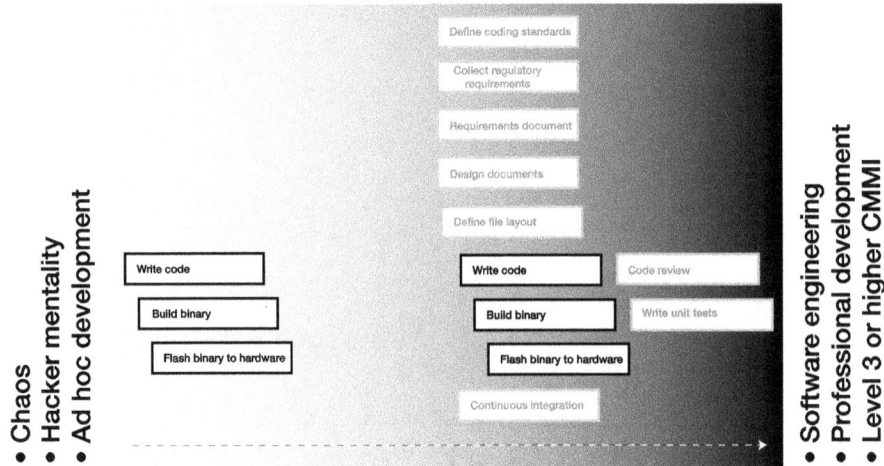

Figure 1-3. *A continuum of software development processes and practices*

There is no perfect set of processes. However, in my career, I have found myself using the same processes and steps over and over again. This book, then, is a collection of the steps and processes that I have found essential for developing embedded software in a commercial environment. I recommend them to you as an effective, efficient way to develop great code. Of course, you can skip any of these recommended steps or phases, but every time you do, there's a good chance that you're buying yourself pain, frustration, and extra work down the road. It is easy to say, "Oh, I can just clean up and refactor this module later so it meets our standards and conventions," but for me, clean-up refactoring is painful, and I have found it often gets skipped for the sake of schedule pressure. Personally, I try very hard not to skip steps because if I do, things don't get done any faster, and all I've done is start the project with technical debt.

In the end, it will come down to how willing you are to take on and adopt the engineering disciplines that these "software recipes" embody. Unfortunately, many people equate discipline with "doing stuff they don't want to do." And, yes, it's not fun writing architecture documentation or automated unit tests and the like, but it's the difference between being a hacker or a professional, spit-and-bailing wire or craftsmanship.

Software Development Life Cycle

Depending on your experience and background, you may have experienced four to eight stages in the software development life cycle (SDLC). This book focuses on the work, or stages, that runs from articulating the initial business needs of the product through the first production release of the software. My definition of the SDLC has the following three software development stages:

- Planning
- Construction
- Release

These three stages are waterfall in nature. That is, you typically don't want to start the construction stage until the planning stage has completed. That said, work within each stage is very much iterative, so if new requirements (planning) arise in the middle of coding (construction), the new requirements can be accommodated in the next iteration through the construction phase. To some, in this day of Agile development, it might seem like a step backward to employ even a limited waterfall approach, but I would make the following counter arguments:

- An embedded project—that is, one with limited resources and infrastructure—absolutely requires a certain amount of upfront planning and architecture before active coding begins.

CHAPTER 1   INTRODUCTION

- 80% or more of the work occurs in the construction stage, which is iterative and fits the Agile model.

- You will experience fewer hiccups in the construction stage if you're building on a solid foundation that was established during the planning stage.

Figure 1-4 outlines my software development life cycle and provides some representative activities that occur in each one. Note that only activities that are the responsibility of the software team are shown. That is, activities related to hardware development or formal software verification are not shown.

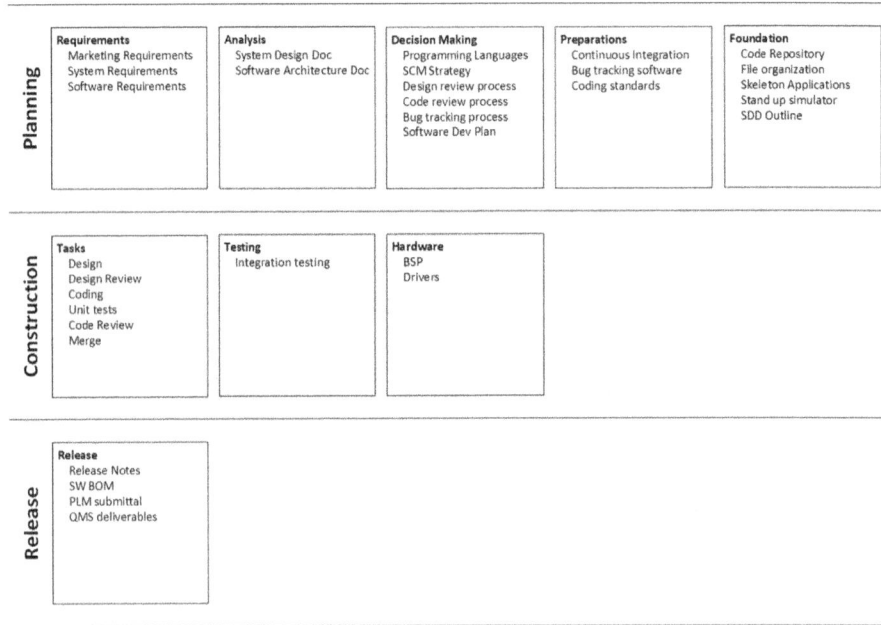

Figure 1-4. Software development life cycle stages

In this cookbook, I illustrate the work of these stages by defining and building a hypothetical Digital Heater Controller (DHC), which I like to call the GM6000. While the GM6000 is hypothetical, the processes, the framework, and the code I provide can be described as "professional

6

grade" and "production quality." That is, everything in this book has been used and incorporated in real-life products. Nevertheless, there are some limitations to the GM6000 project:

- It is only intended to be a representation of a typical embedded project, not an actual product. Some of the requirements may seem unnecessary, but I've included them to illustrate certain concepts or to simplify the construction of the example code.

- Not all the requirements for the GM6000 were designed or coded because if the output of a particular requirement didn't illustrate something new or important, I was inclined to skip it.

Outputs and Artifacts

By applying the processes described in each of these stages, you can generate outputs or artifacts upon which you can build a releasable product. All these processes are codified in a framework that is built on a BSD-licensed, open source software that you have access to and which you can use to quick-start any microcontroller project.

What's different about the framework described in this book—that may not be found in other books about software development life-cycles—is this:

- It is specifically a cookbook for microcontroller applications, even though, having said that, the processes can be applied to software projects large and small.

CHAPTER 1   INTRODUCTION

- This cookbook prescribes the approach of "build and test software first; add hardware second." In real life, this allows you to develop significant amounts of production quality code even before the hardware is available, which dramatically reduces the start-to-release duration of a project.
- This cookbook prescribes continuous integration.
- This cookbook prescribes automated unit tests.

What You'll Need to Know

If you're directly involved in architecting, designing, implementing, or testing embedded software, you should have no problem following the concepts of this book. Additionally, if you have one of the following titles or functions, you might also derive some benefits from this book:

- Software architects and leads—The processes presented here identify the upfront planning and deliverables that can be used as a guide for creating production documentation. Personally, I look at documentation as a tool to be used in the development process, as opposed to busy work or an end-of-the-project scramble to record what was implemented.

- Software engineers—The processes presented here provide a context for processes that software engineers are often asked to follow. They also supply concrete examples of how to write architecture and design documents, write automated unit tests, and develop functional simulators.

- Software managers—The processes presented here provide specifics that can help justify project expenditures for tools like CI build servers or for training. It is material that can be used to champion the idea of doing it right the first time, instead of doing it twice.[1]

Coding in C and C++

The example code and framework code in this cookbook are written in C and C++, but mostly in C++. Nevertheless, if you have experience writing software in C, or a strongly typed programming language, you should be able to follow the examples. If you're skeptical about using C++ in the embedded space, consider that the Arduino UNO framework—written for an ATmega328P microcontroller with only 32KB of flash and 2KB of RAM—is implemented in C++. Nevertheless, there is nothing in the processes presented in this book that requires a specific implementation language.

All the example code and framework code in this book are available on GitHub, and the numerous appendixes in this book contain examples of all prescribed documents.

What Toys You Will Need

Here is a summary of what you will need to build and run the examples in this book and to create the final application code for GM6000:

- C/C++ compiler (e.g., Visual Studio, MinGW, etc.).
- Python 3.8 or higher.

---

[1] Paraphrased from John W. Berman: "There's never enough time to do it right, but there's always enough time to do it over."

CHAPTER 1   INTRODUCTION

- Segger's Ozone debugger software. This is available for Windows, Linux, and macOS (see www.segger.com/products/development-tools/ozone-j-link-debugger/).
- Target hardware.
    - STMicroelectronics' NUCLEO-F413ZH development board.
    - Or Adafruit's Grand Central M4 Express board (which requires a Segger J-Link for programming).

I use Microsoft Windows as the host environment, and I use Windows tools for development. However, the code base itself supports being developed in other host environments (e.g., Linux or macOS). Detailed setup instructions are provided in Appendix A, "Getting Started with the Source Code."

Regulated Industries

Most of my early career was spent working in domains with no or very minimal regulatory requirements. But when I finally did work on medical devices, I was pleased to discover that the best practices I had accumulated over the years were reflected in the quality processes required by the FDA or EMA. Consequently, the processes presented here are applicable to both nonregulated and regulated domains. Nevertheless, if you're working in a regulated industry, you should compare what is presented here against your specific circumstances and then make choices about what to adopt, exclude, or modify to fit your project's needs.

CHAPTER 1   INTRODUCTION

What Is Not Covered

There are several aspects to this software development approach that I don't spend much time defending or explaining. For example, I make the following assumptions:

- Software architecture is done before detailed design and implementation.
- Software architecture and detailed design are two separate deliverables.
- Detailed design is done before coding.
- Unit tests, as well as automated unit tests, are first class deliverables in the development process.
- Continuous integration is a requirement.
- Documentation is a useful tool, not a process chore.

Additionally, while they are worthy topics for discussion, this book only indirectly touches on the following:

- Multithreading
- Real-time scheduling
- Interrupt handling
- Optimizing for space and real-time performance
- Algorithm design
- User interface design
- How to work with hardware peripherals (ADC, SPI, I2C, UART, timers, input capture, etc.)

11

CHAPTER 1   INTRODUCTION

This is not to say that the framework does not support multithreading or interrupt handling or real-time scheduling. Rather, I didn't consider this book the right place for those discussion. To extend the cookbook metaphor a little more, I consider that a list of ingredients. And while ingredients are important, I'm more interested here in the recipes that detail how to prepare, combine, and bake it all together.

Conclusion

Finally, it is important to understand that this book is about how to productize software, not a book on how to evaluate hardware or create a proof of concept. In my experience, following the processes described in this book will provide you and your software team with the tools to achieve a high-quality, robust product without slowing down the project timeline. Again, for a broader discussion of why I consider these processes best practices, I refer you to *Patterns in the Machine*,[2] which makes the case for the efficiency, flexibility, and maintainability of many of these approaches to embedded software development.

---

[2] John Taylor and Wayne Taylor. *Patterns in the Machine: A Software Engineering Guide to Embedded Development.* Apress Publishers, 2021

CHAPTER 2

Requirements

Collecting requirements is the first step in the planning stage. This is where you and your team consolidate the user and business needs into problem statements and then define in rough terms how that problem will be solved. Requirements articulate product needs like

- Functions
- Capabilities
- Attributes
- Capacities

Most of these statements will come from other disciplines and stakeholders, and the requirements will vary greatly in quality and usefulness. Usually, good requirements statements should be somewhat general because the statement shouldn't specify how something should be done, just that it needs to be done. For example, this statement would be far too specific as a requirement:

> *The firmware shall implement a high pass filter using FFT to attenuate low frequencies.*

A better requirement would simply state what needs to be done:

> *The firmware shall remove high frequency interference from the device signal.*

CHAPTER 2   REQUIREMENTS

In the requirements phase, then, the scope of the problem-solving is to "draw the bounding box" for the detailed solution. Here are some examples of how general requirements can be:

- The physical footprint shall be no larger than a bread box.
- The computing platform will be limited to a microcontroller.
- The total bill of materials and manufacturing costs shall not exceed $45.
- The device shall operate effectively in these physical environments: land, sea, and air.

These written requirements become the inputs for the second step in the planning phase. Most of the time, though, the analysis step needs to start before the requirements have all been collected and agreed upon. Consequently, don't burden yourself with the expectation that all the requirements need to be defined before exiting the requirements step. Rather, identify an initial set of requirements with your team as early as possible to ensure there's time to complete the analysis step. The minimum deliverable or output for the requirements step is a draft set of requirements that can be used as input for the analysis step.

Formal Requirements

Typically, requirements are captured in a table form or in a database. If the content of your requirements is presented in a natural language form or story form that is often referred to as a product specification. In my experience, a product specification is a better way to communicate to people an overall understanding of the requirements; however, a list of formal requirements is a more efficient way to track work items and features, especially when it comes to creating test plans and verifications. Either a product specification or a list of requirements constitutes formal requirements.

Generally, when I refer to formal requirements, I simply mean requirements that have been written down. The format is not important if the following minimum attributes are part of the requirements:

- Unique identifier—This identifier can be in any format as long as it is unique across all the entire scope of requirements for the project. After the requirement is written, the identifier should not be changed or reused. For this reason, you do not want to use a document's section numbering as the unique identifier because when the document is modified, the section numbering can change.

- Name—A text label assigned to a requirement that provides a short description or summary of the requirement.

- Description—This is the descriptive text of a requirement. Verbs such as *shall* and *should* are used to indicate whether the requirement is a "must-have" or a "nice-to-have." In addition, requirements must be testable; so phrases such as *shall be easy to use* are problematic. Rather, the description should incorporate measurable criteria such as *shall receive an average usability score of 8 or above in focus group testing*.

- Targeted release—This attribute allows the stakeholders to provide a road map for their product so that the current design cycle can accommodate future functionality.

CHAPTER 2   REQUIREMENTS

Functional vs. Nonfunctional

There are two basic types of requirements: functional and nonfunctional. Functional requirements are those that define what a product or system is supposed to do; nonfunctional requirements (NFRs) define how the product or system should do it. NFRs are sometimes referred to as the "quality attributes" of a system. NFRs are also harder to write due to defining their pass/fail criterion. It is often difficult to articulate the tests that determine if the user interface is "intuitive" or that the user experience with the product is "first class." Some common words that are used in NFRs that should alert you to areas of concern are

- Availability
- Compatibility
- Reliability
- Maintainability
- Manufacturability
- Regulatory
- Scalability

As the name "nonfunctional" implies, the operation of the product is not impacted if one or more NFRs are not met. However, the stakeholder expectations or business needs may not be met if some of the NFRs are not achieved.

Sources for Requirements

Requirements will come to you from various sources and people involved in the product development process. For example, you may get requirements from people in the following roles:

CHAPTER 2 REQUIREMENTS

- Product manager or marketing group—The product manager is typically the primary stakeholder and provides the top-level, most abstract requirements. I label these as Marketing Requirements Specifications (MRS).

- System engineer—The system engineering role is responsible for decomposing the MRS requirements to generate the system-level requirements that constitute a solution to the original MRS requirement. I label these as Product Requirements Specifications (PRS). Nominally the PRS requirements are traceable back to one or more MRS requirements. The PRS is essentially the project team's response to the MRS.

- Engineering (Software, Electrical, Mechanical)—The various engineering disciplines decompose the PRS requirements into yet more detailed requirements that are specific to their disciplines. This is typically the most detailed level of requirements. I label the requirements from software engineers as Software Requirements Specifications (SRS). Nominally the SRS requirements (as well as requirements from other engineering disciplines) are traceable back to either PRS or MRS requirements.

- Other roles (Quality, Regulatory, etc.)—Other functional groups within your company may provide you with requirements, and these requirements should be recorded as either MRS- or PRS-level requirements.

The initial set of requirements coming out of the planning stage will be a mix of MRS, PRS, and SRS requirements. This is to be expected as no development life cycle is truly waterfall.

CHAPTER 2 REQUIREMENTS

Note Capturing and managing requirements is a system engineering role, not a software role. Consequently, a more detailed discussion of requirements, requirements management, and best practices is outside the scope of this book. Nevertheless, it is not unusual for a software engineer to fill the role of the system engineer.

Challenges in Collecting Requirements

In theory, this requirements step should be easy; it is primarily a collection effort where you go gather up all the requirements from your stakeholders. In practice, though, it turns out to be much more difficult because people always seem to want more information before they are willing to make a decision. You may find that you and your software team may find yourselves extracting requirements from stakeholders in the same way a dentist extracts teeth from recalcitrant patients. That is, there may be some browbeating involved in getting the stakeholders to commit to something. And sometimes it can get to the point where you just have to say, "Look, if you want me to build something in this decade, you're going to have to commit: Do you want it this way or do you want it that way?"

You and your software team will also need to make some strategic decisions about how to fill in the gaps from missing requirements. You may have to guess or "make something up" so the downstream work can progress. Filling these gaps is something of a leap of faith, and there is a good chance you'll get it wrong, which means some re-work will be required later in the project. Nevertheless, there are times when you just need to decide *something* so you can set up an implementation path. I have found, though, that if you make these decisions with a good understanding of what the product is supposed to be, the inevitable changes and adaptations that are required after the *real decision* is made will be less significant, less structural, and more cosmetic.

Exiting the Requirements Step

The requirements that are available when the first draft of the software architecture document is generated will only be a subset of the final requirements. In addition, some of the initial requirements will change (or be deleted) as the project moves forward. These changes in requirements dictate that the software architecture document be revisited to make sure it is still appropriate for the newest set of requirements. However, in my experience, if the initial core set of requirements was "mostly correct" in its intent, then the churn on the software architecture document is minimal. This is because the software architecture document is not detailed design; instead, it defines the boundaries of the detailed software solutions.

GM6000

Table 2-1 is the list of initial requirements for a hypothetical heater controller that I like to call the GM6000. This list is intended to illustrate the kinds of requirements that are available when you start to develop the software architecture in the analysis step. As you make progress on the software architecture, additional requirements will present themselves, and you will need to work with your extended team to get the new requirements included in the MRS or PRS requirements documents.

CHAPTER 2   REQUIREMENTS

Table 2-1. *Requirements captured at the start of the analysis step*

Req#	Name	Requirement	Rel[1]
MR-100	Heating system	The Digital Heating Control (DHC) system shall provide indoor heating based on space temperature and a user-supplied heat setting.	1.0
MR-101	Heating enclosures	The DHC shall support at least three different heater enclosures. The heating capacity of each heater enclosure can be different from the other enclosures.	1.0
MR-102	Control board	DHC shall have a single control board that can be installed in many heater enclosures.	1.0
MR-103	Control algorithm	The heater control algorithm in the control board shall accept parameters and configurations that customize the algorithm for a specific heater enclosure.	1.0
MR-104	Provisioning	The DHC control board shall be provisioned to a specific heater enclosure during the manufacturing process. The provisioning shall include the heater control's algorithm parameters and configuration.	1.0
MR-105	Wireless input	The control board shall support connecting to a wireless module for communicating with a wireless temperature input.	2.0
MR-106	Wireless sensor	The DHC system shall support an external, wireless temperature sensor.	2.0

(*continued*)

---

[1] Commercial release, where Rel 1.0 is the initial product release.

CHAPTER 2 REQUIREMENTS

Table 2-1. (*continued*)

Req#	Name	Requirement	Rel[1]
MR-107	User interface	The DHC unit shall support display, LEDs, and user inputs (e.g., physical buttons, keypad membrane, etc.). The arrangement of the display and user inputs can be different between heater enclosures.	1.0
MR-108	User actions	The DHC display, LEDs, and user inputs shall allow the user to do the following: • Turn the heater on and off • Set the maximum fan speed • Specify the temperature set point	1.0
MR-109	User information	The DHC display LEDs shall provide the user with the following information: • Current temperature • DHC on/off state • Active heating state • Fan on/off state • Alerts and failure conditions	1.0
PR-100	Sub-assemblies	The DHC heater closure shall contain the following sub-assemblies: • Control Board (CB) • Heating Element (HE) • Display and User Inputs (DUI) • Blower Assembly (BA) • Power Supply (PS) • Temperature Sensor (TS)	1.0

(*continued*)

Table 2-1. (continued)

Req#	Name	Requirement	Rel[1]
PR-101	Wireless module	The DHC heater closure shall contain the following sub-assemblies: • Wireless Module (WM)	2.0
PR-103	Heater safety	The Heating Element (HE) sub-assembly shall contain a hardware temperature protection circuit that forces the heating source off when it exceeds the designed safety limits.	1.0
PR-105	Heater element interface	The Heating Element (HE) sub-assembly shall have a proportional heating output interface to the Control Board (CB).	1.0
PR-106	Blower assembly interface	The Blower Assembly (BA) sub-assembly shall have a proportional speed control interface to the Control Board (CB).	1.0
PR-107	Temperature sensor	The Temperature Sensor (TS) sub-assembly shall use a thermistor for measuring space temperature.	1.0

A complete set of final requirements for the GM6000 can be found in Appendix H, "GM6000 Requirements."

Summary

The goal of the requirements step is to identify the problem statement presented by the user and business needs. In addition, a high-level solution is identified and proposed for the problem statement. Both the problem statement and the high-level solution are captured in the form of formal requirements.

CHAPTER 2   REQUIREMENTS

INPUTS

- User needs
- Business needs

OUTPUTS

- A subset of the documented final requirements. At a minimum, the subset must be sufficient to complete the analysis step.

CHAPTER 3

Analysis

In the analysis step of the planning stage, you will create three artifacts:

- System architecture (SA)—The system architecture document describes the discrete pieces or units of functionality that will be tied together to make the product. It consists of diagrams with boxes and lines whose semantics usually mean "contains" and "is connected to."

- Software architecture (SWA) documents—The software architecture, on the other hand, provides the designs for the system components that describe how each unit works. These designs usually contain diagrams that are more sophisticated in that they may be structural or behavioral and their lines and boxes often have more particular meanings or rules associated with them (like UML diagrams).

- Requirements trace matrix—The requirements trace matrix is generally a spreadsheet that allows you to map each requirement to the code that satisfies it and the tests that validate it.

In this chapter, I've pulled examples from Appendix I, "GM6000 System Architecture," and Appendix J, "GM6000 Software Architecture," to provide examples of how sections in these documents might look. Be aware that these examples use the "sparse language of work" because the intended

CHAPTER 3   ANALYSIS

audience for these documents is other members of the development team who are expected to be familiar with these details. That is, I may refer to algorithms, standards, or constructs without much if any explanation. For example, when an example document specifies that the "enclosure for the project should be IP51 rated," it does not discuss or explain how the Ingress Protection (IP) rating system works, nor, when a document specifies that the "implementation must guarantee that there are no nested mutex calls when it locks its internal mutex," do I add that "critical sections are evil, and while they're handy-dandy and very easy to use, they will always get you in trouble."

System Engineering

I will note here that system engineering is not a software role. And while it is not unusual for a software engineer to fill the role of the system engineer, a discussion about the intricacies of developing the system architecture is outside the scope of this book. But, as it is an essential input to the software architecture document, Appendix I, "GM6000 System Architecture," provides an example of a system architecture document for the GM6000.

GM6000 System Architecture

Figure 3-1 shows an example of a system-level diagram for the GM6000. In Appendix I, "GM6000 System Architecture," each diagram is followed by a table of supporting text for each label block. However, in this excerpt from the appendix, as well as in all the following excerpts, only a few of the descriptions are shown to give you an idea of the level of detail expected.

CHAPTER 3   ANALYSIS

Digital Heater Controller (DHC)

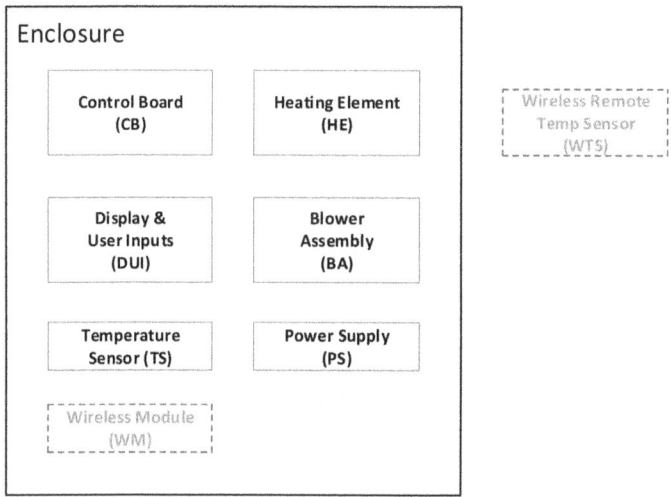

Figure 3-1. *System architecture block diagram*

Component	Description
Enclosure	*The box that contains the product. The enclosure should be IP51 rated.*
Control Board (CB)	*The board that contains the microcontroller that runs the heater controller. The CB contains circuits and other chips as needed to support the microcontroller unit (MCU) and software.*
Display and User Inputs (DUI)	*A separate board that contains the display, buttons, and LEDs used for interaction with the user. This DUI can be located anywhere within the enclosure and is connected to the CB via a wire harness.*
...	*...*

27

CHAPTER 3 ANALYSIS

Software Architecture

There is no canonical definition of software architecture. This cookbook defines software architecture as

> *Identifying the solution at a high level and defining the rules of engagement for the subsequent design and implementation steps.*

From a top-down perspective, software architecture is the top of the software solution pyramid (even though software architecture is not a strictly top-down activity). When creating the software architecture, you will need to make design decisions in the following areas:

- Hardware interfaces.
- Performance constraints.
- Programming languages.
- Subsystems. This includes defining the rules for how these the subsystems will interface with each other and share data.
- Subsystem interfaces.
- Process model.
- Functional simulator.
- Cybersecurity.
- Memory allocation.
- ITC (Inter-thread communication) and IPC (Inter-process communication).

- File and directory organization.
- Localization and internationalization.
- Other areas of concern that are specific to your industry, company, or product. For example, a medical device must have an IEC 62304 software safety classification.

While you're doing all this, it is important to remember that your definitions should be as detail agnostic as possible. I know that sounds strange, but the software architecture is about

> *Defining the logical framework and boundaries for downstream detailed design.*

For example, Figure 3-2, in the "Hardware Interfaces" section that follows, is a hardware block diagram for this book's sample project, the GM6000 digital heater controller. The illustration was taken from the example software architecture document that is provided in Appendix J, "GM6000 Software Architecture." While at first glance it may seem fairly detailed—and it is detailed because it is delineating hardware interfaces and components—upon closer inspection, you will see that no specific hardware part numbers are called out. No specific type of serial bus is specified for communication between components (e.g., I2C, SPI, etc.). While "User Inputs" are called out, no specific type of button nor number of buttons is specified. And even though external storage is present, there is nothing that requires any particular type of storage nor amount.

In summary, then, the goal of this chapter is to describe how you can create the first draft of the software architecture. You will invariably have to create additional drafts as the two key inputs for this step—the extant set of requirements and the system architecture document—will evolve. Unfortunately, in the real world, these inputs are not waterfall handoffs; the details are derived over time during the planning stage.

CHAPTER 3   ANALYSIS

> As time goes on, it is important that when there is a "story" or theory-of-operations description of the system, the team clearly defines and enforces the canonical source for the requirements.

Moving from Inputs to Outputs

In Chapter 2, "Requirements," I provided one block diagram and approximately 20 requirements that were a mix of marketing and engineering requirements. But there are significant requirements and details missing. For example, there is nothing called out for

- A temperature control algorithm (e.g., error vs. PID control)
- The type of display (fixed segment vs. graphic, resolution, color depth, etc.)
- The UI workflow requirements
- The specifics of the interfaces to the Heating Element (HE) and Blower Assembly (BA) sub-assemblies
- Firmware updates
- Diagnostics
- Cybersecurity

Nevertheless, the inputs I provide are sufficient to create the first draft of the software architecture.

The following sections discuss the creation of the content of the software architecture document. While you are performing the analysis and making architectural decisions, you'll discover that there are still a lot of unknown or open questions. Some of these questions may be answered during the planning stage. Some are detailed design questions that will be answered in the construction stage. Either way, keep track of these open questions because they will eventually have to be answered.

CHAPTER 3 ANALYSIS

Hardware Interfaces

Create a hardware block diagram in relation to the microcontroller. That is, outline the inputs and outputs to and from the microcontroller (see Figure 3-2). Whenever possible, omit details that are not critical to understanding the functionality of the inputs and outputs. For example, simply identify that there will be "external serial data storage." Do not call out a specific chip, storage technology (e.g., flash vs. EEPROM), or specific type of serial bus.

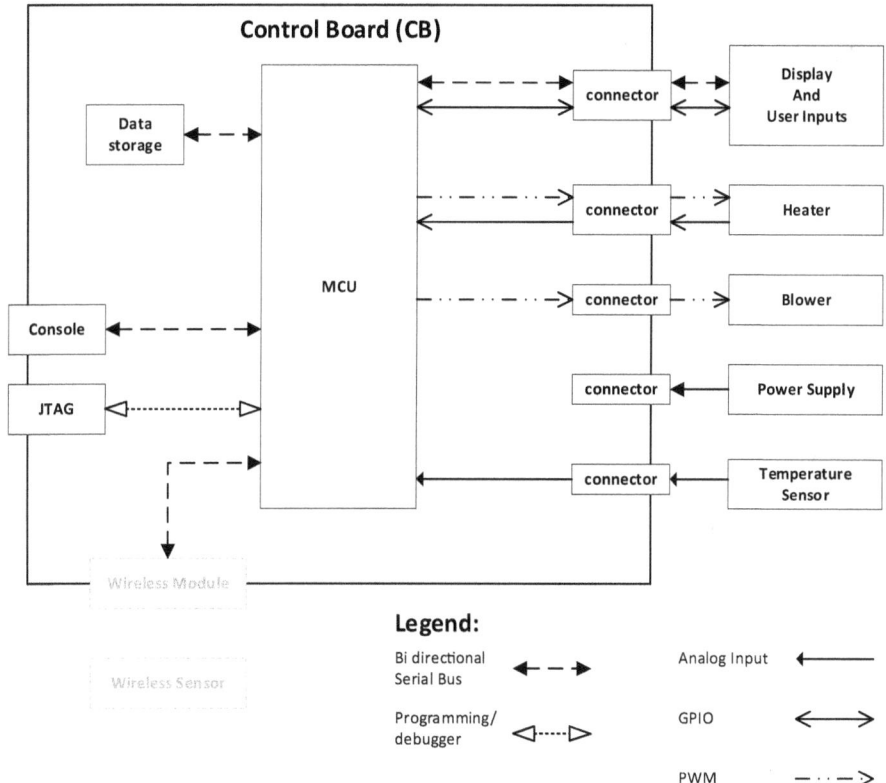

Figure 3-2. Hardware block diagram

CHAPTER 3   ANALYSIS

Component	Description
...	...
Data Storage	Serial persistent data storage for saving configuration, user settings, etc.
...	...

In creating the hardware block diagram, I made the following decisions, which I fed back into the project's requirements prior to exiting the analysis stage:

1. The selected microcontroller must support at least four serial buses (HWR-200).

2. The display will have a serial bus interface (HWR-201).

3. The heater and fan control will be accomplished using a Pulse Width Modulation (PWM) signal (HWR-202, HWR-203).

4. The control board will have UART-based console for provisioning and debugging support (SWR-200, 201, 203).

Performance Constraints

For all of the identified hardware interfaces, you will want to make an assessment of real-time performance and bandwidth usage. Also you should make performance assessments for any applications, driver stacks, crypto routines, etc., that will require significant CPU usage. Since the specifics of these interfaces are still unknown, the assessment will be an approximation—that is, an order-of-magnitude estimate—rather than a

CHAPTER 3 ANALYSIS

precision value. Note that I use the term "real time" to describe contexts where stimuli must be detected and reacted to in less than one second. Events and actions that occur slower than 1 Hz can be achieved without special considerations.

The following are some excerpts from the software architecture document in Appendix J, "GM6000 Software Architecture," that illustrate the performance analysis.

Display

The microcontroller unit (MCU) communicates with the display controller via a serial bus (e.g., SPI or I2C). There is a time constraint in that the physical transfer time for an entire screen's worth of pixel data (including color data) must be fast enough to ensure a good user experience. There is also a RAM constraint with respect to the display in the MCU; it requires that there will be at least one off-screen frame buffer that can hold an entire screen's worth of pixel data. The size of the pixel data is a function of the display's resolution times the color depth. The assessments and recommendations are as follows:

- *The maximum size of the pixel data is limited to 64KB to meet the timing and RAM constraints.*

- *Assuming a 16 MHz serial bus, the wire transfer time for a full screen is 41 msec without accounting for protocol overhead, ISR jitter, thread context switches, etc.*

Temperature Sensor

The space temperature must be sampled and potentially filtered before being used as an input to the control algorithm. However, controlling space temperature is a relatively slow system (i.e., much slower than 1 Hz). Consequently, the assessments and recommendations are as follows:

- *No real-time constraints on space temperature sampling or filtering*

CHAPTER 3   ANALYSIS

Threading

A Real-Time Operating System (RTOS) with many threads will be used. Switching between threads—that is, a context switch—requires a measurable amount of time. This becomes important when there are submillisecond timing requirements and when looking at overall CPU usage. The RTOS also adds timing overhead for maintaining its system tick timer, which is typically interrupt based. The assessments and recommendations are as follows:

- *The RTOS context switching time and tick counter overhead only needs to be considered when there are requirements for response or detection times that are less than 1 msec.*

Programming Languages

Selecting a programming language may seem like a trivial decision, but it still needs to be an explicit decision. The experience of the developers, regulatory considerations, performance, memory management, security, tool availability, licensing issues, etc., all need to be considered when selecting the programming language. The language choice should be documented in the software architecture document as well as in the Software Development Plan.

In most cases, I prefer to use C++. I know that not everyone agrees with me on this, but I make the case for the advantages of using C++ in *Patterns in the Machine*. I mention it here to say that you should not exclude C++ from consideration simply because you are working in a resource-constrained environment.

Subsystems

You will want to decompose the software for your project into components or subsystems. The number and granularity of the components are a choice that you will have to make. Some things to consider when defining subsystems are as follows:

- All of the source code that executes on the microcontroller should be contained within one of the identified subsystems. If you find yourself writing code that does not fit within the description of one of the subsystems, then you need to revise the software architecture document, or reevaluate if the new code is really needed for the project.

- Each subsystem must be traceable back to at least one formal requirement. That is, there must be at least one MRS, PRS, or SRS requirement that the subsystem satisfies or partially satisfies.

- Subsystems are not layers. In some instances, subsystems do map to layers, but they represent functionality.

- When selecting and naming a subsystem, start with a description of the scope of the subsystem. It is sometimes helpful to explicitly call out what is not included in the subsystem.

- Separate subsystems by functionality or behavior, not by anticipated code size. That is, it is okay to have a subsystem that is implemented with a minimal amount of code.

CHAPTER 3   ANALYSIS

- Do not think of subsystems as directories or C++ namespace names. The code for a given subsystem can, and often will be, spread across multiple directories and namespaces.

- There is no minimum or maximum number of subsystems. That said, subsystems such as the Board Support Package (BSP), operating system (OS), operating system abstraction layer (OSAL), drivers, system services, and bootloader are ubiquitous for most microcontroller applications. It is not uncommon for many of the subsystems you identify for a given project to be the same as other projects, even when those projects are completely different.

The GM6000 control board software is broken down into the following subsystems. In Figure 3-3, the subsystems in the dashed boxes represent future or anticipated functionality.

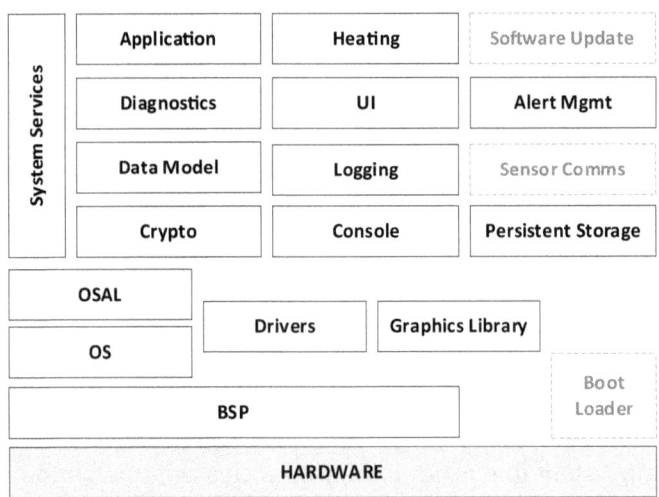

Figure 3-3. Subsystems

CHAPTER 3　ANALYSIS

Here are some excerpts from the software architecture document in Appendix J, "GM6000 Software Architecture," that describe the scope of the subsystems.

Application

The application subsystem contains the top-level business logic for the entire application. This includes functionality such as

- *The top-level state of the entire device*
- *Creating, starting, and stopping all other subsystems*

BSP

The Board Support Package (BSP) subsystem is responsible for abstracting the details of the microcontroller unit (MCU) datasheet. For example, it is responsible for

- *The low-level code that directly configures the MCU's hardware registers*
- *Encapsulating the MCU vendor's supplied SDK, including any modifications or extensions needed*
- *Compiler-dependent constructs (e.g., setting up the MCU's vector table)*

Diagnostics

The diagnostics subsystem is responsible for monitoring the software's health, defining the diagnostics logic, and self-testing the system. This includes features such as power on self-tests and metrics capture.

CHAPTER 3   ANALYSIS

Drivers

The driver subsystem is the collection of driver code that does not reside in the BSP subsystem. Drivers that directly interact with hardware are required to be separated into layers. There should be at least three layers:

- A hardware-specific layer that is specific to a target platform

- A platform-independent layer. Ideally the majority of the business logic is contained in this layer.

- A Hardware Abstraction Layer (HAL) that separates the aforementioned two layers. More specifically, the hardware-specific layer implements the HAL, and the platform-independent layer calls the HAL.

Graphics Library

The graphics library subsystem is responsible for providing graphic primitives, fonts, window management, widgets, etc. The expectation is that the graphic library will be third-party software. The minimum requirements for the graphics library are as follows:

- It is platform independent. That is, it has no direct dependencies on a specific MCU or physical display.

- It supports a bare-metal runtime environment. That is, it can be used with or without an RTOS. This constraint is important because it allows the OSAL's event-based threads to be used directly for events, timers, and ITC messages within the thread where the UI executes. This eliminates the need for an adapter layer to translate the system services events into graphic-library-specific events.

Heating

The heating subsystem is responsible for the closed loop space temperature control. This is the code for the heat control algorithm.

Persistent Storage

The persistent storage subsystem provides the framework, interfaces, data integrity checks, etc., for storing and retrieving data that is stored in local persistent storage. The persistent storage paradigm is a RAM-cached model. The RAM-cached model is as follows:

- *On startup, persistent record entries are read from nonvolatile storage, validated, and loaded into RAM. If the data is invalid, then the associated RAM values are set to factory default values, and the nonvolatile storage is updated with the new defaulted values.*

- *The application updates the entries stored in RAM via an API. When an update request is made, the RAM value is updated, and then a background task is initiated to update the values stored in nonvolatile storage.*

UI

The user interface (UI) subsystem is responsible for the business logic and interaction with end users of the unit. This includes the LCD display screens, screen navigation, consuming button inputs, LED outputs, etc. The UI subsystem has a hard dependency on the graphic library subsystem. This hard dependency is acceptable because the graphic library is platform independent.

CHAPTER 3   ANALYSIS

Subsystem Interfaces

This section is where you define how the various subsystems, components, modules, and drivers will interact with each other. For example, it addresses the following questions:

- Are all the interfaces synchronous?
- What interfaces need to be asynchronous?
- How do drivers interact with application modules?
- Does using the data model architecture make sense?
- Is inter-thread communication (ITC) or inter-process communication (IPC) needed?

Depending on the scope and complexity of the project, there may be one or many interface designs. Do not try to force a single paradigm here. If things are similar but different, they are still different. This is also an area where it helps to have a good understanding of both the detailed design of the project as well as the specific implementation of some of the modules. Taking a deeper dive into the details that are available can be very beneficial at this stage.

The following is a snippet of the "Interfaces" section from the software architecture document in Appendix J, "GM6000 Software Architecture."

Interfaces

The preferred, and primary, interface for sharing data between subsystems will be done via the data model pattern. The secondary interface will be message-based inter-thread communications (ITC). Which mechanism is used to share data will be determined on a case-by-case basis with the preference being to use the data model. However, the decision can be "both" because both approaches can co-exist within a subsystem.

CHAPTER 3 ANALYSIS

The data model pattern supports publish-subscribe semantics as well as a polling approach to sharing data. The net effect of this approach is that subsystems are decoupled. That is, there are no direct dependencies on other subsystems. In Figure 3-4, the arrows represent dependencies between the subsystems. Note that model point data is bidirectional between the subsystems.

A third option for a subsystem interface is a functional API. This should be used for subsystems (e.g., system services) that have no external dependencies with other subsystems and that typically only execute when their APIs are called by other subsystems.

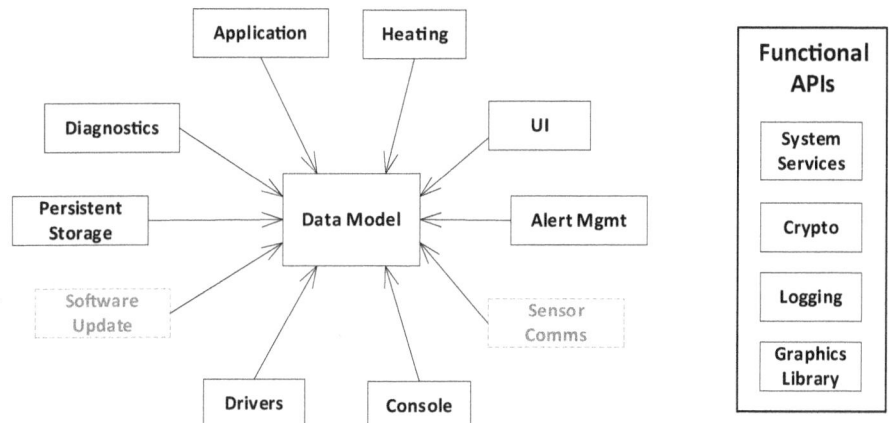

Figure 3-4. *Subsystem interdependencies using the data model*

CHAPTER 3   ANALYSIS

Process Model

The following questions need to be answered in the architecture document:

- Will the application be a bare-metal or main-loop application?
- Will the application use threads?
- Will the application have multiple processes?
    - Is the system architecture a multiprocessor design? (e.g., is it a main board running Linux with an off-board microcontroller that performs all the hard real-time processing?)

If the system uses threads or processes, I recommend that you document why that decision was made. Articulate what problems or requirements having threads solves. If the system uses multiple processors, define the roles and responsibilities of each processor. When multiple threads and processes are being used, the software architecture needs to also address

- Thread and process priorities
- Data integrity when sharing between threads and processes

The following is the "Process Model" section from the software architecture document in Appendix J, "GM6000 Software Architecture."

Process Model

The software will be implemented as a multithreaded application using real-time preemptive scheduling. The preemptive scheduling provides for the following:

- *Decoupling the UI from the rest of the application (with respect to timing and sequencing). This allows the UI to be highly responsive to the user actions without delaying or blocking time-critical business logic.*

- *Using deferred interrupt handlers. A deferred interrupt handler is where the time-consuming portion of the interrupt service routine is deferred to a high-priority thread in order to make the interrupt service routine as short as possible.*

- *Simpler sequential designs that utilize nonbusy, blocking wait semantics*

Thread Priorities

The application shall be designed such that the relative thread priorities between individual threads do not matter with respect to correctness. Correctness in this context means the application would still function, albeit sluggishly, and not crash if all the threads had the same priority. The exception to this rule is for threads that are used exclusively as deferred interrupt handlers.

Data Integrity

Data that is shared between threads must be implemented in a manner to ensure data integrity. That is, read, write, read-modify-write operations must be atomic with respect to other threads accessing the data. The following is a list of allowed mechanisms for sharing data across threads:

CHAPTER 3 ANALYSIS

- *Data is shared using data model point instances. This is the preferred mechanism.*

- *Data is shared using the system services inter-thread-communication (ITC) message passing interfaces. ITC messaging is recommended for when the interface semantics have a many-to-one relationship between the clients and servers and the clients are sending data to the server.*

- *Synchronous ITC messaging—where the client is blocked while the server processes the message—is only allowed when the server actions are well bounded in time and are of short duration. For example, invoking an HTTPS request to an off-board website is considered an unbounded transaction because there are too many variables associated with determining when a request will complete or fail (e.g., TCP retry timing, routing, website availability, etc.).*

- *Asynchronous ITC messaging can always be used.*

- *Encapsulated API is allowed but discouraged. This is where the API implementation uses an internal mutex (which is not exposed to the API's clients) to provide atomic data access. In addition, the internal implementation must guarantee that there are no nested mutex calls when it locks its internal mutex. This approach should only be used as a last resort option and must be clearly documented in the detailed design.*

When sharing data between a thread and an interrupt service routine (ISR), the critical section mechanism shall disable or enable the ISR's specific interrupt. Relying on the MCU's instruction set for atomic read, write, read-modify-write operations to a memory location is strongly discouraged.

If the MCU is used, it must be clearly documented in the detailed design. The following guidelines shall be followed for sharing data between a thread and ISRs:

- *Temporarily suspend thread scheduling before disabling the interrupt, and then resume scheduling after enabling the interrupt. This ensures that there will not be a thread context switch while the thread has disabled the interrupt.*

- *Keep the time that the interrupt is disabled as short as possible. Your process should not be doing anything else except moving data and clearing hardware registers while it has an interrupt disabled.*

- *Only disable or enable a specific interrupt. Never globally disable or enable interrupts.*

Functional Simulator

If your project requires you to implement automated unit tests for your project, you will find that a lot of the work that goes into creating a functional simulator will be done while creating the automated unit tests. The reason is because the automated unit tests impose a decoupled design that allows components and modules to be tested as platform-independent code. Consequently, creating a simulator that reuses abstracted interfaces is not a lot of additional effort—if it is planned for from the beginning of the project. The two biggest pieces of work are as follows:

- Identifying the necessary abstraction layers (OSAL, HAL, etc.)

- Determining the strategy for breaking dependencies on the Board Support Package (BSP)

CHAPTER 3   ANALYSIS

The planning and implementation of this separation strategy results in minimal additional effort to create a functional simulator.

Software architecture decisions that need to be made to implement a functional simulator are as follows:

- What platform will the simulator run on (e.g., Windows, Linux)?

- What portions will be simulated? The entire application? Just the algorithms? The entire system?

- How will the hardware elements be simulated? Mocked drivers? Full hardware emulation? Functional hardware simulation?

- Are there communication channels that need to be simulated?

- Is simulated time needed or desirable? Simulating time is very useful for projects that have algorithms that are time based or where running faster than real time is desirable (e.g., simulating one month of operation in ten minutes).

The following is the "Simulator" section from the software architecture document in Appendix J, "GM6000 Software Architecture."

Simulator

The software architecture and design accommodate the creation of a functional simulator. A functional simulator is the execution of production source code on a platform that is not the target platform. A functional simulator is expected to provide the majority of the functionality but not necessarily the real-time performance of the actual product. Or, more simply, functional simulation enables developers to develop, execute, and

CHAPTER 3   ANALYSIS

test production code without the target hardware. Figure 3-5 illustrates what is common and different between the software built for the target platform and software built for the functional simulator. The architecture for the functional simulator is on the right.

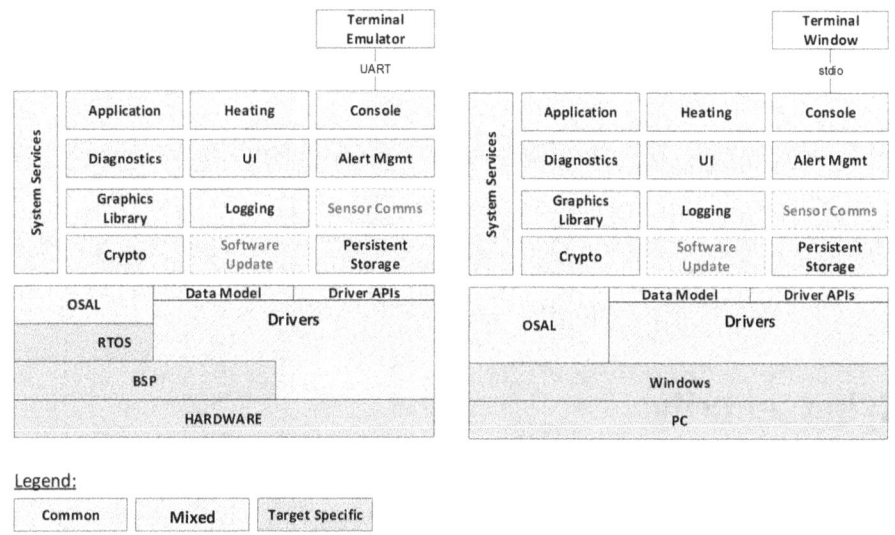

Figure 3-5. *Software architecture with and without a functional simulator*

The functional simulator has the following features, attributes, and limitations:

- *The functional simulator shall be a Windows console executable.*

- *The executable's* stdio *is the stream interface for application's console.*

- *The Windows file system will be used to "mock" the nonvolatile storage of the product.*

- *The bootloader is not simulated.*

47

CHAPTER 3   ANALYSIS

During detailed design of the various drivers, make the decisions as to how each hardware driver will be simulated. Allowed options for simulating hardware are as follows:

- *Mocked–A mocked simulation is where you provide a minimal implementation of the device's HAL interface so that the application compiles, links, and does not cause aberrant behavior at runtime.*

- *Simulated–A simulated device is where only the core functionality of the device is implemented.*

- *Emulated–An emulated device is where you replicate a device's behaviors at its lowest, most basic level.*

Cybersecurity

Cybersecurity may or may not be a large topic for your project. Nevertheless, even if your initial reaction is "there are no cybersecurity concerns for this product," you should still take the time to document why there are no concerns. Also note that I include the protection of personally identifiable information (PII) and intellectual property (IP) as part of cybersecurity analysis.

Sometimes just writing down your reasoning as to why cybersecurity is not an issue will reveal gaps that need to be addressed. Depending on the number and types of *attack surfaces* your product has, it is not uncommon to break the cybersecurity analysis into its own document. And a separate document is okay; what is important is that you do some analysis and document your findings.

A discussion of the best practices and methodologies for performing cybersecurity analysis is beyond the scope of this book. For example, with the GM6000 project, the cybersecurity concerns are minimal. Here is a snippet of the "Cybersecurity" section from the software architecture document that can be found in Appendix J, "GM6000 Software Architecture."

CHAPTER 3 ANALYSIS

Cybersecurity

The software in the GM6000 is considered to be a low-risk target in that it is easier to compromise the physical components of a GM6000 than the software. Assuming that the software is compromised, there are no safety issues because the HE has hardware safety circuits. The worst-case scenarios for compromised software are along the lines of denial-of-service (DoS) attacks, which might cause the DHC to not heat the space, yield uncomfortable temperature control, or run constantly to incur a high energy bill.

No PII is stored in persistent storage. There are no privacy issues associated with the purchase or use of the GM6000.

Another possible security risk is the theft of intellectual property. That is, can a malicious bad actor steal and reverse-engineer the software in the control board? This is considered low risk since there are no patented algorithms or trade secrets contained within the software and the software only has value within the company's hardware. The considered attack surfaces are as follows:

- *Console–The console's command-line interface (CLI) provides essentially super admin access to the software. To mitigate this, the console logic shall require a user to authenticate before being given access to commands.*

  ...

Memory Allocation

The architecture document should define requirements, rules, and constraints for dynamic memory allocation. Because of the nature of embedded projects, the extensive use of dynamic memory allocation is discouraged. When you have a device that could potentially run for years before it is power-cycled or reset, the probability of running out of heap memory due to fragmentation becomes a valid concern. Here is the "Memory Allocation" section from the software architecture document that can be found in Appendix J, "GM6000 Software Architecture."

CHAPTER 3   ANALYSIS

To prevent memory leaks and fragmentation, no dynamic memory allocation is allowed. The application may allocate memory from the heap at startup, but not once the system is "up and running." This practice guarantees the system will not fail over time due to lack of memory.

For objects or structures that must be dynamically created or deleted after startup, the design is required to pre-allocate a memory pool on a per-type basis that will be used to construct the object or structure at runtime.

Inter-thread and Inter-process Communication

As discussed earlier in the "Process Model" section, the architecture may include multiple threads and processes. For this scenario, it is important to clearly define and restrict how inter-thread (ITC) and inter-process (IPC) communications are performed because ITC and IPC are, by definition, primary sources for race conditions and data corruption bugs.

The following is a snippet from the "Message Passing (ITC)" section in the software architecture document in Appendix J, "GM6000 Software Architecture."

Message Passing (ITC)

Data between threads can be shared using message passing. However, there shall be only one message passing framework. The framework has the following requirements and constraints:

- *The message passing model is a client-server model where clients send messages to servers. Messages can be sent asynchronously or synchronously.*

- *Data flow between clients and servers can be unidirectional or bidirectional as determined by the application. Because this is an inter-thread communication, data can be shared via pointers since clients and servers share the same address space.*

- *Data is shared between clients and servers using the concept of a payload. In addition, a convention of "ownership" is used to provide thread-safe access to the payload.*

File and Directory Organization

Source code file organization is very often done organically. That is, developers start writing code and organizing their files based on their immediate needs. File organization is a strategic best practice and should be well-thought-out before any source files are created. The file organization can either hinder or facilitate the construction of the build scripts and in-project reuse. This is especially critical for in-project reuse where you build multiple images and executables from your project's code base. Unit tests and the functional simulators are examples of in-project reuse. A well-thought-out, consistent file organization will also facilitate the creation and maintenance of continuous integration for your project.

The following is a snippet from the *File and Directory Organization* section in the software architecture document in Appendix J, "GM6000 Software Architecture."

CHAPTER 3　ANALYSIS

Source code files shall be organized by dependencies, not by project. Or said another way, the code will be organized by C++ namespaces where namespaces map one to one with directory names. The exceptions to the namespace rule are for the BSP subsystem and third-party packages. In addition to namespaces, the following conventions shall be followed:

- *All in-house developed source code shall be under the top-level* `src/` *directory.*

- `#include` *statements in header files shall contain path information relative to the* `src/` *directory.*

- *There shall not be separate* `include/` *directories to contain header files. That is, do not separate header files and* `.c`|`.cpp` *files into different directories based solely on file type.*

- *Non-namespace directories can be created for organizational purposes. Non-namespace directory names shall be prefixed with a leading underscore.*

...

Localization and Internationalization

Localization and internationalization requirements may seem obvious. That is, you may be planning on creating a product for a single market or region. However, this requirement can change abruptly. Consequently, it is important to state the localization and internationalization requirements just to make sure everyone is on the same page. When it comes to localization, here are some examples of what to identify:

- Does your project need to display something other than numbers?

- Does your project require user input that is not menu driven or numerical? That is, does it require users to enter characters?

- What languages are you required to support? Specify these languages by country. The phrase "English only" is a very different thing than "US English only."

- If your project requires you to display characters, what encoding will you use? 7-bit ASCII has a low overhead, but 8-bit extended ASCII can give you the ability to display accent marks and other non-English characters. UTF-8 allows you to support the display of nearly every character in every language (assuming you can find a font), but it introduces the overhead that there is no longer a one-to-one mapping of the number of bytes to the number of characters in a string.

The following is the *Localization and Internationalization* section from the software architecture document in Appendix J, "GM6000 Software Architecture."

The product is targeted to be sold to North American consumers. The product is built for the US English-speaking market only (as determined by the Product Manager). Consequently, from a software perspective, the 7-bit ASCII character code is sufficient for all text presented to an end user.

CHAPTER 3　ANALYSIS

Requirement Traceability

Requirement traceability refers to the ability to follow the path a requirement takes from design all the way through to a specific test case. There are three types of traceability: forward, backward, and bidirectional. Forward traceability is defined as starting with a requirement and working downward (e.g., from requirements down to test cases). Backward traceability is the opposite (e.g., from test cases up to requirements). Bidirectional is the ability to trace in both directions.

It is not uncommon for SDLC processes to include requirements tracing. In my experience, forward tracing requirements to verification tests is all part and parcel of creating the verification test plan. Forward tracing to design documentation and source code can be more challenging, but it doesn't have to be.

The following steps simplify the forward tracing of requirements to design artifacts (i.e., the software architecture and Software Detailed Design documents) and then to source code:

1. Label all "content section"[1] headings in the software architecture document with a unique identifier that does not change when the document is edited. For example, the GM6000 Software Architecture document uses the prefix SWA-nn to label each subsystem.

---

[1] Content section means any section that is not part of the boilerplate or the housekeeping sections. The introduction, glossary, and change log sections are examples of non-content sections.

2. All *subsystems* identified in the software architecture must be backward traceable to at least one formal MRS, PRS, or SRS requirement.

    a. If you have a subsystem that doesn't trace backward (e.g., you have a missing requirement), you need to revisit the requirements or your subsystem definition. (It's possible the subsystem is not needed.)

3. All SRS requirements must forward trace to at least one labelled section in the software architecture document.

    a. If an SRS requirement doesn't trace, then you need to revisit the requirements and the architecture to determine either what is missing or what is not needed.

There are similar rules for the detailed design document, which also support forward tracing from the software architecture to detailed design sections and then to source code. See Chapter 6, "Foundation," for details.

To see the requirements tracing for the GM6000, see the "Software Requirements Traced to Software Architecture" document in Appendix P, "GM6000 Software Requirements Trace Matrix." You will notice that the trace matrix reveals two orphan subsystems (SWA-12 Bootloader and SWA-26 Software Update). This particular scenario exemplifies a situation where the software team fully expects to create a feature—the ability to update software in the field—but there is no formal requirement because the software team hasn't reminded the marketing team that this would be a good idea ... yet.

Even when your SDLC processes do not require requirements forward traceability to design artifacts, I still strongly recommend that you follow the steps mentioned previously because it is an effective mechanism for closing the loop on whether the software team implemented all the product requirements. It also helps prevent working on features that are not required for release.

CHAPTER 3   ANALYSIS

In a perfect world, all traceable elements would have parents and children. That is, all PRS requirements would have at least one parent MRS requirement and all PRS requirements would have at least one SRS requirement. However, there will always be exceptions. For example, your Quality Management System (QMS) and your SDLC processes essentially impose implicit requirements. Or your SDLC may require design elements that facilitate the construction of automated unit tests. These implicit requirements are often not captured as formal requirements. This means that some common sense needs to be used when performing requirements tracing. Chapter 9, "Requirements Revisited," provides an additional discussion on this topic.

Summary

The initial draft of the software architecture document is one of the major deliverables for the analysis step in the planning stage. As discussed in the "Requirement Traceability" section, there is an auxiliary deliverable to the software architecture document, which is the trace matrix for the software architecture.

INPUTS

- An initial set or draft of the requirements
- An initial draft of the system architecture

OUTPUTS

- The first draft of the system architecture document
- The first draft of the software architecture document
- Requirements trace matrix for the software architecture

CHAPTER 4

Software Development Plan

Nothing in this step requires invention. The work here is simply to capture the stuff that the development team normally does on a daily basis. Creating the Software Development Plan (SDP) is simply making the team's informal processes formal.

The value add of the SDP is that it eliminates many misunderstanding and miscommunication issues. It proactively addresses the "I didn't know I needed to …" problems that invariably occur when you have more than one person writing software for a project. A written and current SDP is especially helpful when a new team member is added to the project; it is a great tool for transmitting key tribal knowledge to a new team member.

A large percentage of the SDP decisions are independent of the actual project. That is, they are part of your company's existing software development life cycle (SDLC) processes or Quality Management System (QMS). This means that work on the SDP can begin early and even be created in parallel with the requirements documents. That said, I recommend that you start the software architecture document before finalizing the first draft of the SDP. The software architecture will provide more context and scope for the software being developed than just the high-level requirements.

Another characteristic of Software Development Plans is that they mostly contain project-agnostic details. They capture processes and best practice details that apply to many projects. After you've created your team's first SDP, you essentially have a template for future SDPs, and 80% of the SDP work on the next project is already done.

It is also very helpful if your organization formalizes their software development processes and best practices. If they do, then the SDP can simply reference those documents instead of re-articulating them.

Project-Independent Processes and Standards

I recommend that you create the following development processes and standards for every project:

- Language programming standards and style guides, which include naming and file organization conventions

- Process descriptions of how you're going to run architecture and design reviews

- Process descriptions of how, and how often, you're going to run source code reviews

- Roles and responsibilities

- Process description of the bug tracking process, which includes how bugs are resolved and verified

- Software Configuration Management (SCM) repository branch model

- A description of how continuous integration (CI) will work

- Unit test requirements, which include how code coverage metrics will be determined

- Software best practices

Project-Specific Processes and Standards

Here are the project-specific topics that need to be addressed in your software planning:

- The SCM repository strategy—The simplest approach is a mono-repository model. However, if your project uses legacy code bases and third-party packages, you may be forced to implement a multi-repository model.

    - The management process for third-party source code and binaries.

- The integration testing and system testing roles and processes that will be performed by the software team—In my experience, this varies a lot depending on the project, team size, and schedules.

- The list of build tools—Typically, these decisions are constrained by your CI server, legacy code bases, and third-party packages.

- The list of release artifacts and the supporting documentation that will be required with each release

CHAPTER 4   SOFTWARE DEVELOPMENT PLAN

Additional Guidelines

You should also reference some additional guidelines that may not be under the control of your software team. For example, some important guidelines may be owned by the quality team, and you can simply include references to those guidelines. However, if those documents don't exist, you will need to create them. I recommended that you develop guidelines for the following items:

- Requirements traceability
- Regulatory concerns
- Development workflow, for example, Agile, Scrum, Waterfall, etc.
- Required architecture, design, and supporting documentation
- Other company or domain-specific quality processes

If these kinds of external guidelines don't exist, that is okay. But it does mean you will need to provide more definition in your SDP for these topics.

Care and Feeding of Your SDP

While fairly static, your SDP will need some care and feeding along the way. When you make changes, it is critical that all the relevant stakeholders—developers, program managers, managers, etc.—are made aware of the changes.

CHAPTER 4 SOFTWARE DEVELOPMENT PLAN

SDP for the GM6000

The following is the outline for the GM6000's SDP. If you use these as templates, feel free to change the organization and formatting. What's important is that you consider the content of each section, even for topics that ultimately do not apply to your project. The complete SDP is provided in Appendix K, "GM6000 Software Development Plan."

1. Document name and version number
2. Overview
3. Glossary
4. Document references
5. Roles and responsibilities
6. Software items
7. Documentation outputs
8. Requirements
9. Software development life cycle processes
10. Cybersecurity
11. Tools
12. SCM
13. Testing
14. Deliverables
15. Change log

Each of these sections should contain links and applicable references to your company's QMS documentation.

CHAPTER 4   SOFTWARE DEVELOPMENT PLAN

Housekeeping

Sections 1–4 and section 15, *Document name and version number, Overview, Glossary, Document references,* and *Change log,* are housekeeping sections for software documentation. They are self-explanatory, and it should be easy to fill in these sections. For example, the *Overview* section is just a sentence or two that states the scope of the document. Here is an example from Appendix K, "GM6000 Software Development Plan":

> *This document captures the software development decisions, activities, and logistics for developing all of the software that executes on the GM6000 Digital Heater Controller's Control Board that is needed to formally test, validate, manufacture, and release a GM6000.*

Roles and Responsibilities

This section identifies the various roles on the team. It describes the responsibility of each role in the software development process and the project as a whole, and it sets common expectations for the entire team. Also be aware that people often perform multiple roles.

Here is an example of a defined role on the team:

- **Software lead**–*Technical lead for all software contained within the GM6000 control board. Responsible for*
    - *Creating software architecture*
    - *Creating software detailed design*
    - *Defining SRS requirements*

- *Resolving software-specific technical issues and decisions*
- *Ensuring the software-specific processes (especially reviews) are followed*
- *Signing off on the final releases*

Also note that when a person is assigned a role, it does not mean that they are the sole author of the document or the deliverable. The responsibility of the role is to ensure the completion of the document and not necessarily to write it themselves.

Software Items

This section identifies what the top-level software deliverables are. For each software item, the following items are called out:

- The verification that is required
- The programming languages that will be used
- The coding standards that will be followed

Here is an example how software items can be identified:

1. *Software that executes on the GM6000 control board when it is shipped to a customer*
    a. *This software item requires formal testing and verification before being released.*
    b. *The software shall be programmed in C/C++ and conform to the SW-1002 Software C/C++ Embedded Coding Standard.*

CHAPTER 4   SOFTWARE DEVELOPMENT PLAN

2. *Manufacturing test software (which executes on the GM6000 control board) that will be used when manufacturing the GM6000*

    a. *This software item will be informally verified by engineering before being released to manufacturing.*

    b. *The software shall be programmed in C/C++ and conform to the SW-1002 Software C/C++ Embedded Coding Standard.*

Documentation Outputs

This section is used to call out non-source code artifacts that the software development team will deliver. It describes who has the responsibility to see that the artifact is completed and delivered and who, if it is a different person, the subject matter expert (SME) is.

Not all the artifacts or documents need to be Word-style documents. For example, Doxygen HTML pages, wiki pages, etc., are acceptable. Depending on your project, you may need to create all these documents, or possibly just a subset. And in some cases, you may need additional documents that aren't listed here. Possible artifacts are

- Software architecture
- Software detailed design
- Doxygen output
- Code review artifacts
- Design review artifacts
- Integration test plans, test procedures, test reports
- Developer environment setup

CHAPTER 4   SOFTWARE DEVELOPMENT PLAN

- Build server setup
- CI setup
- Release notes
- Software Bill of Materials (BOM)
- Release cover page for the Product Lifecycle Management (PLM) system.

Here are some examples from the SDP in Appendix K, "GM6000 Software Development Plan."

1. *The supporting documentation shall be created in accordance with the processes defined in the QMS-010 Software Development Life Cycle Process document.*

2. *A Software Architecture document shall be created and assigned a formal document number. The Software Lead is responsible for this document.*

3. *A Software Detailed Design document shall be created and assigned a formal document number. The Software Lead is responsible for this document.*

4. *The following documentation artifacts are captured in Confluence as wiki pages. The Software Lead is responsible for these items:*

    a. *Instructions on how to set up a developer's local build environment*

    b. *Instructions on how to manage the tools on the build servers*

    c. *Instructions on how to set up the CI platform*

CHAPTER 4   SOFTWARE DEVELOPMENT PLAN

Requirements

This section specifies what requirements documentation (with respect to software) is needed, who is responsible for the requirements, and what is the canonical source for the requirements. The section also includes what traceability processes need to be put in place. Basically, all of the processes discussed in Chapter 3, "Analysis," are captured in the SDP. Here is an example:

1. *The supporting documentation shall be created in accordance with the processes defined in the QMS-004 Requirements Management document.*

2. *The MRS is a formal document (with an assigned number) that captures all the top-level user and business needs. The Product Manager is responsible for this document.*

3. *The PRS is a formal document (with an assigned number) that captures the system-level requirements that are derived from the MRS. The System Engineer is responsible for this document.*

4. *The SRS is a formal document (with an assigned number) that captures the software-level requirements that are derived from the MRS and PRS. The Software Lead is responsible for this document.*

CHAPTER 4   SOFTWARE DEVELOPMENT PLAN

Software Development Life Cycle Processes

This section identifies the different software development phases and workflows for each phase. Ideally this section only consists of references to existing documents. Some of the topics that should be covered are as follows:

- The name and number of development phases
- The workflow for checking and reviewing code
- The workflow for reviewing design documentation
- The bug tracking processes
- The point in the process where formal testing can begin on the code that is being developed
- How the determination will be made that the software is "good enough" to release to manufacturing

Here are examples form the SDP in Appendix K, "GM6000 Software Development Plan."

1. *The software shall be developed in accordance with the processes defined in the QMS-010 Software Development Life Cycle Process document.*

2. *There are four phases: Planning, Construction, Verification, and Release.*

3. *The Planning phase shall consist of requirements gathering, software architecture, planning, and preparing the tools and infrastructure needed for the Construction phase.*

    a. *This process will generally follow an iterative, Agile Kanban process with tasks captured in JIRA.*

CHAPTER 4   SOFTWARE DEVELOPMENT PLAN

    b. All code checked into GitHub during this phase requires a ticket. The ticket workflow shall be the same as the workflow described under the Construction phase.

    c. With respect to software development, the Planning phase is considered waterfall in that the Construction phase shall not begin until the Planning phase has completed.

    d. The Planning phase is exited after the following deliverables have been completed:

- A reviewed first draft of the SWA-1327 GM6000 Software Architecture document
- The foundational skeleton application can be successfully built by the CI server (including automated unit tests)

4. The Construction phase shall consist of detailed design, implementation, testing, and bug fixing.

Cybersecurity

This section identifies the workflows and deliverables—if any—needed to address cybersecurity. Here is an example from the SDP.

1. *The cybersecurity needs of the project shall follow the processes defined in QMS-018 Cyber Security Work Instructions.*

2. *The cybersecurity analysis and control measures shall be documented in the software architecture document. The Software Lead is responsible for the cybersecurity content.*

CHAPTER 4 SOFTWARE DEVELOPMENT PLAN

Tools

This section identifies tools used to develop the software. Because it is sometimes a requirement that you can go back and re-create (i.e., recompile) any released version of the software, it is also important to describe how tools will be archived.

Here is an example from the SDP:

1. *The software that executes on the Control Board hardware shall be compiled with the GCC cross compiler for the specific microcontroller.*

    a. *The version of the compiler shall not be changed during the construction and release phases unless there is a documented compiler bug that impacts the software.*

    b. *The compiler toolchain shall be archived along with the source code in GitHub.*

    c. *The compiler toolchain shall be tagged and labelled when a formal build is performed.*

Software Configuration Management (SCM)

This section specifies the logistics of how you are going to version control your source code, including any third-party packages that will be used. Topics that should be addressed are as follows:

- SCM tools and repository server—For example, GIT, GitHub, etc.

- Repository strategy—For example, a single repository, multiple repositories, etc.

- Management of third-party packages—You might address issues like these:

CHAPTER 4   SOFTWARE DEVELOPMENT PLAN

- Will third-party packages be pulled from the Internet every time a build is done?
- Are there local copies of the packages?
- Are the packages stored in the company's GIT repository?
- Is the local copy forked from the original source?
• Branch strategy—For example, trunk, Git Flow, and merge rules (e.g., for pull requests)
• Versioning strategy—For example, a description of identifiers and SCM labeling

Here are examples from the SDP in Appendix K, "GM6000 Software Development Plan."

1. *GitHub private repositories shall be used to version control all the source code for the project.*

   a. *A single repository shall be used. The repository URL is* `https://github.com/xxxxx/gm6000`*.*

   b. *The repository will also contain all third-party packages and the cross-compiler toolchain used to build binaries for the target hardware.*

2. *The branching strategy shall be a modified trunk-based development model.*

   a. *The* `main` *branch shall be used for all candidate releases.*

   b. *A child branch (off* `main`*), called* `develop,` *shall be used as the stable branch for day-to-day development and pull requests.*

   c. *Each ticket will be used to create a short-lived branch off of the* `develop` *branch. The ticket number shall be part of the branch name.*

CHAPTER 4 SOFTWARE DEVELOPMENT PLAN

Testing

This section specifies details how the testing—which is the responsibility of the software team—will be done. Topics that should be covered are as follows:

- Unit test requirements and code coverage metrics as applicable
- Integration testing requirements
- How third-party packages will be tested
- Use of the non-target-based testing (e.g., using a functional simulator)

Here is an example from the SDP:

1. *The software team is responsible for unit testing and integration testing.*

2. *The source code is organized by namespaces (per SW-1002). Each namespace is required to have at least one unit test for the code it contains.*

   a. *If the namespace has a direct target platform dependency, the unit test shall be a manual test that executes on the target platform.*

   b. *If the namespace contains implementation for the UI, the unit test shall be a manual test that executes either on the target platform or the simulator.*

   Note *The automated unit test requirement is relaxed with respect to the UI because the test infrastructure does not include tools for automated verification of the UI's visual presentation.*

c. *All other namespaces shall have an automated unit that is a stand-alone application that returns pass/fail. Automated unit tests are executed as part of the CI process for all builds. All automated unit tests are required to meet the following code coverage metrics. Note that because of the tools being used (*gcc, gcovr*), the branch coverage metrics are not always correct–the branch coverage threshold is intentionally lower to compensate.*

- *Line coverage >= 80%*
- *Branch coverage >= 60%*

Deliverables

This section summarizes the various deliverables called out in the SDP document. This is essentially the software deliverables checklist for the entire project. Here is an example from the SDP in Appendix K, "GM6000 Software Development Plan":

Deliverable	Phase(s)	Notes
SDP-1328 GM6000 Software Development Plan	Planning Construction	A reviewed first draft is required to exit the planning phase.
SRS-1324 GM6000 Software Requirement Specification	Planning Construction	A reviewed first draft is required to exit the planning phase.
SWA-1327 GM6000 Software Architecture	Planning Construction	A reviewed first draft is required to exit the planning phase.
SWA-1329 GM6000 Software Detailed Design	Construction	
...	...	...

CHAPTER 4   SOFTWARE DEVELOPMENT PLAN

Summary

Don't skip creating an SDP. Lacking a formal SDP simply means that a de facto SDP will organically evolve and be inconsistently applied over the course of the project where it will be a constant source of drama.

INPUTS

- The project's user and business needs
- The company's quality processes
- The company's software development methodology, for example, Agile, waterfall, TDD, etc.
- The software development team's best practices and processes

OUTPUTS

- The first draft of the software development plan document

CHAPTER 5

Preparation

The preparation step is not about defining and developing your product as much as it is about putting together the infrastructure that supports the day-to-day work. The tools that you will be using should have been called out in the Software Development Plan (SDP), but if you have tools that aren't referenced there, this is the time to add them to the SDP along with the rationale for prescribing their use.

The SDP for the GM6000 calls for the following tools:

- Git server—For version control and file management
- JIRA—For ticket tracking and bug tracking
- Confluence—For the wiki server that is used to host some of the supporting documentation
- Jenkins—For continuous integration (CI)

In nearly all companies that I've worked for, tools such as JIRA and Confluence were already in place and were directly supported by the IT team, so it was not something the software team had to worry about. Nevertheless, I still needed to make sure that the team members had accounts and permissions to access the tools and that at least two members of the cross-functional core team had "full access" rights and permissions to the tools and systems, including the ability to create and manage users.

CHAPTER 5   PREPARATION

For actual code development, the companies used the GitHub tools unless they had commercial tools like Perforce or ClearCase. As the GitHub tools are largely free, this chapter prescribes the use of the following tools:

- GitHub public repository—For version control and file management
- GitHub's Projects—For JIRA-like task management and feature tracking
- GitHub Wiki—For Confluence-like documentation and notes

As for continuous integration (CI), many companies do not have CI tools in place, so you and your team may find yourselves needing to implement them with minimal support from IT. For that reason, the book's GitHub wiki pages[1] provide step-by-step instructions for setting up Jenkins to build GM6000 example code. However, the GM6000 only uses a single repository, and it has simple CI requirements. Consequently, the Jenkins setup is basic and does not take advantage of features like pipeline builds and automated deployments.

GitHub Projects

GitHub Projects is an adaptable, flexible tool for planning and tracking your work.[2] It's a free tool that allows you to track issues such as bug reports or tasks or feature requests, and it provides various views to facilitate prioritization and tracking. For example, Figure 5-1 is an example of the Kanban-style view of the GM6000 project. For a given project, the

---

[1] https://github.com/johnttaylor/epc/wiki
[2] https://docs.github.com/en/issues/planning-and-tracking-with-projects/learning-about-projects/about-projects

CHAPTER 5 PREPARATION

issue cards can span multiple repositories, and branches can be created directly from the issue cards themselves. For the details of setting up GitHub Projects, I recommend the "Creating a Project" documentation provided by GitHub.³

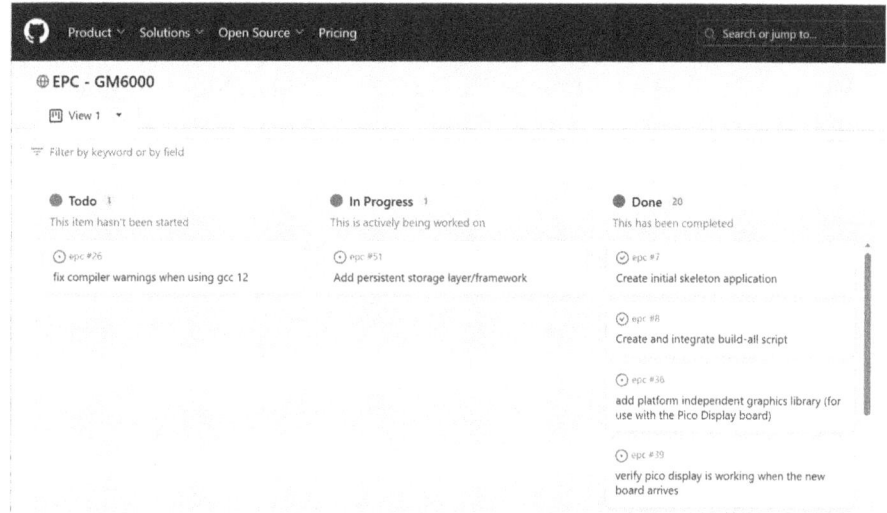

Figure 5-1. Kanban-style view of the GM6000 project

GitHub Wiki

GitHub provides one free wiki per public repository. The following list provides examples of documents you should consider capturing on a Wiki:

- Developer and Build Server setup instructions
- CI Platform setup and maintenance instructions
- Software development tools list

---

³ https://docs.github.com/en/issues/planning-and-tracking-with-projects/creating-projects/creating-a-project

79

CHAPTER 5   PREPARATION

- Software "Bill of Materials" (or some other list of all third-party packages)
- Coding standards
- Work instructions (e.g., instructions for creating releases, shipping hardware to an offshore vendor, etc.)

Figure 5-2 shows an example of a GitHub wiki page for the GM6000 project.

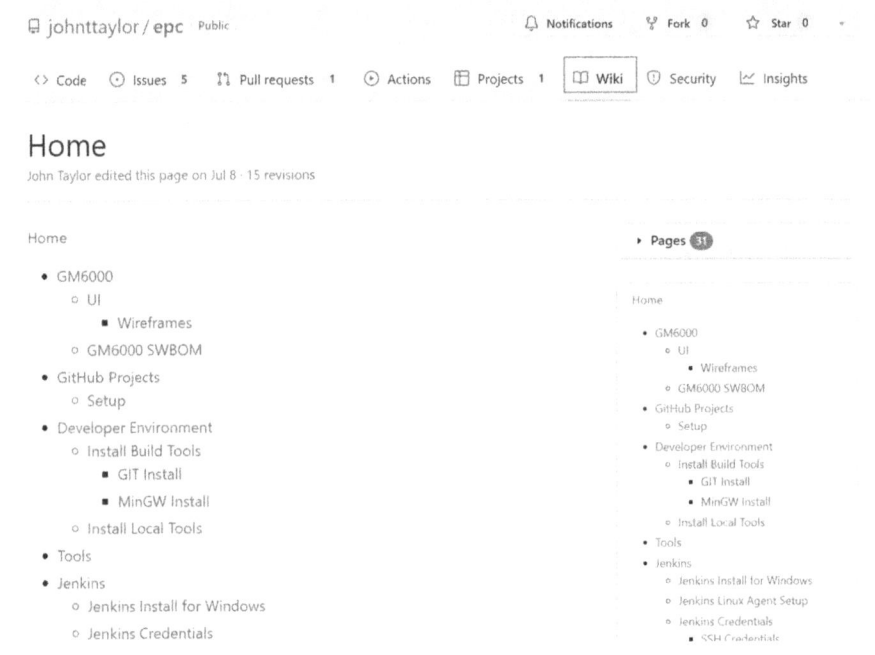

Figure 5-2. *GitHub wiki page for the GM6000 project*

The wiki uses GitHub's markdown language for formatting page content, and it supports storing images as part of a wiki page. The organization of the wiki is flat—there is no direct support for hierarchy of pages—but you can create your own "Custom Side-bar" where you can apply a hierarchy, or table of contents, as shown in Figure 5-3.

CHAPTER 5   PREPARATION

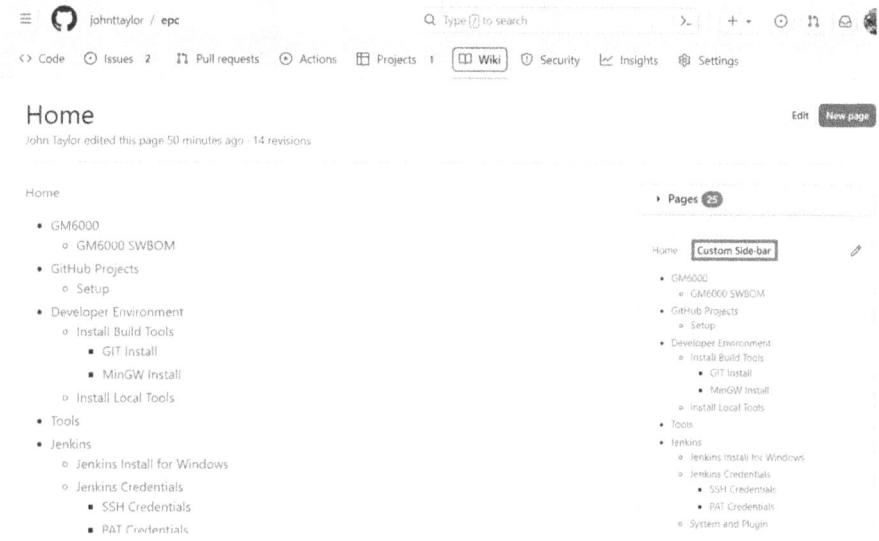

Figure 5-3. *GitHub wiki Custom Side-bar*

The Custom Side-bar is essentially just another wiki page of markdown links that you can indent to indicate hierarchy. The following markdown snippet shows an example of how the side-bar for the GM6000 wiki was defined. Additional help for constructing wiki pages can be found on GitHub's website.[4]

```
[Home](https://github.com/johnttaylor/epc/wiki/Home )
  * [GM6000](https://github.com/johnttaylor/epc/wiki/GM6000)
    * [GM6000 SWBOM](https://github.com/johnttaylor/epc/wiki/
      GM6000---Software-Bill-of-Materials-(SWBOM))
  * [GitHub Projects](https://github.com/johnttaylor/epc/wiki/
    GitHub---Projects)
```

---

[4] https://docs.github.com/en/communities/documenting-your-project-with-wikis/creating-a-footer-or-sidebar-for-your-wiki#creating-a-sidebar

CHAPTER 5   PREPARATION

```
    * [Setup](https://github.com/johnttaylor/epc/wiki/GitHub-
      Projects---Setup)
  * [Developer Environment](https://github.com/johnttaylor/epc/
    wiki/Development-Environment)
    * [Install Build Tools](https://github.com/johnttaylor/epc/
      wiki/Developer---Install-Build-Tools)
      * [GIT Install](https://github.com/johnttaylor/epc/wiki/
        Developer---GIT-Install)
    * [Install Local Tools](https://github.com/johnttaylor/epc/
      wiki/Developer---Install-Local-Tools)
  * [Tools](https://github.com/johnttaylor/epc/wiki/Tools)
```

Continuous Integration Requirements

In a perfect world, there would be a person or team in charge of designing, creating, running, and maintaining the continuous integration hardware and software. If you happen to be in this situation, consult with the CI lead about incorporating some of the requirements listed here into your CI. They are probably doing many of these things already. But if not, collaborate with them on incorporating some of these features:

- Ensure that all individual developer code that gets committed to the Software Configuration Management (SCM) system compiles and passes all automated unit tests. This is considered a basic CI build. In practice, this means CI builds are performed on all pull requests.

- Ensure that a basic CI build completes successfully before the source code for that build is merged into mainline or stable branches.

- Ensure that every CI build builds all unit tests—both manual and automated—along with all the final application executables.
- Ensure that the simulator or simulators—if you have them—build every time.
- Ensure that the build server that is used for the CI builds is the same build server used for creating formal builds from stable branches in the SCM repository.
- Ensure that formal builds, or releases, are done from mainline or some other stable branch. Formal builds are required to pass all automated unit tests just like CI builds.
- Ensure that the formal builds are tagged or labeled in the SCM repository.
- With both CI and formal builds, ensure that all permutations of the final application and simulators and release variants and engineering-only variants get built every time.
- Ensure that build artifacts (e.g., .hex files, .exe files, Doxygen output, etc.) for formal releases are archived so they are retrievable by nondevelopers.
- Incorporate, at your discretion, any automated "smoke tests" or "sanity tests" into the build process. See Chapter 13, "Integration Testing," for additional discussion about automated smoke tests.

CHAPTER 5   PREPARATION

Soapbox: CI is not a simple or free addition to a project. So why do it? The reason to do it is to detect integration errors as quickly as possible. On the surface, this may not sound like a huge win, but CI is a significant net positive when it comes to maintaining stable branches in your SCM. Avoiding the pain of broken builds, and the misery of being bogged down in "merge hell," is more than enough compensation for the effort you put into setting up and maintaining a CI server.

Jenkins

Installing and configuring Jenkins for your specific CI needs is nontrivial. But here is the good news:

- The Jenkins website provides detailed instructions for installing Jenkins on multiple host platforms.[5]

- Jenkins is widely used. This means that there are plenty of plug-ins available, and information about how to do things with Jenkins can often be found with simple Internet searches.

- The book's GitHub Wiki page, `https://github.com/johnttaylor/epc/wiki/All-Things-Jenkins`, provides step-by-step instructions on how to stand up Jenkins.

---

[5] www.jenkins.io/doc/book/installing/

Here are the high-level steps for installing and configuring CI on Jenkins:

1. Install Jenkins—This involves downloading and getting the Jenkins services running. For the GM6000 project, the primary Jenkins controller runs on a Windows PC.

2. Set up Credentials for accessing GitHub—Jenkins accesses GitHub repositories using GitHub APIs.

3. Configure the system, the tools, and the plug-ins.

4. Set up a Linux build agent—A Linux build agent, running on a physical or virtual machine, is required to compile the platform-independent code for a Linux host.

5. Create automation projects—This involves creating jobs that are automatically triggered when pull requests are created and when code is merged to stable branches such as develop and main. These jobs are responsible for building the code, executing the unit tests, generating reports, and archiving build artifacts.

Having two build platforms (Windows and Linux) adds to the complexity of the Jenkins configuration, but in order to keep the GM6000 example code honest, I needed my CI build server to perform native Linux builds.

CHAPTER 5 PREPARATION

Summary

The preparation step in the planning stage is all about enabling software development. Many of the activities are either mostly completed, because the tools are already in place from a previous project, or can be started in parallel with the creation of the Software Development Plan (SDP). So there should be ample time to complete this step before the construction stage begins. But I can tell you from experience, if you don't complete this step before construction begins, you can expect to experience major headaches and rework. Without a working CI server, you may have broken builds or failing unit tests without even knowing it. And the more code that is written before these issues are discovered, the more the work (and pain) needed to correct them increases.

INPUTS

- The initial draft of the Software Development Plan

OUTPUTS

- A Software Configuration Management (SCM) server (e.g., GitHub) for managing the project's source code is up and running.

- User accounts with appropriate permissions have been created for all the software developers on the SCM server. Also, testers should have been given access to the repositories.

- A planning and tracking tool (e.g., JIRA or GitHub Projects) for tracking is up and running, and a project has been created.

CHAPTER 5   PREPARATION

- User accounts have been created for all of the team members (including nonsoftware developers) in the tracking tool.

- A wiki server (e.g., Confluence, or a GitHub wiki) to host lightweight documentation is up and running, and a home page has been created.

- User accounts have been created for all team members (including nonsoftware developers) on the wiki server.

- A continuous integration (CI) server is up and running. This includes creating minimal automation jobs that can check out repository code and execute a script from the repository that returns pass/fail.

CHAPTER 6

Foundation

The foundation step in the planning phase is about getting the day-to-day environment set up for developers so they can start the construction phase with a production-ready workflow. This includes performing tasks, for example:

- Setting up the SCM repositories (e.g., setting up the repository in GitHub)
- Defining the top-level source code organization for the project
- Creating build scripts that can build unit tests and application images
- Creating skeleton applications for the project, including one for the functional simulator
- Creating CI build scripts that are fully integrated and that build all the unit tests and application projects using the CI build server
- Creating the outline for the Software Detailed Design (SDD) document. Because the SDD is very much a living document, as detailed design is done on a just-in-time basis, nothing is set in stone at this point, and you can expect things to change throughout the course of the project. (See Chapter 11, "Just-in-Time Detailed Design," for more details.)

CHAPTER 6   FOUNDATION

SCM Repositories

The SCM tool should have been "stood up" as part of the preparation step. So for the foundation step, it is simply a matter of creating the repository and setting up the branch structure according to the strategy you defined in the SDP.

Source Code Organization

You will need to make several decisions about the layout of your source code tree, and these decisions can have far-ranging consequences. A well-thought-out, consistent file organization facilitates code reuse as well as the creation and maintenance of unit tests. It is also critical to your ability to build multiple images and executables from your code base. These decisions should be captured—actually written down—in the SDD.

Unfortunately, you never get the source code organization quite right on the first pass. However, I have learned from experience that it is best to organize your files by component dependencies—not by project. That is, do not create your directory structure to reflect a top-down decomposition of the project. Rather, organize your code so that the directories reflect the namespaces of your code. By doing this, you can simply inspect the directory structure as a quick visual check that there are no undesired cyclical dependencies. As an example, Figure 6-1 shows an annotated view of the selectively expanded, top-level directory structure for the GM6000 project.

The GM6000 directory structure is more fully documented in Appendix L, "GM6000 Software Detailed Design (Initial Draft)." Additionally, Appendix O, "Software C/C++ Embedded Coding Standard," contains specifics about naming conventions in the source code organization.

CHAPTER 6 FOUNDATION

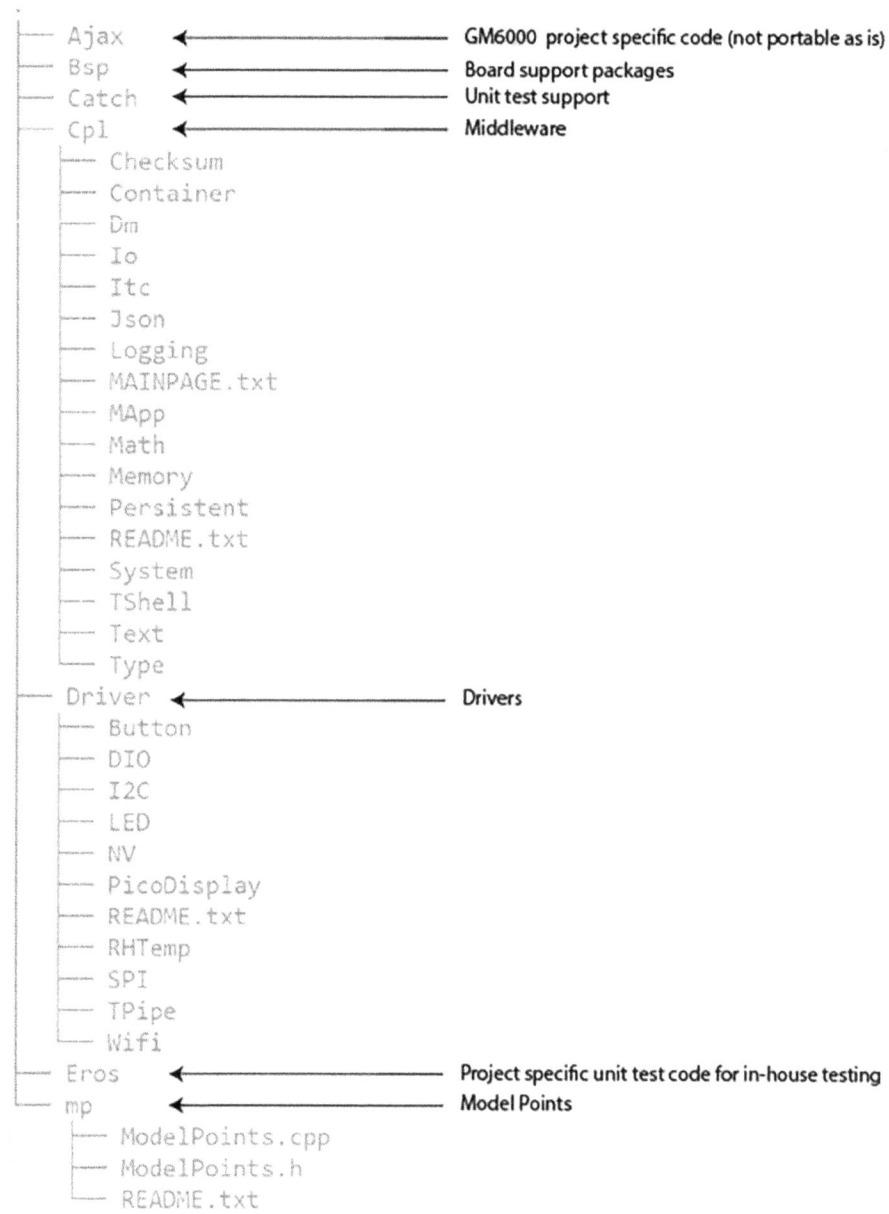

Figure 6-1. *Annotated top-level directory structure for GM6000*

CHAPTER 6 FOUNDATION

Build System and Scripts

Selecting build tools is a decision that impacts the entire life of the project. That is, it is extremely painful to change build systems after you have applications in place and have created a bunch of unit tests. And sometimes, in real life, you just get stuck with something. For example, there may be a component of your project that requires you to use cmake.[1] However, if you do get to choose your own tools, here are some best practices to consider:

- Builds need to be command line based to support automation. This requirement is not absolute, but it is a rare use case where building within a developer's IDE and building from a fully integrated CI tool set will yield the same results. Depending on the IDE, you may be able to launch it from the command line with enough parameters to have it build and exit unassisted. This is okay as long as you always use it in this way.

- The continuous integration build machine and the developers both use the same build scripts. This is an absolute requirement.

- The build tools should create the application (including all variants) and support an unlimited number of unit tests. The build scripts must scale because the number of unit tests or application variants increases over time.

- Adding a new file to the build scripts should require low-to-no effort for the developer. Adding a new directory should also require low effort.

---

[1] https://cmake.org/

CHAPTER 6 FOUNDATION

- For any build script file that is located in the same directory as the source code, the script should not contain any "unique to the final output" details like compiler flags, linker directives, -D symbols, etc. The reason is that any given directory may be built for different output images. For example, it could be built as part of the application and additionally it could be built as part of a unit test image.

- The build scripts should have the ability to selectively build directories. That is, the build scripts should never assume that it is okay to recursively build everything in a directory including all of its subdirectories. Once again, the reason is that, depending on whether the build is creating the application, the functional simulator, or a unit test, the subdirectories that need to be used can differ.

- Build scripts must be constructed such that path information about where a source code file is located is not lost when generating and referencing derived objects. In other words, the build scripts cannot assume or require globally unique file names.

- Build scripts must be constructed such that the generated object files are not placed in the same directory as the source code. This is especially important when building the source code for multiple platforms with different compiler options.

- The build engine should be host, compiler, and target independent. The unit test, functional simulator, and application builds will be built across multiple host environments for multiple target platforms.

CHAPTER 6 FOUNDATION

After you have selected your build tools, you need to create scripts that will build the skeleton applications and unit tests (both manual and automated).

The art of constructing build scripts and using makefiles is out of the scope of this book, simply because of the number of build tools available and the nuances and variations that come with them. Suffice it to say, though, that over the years I have been variously frustrated by many of the build tools that I was either required to use or tried to use. Consequently, I built my own tool—the NQBP2 build engine—which eschews makefiles in favor of a list of directories to build. This tool is freely available and documented on GitHub.

The GM6000 example uses the NQBP2 build engine, and more details about NQBP2 are provided in Appendix F, "NQBP2 Build System."

Skeleton Applications

The skeleton projects provide the structure for all the code developed in the construction phase. There should be a skeleton application for all released images, including target hardware builds and functional simulator builds for the applications. Chapter 7, "Building Applications with the Main Pattern," provides details about creating the skeleton application for the target hardware and the functional simulator.

CI "Build-All" Script

After you have selected your build engine and have created build scripts that can build skeleton applications and unit tests, you will want to create a "build-all" script that builds all the applications and unit tests in the project. Chapter 8, "Continuous Integration Builds," goes into detail about how to create a build-all script. After the build-all script is written, the final step is to integrate it with the CI build server. After this work is done, your CI workflow should be complete (except for maintenance).

The build-all script should be architected such that it does not have to be updated when new applications and unit tests are added to the project.

Software Detailed Design

Creating the outline for the Software Detailed Design (SDD) document is pretty simple after all of the top-level subsystems in the software architecture have been identified. The bulk of the outline for the SDD consists of some boilerplate sections and the subsystems section of the software architecture. Figure 6-2 shows the outline for the GM6000's SDD.

CHAPTER 6 FOUNDATION

1. Document Name and Number
2. Overview
3. Glossary
4. Document References
5. Software Architecture Overview
6. [SDD-35] Source Code
7. [SDD-62] Unit Testing
8. [SDD-31] Sub-Systems
    a. [SDD-10] Alert Management
    b. [SDD-11] Application
    c. [SDD-32] Creation and Start-up
    d. [SDD-12] Boot Loader
    e. [SDD-13] BSP
    f. [SDD-14] Console
    g. [SDD-15] Crypto
    h. [SDD-16] Data Model
    i. [SDD-17] Diagnostics
    j. [SDD-18] Drivers
    k. [SDD-36] Button Driver
    l. [SDD-37] GPIO Output driver
    m. [SDD-39] Pico Display Driver
    n. [SDD-40] PWM driver
    o. [SDD-42] SPI Driver
    p. [SDD-19] Graphics Library
    q. [SDD-20] Heating
    r. [SDD-21] Logging
    s. [SDD-22] OS
    t. [SDD-23] OSAL
    u. [SDD-24] Persistent Storage
    v. [SDD-25] Sensor Communications
    w. [SDD-26] Software Update
    x. [SDD-27] System Services
    y. [SDD-28] UI
9. [SDD-29] Functional Simulator
10. [SDD-30] Engineer Test Application
    a. [SDD-33] Creation and Start-up
11. Change Log

Figure 6-2. *SDD outline for the GM6000*

The *Overview* and *Software Architecture Overview* sections are included to provide some basic context for the design details. Do not make these sections too verbose because the SDD is not the canonical source for the material presented in these sections.

You will also note that there are additional sections that are neither boilerplate nor subsystems. This is okay because the SDD is not restricted to just the top-level subsystems. It contains all of the Software Detailed

Design that the project needs. However, all sections (except housekeeping sections) must be traceable back to a section in the software architecture document. If a detailed design section can't be traced back to the software architecture document, you should stop immediately and resolve the disconnect.

The primary advantage of organizing the SDD according to the subsystems identified in the software architecture document is that you get requirements traceability for free. This is because you have created a one-to-one mapping between the software architecture subsystems and the SDD sections.

The other sections for the SDD outline for the GM6000 are as follows:

- Source code—This section finalizes and documents the top-level source code organization for the entire project. It traces back to *SWA-38 File and Directory Organization.*

- Unit testing—This section defines the naming conventions for unit tests. It traces back to *SWA-42 Unit Testing.*

- Functional simulator—This section captures design details specific to the simulator. It traces back to *SWA-34 Simulator.*

- Engineering test application—This section covers the design details specific to the special test software used for engineering validation and manufacturing testing. It traces back to *SWA-41 Engineering and Manufacturing Testing.*

Summary

The foundation step is the final, gating work that needs to be completed before moving on to the construction phase. The foundation step includes a small amount of design work and some implementation work to get the build scripts to successfully build the skeleton applications and to integrate these scripts with the CI server.

You may be tempted to skip the foundation steps, or to do them later after you started coding the interesting stuff. Don't! The value of the CI server is to detect broken builds immediately. Until your CI server is fully stood up, you won't know if your `develop` or `main` branches are broken. Additionally, skipping building the skeleton applications is simply creating technical debt. The creation and startup code will exist at some point, so doing it first, while planning for known permutations, is a much more efficient and cost-effective solution than organically evolving it over time.

INPUTS

- The initial draft of the Software Development Plan (SDP)
- The initial draft of the software architecture (SWA) document
- The continuous integration (CI) server is running.
- The Software Configuration Management (SCM) server is running.

OUTPUTS

- Skeleton applications for all planned released images. This includes both target hardware and simulator builds.

- Source code repository created and populated with the skeleton applications

- The CI server is able to build all applications and unit tests, tag and label formal builds, and archive build artifacts.

- The first draft of the outline for the Software Detailed Design document. In addition to the outline, the SDD should also include the design for

  - The organization of the source code tree
  - Application creation and startup (i.e., the `main` pattern)

- An updated requirements trace matrix that shows the back trace from SDD sections to the software architecture sections

CHAPTER 7

Building Applications with the Main Pattern

At this point in the process, your principal objective is to set up a process to build your application to run on your hardware. However, you may also want to build variations of your application to provide different features and functionality. Additionally, you may want to create builds that will allow your application to run on different hardware. Consequently, the goal of this chapter is to put a structure in place that lets you build these different versions in an automated and scalable way.

Even if you have only a single primary application running on a single hardware platform, I recommend that you still build a functional simulator for your application. A simulator provides the benefits of being able to run and test large sections of your application code even before the hardware is available. It also provides a much richer debug environment for members of the development team.[1]

The additional effort to create a functional simulator is mostly planning. The key piece of that planning is starting with a decoupled design that can effectively isolate compiler-specific or platform-specific code. The trick, here, is not to do this with IF-DEFs in your function calls.

---

[1] For an in-depth discussion of the value proposition for a functional simulator, I recommend reading *Patterns in the Machine: A Software Engineering Guide to Embedded Development*.

CHAPTER 7　BUILDING APPLICATIONS WITH THE MAIN PATTERN

The IF-DEF approach can be used to manage the platform-specific details at compile time, but the better way to accomplish this is to build your application using the Main pattern, which manages the platform-specific and application-variant-specific details at link time.

About the Main Pattern

By using the Main pattern, the difference between constructing the target application and constructing the function simulator is isolated to the top-level creator. This means that a functional simulator uses over 80% of the same modules as the actual application. But, again, for this wiring magic to work, there must be explicit interface boundaries for all platform-specific functionality. In other words, you've designed your application and drivers to be decoupled from the underlying hardware platform (see Chapter 15, "Drivers," for details). At an implementation level, this generally means that you've separated your hardware-specific, compiler-specific, and application-variant-specific code into different files.

Figure 7-1 illustrates the dependencies of a hypothetical embedded application on its target platform.

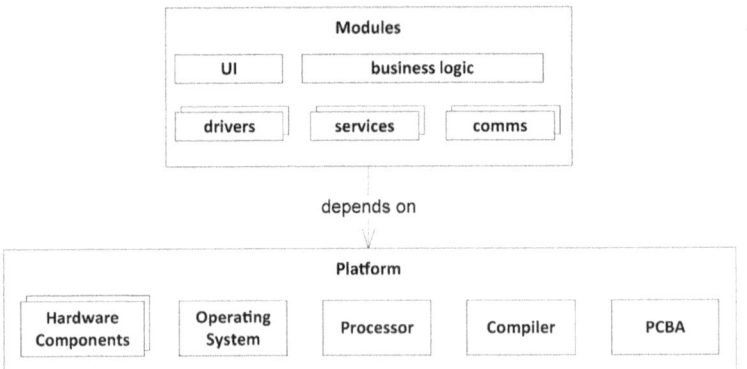

Figure 7-1. *Application platform dependencies*

By using Hardware Abstraction Layer (HAL) interfaces and Operating System Abstraction Layer (OSAL) interfaces, you can decouple the core application from the target platform. Note, however, that the separation of the platform-specific entities can be done with any abstract interface—not just at an HAL or OSAL interface. The concepts of HAL and OSAL interfaces are used here because they are more familiar and conceptually easier to understand. Figure 7-2 shows the same hypothetical embedded application with its hardware dependencies decoupled from the application.

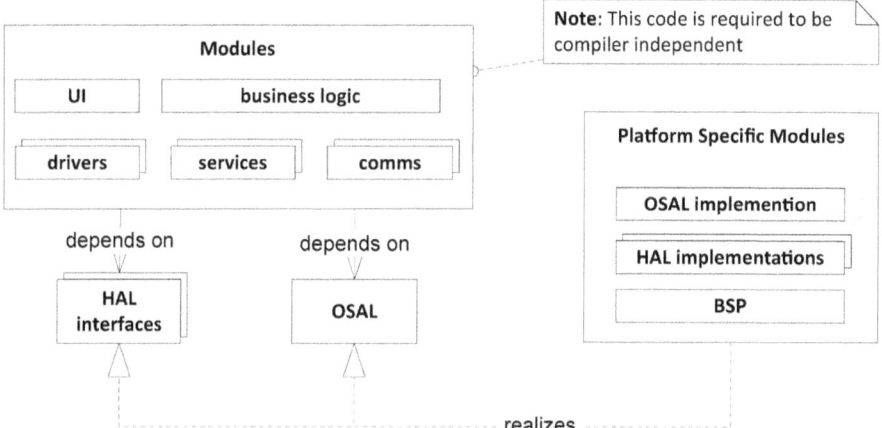

Figure 7-2. *Decoupled application platform dependencies*

Operating System Abstraction Layer

An OSAL provides interfaces for all functionality provided by the underlying operating system. For an embedded system that is using a basic thread scheduler, it would typically include interfaces such as

- Elapsed time (a replacement for the standard C library `clock()` function)
- Non-busy-wait delay (a replacement for the standard C library `sleep()` function)
- Thread management (create, delete, suspend, etc.)
- Mutexes
- Semaphores

You can create your own OSAL or use an open source OSAL such as CMSIS-RTOS2 for ARM Cortex processors. In addition, many microcontroller vendors (e.g. Microchip, TI, etc.) provide an OSAL with their SDKs. The example code for the GM6000 uses the OSAL provided by the CPL C++ class library.

Hardware Abstraction Layer

A HAL interface is an interface with no implementation. That is, the interface is abstract; it defines behavior for a hardware-specific or platform-specific device. At some point in the build process, or at runtime, there will be a binding of a device-specific implementation. A HAL interface is no different than any other abstract interface; prefacing it with HAL is just an attempt to categorize what the interface is abstracting. For example, one could view an OSAL as just a collection of abstract interfaces that define operating system behavior. (See Chapter 15, "Drivers," for more details of HAL interfaces.)

In general, HAL interfaces should be defined or created on an as-needed basis, and they should be created at the level that will provide the most return for the effort. This means that you should not try to create an all-encompassing HAL interface.

CHAPTER 7   BUILDING APPLICATIONS WITH THE MAIN PATTERN

More About Main

After defining your OSAL and HAL interfaces, the next step is to add in the Main pattern. The Main pattern encapsulates all of the platform-specific knowledge and dependencies about how to interconnect the platform-independent modules with the platform-specific modules. The Main pattern consists of

- The resolution of interface references with concrete implementations
- The initialization and shutdown sequencing

In Figure 7-3, the differences between the target application and the functional simulator are contained in the blocks labeled.

- Main
- Platform
- Platform Specific Modules

The core of the application is everything contained in the block labeled Modules, and those modules can stay the same regardless of which Main instance uses it. While the platform and platform-specific blocks, or entities, seem to take up half of the diagram shown in Figure 7-3, in practice, the common entities in Modules constitute over 80% of the code base.

CHAPTER 7　BUILDING APPLICATIONS WITH THE MAIN PATTERN

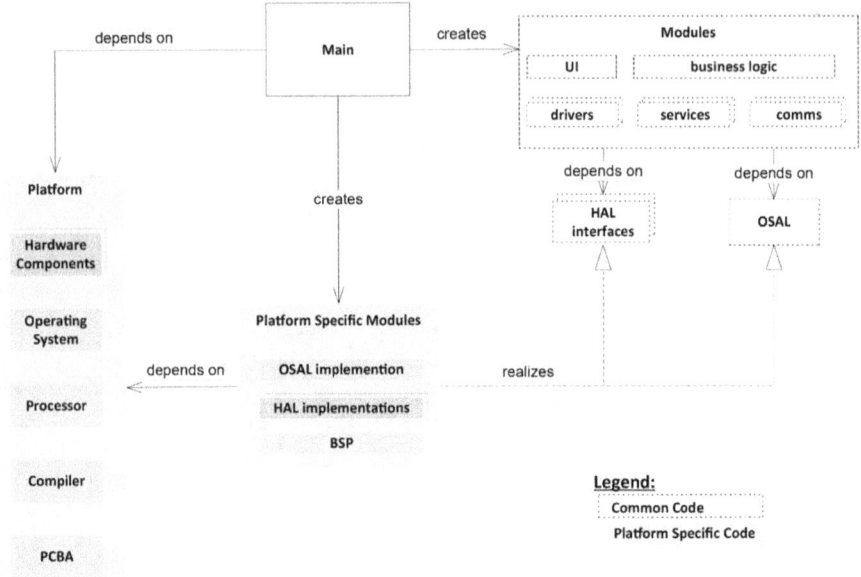

Figure 7-3. Application with Main pattern

Implementing Main

The Main pattern only addresses runtime creation and initialization. Of course, in practice, some of the platform-specific bindings will be done at compile or link time. These bindings are not explicitly part of the Main pattern.

It might be helpful at this point to briefly review how an embedded application gets executed. The following sequence assumes the application is running on a microcontroller:

1. The interrupt service routine for the Reset Vector is executed.

CHAPTER 7 BUILDING APPLICATIONS WITH THE MAIN PATTERN

2. Then the compiler included C/C++ runtime code executes. This includes items such as initialization of static variables, execution of constructors for statically allocated C++ objects, and potentially some minimal board initialization.

3. The `main()` function is called. When and what happens in the `main()` function is obviously application specific. However, in general terms, the following actions occur:

    a. All remaining board, or BSP, initialization is completed.

    b. The OS/RTOS is initialized. The thread scheduler may or may not be started at this time.

    c. Control is turned over to the application.

    d. The various drivers, subsystems, components, and modules are initialized and started.

    e. The application runs. At this point, the application is fully constructed and initialized, interrupts are enabled, and the thread scheduler is running (if there is OS/RTOS).

The Main pattern comes into play in step 3. Here's the annotated version of that step.

3a. All remaining board, or BSP, initialization is completed.	Highly platform-dependent code and should be physically segregated into separate files.
3b. The OS/RTOS is initialized. The thread scheduler may or may not be started at this time.	
3c. Control is turned over to the application.	Common startup source code across different platforms.
3d. The various drivers, subsystems, components, and modules are initialized and started.	
3e. The application runs. At this point, the application is fully constructed and initialized, interrupts are enabled, and the thread scheduler is running (if there is OS/RTOS)	

For steps 3a and 3b, the source code is platform dependent. One approach is to just have a single chunk of code and use an `#ifdef` whenever there are platform deltas. The problem is that `#ifdefs` within function calls do not scale, and your code will quickly become unreadable and difficult to maintain. The alternative is to separate—by platform—the source code into individual files and use link time bindings to select the platform-specific files. This means the logic of determining what hardware-specific and application-specific pieces make up a stand-alone module is moved out of your source code and into your build scripts. This approach declutters the individual source code files and is scalable to many platform variants.

For the remaining steps, 3c, 3d, and 3e, there is value in having a common application startup across different platforms, especially as the amount and complexity of the application startup code increase.

CHAPTER 7 BUILDING APPLICATIONS WITH THE MAIN PATTERN

My claim is that the Main pattern is a scalable way to manage the different combinations without resorting to #ifdefs. And the key decision that you need to make is whether the benefits of having common code across the different common code combinations outweigh the overhead of managing independent applications. In my experience, the answer is usually yes. You want to have as much common code as possible and explicitly (or, manually) manage the combinations.

Figure 7-4 shows high-level pseudocode for how the Main pattern is implemented for the GM6000, the hypothetical heating application that runs both on the target hardware running FreeRTOS and as a functional simulator on a PC.

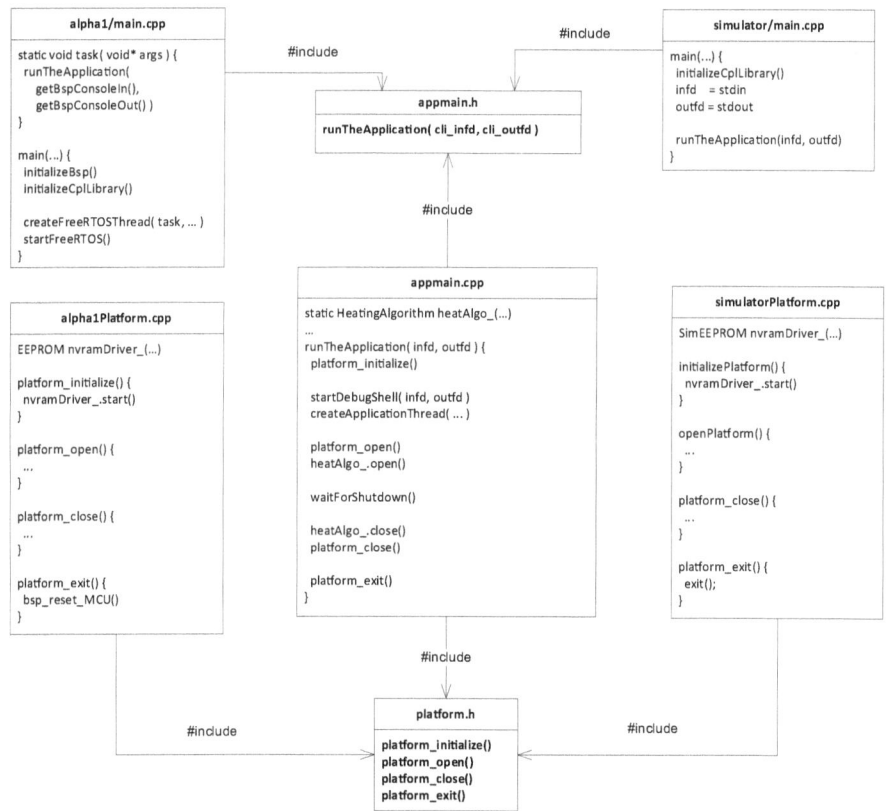

Figure 7-4. *Pseudocode for a Main pattern implementation*

109

CHAPTER 7   BUILDING APPLICATIONS WITH THE MAIN PATTERN

The GM6000 example extends the basic Main pattern to support multiple applications and target hardware variants. However, a concrete example of the basic Main pattern can be found in the main-pattern_initial-skeleton-projects branch in the GitHub repository. The directories of interest are

- src/Ajax/Main
- src/Ajax/Main/_app
- src/Ajax/Main/_plat_alpah1
- src/Ajax/Main/_plat_simulator

Application Variant

It may be that you have a marketing requirement for good, better, and best versions of your application, or it may be that you just need a test-enabled application for a certification process. But whatever the reason for creating additional applications, each separate application will be built from a large amount of common code (see Figure 7-5).

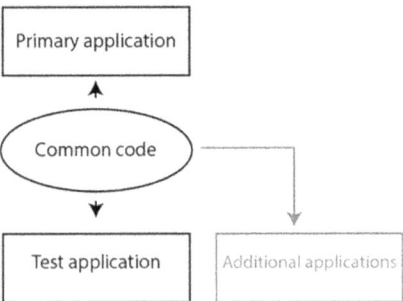

Figure 7-5. *Building multiple applications from common code*

CHAPTER 7   BUILDING APPLICATIONS WITH THE MAIN PATTERN

Additionally, in order for your different applications to execute on your target hardware or simulator, you will need to write additional platform-specific code. But even here there will be a certain amount of common platform code (see Figure 7-6).

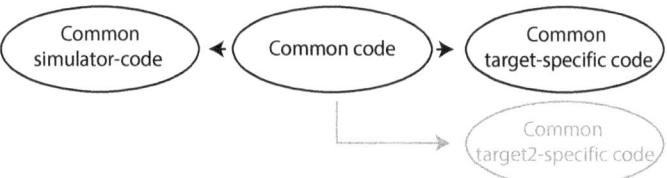

Figure 7-6. *Target-specific common code*

Essentially there are two axes of variance: the Y axis for different application variants and the X axis for different platforms (target hardware, simulator, etc.). Starting with two application variants (a main application and an engineering test application) and two platforms (target hardware and simulator), this yields nine distinct code combinations (see Figure 7-7).

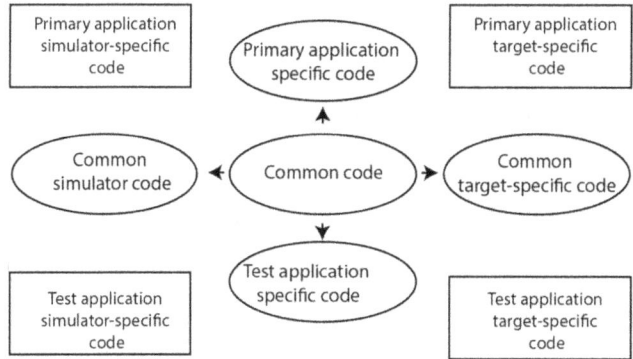

Figure 7-7. *Structure for multiple applications and multiple targets*

Admittedly, these combinations can get a bit overwhelming. As discussed earlier, it is tempting to resort to using #ifdefs to manage the platform, application, or platform-application specific deltas. However, it

111

is better to extend the Main pattern to handle these new combinations. For the GM6000 example, the Main pattern has been extended to build two application variants and three platform variants.

> When your project includes multiple hardware platforms and multiple application variants, the number of different combinations or permutations exists regardless of how you manage the combinations in the source code. Failing to plan for these combinations results in either a rat's nest of `#ifdefs` or duplicate code. However, at the start of the project, you may only have a single hardware platform or single application variant, so it's logical to ask, "How can I plan for the unknown?" My recommendation is to always start with the basic Main pattern: a single application running on the target hardware platform and the simulator. It can be extended later to include new application and hardware variants. The only downside to this just-in-time approach is that the directory and file naming can get a little messy.

Marketing Abstraction Layer

The marketing folks are always changing the names of products and projects, so if I use the product name *du jour* when naming directories, files, and variables, it is unlikely that they will match the final product names. Consequently, to avoid the problems associated with evolving names, I prefer to start with an arbitrary names—in fact, dramatically different names. In the GM6000 project, I chose `Ajax` for the primary application and `Eros` for the test application.

CHAPTER 7   BUILDING APPLICATIONS WITH THE MAIN PATTERN

Ajax Main and Eros Main

Because the Main pattern facilitates the reuse of common components across different application builds and isolates platform dependencies, both applications in the GM6000 project use the Main architectural pattern to build. Additionally, the Main pattern is extended so that much of the creation logic and sequencing business logic can be shared across multiple platforms and application variants. The GM6000 implementation of the Main pattern supports two application variants (product and engineering test) and two[2] platform variants (target hardware and simulator), yielding four possible permutations that need to be considered.

- Ajax (primary application), target build
- Ajax (primary application), simulator build
- Eros (test application), target build
- Eros (test application), simulator build

From past experience, I have found that each of these variants is necessary, even though at the beginning of the project, some of the variants are identical. For example, at the start of the project, there will not be any application differences between the simulator builds for Ajax and Eros.

The details of how to support common Main code across the four permutations are captured in the Software Detailed Design (SDD) document. And, yes, I created the design first, before writing the code. Here is a snippet of Section SDD-32 from the SDD for the Ajax application. Additionally, Figure 7-8 gives you an idea of how the application- and target-specific code is organized in the source tree.

---

[2] The GM6000 example actually supports three different platforms: the simulator and two different hardware boards. To simplify the discussion for this chapter, only two platforms–the simulator and STM32 hardware target–are used. Scaling up to more target platforms or application variants only requires adding "new" code, that is, no refactoring of the existing Main pattern code.

CHAPTER 7   BUILDING APPLICATIONS WITH THE MAIN PATTERN

The implementation of the Main pattern uses internal interfaces so that the core creation and sequencing logic can be common across platform and application variants. There are at least two platforms: the initial NUCLEO-F413ZH board and the function simulator. There are at least two application variants: the Ajax application for the production release of the GM6000 and the Eros Engineering Test software application. The design decision to share the startup code across the different variant was made to avoid maintaining N separate startup sequences.

Per the coding standard, the use of #ifdefs within functions is not allowed. The different permutations are done by defining functions (i.e., internal interfaces) and then static linking the appropriate implementations for each variant.

The following directory structure and header files (for the internal interfaces) shall be used. The directory structure assumes that the build scripts for the different variants build different directories vs. cherry-picking files within a directory.

```
src/Ajax/Main/              // Platform/Application independent implementation
+--- platform.h             // Interface for Platform dependencies
+--- application.h          // Interface for App dependencies
+--- _app/                  // Ajax specific startup implementation
+--- _plat_xxxx/            // Platform variant 1 start-up implementation
|    +--- app_platform.h    // Interface for Platform specific App dependencies
|    +--- _app_platform/    // Ajax-Platform specific startup implementation
+--- _plat_yyyy/            // Platform variant 2 start-up implementation
|    +--- app_platform.h    // Interface for Platform specific App dependencies
|    +--- _app_platform/    // Ajax-Platform specific startup implementation
```

Here is a snippet from SDD-33 from the SDD for the Eros application.

CHAPTER 7   BUILDING APPLICATIONS WITH THE MAIN PATTERN

The Eros application shares, or extends, the Ajax Main pattern (see the "[SDD-32] Creation and Startup (Application)" section). The following directory structure shall be used for the Eros-specific code and extensions to the Ajax startup/shutdown logic.

```
src/Eros/Main/              // Platform/Application Specific implementation
+--- app.cpp                // Eros Application (non-platform) implementation
+--- _plat_xxxx/            // Platform variant 1 start-up implementation
|    +--- app_platform.cpp  // Eros app + specific startup implementation
+--- _plat_yyyy/            // Platform variant 2 start-up implementation
```

	Ajax		
Target	src/Ajax/Main/ _plat_alpha1/ _app_platform/ platform.cpp	src/Ajax/Main/ _app/app.cpp	src/Ajax/Main/ _plat_simulator/ _app_platform/ platform.cpp	**Simulator**
	Ajax App target specific	Ajax App specific	Ajax App Sim specific	
	src/Ajax/Main/ _plat_alpha1/ platform.cpp	src/Ajax/Main/ appmain.cpp	src/Ajax/Main/ _plat_simulator/ platform.cpp	
	common target specific	common	common sim	
	src/Eros/Main/ _plat_alpha1/ app_platform.cpp	src/Eros/Main/app.cpp	src/Eros/Main/ _plat_simulator/ app_platform.cpp	
	Eros App target specific	Eros App Specific	Eros App sim specific	
	Eros		

Figure 7-8. *Source code organization for application and targets*

Build Scripts

After creating the code for the largely empty `Main` pattern, the next step is to set up the build scripts for the skeleton projects. For the GM6000 project, I use the `nqbp2` build system. In fact, all the build examples in the book assume that `nqbp2` is being used. However, you can use whatever collection

CHAPTER 7   BUILDING APPLICATIONS WITH THE MAIN PATTERN

of makefiles or scripts that you are comfortable using. Appendix F, "NQBP2 Build System," provides information on how to use nqbp2 to extract the compiler and link options that are used when building the GM6000 code.

My favorite thing about nqbp2 is the feature that—after a project has been set up—I only have to maintain a list of directories to build. That list is contained in a file called libdirs.b. For the Main pattern this translates to having common libdirs.b files that call out common source code directories.

With nqbp2, a build directory is defined as a directory under the root directories projects/ or tests/. These are the directories where the code is compiled; they contain the build scripts and typically the C/C++ main() entry function. Here are the four build directories for building the Ajax and Eros applications:

- projects/GM6000/Ajax/alpha1/windows/gcc-arm
- projects/GM6000/Ajax/simulator/windows/vc12
- projects/GM6000/Eros/alpha1/windows/gcc-arm
- projects/GM6000/Eros/simulator/windows/vc12

In practice, there are actually more build directories than this because the simulator is built using both the MinGW Windows compiler and the GCC compiler for a Linux host.

Shared libdirs.b files are created for each possible combination of common code. These files are located under the /project/GM6000 tree in various subdirectories.

CHAPTER 7 BUILDING APPLICATIONS WITH THE MAIN PATTERN

File	Contents
common_libdirs.b	Directories (i.e., code) that are common to all variants.
sim_common_libdirs.b	Directories that are common to all simulator variants.
target_common_libdirs.b	Directories that are common to all target variants.
ajax_common_libdirs.b	Directories that are platform independent and common to the Ajax application.
ajax_target_common_libdirs.b	Directories that are target dependent and common to the Ajax application.
ajax_sim_libdirs.b	Directories that are simulator dependent and common to the Ajax application.
Eros_common_libdirs.b	Directories that are platform independent and common to the Eros application.
Eros_target_common_libdirs.b	Directories that are target dependent and common to the Eros application.
eros_sim_libdirs.b	Directories that are simulator dependent and common to the Eros application.

Figures 7-9 and 7-10 are listings of the master `libdirs.b` files for the Ajax target (`alpha1` HW) build and the simulator (Win32-VC) build.

CHAPTER 7 BUILDING APPLICATIONS WITH THE MAIN PATTERN

```
# Common stuffs
../../../ajax_common_libdirs.b
../../../ajax_target_common_libdirs.b
../../../../common_libdirs.b
../../../../target_common_libdirs.b

# target specific stuffs
src/Ajax/Main/_plat_alpha1
src/Ajax/Main/_plat_alpha1/_app_platform

# BSP
src/Cpl/Io/Serial/ST/M32F4
src/Bsp/Initech/alpha1/trace
src/Bsp/Initech/alpha1
src/Bsp/Initech/alpha1/MX
src/Bsp/Initech/alpha1/MX/Core/Src > freertos.c
src/Bsp/Initech/alpha1/console

# SDK
xsrc/stm32F4-SDK/Drivers/STM32F4xx_HAL_Driver/Src >
    stm32f4xx_hal_timebase_rtc_alarm_template.c
    stm32f4xx_hal_timebase_rtc_wakeup_template.c
    stm32f4xx_hal_timebase_tim_template.c

# FreeRTOS
xsrc/freertos
xsrc/freertos/portable/MemMang
xsrc/freertos/portable/GCC/ARM_CM4F

# SEGGER SysVIEW
src/Bsp/Initech/alpha1/SeggerSysView
```

Figure 7-9. Contents of file projects/GM6000/Ajax/alpha1/ windows/gcc-arm/libdirs.b

```
# Use common libdirs.b
../win32_libdirs.b
../../ajax_sim_libdirs.b
../../../ajax_common_libdirs.b
../../../../common_libdirs.b
../../../../sim_common_libdirs.b
```

Figure 7-10. Contents of file projects/GM6000/Ajax/simulator/ windows/vc12/libdirs.b

CHAPTER 7   BUILDING APPLICATIONS WITH THE MAIN PATTERN

Preprocessor

One of the best practices that is used in the development of the GM6000 application is the LConfig pattern.[3] The LConfig pattern is used to provide project-specific configuration (i.e., magic constants and preprocessor symbols). Each build directory has its own header file—in this case, colony_config.h—that provides the project specifics. For example, the LConfig pattern is used to set the buffer sizes for the debug console and the human-readable major-minor-patch version information.

As with the build script, there are common configuration settings across the application and platform variants. Shared colony_config.h files are created for each possible combination.

Simulator

When initially creating the skeleton applications, there are very few differences between the target build and the simulator build. The actual differences at this point are as follows:

- Thread console command—This command is platform specific.

- How the board is initialized—The BSP has to be initialized for the target platform.

- How an application terminates—On the target platform, terminating the application reboots the microcontroller; on the simulator, the executable simply exits.

---

[3] A detailed discussion of the LConfig pattern can be found in *Patterns in the Machine: A Software Engineering Guide to Embedded Development*.

119

Because there are very few differences, it is tempting to skip including the simulator builds as part of creating the skeleton applications. But don't. Supporting a functional simulator has minimal overhead if implemented from the beginning of the project, and it is very painful to retrofit the simulator into the development process later. Not only should you not skip the simulator skeleton builds, but it should also be the first skeleton build you create because typically no target hardware is available yet. Even if the initial target hardware is an off-the-shelf evaluation board, it is still worth your time to build a simulator.

Functionality will be incrementally added to the simulator during the construction stage. As hardware drivers are needed, part of driver design includes specifying how the driver will be simulated.

The Fine Print

Standing up a simulator skeleton application is almost trivial when using the CPL C++ class library (see Appendix E, "CPL C++ Framework," for more details). The CPL class library was specifically designed and built to decouple code from the underlying platform. That is, the class library provides an Operating System Abstraction Layer (OSAL), inter-thread communications, stream interfaces, logging, persistent storage, etc., that have no direct platform dependencies. If you do not use the CPL library, then you either have to build a functional equivalent or use a third-party package for each of these things. I recommend that you do not build it from scratch. The OSAL and other middleware functionality are not particularly rocket science, but it does have a lot of details and nuances that take time to get right.

CHAPTER 7   BUILDING APPLICATIONS WITH THE MAIN PATTERN

Summary

Creating the skeleton applications that include the functional simulator variants is the primary deliverable for the foundation step. The Main pattern is an architectural pattern that is used to allow reuse of platform-independent code across the different platforms and application variants. Constructing the skeleton applications is mostly a boilerplate activity, assuming you have an existing middleware package (such as the CPL C++ class library) that provides interfaces and abstractions that decouple the underlying platform. Avoid the temptation to create the skeleton applications in combination with features, drivers, etc. From my experience, creating the skeletons upfront helps identify all the possible build variants, which helps the implementation of the Main pattern to be cleaner and significantly easier to maintain.

For the GM6000, an example of the initial skeleton applications using the Main pattern with support for multiple applications and target hardware variants can be found on the main-pattern_initial-skeleton-projects branch in the Git repository.

INPUTS

- The initial draft of the Software Development Plan
- The initial draft of the software architecture document
- The initial draft of the Software Detailed Design document

CHAPTER 7   BUILDING APPLICATIONS WITH THE MAIN PATTERN

OUTPUTS

- Skeleton applications that provide the creation and top-level sequencing structure for the various applications
- The functional simulator framework in place
- Updated Software Detailed Design (SDD) document with the Main pattern design

CHAPTER 8

Continuous Integration Builds

This chapter walks through the construction of the "build-all" scripts for the GM6000 example code. The continuous integration (CI) server invokes the build-all scripts when performing pull requests and merging code to stable branches such as `develop` and `main`. At a minimum, the build-all scripts should do the following things:

- Build all unit tests, both manual and automated unit tests
- Execute all automated unit tests and reports pass/fail
- Generate code coverage metrics
- Build all applications. This includes board variants, functional simulator, debug and nondebug versions, etc.
- Run Doxygen (assuming you are using Doxygen)
- Help with collecting build artifacts. What this entails depends on what functionality is or is not provided by your CI server. Some examples of artifacts are
    - Application images
    - Doxygen output
    - Code coverage data

Additionally, your scripts should have the following characteristics:

- The script accepts a unique build-number that is then passed to the application builds. The build-number is used as the canonical version identifier for the applications. By having the CI server generate the canonical build-number, it eliminates the possibility of human errors in setting the canonical identifier (e.g., the developer forgot to increment the version number before checking in their code).

- Adding (or removing) a unit test should not require edits to the build-all script since the number of unit tests will always be increasing as progress is made on the project.

- Adding (or removing) an application image build should not require edits to the build-all script.

- Any and all build, test, or script errors are reported as failures to the CI server.

Unfortunately, the construction of the build-all script is left as an exercise to the reader. I can't provide a universal script because there are just too many dependencies to take into account. For example, the build-all script will be dependent on the host platform, what build engine you are using (traditional makefiles, cmake, nqbp2, etc.), your source code organization, your repository organization (single vs. multiple repositories), etc. What I can do, however, is walk you through the details of the GM6000 build-all scripts to illustrate what is involved.

Example Build-All Scripts for GM6000

The remainder of the chapter discusses the build-all scripts for the GM6000 example. This includes the GM6000's build system, file organization, naming conventions, projects, unit tests, and the build artifacts as they relate to the build-all scripts.

The CI Server

At this point, the CI server should be up and running and should be able to invoke scripts stored in the code repository (see Chapter 5, "Preparation"). In addition, the skeleton applications should have been constructed (see Chapter 6, "Foundation"), and there should be a certain number of existing unit tests that are part of the CPL C++ class library.

The build system used for examples in this book is nqbp2 (see Appendix F, "nqbp2 Build System"). However, the code itself has no direct dependencies on nqbp2, which means you can use a different build system, but you will need to create the build makefiles and scripts.

Directory Organization

The key directories at the root of the source code tree are as follows:

- `src/`—The primary source code directory for the example project
- `xsrc/`—The location of source code for third-party packages

CHAPTER 8   CONTINUOUS INTEGRATION BUILDS

- `top/`—The location of the build-all scripts
- `projects/`—The directory where the applications are built and the released images are created
- `tests/`—The directory where the unit tests are built. This directory should only contain manual or automated unit tests.

To reduce the complexity and maintenance required for the build-all script, two tools from the nqbp2 build system are used: `bob.py` and `chuck.py`. The `bob.py` script recursively finds and executes all `nqbp.py` scripts in a specified directory tree. The `chuck.py` script finds and executes unit tests in a specified directory tree. The list of unit tests to execute is passed as a command-line argument to the `chuck.py` script. These scripts—along with some naming conventions—eliminate the need to enumerate each individual project and unit test in the build-all script because what gets built and executed is discovered when the script runs.

Naming Conventions

You can use whatever naming convention you would like. The important thing is that you should be able to differentiate scripts for different use cases by simply looking at the file name. For example, here are some key use cases to differentiate:

- Manual vs. automated unit tests
- Tests that can, or cannot, execute in parallel with other unit tests
- Tests that can be executed directly vs. tests that need to be executed with a script

For the GM6000 project, there are no mandated naming conventions for executables under the projects/ tree. However, there is a naming convention for unit test executables to simplify executing the unit tests in a CI environment. Admittedly, some of my conventions aren't as intuitive or descriptive as I'd like. My conventions have evolved over time, and some of my unfortunate early naming choices have now become solidified in and across my code bases. Consequently, consider the following conventions as examples of how I solved the problem, not necessarily the only or best way to name things.

Table 8-1 provides a shorthand summary of the naming conventions.

Table 8-1. *Summary of build script naming conventions for unit tests*

Parallel	Not Parallel
a.exe, a.out	aa.exe, aa.out
a.py [runs] b.exe, b.out	aa.py [runs] bb.exe, bb.out

Here is a snippet from the Software Detailed Design document (Appendix M, "GM6000 Software Detailed Design (Final Draft)") that spells out the naming conventions used.

Per the Software Development Plan, all namespaces shall have at least one unit test. The unit tests can be manual or automated (the preference is for automated unit tests). To simplify the CI build process, the following naming conventions are imposed for the unit text executables.

CHAPTER 8   CONTINUOUS INTEGRATION BUILDS

Name		Description
a.exe, a.out	Single lowercase "a" prefix to denote parallel	Scripts used for all automated units that can be run in parallel with other units.
aa.exe, aa.out	Dual lowercase "aa" prefix to denote not parallel	Scripts used for all automated units that cannot be run in parallel with other units. An example here would be a test that uses a hard-wired TCP port number.
b.exe, b.out	Single lowercase "b" prefix to denote parallel and require a script	Scripts used for all automated units that can be run in parallel and that require an external Python script to run. An example here would be piping a golden input file to stdin of the test executable.
bb.exe, bb.out	Dual lowercase "bb" prefix to denote not parallel and require a script	Scripts used for all automated units that cannot be run in parallel and that require an external Python script to run.
a.py	Single lowercase "a" prefix to script to denote it will be running only tests prefixed with single lowercase "b"	Python program used to execute the b.exe and b.out executables.
aa.py	Dual lowercase "aa" prefix to script to denote it will be running only tests prefixed with dual lowercase "bb"	Python program used to execute the bb.exe and bb.out executables.
<all others>		Manual units can use any name for the executable except for the one listed previously.

CHAPTER 8   CONTINUOUS INTEGRATION BUILDS

Windows build_all Script

The Windows `build_all` script is located in the `top/` directory. The script takes two command-line arguments:

- buildNumber—This is the Jenkins project BUILD_NUMBER environment variable.
- branch—This is the branch name. It is only set when building the develop or main branches.

The script performs the following actions:

- It creates the temporary `_artifacts/` directory and ensures that it is empty. This is where Jenkins collects build artifacts.
- It runs Doxygen and copies the output to the `_artifacts/` directory.
- It builds all automated unit tests for the Windows platforms. There are two platforms:
    - Visual Studio compiler
    - MinGW_W64 compiler toolchain. The code coverage metrics are generated from these units.

    Running the same unit test built with different compilers will bring out errors that are masked by a particular compiler. For example, the Visual Studio compiler is notoriously forgiving when it comes to writing non-ISO standard C/C++ code.
- It runs all the unit tests that have been built.
- It builds all target unit tests (e.g., builds that use the GCC-ARM cross compiler). Typically these are manual unit tests.

CHAPTER 8   CONTINUOUS INTEGRATION BUILDS

- It builds all applications under the projects/ directory for all Windows platforms (Windows+MinGW_64, Windows+VC12).

- It builds all applications under the projects/ directory for the hardware target (e.g., projects that use the GCC-ARM cross compiler).

- It copies application images to the _artifacts/ directory. This includes:

  - All target application images (.elf, .hex, .map, .list, etc.)

  - Windows+VC12 simulator images (.exe, .pdb, etc.)

- It builds *debug* versions of all applications under the projects/ directory for the hardware target.

If any of these actions fail, then the build fails.

The script is built so that adding new unit tests (automated or manual) or new applications under the projects/ directory does not require the script to be modified.

If you are adding a new hardware target—for example, changing from the STM32 alpha1 board to the STM32 dev1 board—then a single edit to script is required to specify the new hardware target.

If new build artifacts are needed, then the script has to be edited to generate the new artifacts and to copy the new items to the _artifacts/ directory.

Table 8-2 summarizes where changes need to be made to accommodate changes to the build script.

CHAPTER 8　CONTINUOUS INTEGRATION BUILDS

Table 8-2. *Summary of build script modifications*

Event	Required Change
New Unit Test	Create a new unit test build directory under the tests/ directory.
New Build Artifact	Edit the build-all scripts to generate the new build artifact and copy it to the _artifacts/ directory.
New Target Hardware	Edit the build-all scripts as needed. If the new target is a "next board spin," then only the "_TARGET" and "_TARGET2" variables need to be updated.
New Application	Create the application build directory under the projects/ directory.

None of the aforementioned change scenarios require any modifications to the Jenkins projects that invoke the build_all script. The following are snippets from the top/build_all_windows.bat script file:

```
@echo on
:: This script is used by the CI\Build machine to build the Windows Host
:: projects
::
:: usage: build_all_windows.bat <buildNumber> [branch]

set _TOPDIR=%~dp0
set _TOOLS=%_TOPDIR%..\xsrc\nqbp2\other
set _ROOT=%_TOPDIR%..
set _TARGET=alpha1
set _TARGET2=alpha1-atmel

:: Set Build info (and force build number to zero for "non-official" builds)
set BUILD_NUMBER=%1
set BUILD_BRANCH=none
IF NOT "/%2"=="/" set BUILD_BRANCH=%2
IF "%BUILD_BRANCH%"=="none" set BUILD_NUMBER=0
echo:
echo:BUILD: BUILD_NUMBER=%BUILD_NUMBER%, BRANCH=%BUILD_BRANCH%
```

CHAPTER 8   CONTINUOUS INTEGRATION BUILDS

```
:: Make sure the _artifacts directory exists and is empty
cd %_ROOT%
rmdir /s /q _artifacts
mkdir _artifacts

:: Run Doxygen first (and copy the output to artifacts dir)
cd %_TOPDIR%
run_doxygen.py %BUILD_NUMBER% %BUILD_BRANCH%
IF ERRORLEVEL 1 EXIT /b 1
...

:: Build Mingw projects (just the Win32 builds)
call %_ROOT%\env.bat 3

:: Build NON-unit-test projects
cd %_ROOT%\projects
%_TOOLS%\bob.py -v4 mingw_w64 -c --bldtime -b win32 --bldnum %BUILD_NUMBER%
IF ERRORLEVEL 1 EXIT /b 1

:: Build unit test projects (debug builds for more accurate code coverage)
cd %_ROOT%\tests
%_TOOLS%\bob.py -v4 mingw_w64 -cg --bldtime -b win32  --bldnum %BUILD_NUMBER%
IF ERRORLEVEL 1 EXIT /b 1

:: Run Mingw unit tests
cd %_ROOT%\tests
%_TOOLS%\chuck.py -v --match a.exe --dir mingw_w64
IF ERRORLEVEL 1 EXIT /b 1
%_TOOLS%\chuck.py -v --match aa.exe --dir mingw_w64
IF ERRORLEVEL 1 EXIT /b 1
%_TOOLS%\chuck.py -v --match a.py --dir mingw_w64
IF ERRORLEVEL 1 EXIT /b 1
%_TOOLS%\chuck.py -v --match aa.py --dir mingw_w64
IF ERRORLEVEL 1 EXIT /b 1

:: Generate code coverage metrics
%_TOOLS%\chuck.py -v --dir mingw_w64 --match tca.py rpt --xml jenkins-gcovr.xml
IF ERRORLEVEL 1 EXIT /b 1

...
```

CHAPTER 8   CONTINUOUS INTEGRATION BUILDS

```
:: Skip additional project builds when NOT building develop or main
IF "%BUILD_BRANCH%"=="none" GOTO :builds_done

:: Zip up (NON-debug) 'release' builds
cd %_ROOT%\projects\GM6000\Ajax\%_TARGET%\windows\gcc-arm\_stm32
7z a ajax-%_TARGET%-%BUILD_NUMBER%.zip ajax.*
IF ERRORLEVEL 1 EXIT /b 1
copy *.zip %_ROOT%\_artifacts
IF ERRORLEVEL 1 EXIT /b 1

...

:: Everything worked!
:builds_done
echo:EVERTHING WORKED
exit /b 0
```

Linux build_all Script

The Linux build_all script is located in the top/ directory. The script takes one command-line argument:

- buildNumber—This is the Jenkins project BUILD_NUMBER environment variable.

The script performs the following actions.

- It builds all automated unit tests for the Linux platforms using the GCC compiler.
- It runs all the unit tests that have been built.
- It builds all applications under the projects/ directory for Linux platform.

CHAPTER 8   CONTINUOUS INTEGRATION BUILDS

If any of the actions fail, then the build fails.

The script is designed the same as the Windows `build_all` script so that adding new unit tests or application projects does not require the script to be modified. The Linux `build_all` script is much shorter because only one compiler is used and things like running Doxygen, code coverage, and publishing build artifacts are only done once (in the Windows `build_all` script).

```
# This script is used by the CI/Build machine to build the Linux projects
#
# The script ASSUMES that the working directory is the package root
#
# usage: build_linux.sh <bldnum>
#
set -e

# setup the environment
source ./env.sh default

# Build all test linux projects (only 64bit versions)
pushd tests
$NQBP_BIN/other/bob.py -v4 linux  -gb posix64 --bldtime --bldnum $1

# Run unit tests
$NQBP_BIN/other/chuck.py -v --match a.out --dir _posix64
$NQBP_BIN/other/chuck.py -v --match aa.out --dir _posix64
$NQBP_BIN/other/chuck.py -v --match a.py --dir _posix64
$NQBP_BIN/other/chuck.py -v --match aa.py --dir _posix64

# Build all "projects/" linux projects (only 64bit versions)
popd
pushd projects
$NQBP_BIN/other/bob.py -v4 linux  -gb posix64 --bldtime --bldnum $1
```

CHAPTER 8   CONTINUOUS INTEGRATION BUILDS

Summary

It is critical that the CI server and the CI build scripts are fully up and running before the construction stage begins. By not having the CI process in place, you risk starting the project with broken builds and a potential descent into initial merge hell.

INPUTS

- The CI server is up and running and able to invoke build scripts stored in the GitHub repository.
- The skeleton applications have been created and can successfully build locally on a developer's computer. This includes all of the functional simulator builds, target builds, and all unit tests.

OUTPUTS

- Completed repository-based CI build scripts
- The CI build scripts in the repository fully integrated with the CI server and its automation scripts/projects
- The CI builds are full featured. That is, they support and produce the following outputs on every build.
    - They create Doxygen output.
    - They execute automated unit tests on every build.
    - They gather code coverage metrics from the automated unit tests.

CHAPTER 8   CONTINUOUS INTEGRATION BUILDS

- They tag the develop and main branches in GitHub with the CI build number.
- They archive the build images and other desired outputs for access at a later date. Archiving could involve using sftp or scp, calling RESTful APIs for cloud storage, or even standing up, and writing to, an Amazon S3 file manager.

CHAPTER 9

Requirements Revisited

It is extremely rare that all of the requirements have been defined before the construction phase. In fact, it is not even reasonable to expect that the requirements will be 100% complete before starting implementation. The reason is because unless all of the details are known—and nailing down the details is what you do in the construction phase—it is impossible to have all of the requirements carved in stone. So in addition to design, implementation, and testing, there will inevitably be a continuing amount of requirement work that needs to be addressed. This includes refactoring and clarifying existing requirements as well as developing new requirements. Common sources for new requirements that show up in the construction phase are as follows:

- Feedback from Failure Mode and Effects Analysis (FMEA) or risk control measures

- Feedback from detailed cybersecurity analysis

- Feedback from the detailed designs for software, hardware, mechanical, etc. This is where the wish list of requirements gets reconciled with the real world

- Feedback from voice of the customer (VOC), as well as Alpha and Beta trials

CHAPTER 9   REQUIREMENTS REVISITED

Analysis

There are many types of analysis (e.g., FMEA) that are typically done for an embedded product to ensure it is safe, reliable, compliant with regulatory agencies, and secure. These tests and analysis cover all aspects of the product—mechanical, electrical, packaging, and manufacturing—not just software. This is where many of the edge cases are uncovered and possible solutions are proposed. Often, these solutions take the form of new requirements, which are also sometimes called risk control measures. Typically, these new requirements are product (PRS) or engineering detailed requirements (SRS)—although sometimes they feed back into the marketing (MRS) requirements.

Failure analysis is a system engineering role, not a software role. As such, a detailed discussion of analysis methods, best practices, etc., is outside the scope of this book. However, it is not unusual for a hardware engineer to fill the role of the system engineer when it comes to failure analysis.

It is important to start these analysis activities as soon as possible and to iterate through them as the detailed design evolves. This means some of the analysis occurs before the construction phase. Here is a hypothetical example of a requirement being added late in the process.

RISK CONTROL MEASURE EXAMPLE

The initial PRS (PR-103) and system architecture required a hardware-based protection circuit so that the heating element does not exceed temperature and safety limits. However, while evaluating possible failure modes, it was observed that when the heater safety circuit shut off the heating element, the software would be unaware that there is no active heating. This would have the following impact:

- The software control algorithm would have the potential to "run away" (e.g., integral wind-up[1]) because there is no actual heat.

- An end user would not have any indication that something is wrong with the unit other than they are unable to control space temperature and declare the unit defective.

To mitigate this risk, the following requirement was added as a risk control measure to the PRS:

PR-206: Heater Safety. The Heating Element (HE) sub-assembly shall provide an indication to the Control Board (CB) when it has been shut off due to a safety limit.

Requirements vs. Design Statements

Requirements should be simple to define, but, unfortunately, they are not. The problem is that one stakeholder's "what" is another stakeholder's "how." Consequently, there will always be gaps and overlaps between where requirements end and where detailed designs begin. Nevertheless, it is better to just acknowledge the gaps, rather than go back and forth in an attempt to get the absolute right level of requirements from the stakeholders. The way I acknowledge these gaps is through the use of design statements. They are also useful in situations where high fidelity to details will be needed in the implementation. For example, design statements are perfect for describing all the gory details of the user interface: colors, fonts, layout, text strings, etc.

---

[1] See https://en.wikipedia.org/wiki/Integral_windup

CHAPTER 9   REQUIREMENTS REVISITED

Design Statement for Control Algorithm

The term *design statement* is simply a placeholder for detailed specifications that must be implemented but which are not part of—but rather are derived from—the formal requirements. For example, the definitions of control algorithms are typically specified separately as design statements. The reason is because the stakeholder providing the requirements (e.g., the marketing guy) is not the author (e.g., the guy with a PhD in control theory). In addition, most of the time, the software developer will not be the author of the control algorithm either, so detailed design statements about the algorithm are needed. Here is a hypothetical example of design statements for a control algorithm.

GM6000 HEATING DESIGN STATEMENT EXAMPLE

There is a single PRS requirement for the heating algorithm for the GM6000 example.

PR-207: Temperature Control. *The control algorithm shall maintain the sensed space temperature within ± one degree Celsius of the setpoint under the following conditions:*

- *A constant thermal load on the space.*

- *At least five minutes after the sensed space temperature reached the setpoint temperature.*

- *The sensed space temperature is the measured value (after any SW/HW filtering). That is, it's not the actual, independently measured space temperature.*

A choice was made to use a fuzzy logic controller (FLC) for the core temperature control algorithm instead of simple error or proportional-integral-derivative (PID) algorithms. The details and nuisances of the FLC are nontrivial, so the algorithm design was captured as a separate document (see Appendix N, "GM6000 Fuzzy Logic Temperature Control"). Here is a snippet from the FLC document.

Fuzzification

There are two input membership functions: one for absolute temperature error and one for differential temperature error. Both membership functions use triangle membership sets as shown in Figure 9-1.

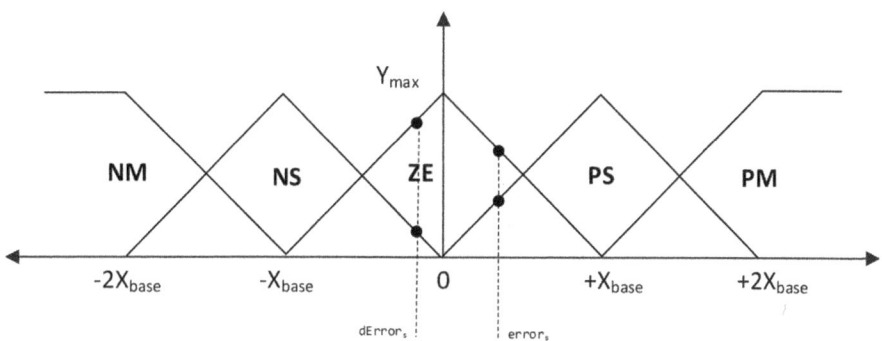

Membership sets:
NM: Negative medium
NS: Negative small
ZE: zero equal (i.e. at setpoint)
PS: Positive small
PM: Positive medium

$X_{base} = Y_{max}$

Figure 9-1. *Membership function*

Absolute error is calculated as

$$\text{error} = \text{temperatureSetpoint} - \text{currentSpaceTemperature}$$
$$\text{error}_s = \text{error} * J_{error}$$

Differential error is calculated as

$$\text{dError} = \text{error} - \text{lastError}$$
$$\text{dError}_s = \text{dError} * J_{derror}$$

The values for Ymax, J_{error}, and J_{derror} are configurable.

The units for the X axis are hundredths degrees Celsius.

The Y axis is unitless. It represents a logical 0.0 to 1.0 weighted membership value.

An input (e.g., `error` or `dError`) is fuzzified by determining its weighted membership in each of the membership sets.

Design Statement for User Interface

As I mentioned previously, user interface details are also candidates for design statements. Of course, one option would be to put all of the UI details into a formal requirement. However, formal requirements have a heavy change control process associated with them, and everyone knows the UI is always being tweaked up until the moment of release. Detailed design statement documents typically have a much lighter change control process and require fewer approvals to update. In my experience, design statements for the UI take the form of wireframe documents and style guides for supporting look and feel.

The formal UI requirements should call out

- Behavior (what controls are available to the user)
- Content (what information needs to be displayed)
- Basic navigation (how to go from one screen to another)

The remaining details (layout, colors, text, fonts, types of controls, etc.) are left to the design statements. With respect to UI requirements, the GM6000 example has four MRS requirements, one PRS requirement, and eight SRS requirements. None of the requirements get into the details of layout, colors, text strings, button assignments, etc.

For example, the `epc` repository's Wiki contains a link to view the wireframes for the UI. Figures 9-2, 9-3, and 9-4 show examples of those design statements.

CHAPTER 9   REQUIREMENTS REVISITED

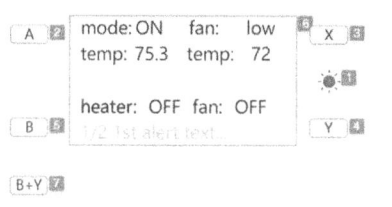

Figure 9-2. Home Screen wireframe

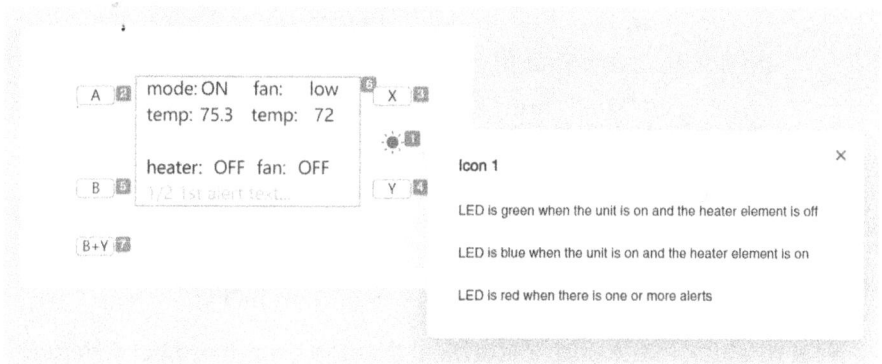

Figure 9-3. Home Screen wireframe with LED details

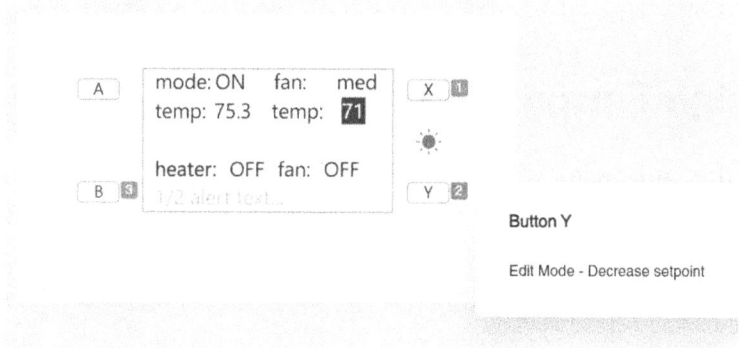

Figure 9-4. Edit Setpoint Screen

143

CHAPTER 9   REQUIREMENTS REVISITED

As a final note about design statements and testing, in most companies, it is assumed that the software test team will be responsible for verifying that the software meets the formal requirements. However, the same cannot be said about design statements. The principal reasons for this are as follows:

1. Schedule pressure—All of the available test resources and time are taken up completing verification of the formal requirements.

2. Lack of pass/fail criteria—Since design statements do not have the rigor (e.g., a unique identifier, or the formalized "shall" and "should" wording) of formal requirements, it is not always clear what needs to be tested and how.

3. Ambiguity over responsibility—It is not always clear who is responsible for testing design statements.

Nevertheless, in the end, it is critical that the overall project schedule accounts for testing design statements. The schedule should identify the individuals responsible for performing the verification as well as provide time for this work to occur. Do not skip testing design statements!

Missing Formal Requirements

Yet another nuisance with requirements is there can be requirements that you are held accountable for that are not part of formal requirements. Typically, these requirements derive from implicit, nonfunctional requirements, or they materialize as the result of a project-level decision.

CHAPTER 9   REQUIREMENTS REVISITED

A nonfunctional requirement (NFR)[2] is a requirement that describes how you should do something instead of what the product does. In my experience, these missing NFRs come from your Quality System Management (QMS) and software development life cycle (SDLC) processes. Here are some examples:

- No dynamic memory allocation is allowed—This is a policy or best practice imposed by your C/C++ coding standard. And the need for a coding standard is dictated by the QMS team. A no-dynamic-memory requirement can also be an explicit requirement. For example, it could be a risk control measure for memory fragmentation leading to uncontrolled execution delays.

- Facilitating automated unit tests—A source code tree organization that facilitates automated unit tests is an NFR dictated by a software development life cycle (SDLC) process.

- Project decisions—Sometimes stakeholders make decisions that impact the design of the software. For example:

    - "The software shall be written in C/C++." This is a command decision made by the software architect or software manager.

    - "The project shall have a functional simulator." Again, this is a decision made by the software architect so that the team can work smarter, not harder, while waiting for hardware to be delivered.

---

[2] See Chapter 2 for discussion of functional vs. nonfunctional requirements.

145

CHAPTER 9 REQUIREMENTS REVISITED

In a perfect world, all the requirements mentioned previously could be included in the formal requirements. In my experience, though, this just adds another level of noise to the formal requirements with a low return on investment. Unless you are in a regulated industry that imposes a high level of rigor, the recommendation is to leave out these NFRs or "missing requirements" and then document the gaps that will inevitably show up in requirements tracing. For the GM6000 example, when backward tracing the software architecture sections to requirements, there are ten sections that trace back to process-related NFRs and two sections that trace back to project decisions that are not captured in the formal requirements.

Requirements Tracing

All functional requirements should be forward traceable to one or more test cases in the verification test plan.[3] If there are test cases that can't be backward traced to requirements, there is disconnect between what was asked for and what is expected for the release. The disconnect needs to be reconciled, not just for the verification testing, but for the software implementation (and the other engineering disciplines) as well. *Reconciled* means that there are no orphans when forward tracing functional requirements to test cases or when backward tracing test cases to requirements. NFRs are not typically included in the verification tracing.

Requirements should also be traced to design outputs. Design outputs include the software architecture and detailed design documents as well as the source code. The importance or usefulness of tracing to design outputs is the same as it is for verification testing; it ensures that you are building everything that was asked for and not building stuff that is not needed. Unlike verification tracing, NFRs should be included in the tracing to design outputs.

---

[3] See Chapter 3, "Analysis," for a discussion of forward and backward requirements tracing.

CHAPTER 9 REQUIREMENTS REVISITED

Requirements tracing to design outputs is not the hard and fast rule that it is for verification testing. However, with some up-front planning, and following the SDLC process steps in order, tracing requirements to design outputs is a straightforward exercise.

Requirements tracing can be done manually, or it can be done using a requirement management tool (e.g., Doors or Jama). The advantage of using requirement management tools is that they are good at handling the many-to-many relationships that occur when tracing requirements and provide both forward and backward traces. The downside to these tools is their cost and learning curve. For the GM6000 project, I manually trace requirements to and from design outputs using a spreadsheet.

The following processes simplify the work needed to forward trace software-related requirements down to source code files:

- Software Detailed Design (SDD) document

    - When creating the SDD, ensure that each content section is backward traceable to a content section in the software architecture document.[4] See Chapter 6, "Foundation," for details on how to do this. When a section doesn't trace, stop and reconcile the disconnect.

    - If a content section has source code, explicitly document the source code directories. See Chapter 11, "Just-in-Time Detailed Design," for information on how to do this.

---

[4] A content section is any section that is not a housekeeping section. For example, the Introduction, Glossary, and Change Log are considered housekeeping sections.

- Software architecture (SWA) document
  - Backward trace all subsystem sections to at least one SRS, PRS, or MRS requirement. See Chapter 3, "Analysis," for details on how to do this. If a section doesn't trace, then stop and reconcile the disconnect.
  - Backward trace the remaining content sections (which are not subsystems) to at least one SRS, PRS, MRS, or a "missing requirement" (e.g., an implicit NFR). If a section doesn't trace, then stop and reconcile the disconnect. Note that when a section traces back to a "missing requirement," document the source of the missing requirement in the trace matrix.
  - Forward trace all software architecture content sections to content sections in the Software Detailed Design document. If a section doesn't trace, then
    i. When the SWA section back traces to a functional requirement, stop and reconcile the disconnect.
    ii. When the SWA section back traces to an NFR, a decision needs to be made if a forward trace to a Software Detailed Design section is needed.
    iii. When the SWA section back traces to a "missing requirement," then it is acceptable to not have a forward trace to a Software Detailed Design section.

CHAPTER 9 REQUIREMENTS REVISITED

After you have completed these steps, you have effectively forward traced the software architecture through detailed design to source code files. The remaining steps are to forward trace requirements (i.e., MRS, PRS, SRS) to sections in the software architecture document.

1. For all software-related MRS requirements, forward trace the MRS requirements to one of the following:

    a. One or more PRS requirements

    b. One or more SRS requirements

    c. One or more content sections in the software architecture document

2. For all software-related PRS requirements, forward trace the PRS requirements to either

    a. One or more SRS requirements

    b. One or more content sections in the software architecture document

3. For all SRS requirements, forward trace to one or more content sections in the software architecture document.

Summary

The formal requirements should avoid excessive design details or specifics whenever possible. The use of design statements should be used to bridge the gap between formal requirements and the details needed by the software team to design and implement the solutions.

CHAPTER 9   REQUIREMENTS REVISITED

Not everything needs to be a formal requirement. There are advantages to having fewer rather than more requirements, and this is where design statements are a great advantage. Nevertheless, the software testing effort must include the verification of formal requirements as well as design statements.

Forward tracing requirements from the MRS and PRS to both formal test cases and design outputs is a tool that ensures all requirements are implemented and verified. It also keeps the team focused on required deliverables and prevents the team from building or testing features that are not essential to the end product.

INPUTS

- All existing requirements as documented at the start of the construction phase
- System architecture (SA) document including ongoing updates to the document
- Software architecture document (SWA) including ongoing updates to the document
- Software Detailed Design (SDD) document including ongoing updates to the document
- Software verification test plan
- Feedback from analysis activities: failure, fault, security, etc.
- Feedback from design validation activities
- Feedback from voice-of-the-customer activities

CHAPTER 9   REQUIREMENTS REVISITED

OUTPUTS

- A final, approved MRS document
- A final, approved PRS document
- A final, approved SRS document
- A final, approved other engineering disciplines detailed requirements documents
- Documented design statements (if used)
- All functional software requirements are forward traceable to one or more test cases in the formal software verification test plan
- (Optional, but recommended) Forward requirements tracing from the MRS and PRS to
    - The detailed engineering discipline requirements (e.g., SRS)
    - Architecture and design documentation
    - Design outputs (e.g., source code)

CHAPTER 10

Tasks

This is the start of the construction phase, and this phase is where the bulk of the development work happens. Assuming that all of the software deliverables from the planning phase were completed, there should now be very few interdependencies when it comes to software work. That is, the simulator has removed dependencies on hardware availability, the UI has been decoupled from the application's business logic, the control algorithm has been decoupled from its inputs and outputs, etc. And since there are now minimal interdependencies, most of the software development can be done in parallel; you can have many developers working on the same project without getting bogged down in merge hell.

The software work, then—the work involved in producing working code—can be broken down into tasks, where each task has the following elements:

1. Requirements
2. A detailed design that has had a peer review
3. Source code and unit tests
4. A code review
5. A source code merge

CHAPTER 10 TASKS

A single task does not have to contain all elements; however, the order of the elements must be honored. For example, there are three types of tasks:

- Requirement task—A requirement task involves identifying, creating, and documenting requirements or design statements. A requirement task only has one element: #1 requirements.

- Design task—A design task involves creating, documenting, and reviewing the detailed design for a set of requirements. A design task has two elements: #1 requirements and #2 design.

- Coding task—A coding task involves writing, testing, and merging code. A coding task always has all five elements.

The tasks as discussed in this chapter are very narrow in scope, and they are limited primarily to generating source code. But there are many other tasks—pieces of work or project activities such as failure analysis, CI maintenance, bug fixing, bug tracking, integration testing, etc.—that still need to be planned, tracked, and executed for the project to be completed.

1) Requirements

The requirements for a task obviously scope the amount of work that has to be done. However, if there are no requirements, then stop design and coding activities and go pull the requirements from the appropriate stakeholders. Also remember that with respect to tasks, design statements are considered requirements.

If there are partial or incomplete requirements for the task, either split the current task into additional tasks: some where you do have sufficient requirements and others where the task is still undefined and ambiguous. Save the undefined and ambiguous tasks for later when they are better and more fully specified. Proceeding without clear requirements puts all of the downstream work at risk.

2) Detailed Design

The detailed design is the "how," and it fills in the gaps from the software architecture to the source code. The detailed design needs to be formally documented and reviewed. The documentation can range from a single sentence to pages of diagrams (e.g., class, sequence, state machine, etc.) and supporting text. For me, it is axiomatic that detailed design is always done before coding. From experience, every time I am tempted to cheat on this rule, nine times out of ten, it turns out to be a mistake. The task eventually required rework or took longer than it would have if I had just done the up-front design. Chapter 11, "Just-in-Time Detailed Design," describes how to perform detailed design.

3) Source Code and Unit Tests

Write your code and test it. Or if you are a proponent of Test-Driven Development (TDD),[1] write the unit tests and then write the code. Or use some combinations of both approaches. Regardless of what you chose, do not skip writing the unit test.

---

[1] Test-Driven Development: https://en.wikipedia.org/wiki/Test-driven_development

Unit tests, whether manual or automated, demonstrate that your code works and meets the requirements of the task. Without unit tests, the program manager, the scrum master, the stakeholders, and the entire company simply have to trust that their software developers are perfect and never make mistakes. Sarcasm aside, requiring unit tests actually makes the timeline shorter because there will be a fewer integration errors downstream. And the later in the process errors are found, the more costly they are in terms of time and effort to correct.

4) Code Review

All code should be reviewed before it is merged into the mainline, release, or stable branches. The Git Pull Request paradigm provides a straightforward and enforceable process for performing code reviews.

5) Merge

Never break the build.

The Definition of Done

While it may seem "over the top" for a team or organization to take the time to explicitly provide a definition of what constitutes "done" for a software task, not having a clear and common definition of "done" is the gateway to technical debt.

For example, consider this scenario. Jim is assigned to write an EEPROM driver. Jim completes the work and tests the driver, but the target hardware is not available, so he writes the code and tests it on an MCU evaluation board, which has a slightly older EEPROM chip (e.g., same family, different storage size). All the tests pass, so Jim claims the EEPROM driver is done. However, there is still more work needed to update (e.g., account for different pin assignments) and verify the driver after the target hardware is received. Consequently, a new task or card should be put into the project backlog to account for the additional work. If this isn't done, bad things happen when the target board is finally available and incorporated into testing. Jim is now fully booked with other tasks and is not "really available" to finish the EEPROM driver. A minor fire drill ensues over priorities for when and who will finish the EEPROM driver.

While this example is admittedly a bit contrived, most software tasks have nuances where there is still some amount of future work left when the code is merged. You will save a lot of time and angst if the development team (including the program manager) clearly defines what done means. My recommendation for a definition of done is as follows:

- All five elements of a coding task are completed.

- New tasks or cards have been created to address and resolve any discrepancies found. Here are some examples of situation where new tasks or cards should be created before signaling that the original task is done.

    - There is a requirement that calls for a user to acknowledge alarms. However, because the UI framework is only partially implemented, the acknowledgment part of the UI will not be implemented at this time. Tasks should be created for implementing the acknowledgment behavior.

    - The current UI wireframes do not support the display of more than two concurrent alarms, but it is possible to have three concurrent alarms. Tasks should be created to update the UI wireframes and to make the UI changes.

- A reviewer observes that certain alarms need to be persistent. Tasks should be created to have a review of the overall system design and define behavior requirements for persistent alarms.
- Nothing more needs to be done to the merged code, unless a bug is uncovered or a requirement changes.

Task Granularity

What is the appropriate granularity of a task? Or, rather, how much time should the task take to complete? Generally, taking into account the five elements of a coding task discussed previously, a task should not take longer than a typical Agile sprint, or approximately two weeks. That said, tasks can be as short as a couple of hours or as long as several weeks. Table 10-1 shows some hypothetical examples of tasks for the GM6000 project.

CHAPTER 10   TASKS

Table 10-1. Examples of task types from the GM6000 project

Task	Task Type	Description
SPI Driver	Coding	The requirement for the task is that the physical interface to the LCD display be an SPI bus.
		1) The detailed design is created. The design is captured as one or more sections in the SDD. These sections formalize the driver structure, including how the SPI interface will be abstracted to be platform independent.
		2) The new sections in the SDD are reviewed.
		3) Before the code is written, a ticket is created, if there is not one already, and a corresponding branch in the repository is created for the code.
		4) The code is written.
		5) As a coding task requires a manual unit test to verify the SPI operation on a hardware platform, the manual unit test or tests are created and run.
		6) After the tests pass, a pull request is generated, the code is reviewed, and any action items arising from the review are resolved.
		7) The code is then merged, and if the CI build is successful, the code is merged into its parent branch.
Control Algorithm Definition	Requirement	There is only one formal requirement (PR-207) with respect to the heater control algorithm.
		The scope of the task is to define the actual control algorithm and document the algorithm as design statements. The documented algorithm design is then reviewed by the appropriate SMEs.

(*continued*)

159

Table 10-1. *(continued)*

Task	Task Type	Description
UI Design	Design	The scope of this task is to design the UI subsystem. It involves collecting numerous UI-specific formal requirements as well as creating (or collecting) the set of wireframe diagrams that comprise the UI.
		The design is captured as one or more sections in the SDD. These sections define the UI threading and event model, determine what is a "screen" with respect to code, define how unit testing will be done, identify (and design) common widgets that are needed (but are not provided by the graphic library), etc. These new sections are then reviewed.

Tasks, Tickets, and Agile

Tasks are schedulable entities. They can be represented by cards in your Agile tool, line items in a Microsoft Project schedule, or issues in GitHub. Each of these tasks should map to a repository branch where the code is checked in prior to being merged into the code base. The specifics of how tasks and tickets are mapped into your workflow are left up to you. However, here are some examples that I have encountered for coding tasks.

JIRA1—Parent card with child cards for task elements

- A story card is created for a task. (This story card is sometimes referred to as an epic.) Then the following subtask cards are created. The story card is completed after all subtasks cards are completed.

    - Requirements
    - Design

CHAPTER 10 TASKS

- Design Review
- Unit Test Implementation
- Code Implementation–This is the ticket card; the name or number of this card is used to create the branch in the repository. This task is completed when the pull request is merged

JIRA2–Single card with a JIRA checklist for task elements

- A single JIRA task or story card is created for the task. A checklist with the following items is added to the card. This is the ticket card; the name or number of this card is used to create the branch in the repository.

    - Requirements
    - Design
    - Design Review
    - Unit Test
    - Code
    - Pull Request and Code Review
    - Merge

Azure DevOps–Parent card with child "ticket" cards

- A product backlog item card is created for the task. This card is used to track the progress of the requirements and design aspects of the task, which may or may not involve creating individual child cards.
- A child task card is created to track the coding. This is the *ticket* card; the name or number of this card is used to create the branch in the repository. This task card is completed when the pull request is merged.

CHAPTER 10 TASKS

Summary

Software tasks are a tool and process for decomposing the software effort into small, well-defined units that can be managed using Agile tools or more traditional Gantt chart–based schedulers. Within a task, there is a waterfall process that starts with requirements, which is followed by detailed design, which is then followed by creating the unit tests and coding.

INPUTS

- All documented requirements including ongoing updates
- Software Development Plan (SDP) including ongoing updates
- System architecture (SA) document including ongoing updates
- Software architecture (SWA) document including ongoing updates
- Software Detailed Design (SDD) document including ongoing updates

OUTPUTS

- Working code
- Unit tests
- Design reviews
- Code reviews

CHAPTER 10   TASKS

- Potential updates to requirements, which may be in MRS, PRS, or SRS documents
- Potential updates to the system architecture (SA) document
- Potential updates to the software architecture (SWA) document
- Updates to the Software Detailed Design (SDD) document
- Updates to design statements when used

CHAPTER 11

Just-in-Time Detailed Design

While defining the overall software architecture is a waterfall process, the planning phase activities, or detailed software design, are made up of many individual activities that are done on a just-in-time basis. As work progresses during the construction phase, the Software Detailed Design is updated along the way. At the start of the construction phase, the state of the Software Detailed Design document should consist of at least

- An overall outline (see Chapter 6, "Foundation")
- The detailed design of the creation, startup, and shutdown of the application (see Chapter 7, "Building Applications with the Main Pattern")

This chapter is not about how to design components; it is about the design process. It is about doing the design in real time and documenting the design such that it does not go stale as the code is written. The purpose of the detailed design is to

- Figure stuff out—If you can't write a description on paper about what it is your coding, then you are not ready to code. The act of coding should be the work of instantiating a solution (i.e., the detailed design) in a programming language, not crafting a solution.

CHAPTER 11 JUST-IN-TIME DETAILED DESIGN

- Provide context that is not explicit in the source code
- Document decisions and any deviations from the software architecture
- Fill in missing requirements and design statements
- Provide a higher level of abstraction for reviews, training, and end-user documentation. No one should have to read your code and reverse-engineer it to figure out how it's designed.

As you put together the detailed design components, you can write for a knowledgeable reader who is

- Familiar with the product and its functionality
- Familiar and conversant with the software and system architecture documents
- Has some experience in embedded software development

Beyond that, there is no one-size-fits-all recipe for doing detailed design. The detailed design for a component can range from a couple of sentences to class diagrams or sequence and state machine diagrams. However, there are few common items that all detailed design components share:

- Every component that needs to be coded can be found in the Software Detailed Design document. This is important because the outline of the SDD plays a key role in tracing requirements (see Chapter 9, "Requirements Revisited"). In other words, if there does not seem to be an appropriate section within the SDD

CHAPTER 11   JUST-IN-TIME DETAILED DESIGN

for the component, something is wrong; you need to revisit the purpose of the component, the requirements, the software architecture, etc., to resolve the disconnect. Do not proceed with the component's detailed design until the disconnect has been resolved.

- All components have a name and a file location. This sounds simple and obvious, but in my experience, this is a good early sanity check for determining the granularity of the component and its dependencies. For example, this step requires you to answer questions like is the component dependent on the MCU or an off-board IC? Is the component specific to the application or is it middleware?

- The simulation approach for each component is specified. For components that directly involve hardware, a decision needs to be made about how the component will be simulated or mocked when building the functional simulator. If a component will not be (or does not need to be) simulated, document that decision.

- No header file details are included in component designs. Avoid putting code fragments or header file details in the SDD because they will quickly be outdated after coding starts. For example, do not include class data members in your class diagram unless they are key to understanding the diagram. For code-level details (e.g., typedefs, enums, structs, etc.), use a documentation tool such as Doxygen that extracts comments from your code base as a companion document to the SDD.

- Duplicate information should not be included in design components. It is always a best practice to ensure there is only one source of information. External information can certainly be referenced but doesn't include details that are already captured in the software architecture document or elsewhere.

Examples

I can't tell you how to do detailed design. There is no one-size-fits-all recipe for doing it, and at the end of the day, it will always be a function of your experience, abilities, and domain knowledge. But I can give examples of what I do. Here are some examples from this design process that I used when creating the GM6000 project.

Subsystem Design

As defined in the software architecture of the GM6000, persistent storage is one of the top-level subsystems identified. It is responsible for "framework, data integrity checks, etc., for storing and retrieving data that is stored in local persistent storage." The snippets that follow illustrate how the subsystem design was documented in the SDD (Appendix M, "GM6000 Software Detailed Design (Final Draft)").

[SDD-24] Persistent Storage

For the most part, this section is simply a copy and paste from the SW architecture document, which of course contradicts the guideline "Duplicate information should not be included in design components." Nevertheless, I included it in the SDD because it provides nontrivial context without requiring the reader to switch to another document.

The Persistent Storage subsystem provides the interfaces, framework, data integrity checks, etc., for storing and retrieving data that is stored in persistent storage. The persistent storage paradigm is a RAM cached model. The RAM cached model has the following behaviors:

1. *On startup, persistent record entries are read from NVRAM, validated, and loaded into RAM.*

    a. *If the loaded data is invalid, then the associated RAM values are set to default/factory values, and the NVRAM storage is updated with new defaulted values.*

2. *The application updates the entries stored in RAM via an API. When an update request is made, the RAM value is updated, and then a background task is initiated to update the values stored in NVRAM.*

Each subsystem or component is responsible for defining the data to be stored as well as providing the initial/factory default values for the data.

[SDD-54] Frequency of Updates

Here is where the analysis and the decision that no wear leveling is required for the application are captured.

The GM6000 uses an off-board EEPROM for its persistent storage. The EEPROM is specified to have at least 1,000,000 write cycles of endurance. The DHC is required to operate for at least five years. This translates to at most 22.8 EEPROM write cycles per hour for the life of the product.

The highest frequency of application data updates to EEPROM is the metrics data, which is every 15 minutes, or 4 writes per hour. Since 4 writes per hour is significantly less than 22.8 writes per hour endurance limit, no wear leveling of the EEPROM will be implemented.

CHAPTER 11   JUST-IN-TIME DETAILED DESIGN

[SDD-55] Records

Here is the design for how persistent storage records are structured and how data integrity and power-failure use cases will be handled.

The application data is persistently stored using records. A record is the unit of atomic read/write operations from or to persistent storage. The CPL C++ class library's persistent storage framework is used. In addition, the library's Model Point records are used, where each record contains one or more model points.

All records are mirrored—two copies of the data are stored—to ensure that no data is lost if there is power failure during a write operation.

All of the records use a 32-bit CRC for detecting data corruption.

Instead of a single record, separate records are used to insulate the data against data corruption. For example, as the Metrics record is updated multiple times per hour, it has a higher probability for data corruption than the Personality record that is written once.

The application data is broken down into the following records:

- *User Settings*
- *Personality (contains customization to the algorithms, model and serial number, unique console password, etc.)*
- *Metrics*

[SDD-55] Records: Class Diagram

This snippet outlines the CPL library design that provides the persistent framework. Capturing the design of third-party code is not something that is frequently done; however, in this case, the decision was made to include it to illustrate exactly what application code is needed and to specify what objects need to be created at startup.

CHAPTER 11 JUST-IN-TIME DETAILED DESIGN

The following diagram illustrates the CPL framework and delineates what components the application provides. Only the classes with bolded outlines need to be implemented; all the other classes are provided by the CPL library.

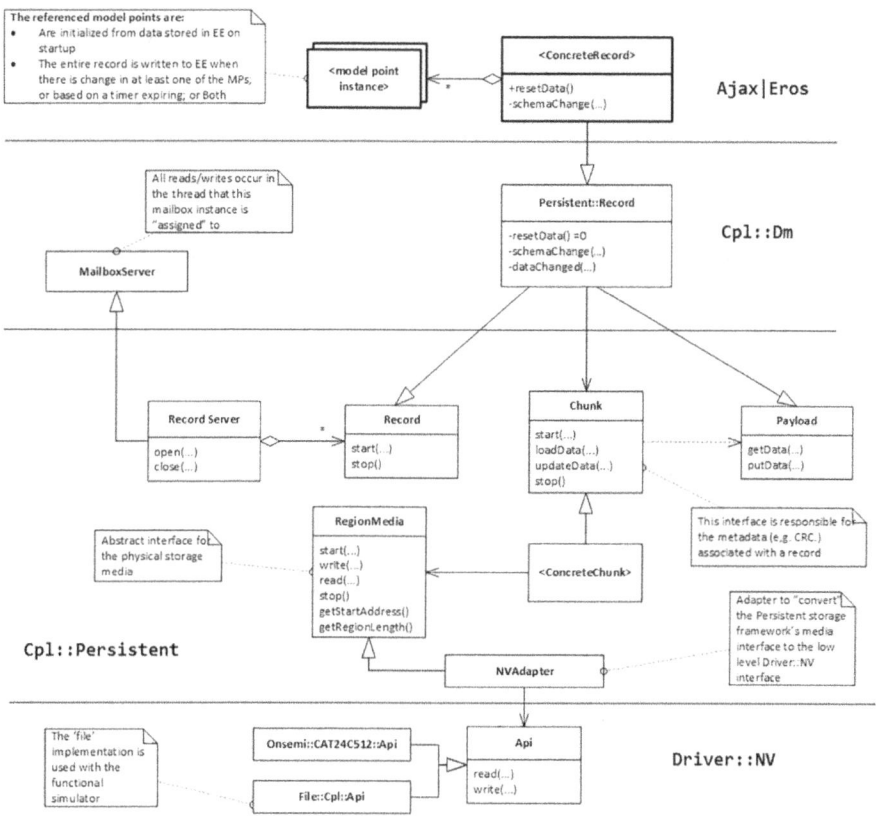

[SDD-55] Records: Location

The content of records is very application specific. Here is how I documented the decision to locate them inside the application `Main/` directories.

CHAPTER 11 JUST-IN-TIME DETAILED DESIGN

The concrete Record instances are defined per project variant (e.g., Ajax vs. Eros), and the source code files are located at

src/Ajax/Main
src/Eros/Main

[SDD-55] Records: Simulator

As the simulator also needs to have working persistent storage, I decided to leverage the existing CPL support to use the local host's file system as the storage media.

The hardware targets have an off-board I2C-based EEPROM IC. The CPL class library Driver::NV::Onsemi::CAT24C512::Api *is used to read and write to the EEPROM.*

The functional simulator uses the provided CPL library Driver::NV::File::Cpl::Api *class, which uses the local host's file system as the physical persistent storage.*

[SDD-56] Memory Map

It's important to do the math to ensure that everything will fit in the EEPROM. This needs to be done early in the project in case a hardware change is needed.

The following table details the offset locations in the EEPROM of the various persistently stored records and data.

Record/Data	Region Start	Region Length	Data Len	Chunk Overhd	Reserved/ Expansion
Personality-A	0	273	193	16	64
Personality-B	273	273	193	16	64
UserSettings-A	546	94	14	16	64
UserSettings-B	640	94	14	16	64

(continued)

CHAPTER 11　JUST-IN-TIME DETAILED DESIGN

Record/Data	Region Start	Region Length	Data Len	Chunk Overhd	Reserved/ Expansion
Metrics-A	734	124	44	16	64
Metrics-B	858	124	44	16	64
Log Entries	982	40704	40704	0	0
LogIndex-A	41686	60	12	16	32
LogIndex-B	41746	60	12	16	32
Allocated		41806	40.8K		
Capacity		65536	64.0K		
Available		23730	23.2K		

I2C Driver Design

The GM6000 has an off-board EEPROM with an I2C interface.

[SDD-53] I2C Driver

This is an example of how only a few sentences are required for the design since the driver is provided by third-party code. The design details also address how the simulator is not supported, and it provides the location of the source code files.

The Driver::I2C abstract interface supplied by the CPL C++ class library will be used for the I2C bus driver. The I2C driver is used to communicate with the following device(s):

- *I2C EEPROM, address 0x50*

The concrete driver for the STM32 microcontroller family uses the ST HAL I2C interfaces for the underlying I2C bus implementation.

For the functional simulator, the EEPROM functionality is simulated at a higher layer (i.e., the `Cpl::Persistent::RegionMedia` *layer).*

The abstract I2C driver interface is located at

`src/Driver/I2C`

The target specific I2C implementation is located at

`src/Driver/I2C/STM32`

Button Driver Design

The initial release of the GM6000 is required to have a graphic display and four discrete momentary buttons for the UX.

[SDD-36] Button Driver

As was the case with the I2C driver, not much is needed for detailed design of the button driver since the driver is supplied by third-party code. However, because the design of the third-party button driver deviates from the GM6000 software architecture, the deviation is documented along with why it is considered acceptable.

The `Driver::Button::PolledDebounced` *driver supplied by the CPL C++ class library will be used for the display's board discrete input buttons. The driver will execute in the driver thread.*

The debounce sampling time is 100 Hz and requires two consecutive samples to match to declare a new button state.

The existing button driver only requires the low-level HAL interface to be implemented for the target platform.

For the functional simulator, the buttons on the display board are simulated using the `TPipe` *implementation of the* `Driver::PicoDisplay` *driver.*

CHAPTER 11   JUST-IN-TIME DETAILED DESIGN

The driver is located at

src/Driver/Button

The target-specific implementation is located at

src/Driver/Button/STM32

Note: The driver deviates from the SWA recommended implementation in that it does not use interrupts to detect the initial button edge. The proposed design meets the SWA requirements of debouncing a button within 50 msec (worse case for the current design is 30 msec), and the continual polling is not overly burdensome for the application. The tradeoff was deemed acceptable because of the simplicity of leveraging existing code instead of writing a more complex driver from scratch.

Fuzzy Logic Controller Design

The GM6000 uses a fuzzy logic controller (FLC) for the core of the heating algorithms. The FLC is documented under the "Heating" subsystem in the SDD.

[SDD-34] Fuzzy Logic Controller

This is an example of where the detailed design of an algorithm was done by a subject matter expert (SME), and the algorithm design is captured outside of the SDD. What the SDD needs is a reference to the external document and the software context for implementing the algorithm.

175

CHAPTER 11   JUST-IN-TIME DETAILED DESIGN

A fuzzy logic controller (FLC) is used to calculate updates to the requested output capacity. It is the responsibility of the control algorithm to call the FLC on a periodic basis. The FLC takes current temperature and temperature setpoint as inputs and generates a delta-change-to-capacity output value every time it is called.

The FLC is implemented per the SWA-1330 GM6000 Fuzzy Logic Temperature Control document. The implementation has the following features:

- *An algorithm supervisor is required to call the FLC and provide the current temperature and heating setpoint on a fixed, periodic basis.*

- *The FLC does not assume any particular unit of measure for temperature and setpoints. It is the responsibility of the algorithm supervisor to ensure consistency of input/output values with respect to units of measure.*

- *The geometry of the membership functions cannot be changed. However, there is a Y axis scaling parameter that is runtime configurable.*

- *All math operations are performed using integer math.*

- *Clients provide a scaling factor that is used during the defuzzification process to compensate for lack of floating arithmetic.*

- *The algorithm supports a single input membership function where the sets are defined by triangles.*

CHAPTER 11   JUST-IN-TIME DETAILED DESIGN

- *The algorithm supports a single centroid output membership function whose output sets have configurable weights.*
- *The algorithm has fixed predefined inference rules.*
- *The algorithm's configurable parameters are provided via a Model Point.*

The source code files are located at `src/Ajax/Heating/Flc`.

Graphics Library

The Graphics Library is a top-level subsystem identified in the software architecture document. The software architecture calls out the Graphics Library subsystem as third-party code.

[SDD-19] Graphics Library

This is an example of documenting a design decision. Specifically it is a decision that is less than optimal, and it should be re-evaluated in future releases.

The SWA requires that the Graphics Library be platform independent and run without an RTOS. There are several commercial libraries that meet these requirements. The decision was made to use the Pimoroni Graphics Library for the following reasons:

- *It is free. The library is open source with an MIT license.*
- *The CPL C++ class library provides a platform-independent port of the Pimoroni Graphics Library.*
- *The Pimoroni library comes with drivers for the ST7789 LCD controller and an RGB LED.*

177

CHAPTER 11   JUST-IN-TIME DETAILED DESIGN

Note: This decision should be revisited for future GM6000 derivatives that have a different display or a more sophisticated UI. The Pimoroni library has the following limitations that do not recommend it as a "foundational" component:

- *No support for Window management*
- *Requires C++14 (or newer) and uses C++ features (e.g., the Standard Template Library) that use dynamic memory*
- *Larger than desired footprint because it pulls in the entire standard C++ library code*

The library is located at

xsrc/pimoroni

Screen Manager Design

The Screen Manager is part of the UI subsystem.

[SDD-44] Screen Manager

This snippet details what the navigation model is and how the application is responsible for defining and changing the home screen.

The UI consists of a set of screens. At any given time, only one screen is active. Each screen is responsible for displaying content and reacting to UI events (e.g., button presses) or model point change notifications from the application.

Navigation between screens uses a stack model. Transitioning to a new screen pushes the current screen onto the navigation stack and then makes the new screen the active screen. Navigating backward is done by popping one or more screens from the navigation stack or clearing the entire navigation stack and making the home screen the active screen.

Which screen instance is the home screen is determined by the contents of a model point instance. This allows the application to change what the home screen is based on the overall state of the application.

There are three special screens that do not follow this paradigm. They are the following:

- The splash screen, which is displayed when the system is starting up

- The shut-down screen, which is displayed when the system is shutting down

- The UI Halted screen, which is displayed when an error occurs that prevents continued operation

[SDD-44] Screen Manager: State Machine

A State Machine diagram is used to model the dynamic nature of the splash, home, halt, and shutdown screens.

The following state machine diagram shows the life cycle of the Screen Manager. **Note**: *The diagram describes the behavior; it is not intended to be an implementation.*

The Screen Manager should be opened as soon as possible during the startup sequence so the Splash screen is displayed instead of a blank or unknown screen contents.

During an orderly shutdown, the application should trigger the "UI-shutdown-Request" as the first step in the shutdown sequence and then close the Screen Manager as late as possible in the shutdown sequence.

CHAPTER 11   JUST-IN-TIME DETAILED DESIGN

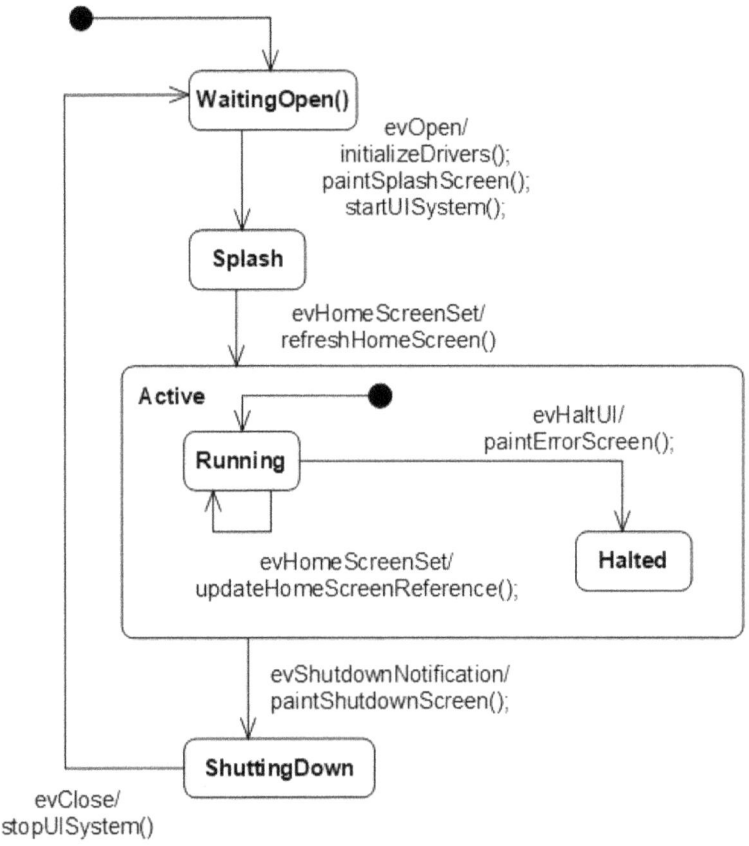

[SDD-44] Screen Manager Class Diagram

The design complexity of the Screen Manager necessitates a class diagram.

The following class diagram identifies the classes and functionality of the Screen Manager. The methods in italics are the public interfaces exposed to the application. Classes in gray/dashed outline are not part of the Screen Manager namespace.

CHAPTER 11 JUST-IN-TIME DETAILED DESIGN

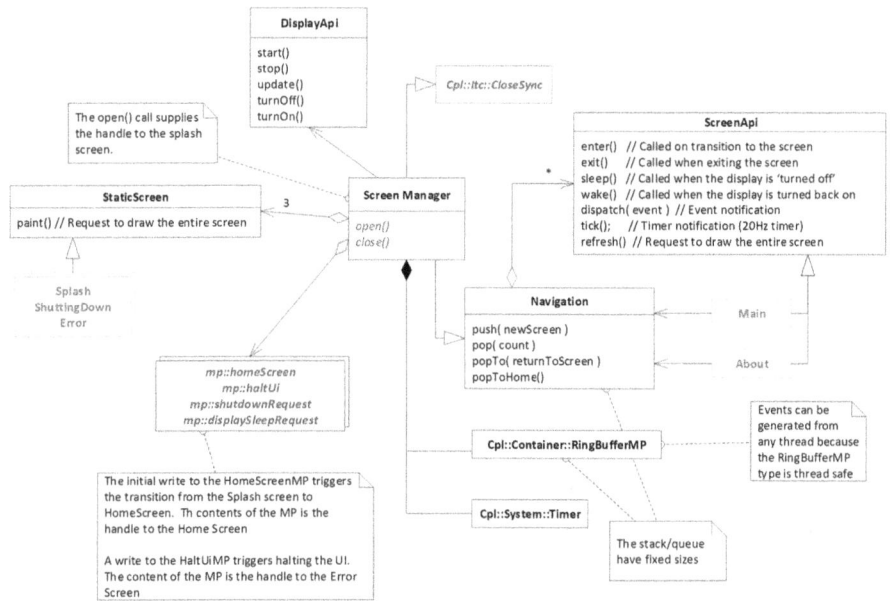

[SDD-44] Screen Manager: Graphics Library

The Screen Manager is platform and hardware independent. No design considerations were needed with respect to the functional simulator, so a simple statement suffices for the design.

The Screen Manager is independent of the graphics library that is used to draw and update the physical display.

[SDD-44] Screen Manager: Location

This statement identifies the Screen Manager's namespace and source code location.

The UI events are application specific. The Screen Manager uses the LHeader pattern for the Event type to decouple itself from the application.

The Screen Manager namespace is `Ajax::ScreenMgr`. *The source code is located at*

src/Ajax/ScreenMgr

Design Reviews

Always perform design reviews and always perform them before coding the component. That is, there should be a design review for each task (see Chapter 10, "Tasks"), and you shouldn't start coding until the design review has been completed. In my experience, design reviews have a bigger return on investment (for the effort spent) than code reviews. The perennial problem with code reviews is that they miss the forest for trees. That is, code reviews tend to focus on the syntax of the code and don't really look at the semantics or the overall design of the software. Code reviews can catch implementation errors, but they don't often expose design flaws. And design flaws are much harder and more expensive to fix than implementation errors.

Do not skip the design review step when the design content is just a few sentences or paragraphs. Holding design reviews is a great early feedback loop between the developers and the software lead.

Review Artifacts

Design reviews can be very informal. For example, the software lead reviews the updated SDD and gives real-time feedback to the developer. However, depending on your QMS or regulatory environment, you may be required to have review artifacts (i.e., a paper trail) that evidence that reviews were held and that action items were identified and resolved. When formal review artifacts are required, it is tempting to hold one or two design reviews at the end of projects. Don't do this. This is analogous to having only a single code review of all the code after you have released the software. Reviews of any kind only add value when performed in real time before coding begins. And, of course, action items coming out of the review should be resolved before coding begins as well.

CHAPTER 11   JUST-IN-TIME DETAILED DESIGN

Here is a description of a lightweight design review process that generates tangible review artifacts. The process is done offline. That is, the reviewers independently review the SDD and then provide written feedback. The process assumes that the Software Detailed Design (SDD) is some sort of shared document (e.g., Google Doc or Microsoft Word).

1. The author, or person responsible for developing the code, updates the SDD document with the design content.

2. The author clears the change history in the document. That is, the author "accepts all changes" and then reenables change tracking.

3. The author sends or publishes the SDD to the reviewers via a shared document link identifying what section or sections should be reviewed. This notice should also contain a timeframe for completing the review.

4. The reviewers independently review the document. Feedback is provided in the shared document. Reviewers should be empowered to correct obvious typos.

5. The reviewers notify the author when they have completed their review.

6. The author reviews the feedback and makes updates as appropriate. All review comments must be addressed by the author, even if the comment is just "no change." The author then notifies the individual reviewers that their comments have been addressed. If the reviewer is satisfied with the resolution, the reviewer marks the comment as resolved.

CHAPTER 11   JUST-IN-TIME DETAILED DESIGN

7. Repeat steps 4–6 until all review comments have been marked as resolved. Marking comments as resolved is absolutely required.

8. After the review has been completed, make a copy of the current SDD and store it in a design review directory. This snapshot copy of the SDD constitutes the review artifact. When archiving the SDD snapshot, it is helpful to identify when the review occurred and what sections were reviewed. This can be as simple as encoding the information in the file name of the archive document.

I have used the aforementioned process on numerous projects, and it works well, but it is not perfect. For example, sometimes the design is sufficiently complex that an in-person meeting is required. Sometimes the reviewers and the author can't agree on how to resolve action items. When these situations occur, remember that the goal is to ensure that the proposed design satisfies the problem statement. It shouldn't be about "I would have solved the problem this way."

Summary

The software detail design process is about decoupling problem-solving from the act of writing source code. When detailed design creates solutions, then "coding" becomes a translation activity of transforming the design into source code. The detailed design process should include the following:

CHAPTER 11   JUST-IN-TIME DETAILED DESIGN

- Design first; then code and test.

- Create an entry for all components in the SDD—not just the complicated ones. This is a necessary aspect for tracing requirements to design elements and source code (see Chapter 9, "Requirements Revisited").

- At minimum view documenting your design as "rubber duck designing",[1] in that by explaining a problem to someone else—or by writing it down—you will often find edge cases, inconsistent logic, missing dependencies, etc.

- Incrementally add to the detailed design in a just-in-time manner. Avoid "big-bang" design efforts.

- Review each individual design increment in real time before coding begins.

INPUTS

- All documented requirements including ongoing updates
- Software Development Plan including ongoing updates
- System architecture document including ongoing updates
- Software architecture document including ongoing updates
- *Software Detailed Design document* including ongoing updates

---

[1] https://en.wikipedia.org/wiki/Rubber_duck_debugging

CHAPTER 11   JUST-IN-TIME DETAILED DESIGN

OUTPUTS

- Potential updates to the MRS, PRS, and SRS documents
- Potential updates to the system architecture document
- Potential updates to the software architecture document
- Updates and reviews to the design statements (if used)
- Updates and reviews to the Software Detailed Design document

CHAPTER 12

Coding, Unit Tests, and Pull Requests

The source code and unit tests are the most visible outputs of the construction phase. However, this chapter is not about how to write source code; rather, it is about the process for writing code, unit testing it, and then merging it into a stable branch. The key thing about this process is that, just like the Software Detailed Design activities, the coding and unit tests are done on a just-in-time basis.

If you followed the steps in Chapter 10, "Tasks," you have already completed these activities:

- A ticket has been created that calls for the source module to be written.

- Requirements for the to-be-written source code have been identified.

- The Software Detailed Design has been created, documented, and reviewed.

CHAPTER 12 CODING, UNIT TESTS, AND PULL REQUESTS

You can now begin the coding and unit testing process. This involves the following:

1. Creating a short-lived branch in the repository for the source code. The branch should have the same name as the ticket.

2. Writing the source code.

3. Writing the unit test code. This step in the process doesn't change whether you are writing platform-dependent or platform-independent code. In either case, unit tests must be written for each component. However, for hardware-specific components, you will need to build a stand-alone test image that you can manually exercise the unit tests against.

4. Creating the unit test project.

5. Iterating through multiple executions of the unit test until all the uncovered bugs are fixed and the desired test coverage has been achieved.

Don't cheat on this process. In my experience, every time I rationalized it was okay to skip or shortcut steps in this process, it always came back to haunt me. I thought I could save myself time, but in the end, it always ended up taking longer than if I had just followed my own rules.

The order that you perform the steps in is entirely up to you. For example, the traditional approach would be to perform the steps in the order listed. But if you're on the Test-Driven Development (TDD) side of the spectrum, the unit test project is created first, then the unit test code is written, and then the code is written. This would then be followed by iterations where the implementation and the test coverage are extended.

My personal approach is somewhere in the middle. That is, I typically write the shell or outline of the code, and then I create the unit test project and write minimum unit test code to make sure that the code I have written compiles and executes. Then I flesh out the remaining functionality incrementally: I iterate through writing code, adding unit test code, and executing the unit tests. In the end, the best suggestion I can make is: test early, test often. Avoid a big-bang approach of writing all the code and then executing all the unit tests.

Check-In Strategies

After the implementation is completed, and the desired test coverage has been achieved, the next step is to check everything into the repository. One advantage of doing the work on a branch is that the developer can check in their work in progress without impacting others on the team. I highly recommend checking in (and pushing) source code multiple times a day. This provides the advantage of being able to revert or back out changes if your latest work goes south. It also ensures that your code is stored on more than one hard drive.

Pull Requests

Use pull requests (PRs) to merge the source on the temporary branch to its parent branch (e.g., `develop` or `main`). Other source control tools provide similar functionality, but for this discussion, my examples will be GitHub specific.[1] The pull request mechanism has the following advantages:

---

[1] If you are not using Git, you may have to augment your SCM's merge functionality with external processes for code reviews and CI integration.

- It identifies any merge conflicts. That is, a PR cannot be completed until all merge conflicts have been resolved.
- It makes the code available to other developers to review and provide feedback in a collaborative environment. The feedback and subsequent discussions are captured and persistently stored, providing artifacts and an audit trail of the code review.
- It notifies code reviewers when the PR is created.
- It allows code updates to be checked in and added to the PR.
- It triggers a continuous integration (CI) build of the submitted code, which includes executing all unit tests (not just the newly submitted tests).
- It enforces approvals and other checks. For example, it can ensure that code is not merged in the parent branch unless the CI build is successful or that a different person approves or signs off on a code review before the code is merged.

The recommended minimum process for a pull request is as follows:

- Require at least one reviewer. If required, specify who that reviewer should be.
- Require that all review comments be successfully resolved before the PR can be merged.
- Require that the CI build has successfully completed (for the latest commit) before the PR can be merged.
- Do not allow any merge conflicts. (The Git server enforce this.)

After the PR has been merged, the ticket can be closed or moved to a ready-for-test-team-validation state depending on your workflow process.

CHAPTER 12　CODING, UNIT TESTS, AND PULL REQUESTS

Granularity

I strongly recommend the best practice of implementing new components in isolation without integrating the component into the application. That is, I recommend that you first go through the coding process—steps 1 through 5—and then create a second ticket to integrate the new component into the actual application or applications. Things are simpler if the scope of the changes is restricted to the integration changes only. Additionally, these are the following benefits:

- It reduces merge conflicts.

- The integration can be deferred until additional required components have been completed. For example, integrating a I2C driver into the application is not required until there is a consumer (e.g., an EEPROM driver) of the I2C driver.

- It allows you to address the multiple permutations inherent in the Main pattern (e.g., common creation, startup, and shutdown).

Examples

The sections that follow provide examples from the GM6000 project using the coding and unit testing process.

I2C Driver

The I2C driver is needed for serial communications to the off-board EEPROM IC used for the persistent storage in the GM6000 application. The class diagram in Figure 12-1 illustrates that there are different implementations for each target platform.

CHAPTER 12   CODING, UNIT TESTS, AND PULL REQUESTS

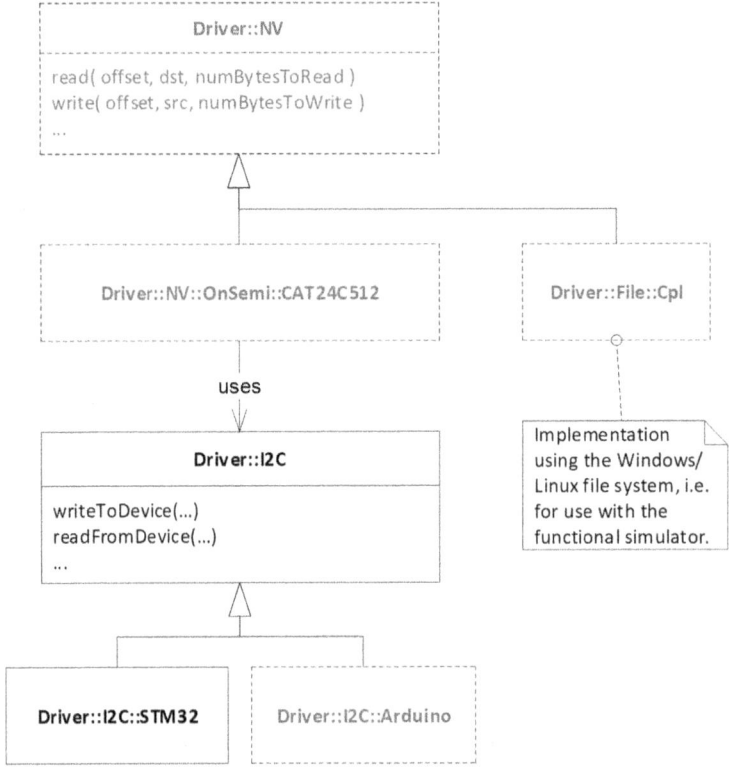

Figure 12-1. *Class diagram for the I2C driver*

Before the coding and unit testing began, the following steps were completed:

- A ticket was created for the driver.

- The requirements were identified. In this case, the requirements were for the persistent storage of the user options and for the heating algorithm customizations where the target hardware has an off-board I2C EEPROM.

CHAPTER 12 CODING, UNIT TESTS, AND PULL REQUESTS

- The detailed design was completed and reviewed. For the I2C driver, there was minimal design because I made the decision to leverage the ST HAL interfaces (see Appendix M, "GM6000 Software Detailed Design (Final Draft)").

At this point, I was ready to start the process. Table 12-1 summarizes the work.

Table 12-1. *Process and work summary for the I2C driver*

Step	Work
Branch	1. Create a branch off of develop for the work. The branch name should contain the ticket card number in its name.
	2. Create the src/Driver/I2C/STM32 directory in the source code tree. The location of the driver was identified during the detailed design step.
Source Code	1. Implement the I2C driver.
	a. Edit the ST Cube MX file to enable and configure the I2C bus. The BSP for the target is located at src/Bsp/Initech/alpha1.
	b. Update the BSP initialization code to call the newly generated MX code for configuring and initializing the I2C bus.
	c. Implement the I2C driver API using the ST HAL APIs.
Unit Test	1. The CPL library contains an existing unit test for I2C drivers that can be used to verify the driver's operation. The unit test code is located at src/Driver/I2C/_0test.

(*continued*)

Table 12-1. (*continued*)

Step	Work
Test Project	1. Create the unit test project and build scripts that are specific to target hardware. The new unit test project is located under the existing tests/Driver directory tree at tests/Driver/I2C/_0test/master-eeprom/NUCLEO-F413ZH-alpah1/windws/gcc-arm. a. Typically, I clone a similar test project directory to start. For the I2C driver's test project, I cloned the tests/Driver/DIO/_0test/out_pwm/NUCLEO-F413ZH-alpah1/windows/gcc-arm. Then I modified the copied files to create a I2C unit test using these steps: • Update the libdirs.b files to include the appropriate I2C directories and to remove the directories specific to the PWM output driver. • Modify main.cpp to call the top-level test function for the driver's unit test. The file was also modified to create a dedicated thread for the unit test to execute in. 2. Compile, link, and download the unit tests. Then verify that the test code passes. Iterate to fix any bug found or to extend the test coverage.

(*continued*)

Table 12-1. (*continued*)

Step	Work
Pull Request	1. Run the top/run_doxgyen.py script to verify that there are no Doxygen errors in the new file. This step is needed because the CI builds will fail when there are Doxygen errors present in the code base. 2. Commit and push the source code. 3. Generate a PR for the branch. The PR triggers a CI build. a. Notify the code reviewers that the code is ready for review. This is done automatically by the Git server when the PR owner selects or assigns reviewers as part of creating the PR. 4. If there are CI build failures, commit and push code fixes to the PR (which triggers a new CI build). 5. Resolve all code review comments and action items. And again, any changes you make to files in the PR trigger a new CI build. 6. After all review comments have been resolved, and the last pushed commit has built successfully, the branch can be merged to develop. The merge will trigger a CI build for the develop branch. 7. Delete the PR branch as it is no longer needed.

At this point, the I2C driver exists and has been verified, but it has not been integrated into the actual GM6000 application (i.e., Ajax or Eros). Additional tickets or tasks are needed to integrate the driver into the Application build.

The I2C driver is intermediate driver in the GM6000 architecture in that it is used by the Driver::NV::Onsemi::CAT24C512 driver. In turn, the NV driver is used by the Cpl::Dm persistent storage framework for reading and writing persistent application records. The remaining tasks would be the following:

CHAPTER 12   CODING, UNIT TESTS, AND PULL REQUESTS

1. Create the STM32 specific unit test project for the CAT24C512 driver and verify that the unit test passes. The CAT24C512 driver exists and has a unit test, but there is no unit test for the STM32 platform. This unit test project works out the kinks in how to create the CAT24C512 driver for the STM32 platform.

2. Integrate the driver into the application. The integration is deferred until task 1 has been completed and there is at least one persistent application record defined (i.e., the first usage of the EEPROM).

Screen Manager

The UI consists of a set of screens. At any given time, only one screen is active. Each screen is responsible for displaying content and reacting to UI events (e.g., button presses) or model point change notifications from the application. The Screen Manager component is responsible for managing the navigation between screens as well as handling the special use cases such as the splash and UI halted screens.

The Screen Manager itself does not perform screen draw operation so it is independent of the Graphics library as well as being hardware independent. Before the coding and unit testing began, the following steps should have been completed:

- A ticket was created for the driver.
- The requirements were identified. In this case, it is the UI wireframes (see the EPC wiki).
- The detailed design was completed and reviewed. From the detailed design, the Screen Manager is responsible for

CHAPTER 12   CODING, UNIT TESTS, AND PULL REQUESTS

- Screen navigation
- Supporting dynamic home screen semantics
- Displaying a splash screen
- Displaying a terminal error screen

At this point, I was ready to start the process of creating the Screen Manager. Table 12-2 summarizes the work.

Table 12-2. Process and work summary for the Screen Manager

Step	Work
Branch	1. Create a GIT branch (off of develop) for the work. The branch name should contain the ticket number in its name.
	2. Create the src/Ajax/ScreenMgr and src/Ajax/ScreenMgr/_0test directories. The location of the Screen Manager was identified during the detailed design step.
Source Code	1. Implement the Screen Manager.
Unit Test	1. Implement the unit test. The unit test is an automated unit test since the Screen Manager has no direct hardware dependencies.

(*continued*)

Table 12-2. (*continued*)

Step	Work

Test Project	1. Create the unit test projects. Since it is an automated unit test, the test needs to be built with three different compilers to eliminate issues that could potentially occur when using the target cross compiler. These are the three compilers I use:
	
	• Microsoft Visual Studio compiler—Used because it provides the richest debugging environment
	
	• MinGW compiler—Used to generate code coverage metrics
	
	• GCC for Linux—Used to ensure the code is truly platform independent
	
	2. I recommend that you build and test with the compiler toolchain that is the easiest to debug with. After all tests pass, then build and verify them with the other compilers. The unit test project directories are as follows:
	
	`tests/Ajax/ScreenMgr/_0test/windows/vc12`
	`tests/Ajax/ScreenMgr/_0test/windows/mingw_w64`
	`tests/Ajax/ScreenMgr/_0test/linux/mingw_gcc`
	
	a. When creating the test project, typically I start by cloning a similar test project directory. For the Screen Manager test projects, I cloned the projects under the `tests/Ajax/Heating/Flc/_0test/` directory tree. I then modified the copied files for the Screen Manager unit test. This included the following changes per compiler variant:
	
	• Updating the `mytoolchain.py` file so that the `unit_test_objects` variable points to the Screen Manager driver's unit test directory. The `unit_test_objects` variable is needed when linking Catch2 test applications with NQBP2.

(*continued*)

CHAPTER 12   CODING, UNIT TESTS, AND PULL REQUESTS

Table 12-2. (*continued*)

Step	Work
	• Updating the `libdirs.b` files to include the appropriate Screen Manager directories and to remove the directories specific to the fuzzy logic controller (FLC) directories.
	3. Compile, link, and execute the unit tests and verify that the test code passes with the targeted code coverage.
	4. Iterate through the process to extend the test coverage and fix any bugs.
Pull Request	1. Run the `top/run_doxgyen.py` script to verify that there are no Doxygen errors in the new file that was added. This step is needed because the CI builds will fail if there are Doxygen errors present in the code base.
	2. Commit and push the source code.
	3. Generate a PR for the branch. The PR triggers a CI build.
	a. Notify the code reviewers that the code is ready for review. This is done automatically by the Git server when the PR author selects or assigns reviewers as part of creating the PR.
	4. If there are CI build failures, commit and push code fixes to the PR (which will trigger new CI builds).
	5. Resolve all code review comments and action items. And again, any changes you make to files in the PR triggers a new CI build.
	6. After all review comments have been resolved and the last pushed commit has built successfully, the branch can be merged to `develop`. The merge will trigger a CI build for the `develop` branch.
	7. Delete the PR branch as it is no longer needed.

At this point, the Screen Manager code exists and has been verified, but it has not been integrated into the actual GM6000 application (i.e., Ajax or Eros). A second ticket is needed to actually integrate the Screen Manager into the application build. For the GM6000 code, I created a second ticket that included the following:

- Integrating the `Driver::PicoDisplay` into the Ajax and Eros applications. It also included integrating the external "Display Simulator" application for the simulator builds of Ajax and Eros.

- Implementing the Splash and Shutdown screens for the Ajax and Eros applications.

- Creating a stub for a Home screen for the Ajax and Eros applications.

Summary

If you wait until after the Software Detailed Design has been completed before writing source code and unit tests, you effectively decouple problem-solving from the act of writing source code. The coding, unit test, and pull request process should include the following:

- Using short-lived branches to isolate the work-in-progress from the rest of the application. The branch should map to the project's ticket workflow. That is, the branch name contains the ticket name.

- Translating the detailed design into source code.

- Verifying the code works by running unit tests. Automate the unit tests wherever there are no direct hardware dependencies.

CHAPTER 12   CODING, UNIT TESTS, AND PULL REQUESTS

- Holding code reviews and documenting them for each ticket. You can use pull requests to enforce code reviews and approvals.

- Requiring all newly committed code to pass the CI build before merging.

- Only allowing trivial merges—merges where there are no merge conflicts—when updating the parent branch (e.g., `develop`).

INPUTS

- All documented requirements including ongoing updates
- Software Development Plan including ongoing updates
- System architecture document including ongoing updates
- Software architecture document including ongoing updates
- Software Detailed Design document including ongoing updates

OUTPUTS

- Source code with unit tests
- Pull requests, which include documented code reviews and successful CI builds
- Merged pull requests

CHAPTER 13

Integration Testing

Integration testing is where multiple components are combined into a single entity and tested. In theory, all of the components have been previously tested in isolation with unit tests, and the goal of the integration testing is to verify that the combined behavior meets the specified requirements. Integration testing also serves as incremental validation of the product as more and more functionality becomes available.

Integration testing is one of those things that is going to happen whether you explicitly plan for it or not. The scope and effort of the integration testing effort can range from small to large, and the testing artifacts that are generated can be formal or informal. Here are some examples of integration testing:

- Testing between system-level components. For example, testing between an IoT device and the cloud

- Testing the combined software being developed by multiple teams. For example, testing the software developed by one team to run on a main CPU board in conjunction with the real-time firmware running on an off-board MCU being developed by another team

- Testing the integration of in-house developed software with software developed by external service organizations

CHAPTER 13   INTEGRATION TESTING

- Testing the integration of various control components into a single control application
- Testing new hardware components and software drivers

Integration testing is not a one-time event or effort. A typical project will have many integration testing efforts as components are continually integrated into increasingly larger components, culminating with the final testing of the entire product or system. At one end of the spectrum, your final project verification may be one giant integration test. At the other end, you may be working in a highly regulated environment that imposes strict integration steps as part of the software development life cycle process.

Regardless of the scope, complexity, or degree of formality, all integration testing follows the following steps:

1. Plan
    a. Define the goal for the test effort.
    b. Define a timeline for the test effort.
2. Develop the code
    a. This includes developing "code under test," potential test harnesses, test scripts, etc.
3. Define use cases or test cases
    a. This includes defining pass/fail criteria.
4. Execute the integration tests
5. Report results

How formal each of these steps is depends on the project, what is being integrated, and the company's Quality Management System (QMS) or regulatory requirements. In my experience, even when it is not dictated

CHAPTER 13   INTEGRATION TESTING

by regulatory requirements, some formality is needed if the project spans multiple teams, especially if the teams are geographically diverse or span organizations. The value of a documented integration test plan is that

- It clearly defines what is and isn't in scope.
- It sets a timeline.
- It sets pass/fail criteria. Or, said another way, it establishes when the integration testing effort ends.
- It specifies who is responsible for defining and executing the test cases.

As mentioned earlier, integration testing will happen organically if it is not explicitly formalized. A principal advantage of formalizing integration testing is that it avoids or reduces the amount drama that naturally occurs between teams and the amount of tension between developers and program managers. In addition, integration events are often viewed as key milestones that have visibility with stakeholders and senior leadership. Taking the time to properly set expectations beforehand more than pays for itself in not having to spend time on damage control.

For the GM6000 project, there is no example integration test plan because it is a single device with a single small development team—namely, me. I performed all of the integration testing either informally or as part of automated integration tests that I wrote to be executed during CI builds. However, a future release of the GM6000 calls for a wireless remote temperature sensor that would likely require more structured integration testing. In this case, I could envision at least three integration test efforts:

1. An RF integration test plan where both the base unit and the wireless sensor are able to pair, transfer data, and unpair. The goal of this test plan would be to evaluate and characterize the RF performance of the two devices.

205

CHAPTER 13   INTEGRATION TESTING

2. A user integration test plan where the procedures for pairing and unpairing are performed. The goal of this test is to verify the procedures and evaluate them for ease of use with respect to the end user. Items such as RF range, temperature control, etc., would be outside the scope of this test effort as would testing the entire UI.

3. A temperature control test plan where the control algorithm uses the remote temperature sensor at various locations throughout the room. The goal of this test is to verify algorithm performance and to identify potential modifications to the control algorithm occasioned by temperature sensor placement.

Continuing with this hypothetical scenario, a minimal formal RF integration testing effort might look like this:

1. The software lead sends an email to the HW lead, System Engineer, Program Manager, etc., that defines the specific RF attributes to be tested: for example, signal to noise, range, bit-error rates, etc. The email also contains the target date for when the testing will begin and how long the test execution will take. While the software lead is responsible for the overall test effort, in this particular scenario, goal definition and test criteria are assigned as a joint effort with the hardware lead.

2. The software team meets to determine the minimum functionality that needs to be implemented on both devices to achieve the stated goals. Work tickets are created for functionality not already completed.

3. The software and hardware leads work together to select an engineer to write the test procedures and define the individual pass/fail requirements. They also identify who will execute the tests. Work tickets are created for the assigned work. The test procedures are defined in a spreadsheet as a high-level list of steps or use cases and include the pass/fail criteria. Note that the documented test procedures provide for a higher degree of confidence in the repeatability of the tests.

4. After the necessary software has been developed, a formal build[1] is created, and the test cases from step 3 are executed. The pass/fail results along with any notes and commentary are recorded in the spreadsheet. Any bugs found are triaged to determine if they need to be fixed in order to continue testing. Blocker bugs are fixed and retested.

Based on the current test results, the software and hardware leads determine if the goals of the testing have been reached. If yes, the software lead sends out an email with test results. Note that the testing goals can be met without all the test cases passing. For example, if the RF range tests fail, and a new antenna design is needed to resolve the issue, testing can be paused until new hardware is received, and then the integration test plan can be re-executed.

---

[1] A formal build is defined as a build of a "stable" branch (e.g., `develop` or `main`) performed on the CI build server where the source code has been tagged and labeled. It is imperative that all non-unit testing be performed on formal builds because the provenance of a formal build is known and labelled in the SCM repository (as opposed to a private build performed on a developer's computer).

CHAPTER 13 INTEGRATION TESTING

Smoke Tests

Smoke or sanity tests are essentially integration tests that are continually executed. Depending on the development organization, smoke tests are defined and performed by the software test team, the development team, or both. In addition, smoke tests can be automated or manual. The automated tests can be executed as part of the CI build or run on demand. If the tests are manual, it is essential that the test cases and steps be sufficiently documented so that the actual test coverage is repeatable over time even when different engineers perform the testing.

One downside to smoke tests is that they can be easily broken as requirements and implementations evolve over time. This means that

- From a project planning perspective, there needs to be time and resources allocated for the care and feeding of the test cases.

- Do not implement the smoke test too early in the project when the code base is relatively immature. When to start implementing smoke testing will always be a project-specific decision. However, always start by testing functionality that is unlikely to change and keep the initial test coverage minimal. You can add more test coverage as the requirements and code mature.

Simulator

A functional simulator can be a no-cost platform for performing automated smoke tests that can be run as part of the CI builds. These automated simulator tests can be simple or complex. In my experience, the only limitation for simulator-based tests that run as part of the CI build is the amount of time they add to the overall CI build time.

CHAPTER 13 INTEGRATION TESTING

The GM6000 project has an automated smoke test and a heating simulation test that run as part of the CI builds. These tests leverage the debug console and the Python pexpect library,[2] which provides control of interactive console applications. An additional Python library, RATT, is used as a thin wrapper on top of pexpect. See Appendix G, "RATT," for an in-depth discussion of the RATT library.

The automated smoke test runs in real time and performs only basic operations (i.e., only a very high-level verification that the build works). The smoke test scripts are located at the src/Ajax/Main/_0test/ directory. The smoke test runs on the Windows simulator and is explicitly called out in the build_all.bat script (see Chapter 8, "Continuous Integration Builds").

The heating simulation test runs in simulated time and verifies the functional behavior of the heating algorithm that is made up of several individual components. The test does not validate the quality or effectiveness of the heating algorithm. As mentioned earlier, this test executes in simulated time, where the test cases advance time per algorithm tick (which is two seconds), allowing you to run several minutes of algorithm time in just a few seconds. The CPL library provides a simulated time feature that is transparent to the application code. The simulated time feature is enabled at link time by selecting the simulated time implementation for the underlying "timing" interfaces in the Cpl::System namespace. At run time, the Cpl::TShell::Cmd::Tick command is used to advance the simulated time. The heating simulator test scripts are located at src/Ajax/Heating/Simulate/_0test. The test executable is built and executed as an automated "unit test" (see Chapter 8, "Continuous Integration Builds").

---

[2] https://pypi.org/project/pexpect/

CHAPTER 13 INTEGRATION TESTING

Summary

Integration testing performed by the software team occurs throughout a project. How formal or informal the integration testing should be depends on what is being integrated. Generally, a more formal integration testing effort is required when integrating components across teams. However, a minimum level of formality should be that the pass/fail criteria is written down.

Continual execution of integration tests, for example, smoke tests or sanity tests, provides an initial quality check of a build. Ideally, these tests would be incorporated in the CI build process.

INPUTS

- All documented requirements including ongoing updates
- Software Development Plan including ongoing updates
- System architecture document including ongoing updates
- Software architecture document including ongoing updates
- Software Detailed Design document including ongoing updates
- Source code

CHAPTER 13   INTEGRATION TESTING

OUTPUTS

- Defined scope and pass/fail criteria for the testing:
    - (Optional) Documented test plan
    - (Optional) Written test cases
    - (Optional) Integration code
- Evaluation and decision regarding the value of automating the testing. If automated testing is determined to be worthwhile, this would be followed by the creation of an automated test suite for regression testing or CI builds.
- Test reports that document the results of the integration tests
- List of executed tests including the backlog tickets or bug cards created for each issue uncovered

CHAPTER 14

Board Support Package

The Board Support Package (BSP) is a layer of software that allows applications and operating systems to run on the hardware platform. Exactly what is included in a BSP depends on the hardware platform, the targeted operating system (if one is being used), and potential third-party packages that may be available for the hardware (e.g., graphics libraries). The BSP for a Raspberry PI running Linux is much more complex than a BSP for a stand-alone microcontroller. In fact, I have worked on numerous microcontroller-based projects that had no explicit concept of a BSP in their design. So while there is no one-size-fits-all definition or template for BSPs in the microcontroller hardware space, ideally a microcontroller BSP encapsulates the following:

- The compiler toolchain, as it relates to the specific MCU
- The MCU's datasheet
- The target board's schematic

CHAPTER 14   BOARD SUPPORT PACKAGE

Compiler Toolchain

The compiler toolchain is all of the glue and magic that has to be in place from when the MCU's reset vector executes up until the application's main() function is called. This includes items, for example:

1. The vector table—The list of function pointers that are called when a hardware interrupt occurs.

2. Minimal MCU and memory configuration—Depending on the MCU, a certain amount of clock configuration and memory access—both RAM and Flash—may be needed before the C/C++ runtime code can be executed.

3. The C/C++ runtime code—The code that executes before main() is called. This code is responsible for setting up the C/C++ environment (e.g., initializing the Data and BSS segments in RAM, invoking static C++ constructors, etc.).

4. The platform dependencies for the C standard library are satisfied. For example, when using the GCC compiler, there needs to be a board-specific implementation for low-level functions such as __io_putchar() and __io_getchar() that read and write characters to and from a UART. These functions are called by the C library's stdio functions.

5. Linker script—This script defines the memory map for the compiler toolchain and the MCU.

CHAPTER 14 BOARD SUPPORT PACKAGE

BSPs are dependent on a specific compiler toolchain as well as MCU and board schematic. Non-ANSI standard compiler features are typically used when implementing the C code for a BSP (e.g., linker script syntax, using GCC's __weak attribute, assembly code, etc.).

Encapsulating the Datasheet

Most MCU vendors provide header files that contain C data structures, functions, and macros to access individual registers and bits within the registers. Ideally, the BSP will further abstract the MCU datasheet and registers by providing functionality based on behavior, not just by hardware register name, for example, the work of configuring the TX and RX pins for a UART. Depending on the MCU, the following configuration is required:

- Configuring the RX as an input pin and selecting the appropriate "pull-up/pull-down/none" options for the pin

- Selecting the RX pin to be used for the UART (i.e., selecting one of many possible pin usages)

- Configuring the TX as an output pin and selecting a drive strength and drive type for the pin

- Selecting the TX pin to be used for the UART (i.e., selecting one of many possible pin usages)

An example of a BSP abstraction for the RX and TX management would be to have single function call that is passed the physical pin assignments for the RX and TX pins, and it would be responsible for knowing which registers, bits, and values (per the datasheet) need to be written to fully configure the specified RX and TX pins.

CHAPTER 14   BOARD SUPPORT PACKAGE

Another example of a BSP abstraction would be setting the baud rate for a UART. Typically, there are multiple registers (clock selection, clock dividers, match registers, etc.) that need to be configured when setting the baud rate. The BSP abstraction would provide a single function call that specifies a desired baud rate, and the BSP would take care of the details.

The goal of defining BSP abstractions is to only provide logical interfaces accessing MCU peripherals instead of dealing directly with MCU's hardware registers. BSP abstractions are not for defining a generalized abstract layer across multiple BSPs. Or said another way, the BSP interfaces should be focused on a specific MCU and PCB with no eye toward potential reuse with other BSPs. In my experience, MCUs and SDKs vary so widely it would be difficult to define common BSP-level abstractions across different MCUs, and it would have very low return on the investment for the work required.

Encapsulating the Board Schematic

Microcontroller projects typically run on custom hardware that is specific to a company's devices and products. The BSP's role is to abstract away the circuit-level details of the schematic. For example:

- Provide logical names (e.g., preprocessor symbols) for the MCU's physical pins

- Provide logical assert and de-assert semantics for physical pin signals (e.g., decouple the knowledge that to assert a Chip Select to an SPI device is a physical low signal)

- Configure the MCU's hardware peripherals per the schematic

BSPs in Practice

As previously mentioned, there is no one size fits all when it comes to microcontroller BSPs. There are two BSPs for the GM6000 project: one is for the ST NUCLEO-F413ZH evaluation board, and the second is for the Adafruit Grand Central M4 Express board. The two BSPs are structured completely differently, and the only thing they have in common is each BSP has `Api.h` and `Api.cpp` files. The BSP for the Nucleo board uses ST's HAL library and Cube MX IDE for low-level hardware functionality. The BSP for the Adafruit Grand Central board leverages the Arduino framework for abstracting the hardware. To illustrate the differences, the following are summaries of the file and directory structure of the two BSPs.

ST NUCLEO-F413ZH BSP

```
src/Bsp/Initech/alpha1/   // Root directory for the BSP
+--- Api.h                // Public BSP interface
+--- Api.cpp              // Implementation for Api.h
+--- ...
+--- stdio.cpp            // C Library support
+--- syscalls.c           // C Library support
+--- ...
+--- mini_cpp.cpp         // C++ support when not linking against stdlibc++
+--- MX/                  // Root directory for the ST Cube MX tool
|    +--- MX.ioc          // MX project file
|    +--- startup_stm32f413xx.s   // Initializes the Data & BSS segments
|    +--- STM32F413ZHTx_FLASH.ld  // Linker script
|    +--- ...
|    \--- Core/           // Contains the MX tool's auto generated code.
|                         // The dir contains the vector table, clock cfg, etc.
|
+--- console/             // Support for the CPL usage of the debug UART
|    +--- Ouptut.h        // Cpl::Io stream instance for the debug UART
|    \--- Ouptut.cpp      // Cpl::Io stream instance for the debug UART
+--- SeggerSysView/       // Run time support for Segger's SysView tool
\--- trace/               // Support for CPL tracing
     \--- Ouptut.cpp      // Tracing using C libray stdio and Cpl::Io streams
```

CHAPTER 14   BOARD SUPPORT PACKAGE

Adafruit Grand Central M4 Express BSP

```
src/Bsp/Initech/alpha1-atmel/   // Root directory for the BSP
+--- Api.h                      // Public BSP interface
+--- Api.cpp                    // Implementation for Api.h
+--- cortex_handlers.c          // Vector table for the MCU
+--- main.cpp                   // Contains main(), calls Arduino's setup() & loop()
+--- sdfat.cpp                  // Support FAT32 file system on the SPI dataflash
+--- wiring.c                   // Low level hardware configuration
\--- FreeRTOS/                  // Source files for FreeRTOS
```

A majority of the Adafruit BSP functionality is performed by the Arduino framework located under the `arduino/hardware/samd/` directory in the EPC repository.

Structure

The structure for BSPs that I recommend is minimal because each BSP is conceptually unique since it is compiler, MCU, and board specific. This structure is a single `Api.h` header file that uses the LHeader pattern and exposes all of the BSP's public interfaces. An in-depth discussion of the LHeader pattern can be found in Appendix D, "LHeader and LConfig Patterns." However, here is a summary of how I used the LHeader pattern in conjunction with BSPs.

1. I created a single `Api.h` header file that is not owned by a specific BSP. This header file will ultimately provide access to a concrete BSP's public interfaces. The GM6000 architecture uses the file `src/Bsp/Api.h`.

a. This file defines a minimal set of common functions that all BSPs should support. In this case, there is a `Bsp_Api_initialize()` function declared.

b. This file contains a `#include "colony_map.h"` statement as dictated by the LHeader pattern. The actual header file that gets included at compile time for this statement is based on each individual project's set of header search paths specified in its make script. This allows individual projects to select a specific BSP.

c. All symbols in the header file should be prefixed with `Bsp_` or `BSP_` to isolate the public BSP interfaces in the global compiler namespace. As an application has only one BSP, there is no need for naming conventions to distinguish between individual concrete BSPs.

2. I created a subdirectory under the `src/Bsp` directory for the new BSP. There are no recommended naming conventions for BSP directories; however, keep in mind that the BSPs are MCU, board, and compiler specific, and your naming convention should accommodate possible BSP variants.

    a. Create a single `Api.h` header file in the preceding directory. This header file contains everything that is needed to expose the public interfaces for the BSP. The public interfaces should include an implementation of the public interfaces defined in 1a.

Figure 14-1 illustrates how referencing a concrete BSP header file is deferred to when a specific project is compiled. Being able to defer which BSP is used is critical in that it allows drivers to be decoupled from a specific BSP. A driver may still be specific to an MCU or off-board IC, but

CHAPTER 14 BOARD SUPPORT PACKAGE

not a BSP. For example, when migrating from using an evaluation board to the first in-house designed board, the existing driver source code does not have to be updated when changing to the in-house board.

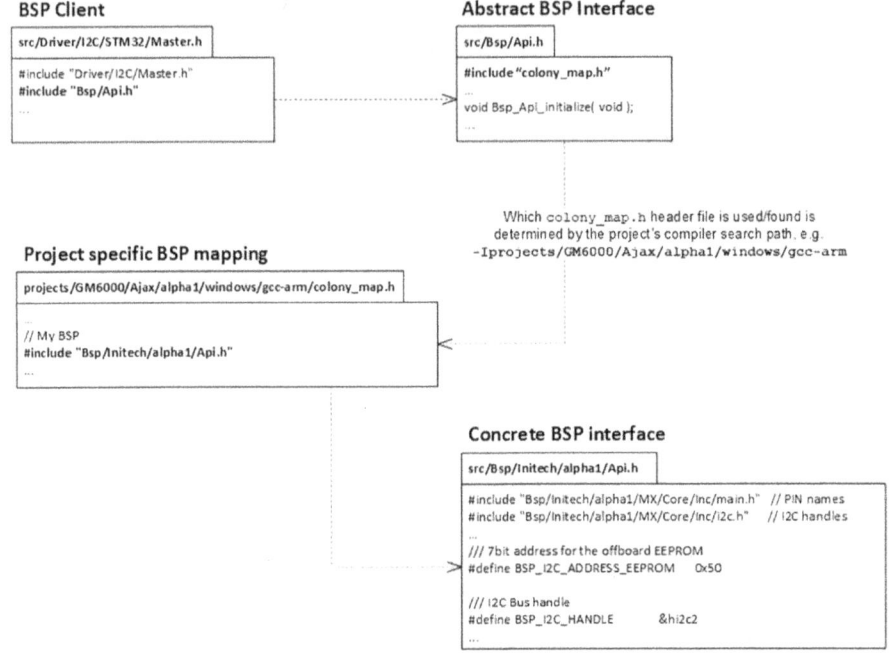

Figure 14-1. LHeader deferred header include

Dos and Don'ts

Here is my short list of dos and don'ts when creating BSPs.

- Build the BSP in a just-in-time manner. That is, only add functionality when there is active development that requires hardware support. For example, you don't need to implement I2C support in the BSP until someone is ready to work on a driver that utilizes an I2C bus.

CHAPTER 14   BOARD SUPPORT PACKAGE

- The initial BSP should contain support for the UART that is used for the debug console and the C library (a.k.a. printf).

- Do not include any C++ code in the BSP's public interface header file (i.e., in Api.h). This allows C modules to #include the BSP's header file and be compiled as a C file. This scenario usually occurs when compiling source code provided by the MCU vendor or third-party packages. Also it is okay to implement a BSP using C++. The only restriction is that the public interface declarations have to be fully C compatible.

- Create a unit test project to verify the basic operation on the hardware when creating a new BSP. Because the BSP deals with the C/C++ runtime code and C library support, the fact that the test project successfully compiles and links is not sufficient to claim victory. For example, if the vector table is not located at the proper memory address, the application will not start or the MCU will immediately crash on boot-up.

- BSPs are very concrete in nature so don't be bogged down with reuse across BSPs or BSP variants. It is okay for copy-paste-edit reuse across BSPs. Or said another way, there is typically very little to no business logic captured in a BSP that warrants the extra effort to make reusable BSP components.

- Keep the BSPs small since they are not reuse friendly. Typically, this means implementing drivers outside of the BSP whenever possible.

CHAPTER 14   BOARD SUPPORT PACKAGE

- BSPs are fairly static in nature. That is, after they are working, they require very little care and feeding. Doing a lot of refactoring or maintenance on existing BSP functionality is a potential indication that there are underlying architecture or design issues.

Bootloader

The discussion so far has omitted any discussion using a bootloader with the MCU. The reason is because designing and implementing a bootloader is outside the scope of this book. However, many microcontroller projects include a bootloader so that the firmware can be upgraded after the device has been deployed. Conceptually a bootloader does the following:

1. It executes when the reset vector is executed.
2. It makes a determination if there is new firmware to load.
    a. If yes, then the MCU application memory is programmed with the new firmware.
3. It verifies that the MCU's application memory contains a valid image.
    a. If yes, the control is transferred to the application; that is, the application's startup code is executed and `main()` is called.

While the aforementioned behavior is straightforward, the implementation details of a bootloader vary greatly. The good news is that bootloaders can be mostly encapsulated in a stand-alone executable that is separate from the BSP. This means the construction of the BSP can be done without having first implemented a bootloader. After the bootloader is in place, the BSP usually requires a few updates because the BSP is no longer

CHAPTER 14 BOARD SUPPORT PACKAGE

the owner of the MCU's vector table. However, the changes are relatively isolated (e.g., an alternate linker script) and usually do not disrupt the existing BSP structure.

If your project requires a bootloader, it is strongly recommended that it is implemented and deployed early in the development cycle. This maximizes the runtime on the bootloader before the first release. This is especially critical if the bootloader itself is not upgradable after the product is deployed.

Summary

The goal of the Board Support Package is to encapsule the low-level details of the MCU hardware, the board schematic, and compiler hardware support into a single layer or component. The design of a BSP should decouple the concrete implementation from being directly referenced (i.e., #include statements) by the drivers and application code that consume the BSP's public interfaces. This allows the client source code to be independent of concrete BSPs. The decoupling of a BSP's public interfaces can be done by using the LHeader pattern.

INPUTS

- All documented requirements including ongoing updates
- Software Development Plan (SDP) including ongoing updates
- System architecture (SA) document including ongoing updates
- Software architecture (SWA) document including ongoing updates
- Software Detailed Design (SDD) document including ongoing updates

CHAPTER 14   BOARD SUPPORT PACKAGE

OUTPUTS

- Working BSP code
- BSP test projects
- Design reviews
- Code reviews
- Potential updates to requirements that may be in MRS, PRS, or SRS documents
- Potential updates to the system architecture (SWA) document
- Potential updates to the software architecture (SA) document
- Updates to the Software Detailed Design document
- Updates to design statements when used

CHAPTER 15

Drivers

This chapter is about how to design drivers that are decoupled from a specific hardware platform that can be reused on different microcontrollers. In this context, reuse means reuse across teams, departments, or your company. I am not advocating designing general-purpose drivers that work on any and all platforms; just design for the platforms you are actively using today.

Writing decouple drivers does not take more effort or time to implement than a traditional platform-specific driver. This is especially true once you have implemented a few decoupled drivers. The only extra effort needed is a mental shift in thinking about what functionality the driver needs to provide as opposed to getting bogged down in the low-level hardware details. I am not saying the hardware details don't matter; they do. But defining a driver in terms of a specific microcontroller register set only pushes hardware details into your application's business logic.

A decoupled driver requires the following:

- A public interface that is defined such that there are no direct hardware dependencies. That is, only the driver's services are defined.

- A layer or mechanism that decouples the driver implementation from a specific hardware platform, for example, a Hardware Abstraction Layer (HAL). Remember that the driver depends on the HAL declarations, not the implementation of the HAL.

CHAPTER 15   DRIVERS

Binding Times

A Hardware Abstraction Layer is created using late bindings. The general idea behind late binding time is that you want to wait as long as possible before binding data or functions to names. Here are the four types of name bindings. However, only the last three are considered late bindings.

- Source time—Source time bindings are made when you edit a source code file. This is reflected primarily in what your #include statements are and how they define data types, as well as numeric and string constants. As source code bindings are bindings that cannot be changed or undone later without editing the file, you want to minimize source time bindings in your HAL interfaces.

- Compile time—Compile-time bindings are late bindings that are made during the compilation stage. The primary mechanisms involved with compile-time bindings are the specification of preprocessor symbols when the compiler is invoked. Oftentimes this is done by setting the compiler's header file search paths. The *LHeader* and *LConfig* patterns (see Appendix D, "LHeader and LConfig Patterns") leverage the header search path mechanism to provide concrete definitions for preprocessor symbols that were declared without any definition provided.

- Link time—Link-time bindings are late bindings that are made during the link stage of the build process. The linker binds names to addresses or binds code with a specific function name. Link-time binding allows a developer to define a function (or set of functions) and then have multiple implementations for those functions. The selection of which implementation to use is specified in the project's build script. (This is why I advocate separate stand-alone build scripts for each variation of a project.)

- Run time—Run-time bindings are late bindings that occur when the application executes. An example of these types of bindings is the C++ polymorphic bindings that occur at run time when a virtual method is called.

Public Interface

Defining a public interface for a driver is a straightforward task. What makes it complicated is trying to do it without referencing any underlying hardware-specific data types. And interacting with the MCU's registers (and its SDK) always involves data types of some kind. For example, when configuring a Pulse Width Modulation (PWM) output signal using the ST HAL library for the STM32F4x, the MCU requires a pointer to a timer block (TIM_HandleTypeDef) and a channel number (of type uint32_t). When using the Arduino framework with the ATSAMD51 MCU, only a simple int is needed. So how do you define a handle that can be used to configure a PWM output signal that is platform independent?

CHAPTER 15   DRIVERS

One way to solve this is by using a forward declaration, for example:

`typedef struct DriverDioPwmConfig_T* DriverDioPwmConfigPtr_T.`

The compiler allows clients (or consumers) to pass around a pointer to a data structure (e.g., `DriverDioPwmConfigPtr_T`) without a concrete type definition because all pointers have the same known storage size. The concrete data type for `DriverDioPwmConfig_T` can then be defined in platform-specific code. The limitations of this approach are as follows:

- It requires memory management for how an instance is created using platform-specific code. For drivers, this is usually not an issue because the Board Support Package (BSP) typically provides the concrete instance.

- A pointer type is cumbersome when the underlying type is an integer or a C++ reference. For example, when using the Arduino framework, the concrete platform type for `DriverDioPwmConfig_T` is an int.

A better approach is to use the LHeader pattern, which uses compile-time bindings to provide a concrete and platform-specific data type for the PWM configuration type. The LHeader pattern eliminates the limitations incurred when using a forward reference. Unfortunately, this comes at the expense of some additional complexity. An in-depth discussion of the LHeader pattern can be found in Appendix D, "LHeader and LConfig Patterns"; however, here is a summary of how the LHeader pattern is used in conjunction with drivers for deferring hardware-specific data types.

1. In the driver's public interface header file (e.g., `src/Driver/DIO/Pwm.h`), use a #include statement—without any path information—that references a header file that does not resolve to any header file in the baseline set of header search file paths. For example:

    ```
    #include "colony_map.h"           // Note: no path specified
    ```

CHAPTER 15   DRIVERS

2. In the public interface header file, use the preprocessor to create a name for the PWM configuration type that maps to another, yet to be resolved, symbol name. For example:

```
/// Defer the definition of the PWM configuration type
#define DriverDioPwmConfig_T    DriverDioPwmConfig_T_MAP
```

3. In the project's build directory, or in a directory that is unique to the project, create a `colony_map.h` header file. This header file then includes a platform-specific header file that maps the `DriverDioPwmConfig_T_MAP` symbol to a concrete type.

4. In the project's build script, add the directory where the `colony_map.h` file (from step 3) is located into the compiler's header search path.

Figure 15-1 illustrates how using the LHeader pattern allows project-specific concrete data types for the PWM configuration data type.

CHAPTER 15 DRIVERS

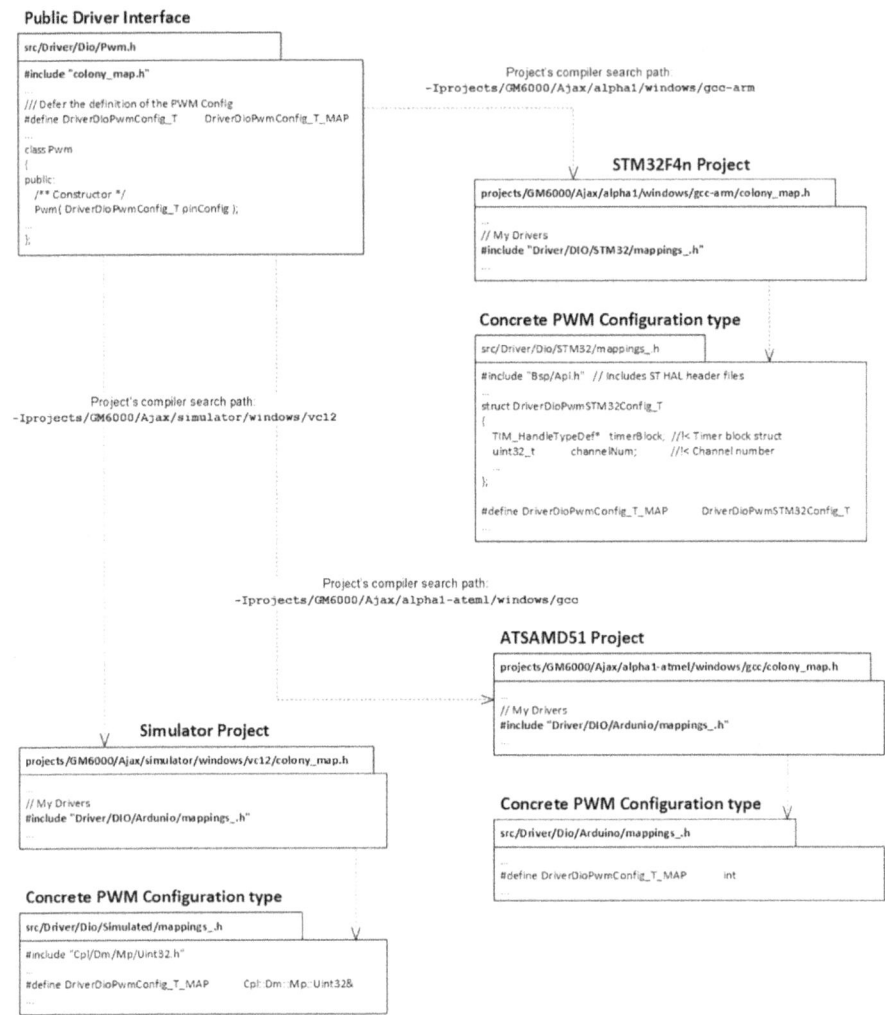

Figure 15-1. PWM compile-time binding using the LHeader pattern

CHAPTER 15   DRIVERS

Hardware Abstract Layer (HAL)

There are numerous ways to create interfaces for a Hardware Abstraction Layer (HAL). The following section covers three ways to create abstract interfaces that decouple a driver from platform-specific dependencies. They are as follows:

- Facade—Using link-time bindings
- Separation of concerns—Using compile-time bindings
- Polymorphic—Using run-time bindings

In this context, an "abstract interface" simply means any interface that defines a behavior that has a late binding. In fact, the same techniques can be used to decouple components throughout the application. In other words, these techniques are not unique to writing hardware-independent drivers.

Facade

A facade driver design is one where the public interface is defined and then each supported platform has its own unique implementation. That is, there is no explicit HAL defined. A simple and effective approach for a facade design is to use a link-time binding. This involves declaring a set of functions (i.e., the driver's public interface) and then having platform-specific implementations for that set of functions. In this way, each platform gets its own implementation. The PWM driver in the CPL class library is an example of an HAL that uses link-time binding. This driver generates a PWM output signal at a fixed frequency with a variable duty cycle controlled by the application.

Figure 15-2 illustrates how a client of the PWM driver is decoupled from the target platform by using link-time bindings.

CHAPTER 15 DRIVERS

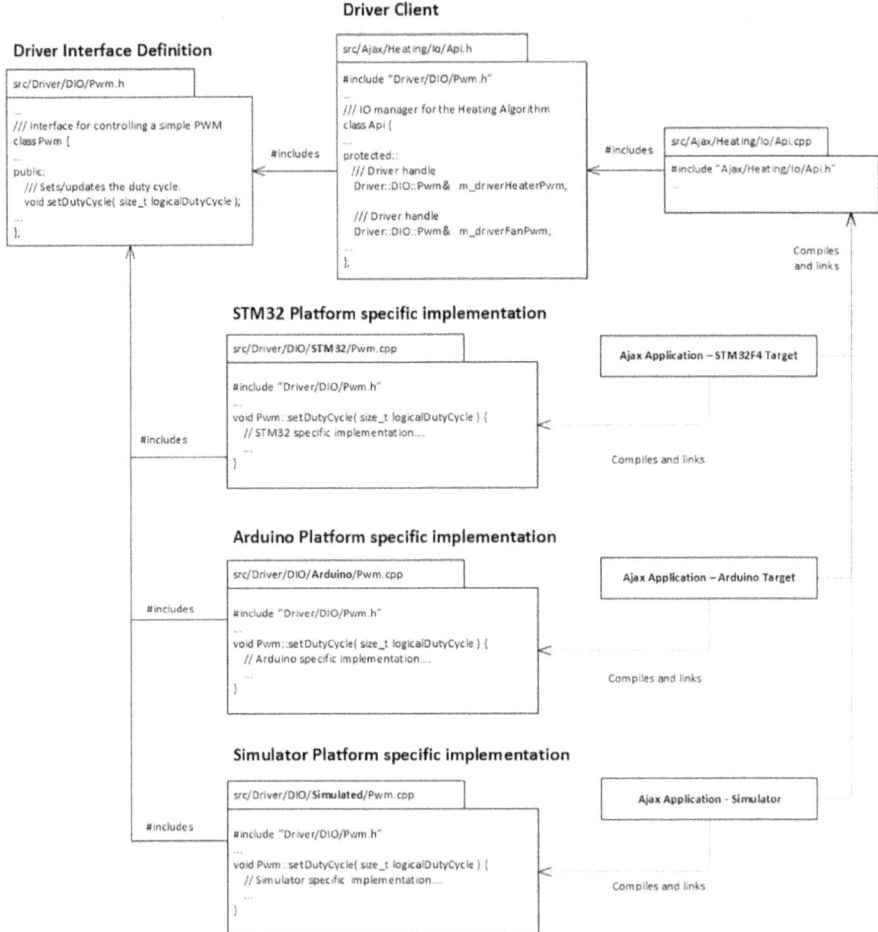

***Figure 15-2.** PWM driver design using a facade and link-time bindings*

CHAPTER 15 DRIVERS

Example PWM Driver

The interface for the PWM driver defines the concrete class Driver::DIO
::PWM that is the public interface for the driver (in the file src/Driver/
DIO/Pwm.h). In addition to link-time binding, the driver design uses the
LHeader pattern for defining a platform-independent PWM configuration
type—DriverDioPwmConfig_T. Figure 15-3 shows the class definition and
the driver's public interface. Note the following:

- Lines 4 and 5 do not contain path information. The build scripts specify the header path for resolving these #include statements.

- Line 8 uses the LHeader pattern to defer the selection of the concrete type for the PWM configuration structure to the application's build script.

- Lines 11–13 show an example of using the LConfig pattern for defining 100% PWM value.

- Lines 23–45 define a concrete class for the PWM driver. The actual implementation will be specified by the application's build script.

CHAPTER 15   DRIVERS

```cpp
1  #ifndef Driver_DIO_Pwm_h_
2  #define Driver_DIO_Pwm_h_
3
4  #include "colony_map.h"
5  #include "colony_config.h"
6
7  /// Defer the definition of the PWM configuration
8  #define DriverDioPwmConfig_T           DriverDioPwmConfig_T_MAP
9
10 /// Value for Maximum Duty/100% cycle
11 #ifndef OPTION_DRIVER_DIO_PWM_MAX_DUTY_CYCLE_VALUE
12 #define OPTION_DRIVER_DIO_PWM_MAX_DUTY_CYCLE_VALUE   0xFFFF
13 #endif
14
15 ///
16 namespace Driver {
17 ///
18 namespace DIO {
19
20 /** This class defines a generic interface for controlling a simple PWM
21     output signal.
22  */
23 class Pwm
24 {
25 public:
26     /** Constructor Note: the 'pinConfig' struct MUST stay in scope as long
27         as the driver is in scope.
28      */
29     Pwm( DriverDioPwmConfig_T pinConfig );
30
31 public:
32     ...
33
34     /** Sets/updates the duty cycle.  A value of 0 is 0% duty cycle.  A
35         value of OPTION_DRIVER_DIO_PWM_MAX_DUTY_CYCLE_VALUE is 100% duty cycle
36      */
37     void setDutyCycle( size_t logicalDutyCycle );
38
39 protected:
40     /// PWM info
41     DriverDioPwmConfig_T    m_pwm;
42
43     /// Started flag
44     bool                    m_started;
45 };
46
47 } // End namespace(s)
48 }
49 #endif  // end header latch
```

Figure 15-3. Partial file listing of epc/src/Driver/DIO/Pwm.h

Each supported hardware platform requires its own implementation of the concrete class. It is the project (or unit test) build scripts that determine which implementation is linked into the executable image. This is why in the repository there are three different implementations of the PWM class in three different directories (see Figure 15-4).

CHAPTER 15 DRIVERS

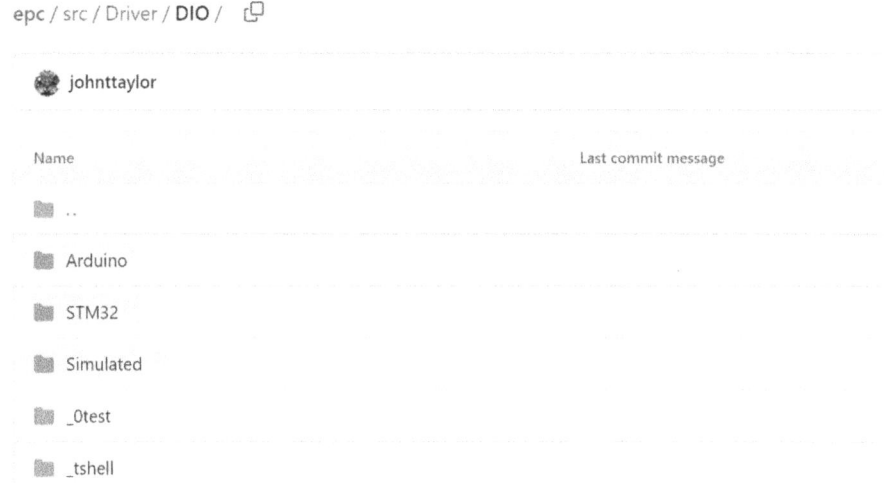

Figure 15-4. *Location of the three different implementations of the PWM class*

In the following three sections, you will see the implementation of the PWM functionality for each of these platforms:

- STM32—See Figure 15-5.
- Arduino—See Figure 15-6.
- Simulated—See Figure 15-7.

The STM32 Implementation of PWM

The implementation relies on the ST HAL library and initialization code generated by the ST Cube MX IDE. The implementation is located at src/Driver/DIO/STM32/Pwm.cpp. Figure 15-5 shows the implementation for the STM32 setDutyCycle() method.

CHAPTER 15 DRIVERS

```cpp
void Pwm::setDutyCycle( size_t logicalDutyCycle )
{
    if ( m_started )
    {
        // The Driver's logical duty-cycle maps the Hardware's duty-cycle range,
        // so I just need to clamp out-of-range values
        if ( logicalDutyCycle > m_pwm.timerBlock->Instance->ARR )
        {
            logicalDutyCycle = m_pwm.timerBlock->Instance->ARR;
        }

        switch ( m_pwm.channelNum )
        {
        case TIM_CHANNEL_1:
            m_pwm.timerBlock->Instance->CCR1 = logicalDutyCycle;
            break;
        case TIM_CHANNEL_2:
            m_pwm.timerBlock->Instance->CCR2 = logicalDutyCycle;
            break;
        case TIM_CHANNEL_3:
            m_pwm.timerBlock->Instance->CCR3 = logicalDutyCycle;
            break;
        case TIM_CHANNEL_4:
            m_pwm.timerBlock->Instance->CCR4 = logicalDutyCycle;
            break;
        default:
            break;
        }
    }
}
```

Figure 15-5. Partial listing of src/Driver/DIO/STM32/pwm.cpp

Arduino Framework Implementation of PWM

The implementation is built on top of the Arduino framework. The implementation is located at `src/Driver/DIO/Arduino/Pwm.cpp`. Figure 15-6 shows the Arduino implementation for the `setDutyCycle()` method.

CHAPTER 15 DRIVERS

```
1 void Pwm::setDutyCycle( size_t logicalDutyCycle )
2 {
3     if ( m_started )
4     {
5         // Scale the logical duty-cycle to the hardware range
6         size_t dutyCycle = (logicalDutyCycle *
7                             (OPTION_DRIVER_DIO_PWM_ARDUINO_MAX_DUTY_CYCLE +1)) /
8                             (OPTION_DRIVER_DIO_PWM_MAX_DUTY_CYCLE_VALUE + 1);
9         if ( dutyCycle >= OPTION_DRIVER_DIO_PWM_ARDUINO_MAX_DUTY_CYCLE )
10        {
11            // At max duty cycle 'force' the output high
12            // Note: Since I am relying on the Arduino framework - I don't have
13            //       detailed knowledge/control of the PWM/Timer peripheral, so
14            //       we brute force the edge cases to ensure all on/off at the
15            //       duty cycle boundaries
16            digitalWrite( m_pwm, HIGH );
17        }
18        else if ( dutyCycle == 0 )
19        {
20            // At min duty cycle 'force' the output low
21            digitalWrite( m_pwm, LOW );
22        }
23        else
24        {
25            // Set the output
26            analogWrite( m_pwm, dutyCycle );
27        }
28    }
29 }
```

Figure 15-6. Partial listing of src/Driver/DIO/Arduino/Pwm.cpp

Simulator Implementation of PWM

The functional simulator implementation uses model points to simulate the PWM output signal. That is, the duty cycle is a simple model point that can be accessed using the debug console. The implementation is located at `src/Driver/DIO/Simulated/Pwm.cpp`. Figure 15-7 shows the simulator implementation for the `setDutyCycle()` method.

CHAPTER 15   DRIVERS

```
1 void Pwm::setDutyCycle( size_t dutyCycle )
2 {
3      if ( m_started )
4      {
5           if ( dutyCycle > OPTION_DRIVER_DIO_PWM_MAX_DUTY_CYCLE_VALUE )
6           {
7                dutyCycle = OPTION_DRIVER_DIO_PWM_MAX_DUTY_CYCLE_VALUE;
8           }
9           m_pwm.write( dutyCycle );
10     }
11 }
```

Figure 15-7. Partial listing of src/Driver/DIO/Simulated/Pwm.cpp

The PWM example is a C++ example. However, the mechanism of link-time binding can easily be done in C. To do this, replace the member functions of the PWM class with C functions that take a pointer to the DriverDioPwmConfig_T structure as one of the function arguments. For example, in C, functions would be defined like this:

```
void pwm_initialize( DriverDioPwmConfig_T* pwmHdl );
bool pwm_start( DriverDioPwmConfig_T* pwmHdl );
void pwm_stop( DriverDioPwmConfig_T* pwmHdl );
void pwm_setDutyCycle( DriverDioPwmConfig_T* pwmHdl, size_t dutyCycle);
```

Separation of Concerns

The "separation of concerns" approach to driver design is to separate the business logic of the driver from the hardware details. This involves creating an explicit HAL interface definition in a header file that is separate from the driver's public interface. The HAL interface specifies basic hardware actions. Or, said another way, the HAL interface should be limited to encapsulating access to the MCU's registers or SDK function

CHAPTER 15 DRIVERS

calls. The implementation of the public driver interface provides the business logic while relying on the HAL interface for interactions with the hardware.

There are several options for how to structure the HAL interface definition. One approach is to use link-time bindings as described in the "Facade" section. Another is to use compile-time binding. An advantage of using compile-time binding is that it provides the least amount of runtime overhead when implementing an HAL interface since it relies solely on the preprocessor.

The implementation for the compile-time binding is to use the same LHeader mechanism that was used in the "Facade" section to include methods not just a data type. The Polled Debounced Button driver in the CPL class library is an example of an HAL using only compile-time bindings. The PolledDebounced driver samples the raw button state at a fixed frequency (determined by the application at run time) requiring N consecutive samples with the same raw button state to declare a change in the logical, or debounced, button state.

Figure 15-8 illustrates how the HAL interface for the Button driver is decoupled from the target platform by using the LHeader pattern.

CHAPTER 15 DRIVERS

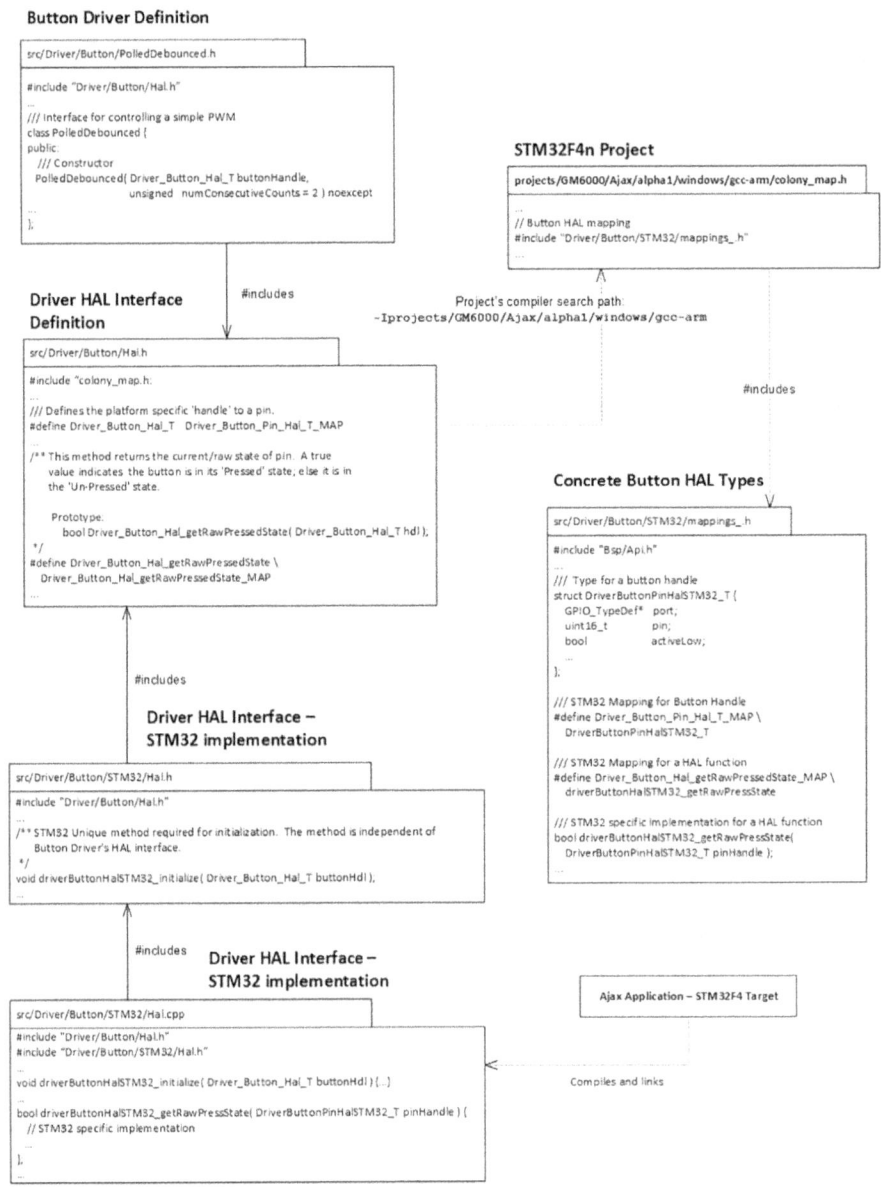

Figure 15-8. Button driver design using separation of concerns and the LHeader pattern

CHAPTER 15 DRIVERS

Example Button Driver

The interface for the Polled Debounced Button driver defines a hardware-independent concrete class `Driver::Button::PolledDebounced` and a separate HAL header file. The HAL header file uses the LHeader pattern to define a hardware-independent data type and behavior (e.g., "get raw button pressed state"). The `PolledDebounced` class implements the driver logic using the abstract interface declared in the HAL header file. Figure 15-9 shows a partial listing for the `PolledDebounced` button class definition in `src/Driver/Button/PolledDebounced.h`. Note the following:

- Line 4 includes the HAL interface. This header file defines the `Driver_Button_Hal_T` structure (using the LHeader pattern).

- Lines 19–33 define the PolledDebounced driver's public interface with no dependencies on the target platform.

CHAPTER 15 DRIVERS

```cpp
#ifndef Driver_Button_PolledDebounced_h_
#define Driver_Button_PolledDebounced_h_

#include "Driver/Button/Hal.h"

namespace Driver { namespace Button {

/** This concrete class implements a button driver where a single button
    is polled and its raw button state is de-bounced.
 */
class PolledDebounced
{
public:
    /** Constructor. The physical button being is sampled is specified by
        'buttonHandle'. The 'numConsecutiveCounts' specifies the number of
        consecutive sample periods - without the raw button state changing -
        to declare a new de-bounced state.
     */
    PolledDebounced( Driver_Button_Hal_T buttonHandle,
                     unsigned            numConsecutiveCounts = 2 ) noexcept;
    ...

public:
    /// This method returns the de-bounced pressed button state.
    inline bool isPressed() noexcept { return m_pressed; }

    /** The application is required to call this method on fixed periodic
        intervals. The raw button state is sampled during this call.
     */
    void sample() noexcept;

    /// Returns the driver's button handle
    inline Driver_Button_Hal_T getHandle() { return m_buttonHdl; }

protected:
    /// Handle to the button
    Driver_Button_Hal_T m_buttonHdl;

    /// Required number of consecutive counts
    unsigned            m_requiredCount;

    /// Consecutive counts
    unsigned            m_counts;

    /// Previous raw state
    bool                m_previousRawPressed;

    /// De-bounced state
    bool                m_pressed;
};

} // End namespace(s)
}
#endif  // end header latch
```

Figure 15-9. Partial file listing of src/Driver/Button/PolledDebounced.h

Figure 15-10 shows a snippet from the HAL header file (located at src/Driver/Button/Hal.h). Note the following:

- Line 4 does not contain path information. The build scripts specify the header path for resolving this #include statement.

- Line 8 uses the LHeader pattern to defer the selection of the concrete type for the Button structure to the application's build script.

- Line 16 defines the HAL interface method as a macro, per the LHeader pattern, to defer the implementation selection to the application's build script.

- There are no create or initialize functions declared. This is intentional since the creation is very platform specific (unless you add additional abstractions such as a factory pattern).[1]

```
1 #ifndef Driver_Button_Hal_h_
2 #define Driver_Button_Hal_h_
3
4 #include "colony_map.h"
5
6 /** This data type defines the platform specific 'handle' to a pin.
7  */
8 #define Driver_Button_Hal_T                     Driver_Button_Pin_Hal_T_MAP
9
10 /** This method returns the current/raw state of pin.  A true value indicates
11     the button is in its 'Pressed' state; else it is in the 'Un-Pressed' state.
12
13     Prototype:
14         bool Driver_Button_Hal_getRawPressedState( Driver_Button_Hal_T hdl );
15  */
16 #define Driver_Button_Hal_getRawPressedState    Driver_Button_Hal_getRawPressedState_MAP
17
18 #endif
```

Figure 15-10. Partial file listing of src/Driver/Button/Hal.h

---

[1] https://en.wikipedia.org/wiki/Factory_method_pattern

CHAPTER 15 DRIVERS

By only including the usage behavior in your HAL interfaces, you can delegate the creation and initialization to platform-specific code on startup (see Chapter 7, "Building Applications with the Main Pattern") without burdening consumers of the driver with platform dependencies. The next step is to implement the abstractions declared in the HAL header file. To accomplish this, you will need to perform the following tasks for each hardware platform:

1. Implement the abstract functions declared in the HAL interface header file. I recommend that you create a pair of files: a header file and a .c|.cpp file. The header file will be used to declare public platform-specific functions that provide functionality that was not defined in the driver's HAL interface (e.g., initialize methods). The .c|.cpp file will contain the platform-specific HAL implementation.

2. Create a mapping header file. This file contains the mapping for the abstract data types and functions.

In the following three sections, you will see the implementation of the button driver functionality for each of these platforms:

- STM32—See Figures 15-11, 15-12, and 15-13.
- Arduino—See Figures 15-14, 15-15, and 15-16.
- Simulated—See Figures 15-17, 15-18, and 15-19.

STM32 MCU Implementation of the Button Driver

The implementation relies on the ST HAL library and initialization code generated by the ST Cube MX IDE. Figures 15-11 through 15-13 show the files that comprise the implementation.

CHAPTER 15 DRIVERS

The src/Driver/Button/STM32/Hal.h is an STM32-specific header file that provides hardware-specific initialization for the button driver. Note the following lines in Figure 15-11.

- Line 4 includes the HAL interface. This header file defines the Driver_Button_Hal_T structure (using the LHeader pattern).

- Line 9 is the STM32-specific driver initialize method. The expectation is that on startup, STM32-specific code would call this method to complete initializing the button driver.

```
1 #ifndef Driver_Button_STM32_Hal_h_
2 #define Driver_Button_STM32_Hal_h_
3
4 #include "Driver/Button/Hal.h"
5
6 /** This method is used to initialize the GPIO for the pin/configuration
7     specified by 'buttonHdl'
8  */
9 void driverButtonHalSTM32_initialize( Driver_Button_Hal_T buttonHdl );
10
11 #endif
```

Figure 15-11. STM32-specific interface for a button driver

The src/Driver/Button/STM32/mappings_.h is used to resolve the LHeader deferred methods and types to an STM32 hardware platform. Note the following lines in Figure 15-12.

- Lines 1 and 47 comprise an additional header latch to break cyclical header file includes when using the LHeader pattern. See the "LHeader Caveats" section for an explanation of why this is needed.

- Lines 3, 4, and 46 are the traditional header latch so that the header is only included once when compiling files.

CHAPTER 15 DRIVERS

- Line 6 is another LHeader pattern usage that allows the STM32 button driver to work with any STM32-based BSP.

- Lines 12–35 define the STM32-specific concrete data type for the instance.

- Line 38 provides the LHeader mapping for the abstract HAL interface to the STM32-specific data structure defined at lines 12–35.

- Line 44 provides the function prototype for the STM32-specific implementation of the abstract HAL interface's `Driver_Button_Hal_getRawPressedState()` method.

- Line 41 provides the LHeader mapping for the abstract HAL interface's `Driver_Button_Hal_getRawPressedState()` method.

Chapter 15 Drivers

```
1  #ifdef Driver_Button_Hal_h_
2
3  #ifndef Driver_Button_STM32_mappings_x_h_
4  #define Driver_Button_STM32_mappings_x_h_
5
6  #include "Bsp/Api.h"
7  #include <stdint.h>
8
9
10 /** Type for a button handle
11  */
12 struct DriverButtonPinHalSTM32_T
13 {
14     GPIO_TypeDef*  port;       //!< Port structure for the Pin
15     uint16_t       pin;        //!< Pin number (within the port)
16     bool           activeLow;  //!< Set to true when the pressed state is ACTIVE_LOW
17
18     /// Constructor
19     DriverButtonPinHalSTM32_T( GPIO_TypeDef*   portStruct,
20                                uint16_t        pinNum,
21                                bool            isActiveLow )
22         : port( portStruct )
23         , pin( pinNum )
24         , activeLow( isActiveLow )
25     {
26     }
27
28     /// Constructor
29     DriverButtonPinHalSTM32_T( const DriverButtonPinHalSTM32_T& other )
30         : port( other.port )
31         , pin( other.pin )
32         , activeLow( other.activeLow )
33     {
34     }
35 };
36
37 /// STM32 Mapping
38 #define Driver_Button_Pin_Hal_T_MAP                    DriverButtonPinHalSTM32_T
39
40 /// STM32 Mapping
41 #define Driver_Button_Hal_getRawPressedState_MAP       driverButtonHalSTM32_getRawPressState
42
43 /// STM32 specific implementation for getting the raw button state
44 bool driverButtonHalSTM32_getRawPressState( DriverButtonPinHalSTM32_T pinHandle );
45
46 #endif  // end header latch
47 #endif  // end Interface latch
```

Figure 15-12. STM32 LHeader mappings for the button driver

The `src/Driver/Button/STM32/Hal.cpp` file implements the HAL interface for the STM32 platform. Note the following lines in Figure 15-13.

- Line 1 includes the abstract HAL interface definition.
- Line 2 includes the STM32 button driver interface definition.

247

CHAPTER 15 DRIVERS

- Lines 4–7 are the STM32 implementation of the method declared in the header file from line 2.

- Lines 9–19 are the implementation of the abstract HAL interface.

```
1 #include "Driver/Button/Hal.h"
2 #include "Hal.h"
3
4 void driverButtonHalSTM32_initialize( Driver_Button_Hal_T buttonHdl )
5 {
6     // Currently all initialize is done via the STM32 MX tool and the BSP
7 }
8
9 bool driverButtonHalSTM32_getRawPressState( DriverButtonPinHalSTM32_T pinHandle )
10 {
11    if ( pinHandle.activeLow )
12    {
13        return HAL_GPIO_ReadPin( pinHandle.port, pinHandle.pin ) ? false : true;
14    }
15    else
16    {
17        return HAL_GPIO_ReadPin( pinHandle.port, pinHandle.pin )? true: false;
18    }
19 }
```

Figure 15-13. STM32 HAL button driver implementation

Arduino Framework Implementation of the Button Driver

The implementation is built on top of the Arduino framework. Figures 15-14 through 15-16 show the files that comprise the implementation.

The src/Driver/Button/Arduino/Hal.h is an Arduino-specific header file that provides hardware-specific initialization for the button driver. Note the following lines in Figure 15-14.

- Line 4 includes the HAL interface. This header file defines the Driver_Button_Hal_T structure using the LHeader pattern.

- Line 10 is the Arduino-specific driver initialization method. The expectation is that on startup, Arduino-specific code would call this method to complete the initialization of the button driver.

CHAPTER 15 DRIVERS

```
1 #ifndef Driver_Button_Arduino_Hal_h_
2 #define Driver_Button_Arduino_Hal_h_
3
4 #include "Driver/Button/Hal.h"
5
6
7 /** This method is used to initialize the GPIO for the pin/configuration specified
8     by 'buttonHdl'
9  */
10 void driverButtonHalArduino_initialize( Driver_Button_Hal_T buttonHdl );
11
12 #endif
```

Figure 15-14. *Arduino framework-specific interface for a button driver*

The src/Driver/Button/Ardunio/mappings_.h is used to resolve the LHeader deferred methods and types to the Arduino framework. Note the following lines in Figure 15-15.

- Lines 1 and 45 comprise an additional header latch to break cyclical header file includes when using the LHeader pattern. See the "LHeader Caveats" section on why this is needed.

- Lines 3, 4, and 44 are the traditional header latch so that the header is only included once when compiling files.

- Line 6 is another LHeader pattern usage that allows the Arduino button driver to work with an Arduino framework-based BSP.

- Lines 9–32 define the Arduino-specific concrete data type for the button instance.

- Line 36 provides the LHeader mapping for the abstract HAL interface to the Arduino framework-specific data structure defined at lines 9–32.

CHAPTER 15 DRIVERS

- Line 42 provides the function prototype for the Arduino framework-specific implementation of the abstract method for Driver_Button_Hal _getRawPressedState().

- Line 39 provides the LHeader mapping for the abstract method for Driver_Button_Hal _getRawPressedState().

```
1 #ifdef Driver_Button_Hal_h_
2
3 #ifndef Driver_Button_Arduino_mappings_x_h_
4 #define Driver_Button_Arduino_mappings_x_h_
5
6 #include "Bsp/Api.h"
7
8 /// Type for a button handle
9 struct DriverButtonPinHalArduino_T
10 {
11     int      pin;          //!< Arduino Pin number
12     uint32_t mode;         //!< Pin Mode: Values: INPUT, INPUT_PULLUP, INPUT_PULLDOWN
13     bool     activeLow;    //!< Set to true when the pressed state is ACTIVE_LOW
14
15     /// Constructor
16     DriverButtonPinHalArduino_T( int      pinNum,
17                                  uint32_t pinMode,
18                                  bool     isActiveLow )
19         : pin( pinNum )
20         , mode( pinMode )
21         , activeLow( isActiveLow )
22     {
23     }
24
25     /// Constructor
26     DriverButtonPinHalArduino_T( const DriverButtonPinHalArduino_T& other )
27         : pin( other.pin )
28         , mode( other.mode )
29         , activeLow( other.activeLow )
30     {
31     }
32 };
33
34
35 /// Arduino Mapping
36 #define Driver_Button_Pin_Hal_T_MAP                    DriverButtonPinHalArduino_T
37
38 /// Arduino Mapping
39 #define Driver_Button_Hal_getRawPressedState_MAP       driverButtonHalArduino_getRawPressState
40
41 /// Arduino specific implementation for getting the raw button state
42 bool driverButtonHalArduino_getRawPressState( DriverButtonPinHalArduino_T pinHandle );
43
44 #endif  // end header latch
45 #endif  // end Interface latch
```

Figure 15-15. Arduino framework LHeader mappings for the button driver

CHAPTER 15 DRIVERS

The `src/Driver/Button/Arduino/Hal.cpp` file implements the HAL interface for the Arduino framework. Note the following lines in Figure 15-16.

- Line 1 includes the abstract HAL interface definition.
- Line 2 includes the Arduino framework button driver interface definition.
- Lines 5–8 comprise the implementation of the Arduino framework for the method declared in the header file from line 2.
- Lines 10–15 comprise the implementation of the abstract HAL interface.

```
1 #include "Driver/Button/Hal.h"
2 #include "Hal.h"
3 #include <stdint.h>
4
5 void driverButtonHalArduino_initialize( DriverButtonPinHalArduino_T buttonHdl )
6 {
7     pinMode( buttonHdl.pin, buttonHdl.mode );
8 }
9
10 bool driverButtonHalArduino_getRawPressState( DriverButtonPinHalArduino_T pinHandle )
11 {
12     uint32_t phy = digitalRead( pinHandle.pin );
13     bool     log = phy == HIGH ? true : false;
14     return pinHandle.activeLow ? !log : log;
15 }
```

Figure 15-16. Arduino framework HAL button driver implementation

Simulator Implementation of the Button Driver

The GM6000 functional simulator uses an external C# executable to emulate the LCD display and its associated buttons. The simulator uses a TPipe driver to communicate with the external executable. TPipe is a platform-independent driver in the CPL class library for point-to-point, full-duplex, text-based stream, which is used to pass commands between two end points (see `src/Driver/TPipe`). As the TPipe driver only supplies

251

CHAPTER 15 DRIVERS

the communication tunnel, a TPipe-aware button driver is also needed. The implementation of this button driver consists of the files shown in Figures 15-17 through 15-19.

The src/Driver/Button/TPipe/Hal.h is a TPipe-specific header file that provides hardware-specific initialization for the button driver. Note the following lines in Figure 15-17.

- Line 4 includes the HAL interface. This header file defines the Driver_Button_Hal_T structure (using the LHeader pattern).

- Line 13 is the TPipe-specific driver initialize method. The expectation is that on startup, this method is called to complete initializing the button driver.

```
 1 #ifndef Driver_Button_TPipe_Hal_h_
 2 #define Driver_Button_TPipe_Hal_h_
 3
 4 #include "Driver/Button/Hal.h"
 5 #include "Cpl/Container/Map.h"
 6 #include "Driver/TPipe/RxFrameHandlerApi.h"
 7
 8 ...
 9
10 /** This method is used to register the button driver with the TPipe to
11     receive button events.  This method is called once - NOT per button/button-handle.
12 */
13 void driverButtonHalTPipe_initialize( Cpl::Container::Map<Driver::TPipe::RxFrameHandlerApi>&
14                                       tpipeRxFrameHandlerList );
15
16 #endif
```

Figure 15-17. TPipe-specific interface for a button driver

The src/Driver/Button/TPipe/mappings_.h is used to resolve the LHeader deferred methods and types on the simulator platform. Note the following lines in Figure 15-18.

- Lines 1, 2, and 13 are the traditional header latch so that the header is only included once when compiling files.

- Line 5 provides the LHeader mapping for the abstract HAL interface to the TPipe-specific data type.

CHAPTER 15 DRIVERS

- Line 11 provides the function prototype for the TPipe-specific implementation of the abstract HAL interface's `Driver_Button_Hal_getRawPressedState()` method.

- Line 8 provides the LHeader mapping for the abstract method `Driver_Button_Hal_getRawPressedState()`.

```
1 #ifndef Driver_Button_TPipe_mappings_x_h_
2 #define Driver_Button_TPipe_mappings_x_h_
3
4 /// TPipe Mapping
5 #define Driver_Button_Pin_Hal_T_MAP                 const char*
6
7 /// TPipe Mapping
8 #define Driver_Button_Hal_getRawPressedState_MAP    driverButtonHalTPipe_getRawPressState
9
10 /// TPipe specific implementation for getting the raw button state
11 bool driverButtonHalTPipe_getRawPressState( const char* buttonName );
12
13 #endif  // end header latch
```

Figure 15-18. *TPipe LHeader mappings for the button driver*

The `src/Driver/Button/TPipe/Hal.cpp` file implements the HAL interface for the simulator platform. Note the following lines in Figure 15-19.

- Line 1 includes the abstract HAL interface definition.

- Line 2 includes the TPipe button driver interface definition.

- Lines 10–32 implement the required TPipe child class for the `Driver::TPipe::RxFrameHandlerApi` interface.

- Line 35 is used to store a pointer to the single instance of class defined in lines 10–32.

- Lines 37–41 are the implementation of the TPipe method defined in the header file from line 2.

- Lines 43–51 comprise the implementation of the abstract HAL interface.

253

CHAPTER 15   DRIVERS

```
1 #include "Driver/Button/Hal.h"
2 #include "Hal.h"
3 #include "Driver/TPipe/RxFrameHandler.h"
4 #include "Cpl/Text/Tokenizer/Basic.h"
5 #include "Cpl/Text/FString.h"
6 #include "Cpl/System/Mutex.h"
7 #include "Cpl/System/Assert.h"
8 #include <memory.h>
9
10 class ButtonFrameHandler : public Driver::TPipe::RxFrameHandler
11 {
12 public:
13     ...
14
15     /// Constructor
16     ButtonFrameHandler( Cpl::Container::Map<Driver::TPipe::RxFrameHandlerApi>& tpipeRxFrameHandlerList )
17         : RxFrameHandler( tpipeRxFrameHandlerList, OPTION_DRIVER_BUTTON_HAL_TPIPE_COMMAND_VERB )
18     {
19     }
20
21     /// See Driver::TPipe::RxFrameHandlerApi
22     void execute( char* decodedFrameText ) noexcept
23     {
24         ...
25     }
26
27     ///
28     bool getButtonState( const char* buttonName )
29     {
30         ...
31     }
32 };
33
34
35 static ButtonFrameHandler* rxFrameHandler_;
36
37 void driverButtonHalTPipe_initialize( Cpl::Container::Map<Driver::TPipe::RxFrameHandlerApi>& tpipeRxFrameHandlerList )
38 {
39     CPL_SYSTEM_ASSERT( rxFrameHandler_ == nullptr ); // Only call this function once
40     rxFrameHandler_ = new(std::nothrow) ButtonFrameHandler( tpipeRxFrameHandlerList );
41 }
42
43 bool driverButtonHalTPipe_getRawPressState( const char* buttonName )
44 {
45     if ( rxFrameHandler_ )
46     {
47         return rxFrameHandler_->getButtonState( buttonName );
48     }
49
50     return false;
51 }
```

Figure 15-19.   TPipe HAL button driver implementation

LHeader Caveats

At this point, I should note that the LHeader pattern has an implementation weakness. It breaks down in situations where interface A defers a type definition using the LHeader pattern, and interface B also defers a type definition using the LHeader pattern, and interface B has a dependency on interface A. This use case results in a "cyclic header include scenario," and the compile will fail. This problem can be solved by adding an additional header latch using the header latch symbol defined in the HAL header file to the platform-specific mappings header file. Figure 15-12 shows an example of the additional header latch from STM32 mapping header file for the Button driver, and Appendix D, "LHeader and LConfig Patterns," provides additional details.

Unit Testing

All drivers should have unit tests. These unit tests are typically manual unit tests because they are built and executed on a hardware target.[2] One advantage of using the separation of concerns paradigm for a driver is that you can write automated unit tests that run as part of CI builds. For example, with the Button driver, there are two separate unit tests:

- One test is designed as a manual test and runs on target hardware (see `src/driver/Button/_0test/_hw/test.cpp`). In addition, the same manual unit test can run on multiple hardware targets. That is, each hardware target used for testing has its own unit test project that shares common unit test code.

- The second test is designed as an automated unit and runs as a command-line executable under Windows and Linux (see `src/driver/Button/_0test/polleddebounced.cpp`). The automated unit test mocks the hardware by having a Boolean array hold the button state.

---

[2] In my experience, test automation involving target hardware is an exception because of the effort and expenses involved.

CHAPTER 15 DRIVERS

Polymorphism

A polymorphic design is similar to a facade design, except that it uses run-time bindings for selecting the concrete hardware-specific implementation. A polymorphic design is best suited when using C++.[3] The I2C driver is an example of a polymorphic Hardware Abstraction Layer. It encapsulates an I2C data transfer from an I2C master to an I2C slave device.

Figure 15-20 is a class diagram of I2C driver abstract interface and concrete child classes.

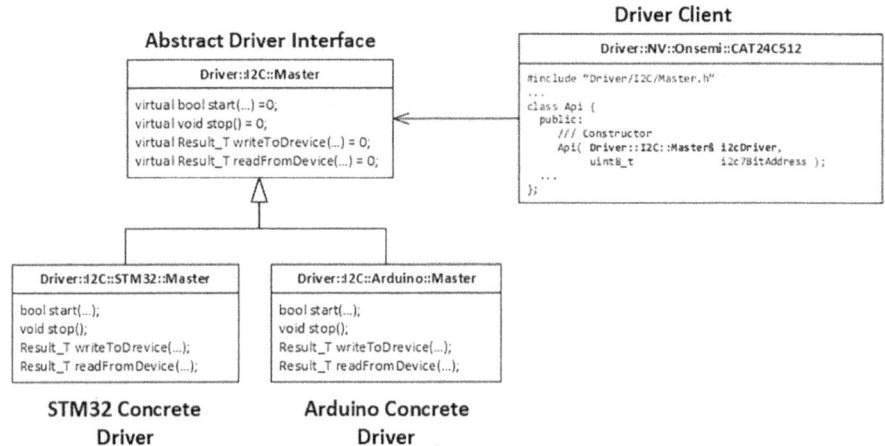

Figure 15-20. I2C driver class diagram

---

[3] It is possible to implement run-time polymorphism in C. For example, the original CFront C++ compiler translated the C++ source code into C code and then passed it to the C compiler. I recommend that you use C++ instead of hand-crafting the equivalent of the vtables in C.

256

There is no simulated implementation of the I2C driver in the CPL class library. The reason is because the I2C driver and the SPI driver are intermediary drivers. That is, the other drivers (like the EEPROM driver) are the immediate clients of the I2C/SPI drivers. The client drivers are what need to be simulated.

Example I2C Driver

The public interface for the I2C driver is the abstract C++ class `Driver::I2C::Master` in file `src/Driver/I2C/Master.h`. Figure 15-21 shows the abstract class definition.

CHAPTER 15 DRIVERS

```cpp
#ifndef Driver_I2C_Master_h_
#define Driver_I2C_Master_h_

#include <stdint.h>
#include <stdlib.h>

namespace Driver { namespace I2C {

/** This class defines a non-platform specific interface for an I2C master device
    driver.  The intended usage is to create ONE driver per physical I2C bus, i.e.
    the driver instance can be shared with multiple clients.

    The driver is NOT thread safe.  It is the responsibility of the Application
    to ensure thread safety when driver is used and/or shared with multiple
    clients.
 */
class Master
{
public:
    /// Result codes
    enum Result_T {
        eSUCCESS = 0,    //!< Operation was successful
        ...
        eERROR           //!< Generic/non-classified error
    };

public:
    /** This method is used initialize/start the driver.  To 'restart' the driver,
        the application must call stop(), then start().

        The method returns true if successful; else false is returned when an
        error occurred.  If false is returned, future read/write calls will always
        return a failure.
     */
    virtual bool start() noexcept = 0;

    /// This method is used to stop/shutdown the driver.
    virtual void stop() noexcept = 0;

public:
    /** This method writes 'numBytesToTransmit' from 'srcData' to the I2C
        peripheral device.

        If 'noStop' is true, the driver retains control of the bus at the end
        of the transfer (no Stop is issued), and the next I2C transaction will
        begin with a Restart rather than a Start.
     */
    virtual Result_T  writeToDevice( uint8_t        device7BitAddress,
                                     size_t         numBytesToTransmit,
                                     const void*    srcData,
                                     bool           noStop = false ) noexcept = 0;

    /** This method reads 'numBytesToRead' bytes from the I2C peripheral device
        into 'dstData'. The application is RESPONSIBLE for ensure that 'dstData'
        is AT LEAST 'numBytesToRead' in size.
        ...
     */
    virtual Result_T readFromDevice( uint8_t        device7BitAddress,
                                     size_t         numBytesToRead,
                                     void*          dstData,
                                     bool           noStop = false ) = 0;
public:
    /// Virtual destructor
    virtual ~Master() {}
};

}}      // end namespaces
#endif  // end header latch
```

Figure 15-21. Partial file listing of src/Driver/I2C/Master.h

CHAPTER 15 DRIVERS

Each supported hardware platform requires its own concrete child class of the `Driver::I2C::Master` class shown in Figure 15-21. In addition to providing the implementation for the pure virtual methods, the child class contains platform-specific methods, data types, etc. This means that instances of the driver are created in platform-specific code on startup (see Chapter 7, "Building Applications with the Main Pattern").

In the following two sections, you will see the implementation of the I2C driver functionality for each of these platforms:

- STM32—See Figure 15-22.
- Arduino—See Figure 15-23.

STM32 Implementation of the I2C Driver

The implementation relies on the ST HAL library and initialization code generated by the ST Cube MX IDE. The implementation is found in the files `src/Driver/I2C/STM32/Master.h` and `src/Driver/I2C/STM32/Master.cpp`. Figure 15-22 shows a snippet from the `Master.h` file. Note the following:

- Line 4 includes the abstract I2C class to be implemented.
- Line 5 is another LHeader pattern usage that allows the STM32 I2C driver to work with any STM32-based BSP.

259

CHAPTER 15 DRIVERS

```cpp
#ifndef Driver_I2C_STM32_Master_h_
#define Driver_I2C_STM32_Master_h_

#include "Driver/I2C/Master.h"
#include "Bsp/Api.h"    // Pull's in the ST HAL APIs

namespace Driver { namespace I2C { namespace STM32 {

/** This class implements the I2C interface for the STM32 family of
    micro-controller using the ST's MX Cube/IDE to configure the SPI peripherals
    and IO pins
    ...
 */
class Master : public Driver::I2C::Master
{
public:
    /** Constructor. The 'i2cInstance' MUST have already been initialize, i.e.
        the low level MX_I2Cx_Init() from the ST HAL APIs has been called
        ...
     */
    Master( I2C_HandleTypeDef* i2cInstance,
            uint32_t           timeoutMs = 50 );     // Default timeout is 50ms
public:
    /// See Driver::I2C::Master
    bool start() noexcept;

    /// See Driver::I2C::Master
    void stop() noexcept;

    /// See Driver::I2C::Master
    Result_T writeToDevice( uint8_t      device7BitAddress,
                            size_t       numBytesToTransmit,
                            const void*  srcData,
                            bool         noStop = false ) noexcept;

    /// See Driver::I2C::Master
    Result_T readFromDevice( uint8_t  device7BitAddress,
                             size_t   numBytesToRead,
                             void*    dstData,
                             bool     noStop = false );
    ...
protected:
    /// Handle the low-level ST HAL driver instance
    I2C_HandleTypeDef*  m_i2cDevice;

    /// Timeout period for a SPI transaction
    uintptr_t           m_timeout;

    /// Track my started state
    bool                m_started;
};

}}}    // end namespaces
#endif // end header latch
```

Figure 15-22. Partial file listing of src/Driver/I2C/STM32/Master.h

CHAPTER 15 DRIVERS

Arduino Framework Implementation of the I2C Driver

The implementation is built on top of the Arduino framework. The implementation is located in src/Driver/I2C/Arduino/Master.h and src/Driver/I2C/Arduino/Master.cpp. Figure 15-23 shows a snippet from the Master.h file. Note the following:

- Line 4 includes the abstract I2C class to be implemented.

- Line 5 is another LHeader pattern usage that allows the Arduino framework I2C driver to work with any Arduino-based BSP.

- Line 6 includes the Arduino I2C driver.

CHAPTER 15　DRIVERS

```
1  #ifndef Driver_I2C_Arduino_Master_h_
2  #define Driver_I2C_Arduino_Master_h_
3
4  #include "Driver/I2C/Master.h"
5  #include "Bsp/Api.h"     // Pull's in (the core) Arduino APIs
6  #include <Wire.h>
7
8  namespace Driver { namespace I2C { namespace Arduino {
9
10 /** This class implements the I2C interface using the Arduino framework and/or
11     APIs.
12     ...
13  */
14 class Master : public Driver::I2C::Master
15 {
16 public:
17     /// Constructor.
18     Master( TwoWire& i2cInstance = Wire,
19             uint32_t timeoutMs   = 50 );    // Default timeout is 50ms
20 public:
21     /// See Driver::I2C::Master
22     bool start() noexcept;
23
24     /// See Driver::I2C::Master
25     void stop() noexcept;
26
27     /// See Driver::I2C::Master
28     Result_T writeToDevice( uint8_t      device7BitAddress,
29                             size_t       numBytesToTransmit,
30                             const void*  srcData,
31                             bool         noStop = false ) noexcept;
32
33     /// See Driver::I2C::Master
34     Result_T readFromDevice( uint8_t     device7BitAddress,
35                              size_t      numBytesToRead,
36                              void*       dstData,
37                              bool        noStop = false );
38     ...
39 protected:
40     /// Handle an Ardunio driver instance
41     TwoWire&  m_i2cDevice;
42
43     /// Current Baud rate
44     uint32_t m_baudRate;
45
46     /// Current timeout
47     uint32_t m_timeout_ms;
48
49     /// Track my started state
50     bool      m_started;
51 };
52
53 }}}      // end namespaces
54 #endif   // end header latch
```

Figure 15-23. Partial listing of src/Driver/I2C/Arduino/Master.h

Dos and Don'ts

There is no silver bullet when it comes to driver design. That said, I recommend the following best practices:

- When designing a new driver, base your design on your current hardware platform, BSP, and application needs. This minimizes the amount of glue logic that is needed for the current project. It also avoids having to "guesstimate" the nuances of future hardware platforms and requirements. Don't spend a lot of effort in coming up with an all-encompassing interface or HAL definition. Don't overdesign your driver, and don't include functionality that is not needed by the application. For example, if your application needs a UART driver that never needs to send or receive a break character,[4] do not include logic for supporting break characters in your UART driver.

- Always include a start() or initialize() function even if your initial implementation does not require it. In my experience, as a driver and the application mature, you typically end up needing some initialization logic. I also recommend always including a stop() or shutdown() function as well.

- If you have experience writing the driver on other platforms, leverage that knowledge into current driver design.

---

[4] A break character consists of all zeros and must persist for a minimum of 11 bit times before the next character is received. A break character can be used as an out-of-band signal, for example, to signal the beginning of a data packet.

- Don't optimize until you have to. A product with a simpler driver that has good-enough performance and ships on time is a very good thing. For example, in the GM6000 example, the space or room temperature changes slowly (e.g., seconds to minutes). A polled ADC driver, then, is sufficient; there is no need to build an interrupt-driven ADC driver with KHz sampling.

- Separate creation from usage when it comes to driver interfaces. That is, have one header file (or interface) for creating the driver and a second header file that contains the runtime functionality of the driver. Creating a driver instance is almost always platform specific, which means the code that creates the driver cannot be reused on other platforms. Nevertheless, in embedded applications, drivers are only created once on startup, so reuse is not as important. However, there is a lot of value in being able to reuse the run-time behavior of a driver (e.g., sending/receiving data over an I2C bus). The return on investment for decoupling the run-time behavior of a driver from the underlying hardware platform is high; decoupling the creation of driver is typically low. Separate interfaces make it possible to skip the effort of implementing decoupled driver creation.

- Do not create a single, unified, all-encompassing HAL interface. HAL interfaces should be created on a per-driver basis. A fat HAL interface definition imposes an all or nothing restriction when attempting to reuse the drivers that rely on the fat HAL interface.

- It is better to have many different drivers that do similar tasks, instead of a single all-purpose, all-encompassing driver. For example, I created the `PolledDebounced` button driver for the example code because that is all the application required, and it was simple. However, when presented with more complex button requirements like a 3 x 4 button array, the `PolledDebounced` button driver should not be used. Instead, a new button driver should be created that performs row and column GPIO multiplexing for the button array. Also, by creating a separate driver, you don't have to worry about breaking the existing products that use the `PolledDebounced` driver.

Summary

A decoupled driver design allows reuse of drivers across multiple hardware platforms. A driver is decoupled from the hardware by creating a Hardware Abstraction Layer (HAL) for its run-time usage. The following late binding strategies can be used for the construction of the HAL interfaces:

- Facade—Using link-time bindings
- Separation of concerns—Using compile-time bindings
- Polymorphic—Using run-time bindings

Additional benefits of decouple driver design are as follows:

- The HAL interface facilitates simulating or mocking drivers when building a functional simulator.
- It allows the construction of automated unit tests that can be run as part of the CI build without having hardware automation.

CHAPTER 15   DRIVERS

INPUTS

- All documented requirements including ongoing updates
- Software Development Plan (SDP) including ongoing updates
- System architecture (SA) document including ongoing updates
- Software architecture (SWA) document including ongoing updates
- Software Detailed Design (SDD) document including ongoing updates

OUTPUTS

- Working driver code
- Unit tests
- Design reviews
- Code reviews
- Potential updates to requirements that may be in MRS, PRS, or SRS documents
- Potential updates to the system architecture (SWA) document
- Potential updates to the software architecture (SA) document
- Updates to the Software Detailed Design document
- Updates to design statements when used

CHAPTER 16

Release

For most of the construction stage, you are focused on writing and testing and optimizing your software. And as the product gets better and better and the bugs get fewer and fewer, you start to have the sense that you're almost done. However, even when you finally reach the point when you can say "the software is done," there are still some last-mile tasks that need to be completed in order to get the software to your customers. These mostly not-coding-related tasks comprise the release activities of the project.

The release stage of the project overlaps the end-of-construction stage. That is, about the time you start thinking about creating a release candidate, you should be starting your release activities. Ideally, if you've followed the steps in this cookbook, your release activities will simply involve collecting, reviewing, and finalizing reports and documentation that you already have. If not, you'll get to experience the angst and drama of a poorly planned release: fighting feature creep, trying to locate licenses, fighting through installation and update issues, etc. If you find yourself in the position of struggling with the logistics of releasing your software, it means you probably "cheated" during the planning and construction stages and built up technical debt that now has to be retired before shipping the software. My recommendation is if you are working with an Agile methodology, you practice "releasing" the software at the end of each sprint. That is, when you estimate you have about three sprints left to finish the project, go through all the release activities as if you were going to release the product.

CHAPTER 16   RELEASE

The work items for the release stage are as follows:

- Tightening up change management—Your change management process needs to prevent unnecessary changes from being made as you work toward the gold release. The goal is to get to a "code freeze," where there are no more changes because every change requires more testing and has the potential to introduce new bugs.

- Generating a Software Bill of Materials—The Software Bill of Materials (SBOM) is a list of all third-party packages, including licensing and version information, that are contained with the released software. The SBOM is used to verify that software licensing of all the packages is "good to go." The SBOM is also used to track Common Vulnerabilities and Exposures[1] (CVEs) for the packages after the release.

- Creating an anomalies list—The anomalies list is an exhaustive list of known bugs and issues for a release. Generally, this is a development document, and it is the tool that the team and product stakeholders use to make the ship-don't-ship decision.

- Generating release notes—These may take the form of internal release notes or customer release notes. Release notes may use the anomalies list as input but usually add additional details—especially about workarounds that may be available. Internal release notes are created on a regular basis. For example, every

---

[1] The US National Institute of Standards and Technology (NIST) department maintains a database of known CVEs. See https://nvd.nist.gov/vuln

formal CI build that is handed off to QA for testing benefits from internal release notes. Customer release notes, however, only need to be generated when a release is deployed as an early-access release (e.g., Alpha or Beta release) or as a general availability (GA) release to the end customer. Customer release notes are oftentimes derived from internal release notes, but they are usually edited for simplicity as well as to "properly position sensitive limitations of the software." In other words, you generally want to edit your dirty laundry out of the customer release notes.

- Deploying the application—The deployment step includes making the software images available to manufacturing who will use them when physically assembling the product. Additionally, these images may be placed on servers that are responsible for providing over-the-air (OTA) updates to previously sold products.

- Completing QMS deliverables—Depending on your QMS process, there can be many non-software artifacts that must be completed with each gold release (e.g., requirements tracing documentation, design documentation, design and code review artifacts, etc.)

- Archiving the build tools—This involves archiving all the components that were used to build the release software and archiving them so that, if necessary, an identical version of the release can be built at a later time.

CHAPTER 16 RELEASE

While the work involved in the release stage of a project is not particularly complex or difficult, it can still take a substantial amount of time to perform it. Make sure you have allocated resources and time for all the release activities in your project schedule—especially the tasks that occur after the product has technically shipped.

About Builds and Releases

Not every build gets released, but every release is a build—it just gets gussied up a bit. That being said, it is helpful to establish a common understanding with stakeholders about what constitutes different builds and releases.

Generally, there are three types of builds:

- Private build—A build that is performed on a developer's build machine. The build scripts for a developer build are responsible for setting the build number to zero to identify that it is not a formal build. In addition, the provenance of actual source code used for a private build is assumed to be unknown in that it may or may not have been locally edited prior to the actual build. Consequently, private builds should never be used for any formal testing or design verification. There can be hundreds of private builds floating around in different development environments and on different team member's machines.

- CI build—A build performed on the build server for each pull request. Because there can be many CI builds per single pull request (e.g., a build needs to be fixed or a test error needs to be corrected or a change is required because of code review feedback),

CI builds should not be consumed outside of the CI environment. That is, if someone needs to use a CI build, even for a quick and dirty test, the CI build should be turned into a formal build. The build script or build process for a CI build is also responsible for setting the build number to zero to identify that it is not a formal build.

- Formal build—A build performed on the build server of a stable branch that has a canonical build number. Furthermore, an SCM tag or label should be created to identify all of the source code used for the build. Formal builds are deployable in the sense that they have known (and documented) provenance, which is critical for logging bugs against the build. Without this formality, any bugs identified could be false positives in that the bugs could be a result of changes that were rejected during the pull request and code review process. Whether or not a formal build can be a release candidate is dependent on your branching strategy for stable branches.

When discussing releases, all release builds must be formal builds and have a human-friendly version identifier. Generally, there are four different types of releases:

- Working release—A formal build that is deployed to the test team during the construction stage for test case development and early verification. Working releases can also be deployed externally for activities such EMC (Electromagnetic Compatibility) and regulatory testing. Which SCM branch a working release is built from is dependent on your branching strategy. For the GM6000 example, working releases are built from the `develop` branch.

- Early-access release (Alpha, Beta Release)—A formal build that is deployed to a select, and restricted, number of customers or field sites. These builds are typically not feature complete and have undergone less change control rigor than a candidate release. What SCM branch early-access releases are built from is dependent on your branching strategy. For the GM6000 example, early-access releases are built from the `main` branch.

- Candidate release—A formal build that is feature complete. Additionally, there is an expectation that the release can successfully pass all formal testing and verification. Which SCM branch candidate releases are built from is dependent on your branching strategy. For the GM6000 example, candidate releases are built from the `main` branch.

- Gold Release—A gold release is the candidate release that has been declared ready to ship by the stakeholders.

A human-readable version number (e.g., 1.4.0) is not used as the canonical identifier for releases. This is because at build time, it is unknown whether or not the release can be deployed to a customer either as an early-access release or a gold release. This is why the build number is used as the canonical version identifier. The human-readable version number should only be changed after early-access or GA releases are deployed.

Tightening Up the Change Control Process

During the construction stage, the software team is largely left alone to determine when and what work, features, and changes are made to the code base. However, as the project enters the release stage of the project, unbounded changes become counterproductive since every change has the potential to introduce new bugs and trigger additional regression testing. To limit the number of changes and to focus the work on "only what is needed" for release, you need to define a formal, well-advertised process for how all forthcoming code changes will be approved. Typically, this takes the form of establishing a Change Control Board (CCB) that is made up of a limited number of stakeholders. CCB meets regularly to review the state of the software along with the anomalies list (i.e., the known bug list) in order to approve code changes.

The CCB is also responsible for reviewing and approving the scope of any regression testing activities that are needed as a result of source code changes. Or said another way, when approving changes, the CCB needs to consider what the impact every change will have on the testing and verification efforts.

In my experience, how strict the CCB is with respect to approving changes varies over time. When the CCB is first put in place, the board typically accepts all of the recommendations from the software lead and the project manager on what should be changed. As the project approaches its first candidate release, the CCB becomes more conservative with respect to approving recommendations. Eventually, the CCB evolves into a single stakeholder who approves the changes and who ultimately will designate a candidate release as a gold release.

Obviously, it is best to define the CCB process before your project gets to the release stage because de facto CCB processes form organically. There are always competing must-have priorities, bug fixes, feature creep, etc., across all the stakeholders, which results in there always being one more software change request. The CCB process (formal or informal) provides the discipline to stop changes so the software can finally ship.

There is an assumption that when the project enters the release stage, any work for the next release or next product variant is isolated from the code that is getting ready to ship. Typically, this is done by having separate branches in the SCM repository for the upcoming release and the follow-on release. After the current release is completed, the source code from the gold release is reconciled with the follow-on release.

Software Bill of Materials (SBOM)

When I first started as an embedded developer many decades ago, it was rare to have any third-party software items included in a product's code base. The exception was usually a minimal amount of software provided by the microcontroller vendor. In today's environment, it is rare to not include third-party packages. In fact, I was surprised to see, for example, that for the GM6000 project there were nine third-party packages used in the GM6000 code base.

The Software Bill of Materials (SBOM), then, is used to identify all third-party software included in the released product. For each item in the SBOM, the item's software licensing and version information is captured. The software licensing information is needed to ensure that all conditions for the item's license have been met (e.g., complying with GPL requirements or having purchased the required licenses). The version information from the SBOM is used when monitoring the item for bugs and CVEs. Additionally, there can be other potential concerns with respect to third-party software such as export restrictions on encryption technology.

CHAPTER 16   RELEASE

It should be obvious that the SBOM should be created as you go. That is, the process should start when external packages are first incorporated into the code base, not as a "paperwork" item during the release stage. For non-open-source licensing, purchasing software licenses takes time and money, and you need to make sure that money for those purchases is budgeted. Your company's legal department needs to weigh in on what is or is not acceptable with respect to proprietary and open source licenses. Or, said another way, make sure you know, and preferably have some documentation on, your company's software licensing policies. Don't assume something is okay because it is widely used in or around your company because nothing is as frustrating as the last-minute scramble to redesign (and retest) your application because one of your packages has unacceptable licensing terms.

The SBOM is not difficult to create since it is essentially just a table that identifies which third-party packages are used along with their pertinent information. My recommendations for creating and maintaining the SBOM are as follows:

- Initially create the SBOM as a living document (e.g., as a Wiki page) and update it as third-party packages are added to the code base.

- As entries are added to the SBOM, have the new items reviewed by the appropriate stakeholders (e.g., legal team, your manager, the project manager, etc.) to ensure that the licensing terms are acceptable, and that money is budgeted for purchasing the license.

- Depending on your QMS process, you may need to convert the working SBOM into a formal document prior to completing the release stage. See Appendix Q, "GM6000 Software Bill of Materials," for an example of a formal SBOM document.

CHAPTER 16   RELEASE

Anomalies List

By definition, your bug tracking tool is the canonical source for all known defects. The anomalies list is simply a snapshot in time of the known defects and issues for a given release. In theory, the anomalies list for any given release could be extracted from the bug tracking tool, but having an explicit document that enumerates all of the known defects for a given release simplifies communications within the cross-functional team and with the leadership team. When an anomalies list needs to be generated should be defined by your QMS process; however, as it is a key tool in determining if a release is ready for early access or GA, you may find yourself generating the list more frequently at the end of the project.

Release Notes

Internal release notes should be generated every time a formal build is deployed to anyone outside of the immediate software team. This means you need release notes for formal builds that go to testers, hardware engineers, QA, etc. Simply put, the internal release summarizes what is and what is not the release. It is important to remember that when writing the internal release notes, the target audience is everyone on the team—not just the software developers. The software lead or the "build master" is typically responsible for generating the internal release notes.

There should be a line or bullet item for every change (from the previous release) that is included in the current release. There should be an item for every pull request that was merged into the release branch. Internal release notes can be as simple as enumerating all of the work item tickets and bug fixes—preferably with titles and hyperlinks—that went into the release. Remember, if you are following the cookbook, there will be a work item or bug tickets created for each pull request. One advantage of referencing work or bug tickets is that individual tickets will contain additional information, context, comments, steps to reproduce, etc., which means all that detail can stay there and not be included in the release notes.

In addition to the changes and bug fixes, the release notes should include a section about "known issues" that includes items such as

- Missing or incomplete functionality
- Performance issues
- Workarounds for existing bugs

A comprehensive and verbose list of known issues makes for better team communication, and it heads off any premature bug reporting about missing functionality.

Customer-facing release notes are only required when a release (alpha, beta, or gold) is deployed to an end customer. These release notes are usually derived from the internal release notes, but they are simplified and sanitized. However, depending on your relationship with your customers or partners, the customer release notes for alpha and beta releases may just be the internal release notes.

Deployment

In most cases, the embedded software you create is sold with your company's custom hardware. This means that deploying your software requires making the images available to your company's manufacturing process. Companies that manufacture physical products typically track customer-facing releases in a Product Lifecycle Management (PLM) tool such as Windchill or SAP that is used to manage all of the drawings and bill of materials for the hardware. With respect to embedded software, the software images and their respective source files are bill-of-material line items or sub-assemblies tracked by the PLM tool. Usually, the PLM tool contains an electronic copy of the release files. As PLM tools have

CHAPTER 16 RELEASE

a very strict process for adding or updating material items, the process discourages frequent updates, so you don't want to put every working release or candidate release into the PLM system—just the alpha, beta, and gold releases.

These processes are company and PLM tool specific. For example, at one company I worked for, the PLM tool was Windchill, but since the software images were zipped snapshots of the source code (i.e., very large binary files), the electronic copies of the files were formally stored in a different system and only a cover sheet referencing the storage location was placed in Windchill.

Typically, the following information is required for each release into the PLM system:

- A brief summary or description of the release
- An electronic copy of the software images with a checksum (MD5 or SHA512) for each item
- Version identifiers for all software images
- The SCM tag or label associated with the release build
- A snapshot of all the source code files that make up the release (with an MD5 checksum for the compressed file)
- (Optional) Build instructions for release
- (Optional) Programming instructions for the manufacturing process

Over-the-Air (OTA) Updates

In addition to deployment of images to manufacturing, you may be able to update hardware in the field through a variety of methods. The methods used by field engineers will be similar to those used by engineering and

CHAPTER 16 RELEASE

QA to test the product. However, if customers will initiate and deploy the update, you will need to have developed, tested, and documented a straightforward process for accomplishing this. Typically, anything requiring more than connecting a standard USB cable to a computer to perform the update is a bad idea for customer deployment.

With the right network connectivity (Wi-Fi or cellular), you might also deploy updates using over-the-air (OTA) strategies. For this scenario, there is the additional step of deploying the software images to a server that is responsible for delivering the OTA updates to products in the field. This includes the code that instructs the hardware how to swap in, use, and then load the new image. Regardless of how your software updates itself with a new image, the process should have been included in the definition and design of the product.

The same care and due diligence that went into updating the PLM system for manufacturing with a new release should be applied when releasing images to the OTA server. The last thing you want is a self-made crisis of releasing the wrong or bad software to the field. Since almost all embedded software interacts with the physical world, a bad release can have negative real-world consequences for a period of time before a fixed release can be deployed (e.g., no heating for an entire building for days or weeks in the middle of winter). Or, worst case, the OTA release "bricks" the hardware, requiring field service personnel to resurrect the device.

CHAPTER 16   RELEASE

QMS Deliverables

While the Quality Management System (QMS) deliverables do not technically gate the building and testing of a release, the required processes can delay shipping the software to customers. What is involved in the QMS deliverables is obviously specific to your company's defined QMS processes. On one end of the spectrum, there are startup companies that have no QMS processes, and all that matters is shipping the software. On the other end, there are the regulated industries, such as medical devices, that will have quite verbose QMS processes. If you have no, or minimal, QMS processes defined, I recommend the following process be followed and the following artifacts be generated for each gold release.

1. Finalize and publish final drafts of the following documents:

    - Software Development Plan (SDP)
    - Formal requirements (MRS, PRS, SRS, etc.)
    - System architecture
    - Software architecture
    - Software Detailed Design
    - Software coding standards
    - Developer environment setup
    - Build server setup
    - CI setup

    In theory, if you have been following the cookbook, this should be limited to closing out a few remaining TBDs or action items and should not require a large amount of effort. It should not involve "big-bang" document reviews.

CHAPTER 16   RELEASE

2. Archive existing quality artifacts. Do not go back and attempt to create missing artifacts. Just archive what artifacts you do have. You can note missing artifacts as lessons learned for the next project. Additional quality artifacts you might archive are as follows:

    - Design review artifacts

    - Code review artifacts, where individual documents were created per the review. You can skip this step if you are using a collaborative tool for code reviews (such as GitHub's pull request process) because you can always retrieve or review the code review comments and actions at a later date using the tool.

    - Doxygen output for the release code base (if using Doxygen)

    - Any software integration testing artifacts such as test plans, test cases, and test reports

    - Any formal software testing artifacts such as test plans, test cases, and test reports

3. Archive all items that are release deliverables as described in your Software Development Plan.

4. Create a master index of the locations of your quality documentation and artifacts. Also include links and references to any Wiki pages that were used to support the software development. Be sure to only store the master index, documents, and build artifacts in a single location on shared storage. There should never be confusion about where to find the "one true source" for the aforementioned content.

CHAPTER 16   RELEASE

Archiving Build Tools

The product lifetimes for embedded software applications are often a decade or more. A lot can happen over that time period that could trigger the need to rebuild or patch a previously deployed release, and there is no guarantee that the same compiler, CASE tool, third-party SDK, operating system, etc., that were used for the original release will still be available N years later.

For example, while working at an engineering service company several years ago, the company took on a project to update a customer's existing product for hardware end-of-life issues. Part of the work involved making changes to the existing software to support the new hardware components. Because of the age of the product, this required setting up a build environment using Visual Studio 2008, Service Pack 1. Fortunately, in this case, Visual Studio 2008 was still available from Microsoft, albeit through their MSDN subscription program.

If you've followed the steps in this cookbook, archiving the build tools simply means archiving your CI build server after each GA release.[2] Another advantage of archiving the build server is that the host operating system also gets archived. For example, I have worked on projects where the build tools only ran on Windows XP—and this was well after Microsoft had deprecated support for Windows XP.

---

[2] Archiving a build server can take many forms. For example, if the build server is a VM, then creating a backup or snapshot of VM is sufficient. If the build server is a Docker container, then backing up the Docker file or Docker image is sufficient. For a physical box, creating images of the box (using tools like Ghost, AOMEI, or True Image) could be an option. Just make sure that the tool you use has the ability to restore your image to a machine that has different hardware than the original box.

Summary

The start of the release stage overlaps the end of the construction phase and finishes when a gold release is approved. The release stage has several deliverables in addition to the release software images. Ideally, the bulk of the effort during the release stage is focused on collecting the necessary artifacts and quality documents, and not the logistics and actual work of creating and completing them.

Ensure that you have a functioning Change Control Board in place for the end-game sprints in order to prevent feature creep and never-ending loops of just-one-more-change and to reduce your regression testing efforts.

Finally, put all end-customer release images and source code into your company's PLM system to be included as part of the assembled end product.

INPUTS

- Final source code, that is, the code base, is closed to unauthorized changes
- Current defect list
- Project documentation and artifacts (e.g., requirements documents, Software Development Plan, Software Detailed Design, integration test reports, etc.)

OUTPUTS

- Release notes (both internal and customer facing)
- Software Bill of Material (SBOM)

CHAPTER 16   RELEASE

- Anomalies list (i.e., the list of known defects at the time of release)
- Archived source code. This includes tagging and labeling branches in your SCM repositories as well as storing them in the company's PLM system (when applicable)
- Archived images, executables, etc., that are required for manufacturing. Typically, these are released into the company's PLM system
- Final revisions of the project documentation. This includes items such as the following list. The company's QMS will define the definitive list of documentation and artifacts
    - Requirements and requirements tracing
    - Software Development Plan
    - Software architecture
    - Software Detailed Design
    - Software coding standards
    - Doxygen output
    - Code review artifacts
    - Design review artifacts
    - Integration test plans, test procedures, and test reports
    - Software test plans, test procedures, and test reports
    - Developer environment setup
    - Build server setup
    - CI setup

APPENDIX A

Getting Started with the Source Code

The source code for the GM6000 example project can be found on GitHub in the following repository: `https://github.com/johnttaylor/epc`. The example code executes on two hardware platforms: the ST NUCLEO-F413ZH and Adafruit Grand Central M4 Express evaluation boards. The GM6000 example also contains a functional simulator. The simulator can be built and executed for both Windows and Linux hosts. This appendix will take you through how to build for both the hardware targets and the functional simulator.

The code base is IDE agnostic in that no specific IDE is required to build or compile the code, and all builds are done via the command line. An IDE is only required for debugging. That said, the `epc` repository does contain a Visual Studio solution and project files, which are configured to take advantage of Visual Studio's IntelliSense and auto-completion. In addition, there is support for using VS Code's *clangd* auto-complete and formatting as well as GDB debugging.

The build engine for the example code is NQBP2. NQBP2 is Python based, and it leverages Google's Ninja build tool for fast, parallel builds. A detailed discussion of NQBP2 can be found in Appendix F, "NQBP2 Build System."

APPENDIX A   GETTING STARTED WITH THE SOURCE CODE

The latest instructions for setting up your development environment can be found on the `epc` repository's GitHub Wiki page: https://github.com/johnttaylor/epc/wiki/Development-Environment.

Repository Organization

A single GitHub repository stores all of the source code that is used to build the GM6000 example project. This means that all third-party code has been copied into the `epc` repository and was incorporated using the open source tool Outcast.[1] The following is the top-level directory structure of the repository.

```
<root>/epc         // Root of the epc repository
+-- arduino/       // External colony.aruduino repo (using Outcast)
+-- docs/          // Contains the Doxygen output
+-- pkg.info/      // Stores the Outcast 'mapping' information
+-- pkgs.overlaid/ // Additional Outcast information (for 'overlay' repos)
+-- projects/      // Application build directory tree
+-- scripts/       // Collection of utility scripts (e.g. common RATT scripts)
+-- src/           // The principal source code tree
+-- tests/         // Unit test build directory tree
+-- top/           // Contains scripts related to the build/CI environments
\-- xsrc/          // External code/repos (using Outcast)
```

---

[1] https://github.com/johnttaylor/Outcast

APPENDIX A   GETTING STARTED WITH THE SOURCE CODE

Windows

This section details the Windows specific instructions.

Prerequisites for Windows

The following is the minimal set of tools that need to be installed in order to compile the automated unit tests and the functional simulator under Windows as well as to cross-compile for the hardware targets.

- Python 3.8.5 or newer—Detailed installation instruction can be found on the Wiki page: https://github.com/johnttaylor/epc/wiki/Installing-Developer-Tools:-Common#installing-python. Make sure you add Python to the system's command path.

- At least one compiler—The code base supports using the Visual Studio compiler as well as the MinGW-w64 compiler (a.k.a. GCC for Windows). The Visual Studio compiler provides a better debugging experience, while the MinGW compiler is used to generate code coverage metrics.

- Microsoft Visual Studio—The community edition is free and works well. You need a version of Visual Studio that supports the C++11 language standard. If you only want to use and install one compiler, this is the one I recommend. Detailed installation instruction can be found on the Wiki page: https://github.com/johnttaylor/epc/wiki/Installing-Developer-Tools:-Common#installing-visual-studio.

APPENDIX A   GETTING STARTED WITH THE SOURCE CODE

- GCC for Windows—This is also known as the MinGW-w64 compiler. You will need to install a version of the compiler toolchain that supports generating both 32-bit and 64-bit applications because the `mingw_w64` build scripts default to 32-bit builds. Detailed installation instruction can be found on the Wiki page: `https://github.com/johnttaylor/epc/wiki/Developer---MinGW-Install`.

The GCC cross compiler for the ARM Cortex M/R is included as part of the epc repository (xsrc/stm32-gcc-arm) and does not need to be installed. This compiler is used for both the ST NUCLEO-F413ZH and Adafruit Grand Central M4 Express targets.

Getting the Source Code on Windows

Clone the epc repository (`https://github.com/johnttaylor/epc`) to your machine. The repository can be installed anywhere. However, the root path to the repository location cannot contain any spaces.

Here is an example of how you might clone the repository.

```
C:\>mkdir work
C:\>cd work
C:\work>git clone https://github.com/johnttaylor/epc
```

Compiler Configuration on Windows

At the root of the repository, there is a script, `env.bat`, that is used to configure the working environment for a Windows host. This script must be run once per terminal session to properly set environment variables

APPENDIX A GETTING STARTED WITH THE SOURCE CODE

and to specify which compiler to use. You should not have to edit the env.bat script (though you are welcome to customize it). The env.bat script calls helper scripts that configure the individual compilers. You will need to modify these helper scripts for each installed compiler.

These helper scripts are located in the top\compilers\ directory. There needs to be a Windows batch file for each installed compiler. The individual batch files are responsible for updating the environment for that compiler with such things as adding the compiler to the Windows command path, setting environment variables needed by the compiler or debug tools, etc.

In addition, each script provides a "friendly name" that is used to identify the compiler when running the env.bat file. The actual batch file script names are not important. That is, it does not matter what the file names are as long as you have a unique file name for each script.

Here is an example of the top\compilers\01-vcvars32-vc17.bat file. In line 2 of Figure A-1, you can see where the friendly name is set. And line 4 simply calls the batch file supplied by Visual Studio. You will need to edit lines 2 and 4 to match your local installation.

```
1    ::@echo off
2    IF "/%1"=="/name" ECHO:Visual Studio VC17 (32bit) compiler for Windows & exit /b 0
3
4    call "C:\Program Files\Microsoft Visual Studio\2022\Community\VC\Auxiliary\Build\vcvars32.bat"
```

Figure A-1. *The 01-vcvars32-vc17.bat file*

Figure A-2 provides an example of the top\compilers\03-mingw64-10.0.3-2.bat batch file. You will need to edit lines 2, 4, and 5 to match your local installation.

APPENDIX A   GETTING STARTED WITH THE SOURCE CODE

```
1    @echo off
2    IF "/%1"=="/name" ECHO:MINGW64 v10.3.0-2 compiler for Windows (32bit and 64 bit) & exit /b 0
3
4    call set PATH=C:\TDM-GCC-64\bin;%PATH%
5    echo:MinGW-x64 Compiler Environment set (v10.3.0-2 32bit and 64bit)
```

Figure A-2. The 03-mingw64-10.0.3-2.bat file

There is no naming convention for the file names for these scripts. However, I do recommend that you prefix the name with a numeric number, for example, "01". The reason is because by doing this, the compiler scripts are always listed in the same order when you add a new compiler.

In a team environment, it would be a bit cumbersome to have developers edit build files to specify the compiler locations on their individual machines. However, in my experience, this can be addressed by requiring that all the members of the team install their compilers and tools to the same location. If you take this approach, this is an excellent item to add to your Software Development Plan.

Building on Windows

Developers can build the applications and unit tests. All application builds are performed under the projects\ directory tree. All unit test builds are performed under the tests\ directory tree. While there is a limited amount of source code under the projects\ and tests\ directories, the bulk of the source code is under the src\ and xsrc\ directories.

APPENDIX A   GETTING STARTED WITH THE SOURCE CODE

Building the Functional Simulator

All builds are performed on the command line. Use the following steps to build the functional simulator for the GM6000 Ajax application.

1. Open a terminal window (i.e., run cmd.exe).
2. Navigate to the root directory of the cloned epc repository and run the env.bat file. The output of this command may look something like this:

   ```
   c:\>cd work\epc
   c:\work\epc>env.bat
   NO TOOLCHAIN SET

   1 - Visual Studio VC17 (32bit) compiler for Windows
   2 - Visual Studio VC17 (64bit) compiler for Windows
   3 - MINGW64 v10.3.0-2 compiler for Windows (32bit
       and 64 bit)
   4 - GCC-ARM compiler for Grand Central BSP 1.6.0
   5 - GCC-ARM (none-eabi) compiler for STM32
   c:\work\epc>
   ```

   Running the script without any arguments will display the list of available compilers. To select a compiler toolchain, run the script again with the number of the compiler toolchain you want to use. For example, the following selects the Visual Studio compiler (32-bit version):

   ```
   c:\work\epc>env.bat 1
   ********************************************************
   ** Visual Studio 2022 Developer Command Prompt v17.3.6
   ** Copyright (c) 2022 Microsoft Corporation
   ********************************************************
   ```

291

APPENDIX A   GETTING STARTED WITH THE SOURCE CODE

```
[vcvarsall.bat] Environment initialized for: 'x86'
c:\work\epc>
```

The env.bat shell script only needs to be run once per command window per compiler. To select a different compiler, simply re-run the env.bat script again and specify a different number. Depending on how the compiler environment is set up, you may not always be able to run the env.bat an unlimited number of times for a given compiler because the environment space gets used up. If this happens, simply close your terminal window and open a new command window.

3. Navigate to the build directory for the GM6000 Ajax simulator using the Visual Studio compiler and run the build script: nqbp.py. The output of the build will be located in the subdirectory _win32\.

```
c:\work\epc>cd projects\GM6000\Ajax\simulator\
windows\vc12
c:\work\epc\projects\GM6000\Ajax\simulator\windows\
vc12>nqbp.py
=========================================================
= START of build for: ajax-sim.exe
= Project Directory:   C:\work\epc\projects\GM6000\Ajax\
  simulator\windows\vc12
= Toolchain:      VC++ 12, 32bit (Visual Studio 2013)
= Build Configuration: win32
= Begin (UTC):    Sat, 02 Mar 2024 19:32:25
= Build Time:     1709407945 (65e37ec9)
=========================================================
[266/266] Linking: ajax-sim.exe
```

APPENDIX A   GETTING STARTED WITH THE SOURCE CODE

```
============================================================
= END of build for:  ajax-sim.exe
= Project Directory:  C:\work\epc\projects\GM6000\Ajax\
                      simulator\windows\vc12
= Toolchain:      VC++ 12, 32bit (Visual Studio 2013)
= Build Configuration: win32
= Elapsed Time (hh mm:ss): 00 00:16
============================================================
c:\work\epc\projects\GM6000\Ajax\simulator\windows\
vc12>dir _win32
03/02/2024 02:32 PM    <DIR>          .
03/02/2024 02:32 PM    <DIR>          ..
03/02/2024 02:32 PM            98,632 .ninja_deps
03/02/2024 02:32 PM            45,433 .ninja_log
03/02/2024 02:32 PM         2,990,080 ajax-sim.exe
03/02/2024 02:32 PM        10,202,952 ajax-sim.ilk
03/02/2024 02:32 PM        27,668,480 ajax-sim.pdb
03/02/2024 02:32 PM           195,812 build.ninja
03/02/2024 02:32 PM           469,107 main.obj
02/25/2024 01:12 PM    <DIR>          src
03/02/2024 02:32 PM         1,567,744 vc140.idb
03/02/2024 02:32 PM         2,740,224 vc140.pdb
02/25/2024 01:12 PM    <DIR>          xsrc
```

The same steps are used to build all applications and unit tests.

Building for the Hardware Targets on Windows

The same process is used to build hardware targets as is used to build the functional simulator and automated unit tests. The only difference is the compiler selected. Use the following steps to build the images for the STM32 hardware target.

APPENDIX A   GETTING STARTED WITH THE SOURCE CODE

1. Open a terminal window (i.e., run cmd.exe).

2. Navigate to the root directory of the cloned epc repository and run the env.bat file. The output of the command may look something like this:

   c:\>**cd work\epc**
   c:\work\epc>**env.bat**
   NO TOOLCHAIN SET

   1 - Visual Studio VC17 (32bit) compiler for Windows
   2 - Visual Studio VC17 (64bit) compiler for Windows
   3 - MINGW64 v10.3.0-2 compiler for Windows (32bit and 64 bit)
   4 - GCC-ARM compiler for Grand Central BSP 1.6.0
   5 - GCC-ARM (none-eabi) compiler for STM32
   c:\work\epc>**env.bat 5**
   GCC Arm-none-eabi Environment set to xsrc\stm32-gcc-arm\bin
   c:\work\epc>

3. Navigate to the build directory under the alpha1 target where the GCC cross compiler is located and run the build script: nqbp.py. The output of the build will be written to the subdirectory _stm32\.

   c:\work\epc>**cd projects\GM6000\Ajax\alpha1\windows\gcc-arm**
   c:\work\epc\projects\GM6000\Ajax\alpha1\windows\gcc-arm>**nqbp.py**
   ===
   = START of build for: ajax
   = Project Directory: C:\work\epc\projects\GM6000\Ajax\alpha1\windows\gcc-arm

APPENDIX A   GETTING STARTED WITH THE SOURCE CODE

```
= Toolchain:        GCC Arm-Cortex (none-eabi) Compiler
= Build Configuration: stm32
= Begin (UTC):      Sun, 17 Mar 2024 15:32:24
= Build Time:       1710689544 (65f70d08)
========================================================
[357/358] Generic Command:
  text    data    bss     dec     hex filename
 524596   2212   88312  615120   962d0 ajax.elf
[358/358] Objdmp: ajax.elf TO ajax.list
========================================================
======================
= END of build for:  ajax
= Project Directory: C:\work\epc\projects\GM6000\Ajax\
                     alpha1\windows\gcc-arm
= Toolchain:        GCC Arm-Cortex (none-eabi) Compiler
= Build Configuration: stm32
= Elapsed Time (hh mm:ss): 00 00:53
========================================================
c:\work\epc\projects\GM6000\Ajax\alpha1\windows\gcc-
arm>dir _stm32
03/17/2024 11:33 AM    <DIR>          .
03/17/2024 11:33 AM    <DIR>          ..
03/17/2024 11:33 AM           426,776 .ninja_deps
03/17/2024 11:33 AM           114,347 .ninja_log
03/17/2024 11:33 AM           526,820 ajax.bin
03/17/2024 11:33 AM         8,459,972 ajax.elf
03/17/2024 11:33 AM         1,481,867 ajax.hex
03/17/2024 11:33 AM         9,817,733 ajax.list
03/17/2024 11:33 AM         8,281,873 ajax.map
03/17/2024 11:32 AM           641,495 build.ninja
03/17/2024 11:33 AM         1,414,640 main.o
```

APPENDIX A   GETTING STARTED WITH THE SOURCE CODE

```
03/17/2024  11:33 AM          10,113 main.o.d
12/30/2023  03:03 PM    <DIR>        src
12/30/2023  03:03 PM    <DIR>        xsrc
```

The same steps can be used for the Grand Central hardware, except that in step 2 you would select "GCC-ARM compiler for Grand Central BSP 1.6.0" and in step 3 you would change to the projects\GM6000\Ajax\alpha1-atmel\gcc\ directory.

Build Directories on Windows

A build directory is any subdirectory under the projects\ and tests\ parent directories that contains an nqbp.py build script. Because a given project or unit test can be compiled with multiple compilers on multiple hosts, there can be many build directories for a single application or unit test. The following list is the compiler naming convention for build directories with respect to a Windows host PC.

- windows\vc12—Any Visual Studio compiler that supports C++11

- windows\mingw_w64—Any MinGW_w64 compiler that supports C++11

- windows\gcc—The ARM Cortex M/R Cross compiler for an ATSAM51 Arduino target

- windows\gcc-arm—The ARM Cortex M/R Cross compiler for an STM32 target

APPENDIX A   GETTING STARTED WITH THE SOURCE CODE

Linux

This section details the Linux specific instructions.

Prerequisites for Linux

The following is the minimal set of tools that are required in order to compile and execute the automated unit tests and the functional simulators under Linux.

- Python 3.8.5 or newer—For example, you could install this using a command similar to this:

    ```
    sudo apt install python3
    ```

- The GCC compiler—Install the entire GCC toolchain and tools. For example, you could use a command similar to this:

    ```
    sudo apt install build-essential
    ```

After installation, it is assumed that the GCC compiler is in the command path.

Currently, the epc repository does not directly support cross compiling on a Linux host for the ARM Cortex M/R targets. This is not a limitation of the tools or code base. It is simply the result of a decision to not create the build directories and build scripts for these targets.

APPENDIX A   GETTING STARTED WITH THE SOURCE CODE

Getting the Source Code on Linux

Clone the epc repository (https://github.com/johnttaylor/epc) to your PC. The repo can be installed anywhere on your box. However, the root path to the repo location cannot contain any spaces. For example:

```
~$ mkdir work
~$ cd work
~/work$ git clone https://github.com/johnttaylor/epc
```

Compiler Configuration on Linux

At the root of the repository, there is a script, env.sh, that is used to configure the working environment. This script must be run once per terminal session to properly set environment variables and to specify the compiler to use. You should not have to edit the env.sh script (though you are welcome to customize it). The env.sh script defaults to calling the native GCC compiler helper. However, it supports an optional argument that is used to set the path to an alternate gcc installation.

Building on Linux

All application builds are performed under the projects/ directory tree. All unit test builds are performed under the tests/ directory tree. While there is a limited amount of source code under the projects/ and tests/ directories, the bulk of the source code is under the src/ and xsrc/ directories.

All builds are performed on the command line. Use the following steps to build the functional simulator for the GM6000 Ajax application.

1. Open a terminal window.

APPENDIX A   GETTING STARTED WITH THE SOURCE CODE

2. Run the env.sh script using the source shell command. The output of the command may look something like this:

   ```
   ~$ cd work/epc
   ~/work/epc$ source env.sh
   Environment set (using native GCC compiler)
   gcc (Debian 10.2.1-6) 10.2.1 20210110
   Copyright (C) 2020 Free Software Foundation, Inc.
   This is free software; see the source for copying
   conditions. There is NO
   warranty; not even for MERCHANTABILITY or FITNESS FOR A
   PARTICULAR PURPOSE.
   ```

3. Navigate to the build directory for the GM6000 Ajax simulator using the GCC compiler and run the build script nqbp.py. The output of the build will be located in the subdirectory _posix64/.

   ```
   ~/work/epc$ cd projects/GM6000/Ajax/simulator/linux/gcc
   ~/work/epc/projects/GM6000/Ajax/simulator/linux/gcc$ nqbp.py
   =======================================================
   = START of build for:   ajax-sim
   = Project Directory:    ~/work/epc/projects/GM6000/Ajax/
                           simulator/linux/gcc
   = Toolchain:            GCC
   = Build Configuration:  posix64
   = Begin (UTC):          Sun, 31 Mar 2024 14:16:31
   = Build Time:           1711894591 (6609703f)
   =======================================================
   [282/282] Linking: ajax-sim
   =======================================================
   ```

APPENDIX A   GETTING STARTED WITH THE SOURCE CODE

```
        = END of build for:     ajax-sim
        = Project Directory:    ~/work/epc/projects/GM6000/Ajax/
                                simulator/linux/gcc
        = Toolchain:            GCC
        = Build Configuration: posix64
        = Elapsed Time (hh mm:ss): 00 00:08
        ===========================================================
        ~/work/epc/projects/GM6000/Ajax/simulator/linux/gcc$
        ls -l _posix64/
        total 1412
        -rwxr-xr-x 1 john john 1206488 Mar 31 10:16 ajax-sim
        -rw-r--r-- 1 john john  186928 Mar 31 10:16 build.ninja
        -rw-r--r-- 1 john john   30728 Mar 31 10:16 main.o
        -rw-r--r-- 1 john john    6966 Mar 31 10:16 main.o.d
        drwxr-xr-x 6 john john    4096 Mar 31 10:16 src
        drwxr-xr-x 5 john john    4096 Mar 31 10:16 xsrc
```

The same steps are used to build all applications and unit tests.

Build Directories on Linux

A build directory is any subdirectory under the projects/ and tests/ parent directories that contains an nqbp.py build script. Because a given project or unit test can be compiled with multiple compilers on multiple hosts, there can be many build directories for a single application or unit test. The following list is the compiler naming convention for build directories with respect to a Linux host PC.

- linux/gcc—Any GCC compiler that supports C++11

Currently, there are no projects or build scripts for cross compiling on a Linux host.

APPENDIX A   GETTING STARTED WITH THE SOURCE CODE

Additional Tools

Up until now, this discussion has been about building GM6000 applications and unit tests. However, if you are planning to

- Run on the target hardware
- Run the CI "build-all" scripts locally on your box
- Run Doxygen before submitting a pull request

then additional steps are required. What follows are the additional tools that need to be installed.

STM32 Cube IDE

The STM32 Cube IDE application is used to program and debug code on the NUCLEO-F413ZH development board. Detailed installation instructions for STM32 Cube IDE can be found on the Wiki page: `https://github.com/johnttaylor/epc/wiki/Installing-Developer-Tools:-Development-Machine#stm32-cube-ide`. Accept the default install options.

The Segger tool suite (J-Link, Ozone, etc.) can also be used for programming and debugging. I recommend using the Segger tools instead of the STM32 IDE because the Segger tools are microcontroller vendor agnostic and provide a richer feature set for development.

STM32 Cube MX

The STM32 Cube MX is a GUI application used for the low-level MCU configuration. That is, you need it when creating and updating the BSPs for the STM32 target hardware. The following steps show how to install the

APPENDIX A   GETTING STARTED WITH THE SOURCE CODE

MX tool on Windows. Detailed installation instructions for STM32 Cube MX can be found on the Wiki page: https://github.com/johnttaylor/epc/wiki/Installing-Developer-Tools:-Development-Machine#stm32-cube-mx. Accept the default install options.

Segger Tools

If you plan on using the STM32 IDE for programming and debugging, you can skip the following discussions of Segger tools.

Segger J-Link Tools

If you are programming ARM7 Cortex-M microcontrollers, you will also need to install Segger's tools for programming microcontrollers and use a J-Link programmer. Even without a J-Link programmer, the Segger tools can be used to program and debug the NUCLEO-F413ZH board. However, a J-Link programmer is required to program and debug on the Adafruit Grand Central M4 Express board. The following steps describe how to install the J-Link tools on a Windows box:

1. Install the J-Link software. Detailed installation instruction can be found on the Wiki page: https://github.com/johnttaylor/epc/wiki/Installing-Developer-Tools:-Development-Machine#segger-j-link-tools.

2. Reprogram the Nucleo's on-board ST-LINK chip.

    a. Download the "ST-LINK Re-flash Utility" application from www.segger.com/products/debug-probes/j-link/models/other-j-links/st-link-on-board/.

    b. Follow the instruction on the Segger website to re-flash the ST-LINK chip on your NUCLEO-F413ZH development board for use with the Segger tools.

APPENDIX A   GETTING STARTED WITH THE SOURCE CODE

Segger Ozone Debugger

Segger provides a stand-alone debugger for ARM and RISC-V microprocessors. Detailed installation instruction for Ozone can be found on the Wiki page: https://github.com/johnttaylor/epc/wiki/Installing-Developer-Tools:-Development-Machine#segger-ozone-debugger.

Segger SystemView

Segger's SystemView is a real-time recording and visualization tool for embedded systems that reveals the true runtime behavior of an application. Or said another way, it is a handy-dandy tool for evaluating and troubleshooting CPU usage and performance. Detailed installation instruction for SystemView can be found on the Wiki page: https://github.com/johnttaylor/epc/wiki/Installing-Developer-Tools:-Development-Machine#segger-systemview. Accept the default install options.

Terminal Emulator

A terminal emulator is required to connect to the target's hardware serial port debug console. You can use any terminal emulator, not just one of the ones listed here.

PuTTY

Detailed installation instructions for PuTTY can be found on the Wiki page: https://github.com/johnttaylor/epc/wiki/Installing-Developer-Tools:-Development-Machine#putty. Accept the default install options.

APPENDIX A   GETTING STARTED WITH THE SOURCE CODE

Tera Term

Detailed installation instructions for Tera Term can be found on the Wiki page: `https://github.com/johnttaylor/epc/wiki/Installing-Developer-Tools:-Development-Machine#tera-term`. Accept the default install options.

Doxygen

Doxygen is an automated code documentation tool that is used to generate detailed documentation directly from the code base. To achieve this, you need to install

- Doxygen
- Graphviz
- Microsoft Help Compiler

Detailed installation instructions for Doxygen can be found on the Wiki page: `https://github.com/johnttaylor/epc/wiki/Installing-Developer-Tools:-Common#installing-doxygen`.

The `run_doxygen.py` script takes optional command arguments to pass a build number and build branch. The script embeds the build number and branch into the output.

Code Coverage

The GCC compiler and the Python `gcovr` library are used to generate code coverage metrics when running the automated unit tests. The code coverage metrics are collected and reported as part of the CI builds. The developer can run code coverage reports on a per-unit-test basis before submitting a pull request.

APPENDIX A   GETTING STARTED WITH THE SOURCE CODE

The following steps show how to set up and generate coverage metrics for a unit test on a Windows box. The process is the same on Linux.

1. Install the MinGW compiler for Windows (or GCC under Linux). See the previous setup instructions for installing the compiler.

2. Install the Python gcovr library. Detailed installation instruction can be found on the Wiki page: https://github.com/johnttaylor/epc/wiki/Installing-Developer-Tools:-Common#installing-gcovr.

3. Build an automated unit test using the MinGW (or GCC) compiler. Note that if you pass the -g option to the nqbp.py script, it creates a debug build.

```
c:\>cd work\epc
c:\work\epc>env.bat
NO TOOLCHAIN SET

1 - Visual Studio VC17 (32bit) compiler for Windows
2 - Visual Studio VC17 (64bit) compiler for Windows
3 - MINGW64 v10.3.0-2 compiler for Windows (32bit
    and 64 bit)
4 - GCC-ARM compiler for Grand Central BSP 1.6.0
5 - GCC-ARM (none-eabi) compiler for STM32
c:\work\epc>env.bat 3
MinGW-x64 Compiler Environment set (v10.3.0-2 32bit
and 64bit)
c:\work\epc>cd tests\Ajax\Alerts\_0test\windows\mingw_w64
```

APPENDIX A GETTING STARTED WITH THE SOURCE CODE

```
c:\_workspaces\zoe\epc\tests\Ajax\Alerts\_0test\
windows\mingw_w64>nqbp.py -g
==========================================================
= START of build for:  a.exe
= Project Directory:   C:\work\epc\Ajax\Alerts\_0test\
                       windows\mingw_w64
= Toolchain:        Mingw_W64
= Build Configuration: win32
= Begin (UTC):      Sat, 02 Mar 2024 21:33:26
= Build Time:       1709415206 (65e39b26)
==========================================================
[110/110] Linking: a.exe
==========================================================
= END of build for:  a.exe
= Project Directory:   C:\work\epc\Ajax\Alerts\_0test\
                       windows\mingw_w64
= Toolchain:        Mingw_W64
= Build Configuration: win32
= Elapsed Time (hh mm:ss): 00 00:25
==========================================================
```

4. Run the unit test.

   ```
   c:\work\epc\tests\Ajax\Alerts\_0test\windows\mingw_
   w64>_win32\a.exe
   ==========================================================
   All tests passed (22 assertions in 1 test case)
   ```

5. Generate line coverage metrics. Note: The
   -f.*Ajax.Alerts.* argument is a regular
   expression to filter the output to just the files in the
   Ajax::Alerts namespace.

APPENDIX A   GETTING STARTED WITH THE SOURCE CODE

```
c:\work\epc\tests\Ajax\Alerts\_Otest\windows\mingw_
w64>tca.py rpt
-f.*Ajax.Alerts.*
--------------------------------------------------------
              GCC Code Coverage Report
Directory: ../../../../../src
--------------------------------------------------------
File                      Lines  Exec  Cover  Missing
--------------------------------------------------------
C:/work/epc/src/Ajax/Alerts/Summary.cpp
                           50    44    88%   41-43,65-67
--------------------------------------------------------
TOTAL                      50    44    88%
--------------------------------------------------------
```

6. Generate branch coverage metrics.

```
c:\work\epc\tests\Ajax\Alerts\_Otest\windows\
mingw_w64>tca.py rpt --branch
-f.*Ajax.Alerts.*
--------------------------------------------------------
              GCC Code Coverage Report
Directory: ../../../../../src
--------------------------------------------------------
File                   Branches  Taken  Cover  Missing
--------------------------------------------------------
C:/work/epc/src/Ajax/Alerts/Summary.cpp
                          28     24    85%   39,53,63,136
--------------------------------------------------------
TOTAL                     28     24    85%
--------------------------------------------------------
```

APPENDIX A   GETTING STARTED WITH THE SOURCE CODE

RATT

The RATT test engine is a set of Python scripts that are used to automate user interactions over IO streams such as

- Serial ports
- TCP sockets
- `stdin` and `stdout`

RATT is built on top of the Python `pexpect` library and can be found in the epc repository in the `xsrc/ratt/` directory. For example, the automated "smoke test" for the GM6000 Ajax application is a collection of RATT scripts that interact with the functional simulator's debug console.

The following steps show how to set up and run a RATT script on Windows. The process is the same on Linux box.

1. Install the Python pexpect library. Detailed installation instructions can be found on the Wiki page: `https://github.com/johnttaylor/epc/wiki/Installing-Developer-Tools:-Common#installing-pexepect`.

2. Run the Ajax smoke test script to verify that RATT is working.

Note   The `a.py` script requires that the command-line environment be first properly configured by running the `env.bat` script.

```
c:\>cd work\epc
c:\work\epc>env.bat 1
**********************************************************
** Visual Studio 2022 Developer Command Prompt v17.3.6
```

APPENDIX A   GETTING STARTED WITH THE SOURCE CODE

```
** Copyright (c) 2022 Microsoft Corporation
***********************************************************
[vcvarsall.bat] Environment initialized for: 'x86'
c:\>cd projects\GM6000\Ajax\simulator\windows\vc12
c:\work\epc\projects\GM6000\Ajaxsimulator\windows\
vc12>nqbp.py
===========================================================
= START of build for: ajax-sim.exe
= Project Directory:  C:\work\epc\projects\GM6000\Ajax\
                      simulator\windows\vc12
= Toolchain:     VC++ 12, 32bit (Visual Studio 2013)
= Build Configuration: win32
= Begin (UTC):     Sat, 02 Mar 2024 23:18:10
= Build Time:      1709421490 (65e3b3b2)
===========================================================
[282/282] Linking: ajax-sim.exe
===========================================================
= END of build for:   ajax-sim.exe
= Project Directory:  C:\work\epc\projects\GM6000\Ajax\
                      simulator\windows\vc12
= Toolchain:     VC++ 12, 32bit (Visual Studio 2013)
= Build Configuration: win32
= Elapsed Time (hh mm:ss): 00 00:17
===========================================================
c:\work\epc\projects\GM6000\Ajax\simulator\windows\
vc12>a.py
------------ START: Ratt, ver=2.0.0. Start
             time=2024-03-02_18.19.50
------------ RUNNING SUITE CASE: c:\work\epc\src\Ajax\
             Main\_0test\provision_suite.py
```

309

APPENDIX A   GETTING STARTED WITH THE SOURCE CODE

```
STARTING: provision_suite ...
COMPLETED: provision_suite.
------------ TEST SUITE PASSED.
------------ END: End time=2024-03-02_18.19.54,
             delta=0.07 mins

------------ START: Ratt, ver=2.0.0. Start
time=2024-03-02_18.19.54
------------ RUNNING SUITE CASE: c:\work\epc\src\Ajax\
             Main\_0test\test_suite.py
STARTING: test_suite ...
..STARTING: tc_basic_heating ...
..COMPLETED: tc_basic_heating.
COMPLETED: test_suite.
------------ TEST SUITE PASSED.
------------ END: End time=2024-03-02_18.20.13,
             delta=0.31 mins
c:\work\epc\projects\GM6000\Ajax\simulator\
windows\vc12>
```

State Machine Tools

The GM6000 example code makes use of commercial tools for drawing state machine diagrams and autogenerating code based on those diagrams. These tools are only needed when modifying an existing state diagram or creating a new state diagram. These tools are not open source and require commercial licenses. The tools are as follows:

1. Cadifra—A UML Editor that is used to create and edit UML state machine diagrams. Detailed installation instructions can be found on the

APPENDIX A   GETTING STARTED WITH THE SOURCE CODE

Wiki page: https://github.com/johnttaylor/ epc/wiki/Installing-Developer-Tools:- Development-Machine#cadifra-uml-editor.

2. SinelaboreRT—A JAVA application that auto- generates code for state machines that were drawn using UML notation. Detailed installation instructions can be found on the Wiki page: https://github.com/johnttaylor/epc/wiki/ Installing-Developer-Tools:-Development- Machine#sinelaborert-uml-state-diagrams.

3. genfsm.py—A script that is used to invoke the Sinelabore tool. In addition, the genfsm.py script performs some additional processing to the Sinelabore output for integration with the CPL C++ class library. Every directory that contains at least one state diagram must also have a genfsm.py script. The genfsm.py script needs to be customized for each specific directory and namespace. The following bolded items identify what needs to be customized:

File: src/Ajax/Heating/Supervisor/genfsm.py

```
#!/usr/bin/python3
"""Invokes NQBP's genfsm_base.py script. To run 'GENFSM' copy this file
   To your source directory. Then edit the local script to generate one or
   more Finite State Machines (FSMs)
"""

import os
import sys

# Make sure the environment is properly set
NQBP_BIN = os.environ.get('NQBP_BIN')
```

APPENDIX A   GETTING STARTED WITH THE SOURCE CODE

```
if ( NQBP_BIN == None ):
  sys.exit( "ERROR: The environment variable NQBP_BIN is not set!" )
sys.path.append( NQBP_BIN )

# Find the Package & Workspace root
from other import genfsm_base
sys.argv.append('')
sys.argv.append('')
sys.argv.append('')

###############################################################
# BEGIN EDITS HERE
###############################################################

# Generate FSM#1
sys.argv[1] = '-d 4'  # Size of the event queue
sys.argv[2] = 'Fsm'   # Name of Cadifra diagram (without .extension)
sys.argv[3] = 'Ajax::Heating::Supervisor' # Namespace
genfsm_base.run( sys.argv )
```

Outcast

Outcast is an experimental tool suite for managing source code packages for reuse by other packages. Outcast is used to incorporate external repositories such as the CPL C++ class library (`colony.core`) and NQBP2 (`nqbp2`) into the epc repository so that day-to-day development in the epc is a mono-repository work flow. The Outcast tool only needs to be used when adding or upgrading external packages.

If you need to install the Outcast because you are adding or upgrading external packages, detailed installation instruction for Outcast can be found on the Wiki page: `https://github.com/johnttaylor/epc/wiki/Installing-Developer-Tools:-Development-Machine#outcast`. Make sure you add Outcast's `bin/` directory to the system's command path.

APPENDIX B

Running the Example Code

This appendix describes how to run the Ajax and Eros applications in the GM6000 project. The Ajax application is the image that is provisioned into the GM6000 product when it ships. The Eros application is an engineering test application for exercising and validating the hardware.

The developer's primary interaction with these example applications is through the debug console. With only a few exceptions, all of the console commands are the same whether running on the target hardware or the simulator.

Ajax Application

The Ajax application has a live debug console. However, the console is password protected. The password for each individual board is set during the provisioning when units are manufactured.

APPENDIX B   RUNNING THE EXAMPLE CODE

Provisioning

The Ajax application requires that each control board be provisioned during the manufacturing process. The provisioning step is used to store the following data in nonvolatile storage:

- Model number
- Serial number
- Console password (unique per unit)
- Heating algorithm configuration

During development, developers will need to provision their targets (at least once) using the prov console command before running the Ajax application. The Eros application contains the prov console command, while the Ajax application does not. However, the debug build of the Ajax application[2] does contain the prov console command to simplify development. To provision a target:

1. Run the Eros application and execute the prov console command
2. Or run the debug version of the Ajax application and execute the prov console command:

   a. Restart the Ajax application.

The following is an example of provisioning using the debug version of the Ajax application running on the functional simulator without the simulated display running.

---

[2] To build the debug version of any application or unit test, use the -g option when invoking the build script. For example, nqbp.py -g.

APPENDIX B   RUNNING THE EXAMPLE CODE

C:\work\epc\projects\GM6000\Ajax\simulator\windows\vc12>_
win32**ajax-sim.exe**

WARNING. Failed to connected to the Display Simulation.
(host=127.0.0.1, port=5010).
        Running without Simulated display.

AJAX: appvariant_initialize0( )
>> 00 00:00:02.158 (METRICS) METRICS:POWER_ON. Boot count = 7

--- Your friendly neighborhood Tshell. ---

$> >> 00 00:00:02.564 (ALERT) ALERT:FAILED_SAFE. Cleared
>> 00 00:00:04.166 (INFO) User Record size: 14 (30)
>> 00 00:00:04.166 (INFO) Metrics Record size: 39 (55)
>> 00 00:00:04.167 (INFO) Personality Record size: 193 (209)
>> 00 00:00:04.168 (INFO) Log Entry size: 159
$> **help prov**
prov <modelNumber> <serialNumber> <consolePwd> <h-outS>
<h-maxY> <h-errS> <h-dErrS> <h-outK0> <h-outK1> <h-outK2>
<h-outK3> <h-outK4> <fanLow> <fanMed> <fanHi> <maxCap>
   Provisions the GM6000 with its personality

$> **prov T-101 SN800 Was.Here1234! 1000 1000 5 5 -20 -10 0 10 20   39322 52429 65536 60000**
Model Number: T-101
Serial Number: SN800
Console Pwd: Was.Here1234!
<h-outS>:   1000
<h-maxY>:   1000
<h-errS>:   5
<h-dErrS>:   5
<h-outK0>:   -20
<h-outK1>:   -10

APPENDIX B   RUNNING THE EXAMPLE CODE

```
<h-outK2>:        0
<h-outK3>:        10
<h-outK4>:        20
<fanLow>:         39322
<fanMed>:         52429
<fanHi>:          65536
<maxCap>:         60000
$>bye app
$> >> 00 00:02:20.042 (METRICS) METRICS:SHUTDOWN. Boot
count = 7
c:\work\epc\projects\GM6000\Ajax\simulator\windows\vc12>
```

The functional simulator's persistent storage is realized with a file-based implementation of the NV driver. The file-based NV driver uses a file eeprom.bin in the working directory where the Ajax application is launched. The eeprom.bin file can be copied or moved to work with both the Ajax and Eros functional simulators.

Console Password

The Ajax application's debug console is password protected. To gain access to the debug console, the user must log in using the user console command. Per the GM6000 requirements, no help or error messages are displayed on the debug console until a user successfully logs in. The following is an example of logging into the release version of the Ajax application running on a functional simulator without the simulated display running.

APPENDIX B RUNNING THE EXAMPLE CODE

The username to use when logging in is dilbert, and, in the provisioning step, the password was set to "Was.Here1234".

C:\work\epc\projects\GM6000\Ajax\simulator\windows\vc12>**_win32\ ajax-sim.exe**

```
WARNING. Failed to connected to the Display Simulation.
(host=127.0.0.1, port=5010).
        Running without Simulated display.
AJAX: appvariant_initialize0()
>> 00 00:00:02.149 (METRICS) METRICS:POWER_ON. Boot count = 8
>> 00 00:00:02.552 (ALERT) ALERT:FAILED_SAFE. Cleared
>> 00 00:00:04.206 (INFO) User Record size:        14 (30)
>> 00 00:00:04.206 (INFO) Metrics Record size:     39 (55)
>> 00 00:00:04.208 (INFO) Personality Record size: 193 (209)
>> 00 00:00:04.213 (INFO) Log Entry size:          159
```
help   # Command is ignored until a successful login
user login dilbert Was.Here1234!
$> **help**
```
bye [app [<exitcode>]]
dm ls [<filter>]
dm write {<mp-json>}
dm read <mpname>
dm touch <mpname>
help [* | <cmd>]
log [*|<max>]
log <nth> (*|<max>)
log clear
rnd <numBytes>
threads
tprint ["<text>"]
trace [on|off]
```

APPENDIX B RUNNING THE EXAMPLE CODE

```
trace section (on|off) <sect1> [<sect2>]...
trace threadfilters [<threadname1> [<threadname2>]]...
trace level (none|brief|info|verbose|max)
trace here|revert
ui <event>
user login <username> <password>
user logout
$>
```

The debug version of the Ajax application does not require a login to the debug console. This is done to simplify development.

Functional Simulator

The functional simulator can run with or without a simulated display. The simulated display is provided by a C# Windows application (see Figure B-1). The simulated display emulates the physical display at the pixel data level. That is, the raw pixel data is transferred from the functional simulator via sockets to the C# Windows application. The C# Windows application also emulates the button inputs and the RGB LED output that is part of the physical display board. The mouse or keyboard can be used to "press the buttons." However, only the keyboard can be used to press multiple buttons simultaneously (e.g., the B+Y key combination).

APPENDIX B   RUNNING THE EXAMPLE CODE

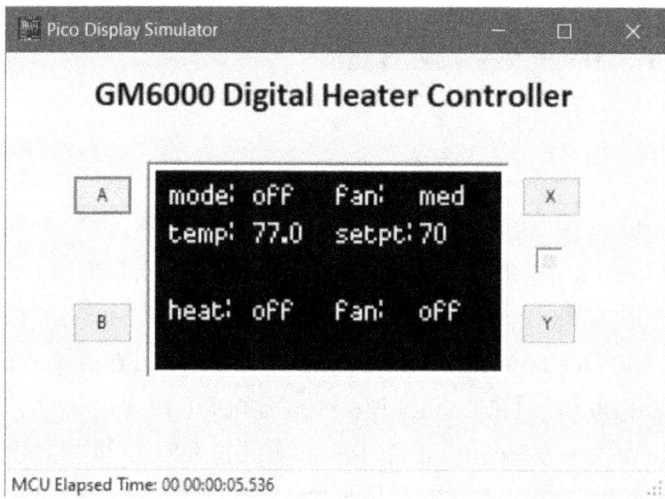

Figure B-1. *Simulated display with the Ajax application*

The epc repository contains a pre-built simulated display in the projects\pico-display-simulator\simulator\bin\Release. The C# Visual Studio solution for the simulated display is in the projects\pico-display-simulator directory.

When running the functional simulator on a Windows host, there is a helper script in the Ajax build directory named go.bat that launches both the simulated display and the functional simulator together. For example:

```
c:\work\epc\projects\GM6000\Ajax\simulator\windows\vc12>go.bat
Launching display simulator...

Waiting for 1 seconds, press a key to continue ...

AJAX: appvariant_initialize0()
>> 00 00:00:00.133 (METRICS) METRICS:POWER_ON. Boot count = 9
>> 00 00:00:00.519 (ALERT) ALERT:FAILED_SAFE. Cleared
>> 00 00:00:02.184 (INFO) User Record size:        14 (30)
>> 00 00:00:02.184 (INFO) Metrics Record size:     39 (55)
>> 00 00:00:02.186 (INFO) Personality Record size: 193 (209)
```

319

APPENDIX B RUNNING THE EXAMPLE CODE

```
>> 00 00:00:02.191 (INFO) Log Entry size:            159
user login dilbert Was.Here1234!
$>
```

If you have not previously provisioned the simulator, the UI will display a hard error that the unit is not provisioned, and you can't log in because there is no valid command console password. To provision the simulator, run the Eros simulator (or a debug build of the Ajax simulator). Then copy the Eros simulator's `eeprom.bin` file that contains the provision information to the Ajax build directory. For additional details, see the "Provisioning" discussion in the "Eros" section.

Here is a list of command-line options supported by the Ajax functional simulator:

```
c:\work\epc\projects\GM6000\Ajax\simulator\windows\vc12>_win32\
ajax-sim.exe -h
Ajax Simulation.

   Usage:
     ajax-sim [options]

   Options:
     -s HOST          Hostname for the Display Simulation.
                      [Default: 127.0.0.1]
     -p PORT          The Display Simulation's Port number
                      [Default: 5010]
     -e               Generate a POST failure on start-up
     -t ADCBITS       Sets the initial mocked ADCBits value
                      (only valid when the House Simulator is
                      NOT compiled) [Default: 2048]
```

```
-o ODT          Sets the initial Outdoor Temp value
                (only valid when the House Simulator is
                compiled) [Default: 70]
-v              Be verbose
--help          Show this screen.

Note: No 'Display simulation' is required.
```

The Windows-based simulated display can be used with the functional simulator running under Linux because the interface between the functional simulator and the simulated display is via TCP sockets. Use the `-s` and `-p` options with the `ajax-sim` command to specify the IP address and port number for the simulated display.

Hardware Target

The Ajax application can execute on the STM32 and Adafruit evaluation boards without any extra hardware such as the display board, EEPROM, temperature sensor, etc. However, depending on what the missing hardware is, the functionality of the application will be restricted. Figure B-2 is a block diagram of the hardware for the GM6000's pancake control board.

APPENDIX B   RUNNING THE EXAMPLE CODE

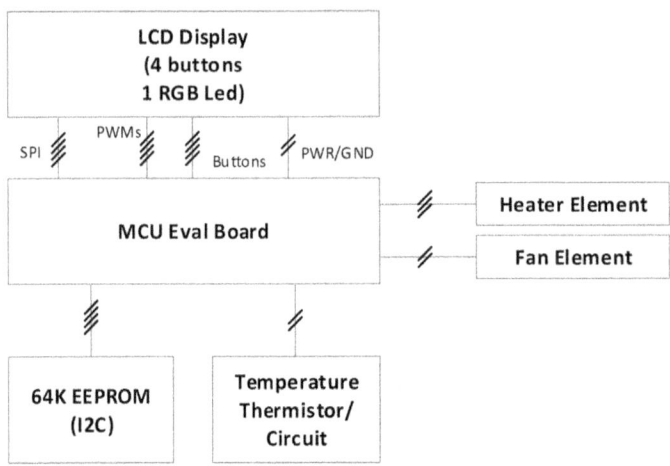

Figure B-2. *Block Diagram for the GM6000 pancake board*

The MCU pinout for the pancake board can be found at the following Wiki pages in the epc repository:

>ST NUCLEO-F413ZH evaluation board–
>https://github.com/johnttaylor/epc/wiki/
>STM32%E2%80%90Alpha-board-Pin-Out

>Adafruit Grand Central M4 Express evaluation board–https://github.com/johnttaylor/epc/wiki/Adafruit%E2%80%90Grand%E2%80%90Central%E2%80%90Alpha-board-Pin-Out

>Schematic for the temperature thermistor circuit–
>https://github.com/johnttaylor/epc/wiki/
>Temperature-Circuit

APPENDIX B   RUNNING THE EXAMPLE CODE

I recommend that you build and run the debug version of the Ajax application during development (e.g., nqbp.py -g). The reason is because the debug version of the application contains the prov console command and does not require the developer to log in into the console.

Console Commands

This section covers the basic debug console commands. The commands and behavior are the same whether running on the target or the functional simulator. A full list of console commands supported at runtime can always be obtained by using the following help commands:

- help
- help *
- help <cmd>

Here is an example of the output of the help command:

```
$> help
bye [app [<exitcode>]]
dm ls [<filter>]
dm write {<mp-json>}
dm read <mpname>
dm touch <mpname>
help [* | <cmd>]
log [*|<max>]
log <nth> (*|<max>)
log clear
nv ERASE
```

```
nv read <startOffSet> <len>
nv write <startOffset> <bytes...>
nv test (aa|55|blank)
prov <modelNumber> <serialNumber> <consolePwd> <h-outS>
<h-maxY> <h-errS> <h-dErrS> <h-outK0> <h-outK1> <h-outK2>
<h-outK3> <h-outK4> <fanLow> <fanMed> <fanHi> <maxCap>
rnd <numBytes>
threads
tprint ["<text>"]
trace [on|off]
trace section (on|off) <sect1> [<sect2>]...
trace threadfilters [<threadname1> [<threadname2>]]...
trace level (none|brief|info|verbose|max)
trace here|revert
ui <event>
user login <username> <password>
user logout
$>
```

I recommend that you create a text file to store a list of commonly used console commands and then copy and paste from the text file into the terminal window attached to the console.

Heating Mode, Fan Mode, and Setpoint

The heating and fan modes, and the heating setpoint, can be monitored and set using the data model dm console command.

APPENDIX B RUNNING THE EXAMPLE CODE

The following commands are used to display the current settings:

dm read heatingMode
dm read fanMode
dm read heatSetpoint

Example:

```
$> dm read heatingMode
{
  "name": "heatingMode",
  "valid": true,
  "type": "Cpl::Dm::Mp::Bool",
  "seqnum": 2,
  "locked": false,
  "val": false
}
$>dm read fanMode
{
  "name": "fanMode",
  "valid": true,
  "type": "Ajax::Dm::MpFanMode",
  "seqnum": 2,
  "locked": false,
  "val": "eMEDIUM"
}
$> dm read heatSetpoint
{
  "name": "heatSetpoint",
  "valid": true,
  "type": "Cpl::Dm::Mp::Int32",
```

APPENDIX B RUNNING THE EXAMPLE CODE

```
    "seqnum": 2,
    "locked": false,
    "val": 7000
  }
$>
```

The following commands are used to configure the heating mode, fan mode, and heating setpoint. In the following examples, the heating mode is turned *on*, the fan mode is set to *high*, and the heating setpoint is set to 72.5° F.

```
dm write {name:"heatingMode",val:true}
dm write {name:"fanMode",val:"eHIGH"}
dm write {name:"heatSetpoint",val:7250}
```

Example output:

```
$> dm write {name:"heatingMode",val:true}
>> 00 00:11:05.661 (Ajax::Ui::Home) heat mode changed
$> dm write {name:"fanMode",val:"eHIGH"}
>> 00 00:11:12.682 (Ajax::Ui::Home) fan mode changed
$> dm write {name:"heatSetpoint",val:7250}
>> 00 00:11:18.309 (Ajax::Ui::Home) setpoint changed
$> dm read heatingMode
{
  "name": "heatingMode",
  "valid": true,
  "type": "Cpl::Dm::Mp::Bool",
  "seqnum": 7,
  "locked": false,
  "val": true
}
$> dm read fanMode
```

```
{
  "name": "fanMode",
  "valid": true,
  "type": "Ajax::Dm::MpFanMode",
  "seqnum": 7,
  "locked": false,
  "val": "eHIGH"
}
$> dm read heatSetpoint
{
  "name": "heatSetpoint",
  "valid": true,
  "type": "Cpl::Dm::Mp::Int32",
  "seqnum": 7,
  "locked": false,
  "val": 7250
}
$>
```

Temperature

The dm console command is used to monitor the indoor temperature. The command can also be used to override or force a specific indoor temperature. The following command is used to display the current indoor temperature:

dm read onBoardIdt

Example output:

```
$> dm read onBoardIdt
{
  "name": "onBoardIdt",
  "valid": true,
```

APPENDIX B RUNNING THE EXAMPLE CODE

```
  "type": "Cpl::Dm::Mp::Int32",
  "seqnum": 1087,
  "locked": false,
  "val": 7579
}
$>
```

The following commands are used to override the current indoor temperature to 72.33° F and then restore it to the value being reported by the sensor. The locked attribute of the model point is used to force a temperature value that will not be overwritten by the temperature sensor driver.

dm write {name:"onBoardIdt",val:7233,locked:true}
dm write {name:"onBoardIdt",locked:false}

Example output:

```
$> # Temperature as being reported by the physical sensor
$> dm read onBoardIdt
{
  "name": "onBoardIdt",
  "valid": true,
  "type": "Cpl::Dm::Mp::Int32",
  "seqnum": 1374,
  "locked": false,
  "val": 7582
}
$> # Forced temperature value
$> dm write {name:"onBoardIdt",val:7233,locked:true}
$> dm read onBoardIdt
{
  "name": "onBoardIdt",
  "valid": true,
```

```
  "type": "Cpl::Dm::Mp::Int32",
  "seqnum": 1377,
  "locked": true,
  "val": 7233
}
$> # Temperature as reported by the physical sensor
$> dm write {name:"onBoardIdt",locked:false}
$> dm read onBoardIdt
{
  "name": "onBoardIdt",
  "valid": true,
  "type": "Cpl::Dm::Mp::Int32",
  "seqnum": 1381,
  "locked": false,
  "val": 7587
}
$>
```

Overriding, or forcing a model point value, can be applied to all model points. For example, this command forces the fan PWM value to 50% duty cycle, which in turn drives the physical fan PWM output signal to 50% duty cycle:

```
dm write {name:"cmdFanPWM",val:32765,locked:true}
```

APPENDIX B RUNNING THE EXAMPLE CODE

Heating and Fan PWM Outputs

The dm console command is used to monitor the PWM output values for the Heating element and Fan speed. The following commands are used to display the current settings:

dm read cmdHeaterPWM
dm read cmdFanPWM

Example output:

```
$> dm read cmdHeaterPWM
{
  "name": "cmdHeaterPWM",
  "valid": true,
  "type": "Cpl::Dm::Mp::Uint32",
  "seqnum": 34,
  "locked": false,
  "val": 0
}
$> dm read cmdFanPWM
{
  "name": "cmdFanPWM",
  "valid": true,
  "type": "Cpl::Dm::Mp::Uint32",
  "seqnum": 8,
  "locked": false,
  "val": 0
}
```

Generating UI Events from the Console

The console command ui is used to trigger button events. This command is very helpful when writing automated test scripts that exercise the user interface. The syntax for the ui command is as follows:

```
$> help ui
ui <event>
   Generates UI events. Supported events are:
     btn-a    -->AJAX_UI_EVENT_BUTTON_A
     btn-b    -->AJAX_UI_EVENT_BUTTON_B
     btn-x    -->AJAX_UI_EVENT_BUTTON_X
     btn-y    -->AJAX_UI_EVENT_BUTTON_Y
     btn-esc  -->AJAX_UI_EVENT_BUTTON_ESC
     nop      -->AJAX_UI_EVENT_NO_EVENT
```

Example for using the ui command to change the Heating mode by triggering a UI event for button-A UI:

```
$> # Current Heating is turned off
$> dm read heatingMode
{
  "name": "heatingMode",
  "valid": true,
  "type": "Cpl::Dm::Mp::Bool",
  "seqnum": 8,
  "locked": false,
  "val": false
}
$> # Toggle the heating mode by emulating pressing the A button
$> ui btn-a
Generated event: btn-a
>> 00 00:51:52.576 (Ajax::Ui::Home) heat mode changed
$> dm read heatingMode
```

APPENDIX B   RUNNING THE EXAMPLE CODE

```
{
  "name": "heatingMode",
  "valid": true,
  "type": "Cpl::Dm::Mp::Bool",
  "seqnum": 9,
  "locked": false,
  "val": true
}
$> # Toggle the heating mode by emulating pressing the A button
$> ui btn-a
Generated event: btn-a
>> 00 00:52:01.876 (Ajax::Ui::Home) heat mode changed
>> 00 00:52:01.878 (INFO) INFO:HEATING_ALGO. Heating mode
unexpectedly disabled, generating Fsm_evDisabled event.
$> dm read heatingMode
{
  "name": "heatingMode",
  "valid": true,
  "type": "Cpl::Dm::Mp::Bool",
  "seqnum": 10,
  "locked": false,
  "val": false
}
$>
```

General-Purpose Commands

There are several non-application-specific console commands that are very helpful. The threads command displays a list of all threads created by the application. When running on a target with FreeRTOS, the output also contains the stack usage per thread. This allows the developer to evaluate if the stack size for a given thread is sufficient.

APPENDIX B   RUNNING THE EXAMPLE CODE

Here is an example of how this looks with FreeRTOS running on the STM32 board. The stack column is the thread's stack high water mark in words (the smaller the value, the closer the stack is to overflowing).

```
$> threads
```

Name	R	ID	Native Hdl	Pri	State	Stack
----	-	--	----------	---	-----	-----
main	Y	0x20016d90	0x20016d90	3	Blckd	684
UI	Y	0x200195b8	0x200195b8	4	Ready	543
APP	Y	0x20018480	0x20018480	3	Ready	630
NVRAM	Y	0x2001a6e8	0x2001a6e8	1	Ready	795
TShell	Y	0x2001b9a8	0x2001b9a8	4	Run	585

```
Total number of threads: 5
$>
```

The trace command is used to control the CPL library's printf tracing at runtime. The command is used to

- Enable and disable tracing
- Enable and disable which sections are printed
- Support filtering the trace statements by thread

Example output:

```
$> help trace
trace [on|off]
trace section (on|off) <sect1> [<sect2>]...
trace threadfilters [<threadname1> [<threadname2>]]...
trace level (none|brief|info|verbose|max)
trace here|revert
```

333

APPENDIX B   RUNNING THE EXAMPLE CODE

Enables/Disables the Cpl::System::Trace engine and manages the section', information level, and thread filter options. See the Cpl::System::Trace interface for details on how the trace engine works.

$> **trace**

```
TRACE: Currently Enabled Sections:
----------------------------------
CRITICAL
WARNING
ALERT
EVENT
INFO
METRICS
*Ajax::Ui

TRACE: Currently Enabled Thread Filters:
----------------------------------------

TRACE: Runtime state:= ENABLED, Info Level:= BRIEF
$>
```

The log command is used to display the application's persistent stored log entries and to clear the log file.

Example output:

$> **help log**
```
log [*|<max>]
log <nth> (*|<max>)
log clear
  Displays and clear stored log records entries. Records are
  always displayed newest entry first. The output format is:
  "[<entrykey>] (<entryTimestamp>) <CATID>:<MSGID>. <text>"
```

334

APPENDIX B RUNNING THE EXAMPLE CODE

- 'log' with no arguments displays the newest entry.
- 'log *' displays all entries.
- 'log <max>' displays at most <max> entries.
- 'log <nth> *' displays all log entries starting with the <nth> record.
- 'log <nth> <max>' displays up to <max> entries starting with <nth> record.

```
$> log *
[10] (   3121877) INFO:HEATING_ALGO. Heating mode unexpectedly
    disabled, generating Fsm_evDisabled event.
[f]  (   3093309) INFO:HEATING_ALGO. Heating mode unexpectedly
    disabled, generating Fsm_evDisabled event.
[e]  (    657164) INFO:HEATING_ALGO. Heating mode unexpectedly
    disabled, generating Fsm_evDisabled event.
[d]  (    513590) INFO:HEATING_ALGO. Heating mode unexpectedly
    disabled, generating Fsm_evDisabled event.
[c]  (       566) ALERT:FAILED_SAFE. Cleared
[b]  (       436) METRICS:POWER_ON. Boot count = 6
[a]  (    963162) METRICS:SHUTDOWN. Boot count = 5
[9]  (    483583) INFO:HEATING_ALGO. Heating mode unexpectedly
    disabled, generating Fsm_evDisabled event.
[8]  (       566) ALERT:FAILED_SAFE. Cleared
[7]  (       436) METRICS:POWER_ON. Boot count = 5
[6]  (     15919) METRICS:SHUTDOWN. Boot count = 4
[5]  (       566) ALERT:FAILED_SAFE. Cleared
[4]  (       436) METRICS:POWER_ON. Boot count = 4
[3]  (       434) METRICS:POWER_ON. Boot count = 3
[2]  (       434) METRICS:POWER_ON. Boot count = 2
[1]  (       610) METRICS:POWER_ON. Boot count = 1
16 log records
$>
```

The bye command is used to exit the application. When running on the target, the bye command causes a warm reboot. When running the simulator, the bye command exits the application.

Example output:

```
$> help bye
bye [app [<exitcode>]]
  Requests the  shell to exit. If the optional argument
  'app' is specified then the application is exited with the
  specified <exitcode>. The default <exitcode> is '0'.

$> # Reboot the target
$> bye app
$> >> 00 01:15:09.054 (METRICS) METRICS:SHUTDOWN. Boot count = 6
>> 00 00:00:00.436 (METRICS) METRICS:POWER_ON. Boot count = 7

--- Your friendly neighborhood TShell. ---
```

Eros

The Eros application has a live debug console. Unlike the Ajax application, the console is not password protected. The Eros application is intended to be used during the manufacturing process to provision each unit as well as to perform "design verification testing" of the heating system.

APPENDIX B   RUNNING THE EXAMPLE CODE

Provisioning

The provisioning step is used to store the following data in nonvolatile storage:

- Model number
- Serial number
- Console password (unique per unit)
- Heating algorithm configuration

The following is an example of provisioning using the Eros application running on a functional simulator (without the simulated display running).

```
c:\work\epc\projects\GM6000\Eros\simulator\windows\vc12>_win32\
eros-sim.exe

WARNING. Failed to connected to the Display Simulation.
(host=127.0.0.1, port=5010).
         Running without Simulated display.
>> 00 00:00:02.193 (METRICS) METRICS:POWER_ON. Boot count = 1

--- Your friendly neighborhood TShell. ---

>> 00 00:00:04.247 (INFO) User Record size:       14 (30)
>> 00 00:00:04.247 (INFO) Metrics Record size:    39 (55)
>> 00 00:00:04.248 (INFO) Personality Record size: 193 (209)
>> 00 00:00:04.249 (INFO) Log Entry size:         159
$$> help prov
prov <modelNumber> <serialNumber> <consolePwd> <h-outS>
<h-maxY> <h-errS> <h-dErrS> <h-outK0> <h-outK1> <h-outK2>
<h-outK3> <h-outK4> <fanLow> <fanMed> <fanHi> <maxCap>
   Provisions the GM6000 with its 'personality'
```

APPENDIX B   RUNNING THE EXAMPLE CODE

```
$$> prov T-101 SN800 Was.Here1234! 1000 1000 5 5 -20 -10 0 10
20  39322 52429 65536 60000
Model Number:     T-101
Serial Number:    SN800
Console Pwd:      Was.Here1234!
<h-outS>:         1000
<h-maxY>:         1000
<h-errS>:         5
<h-dErrS>:        5
<h-outK0>:        -20
<h-outK1>:        -10
<h-outK2>:        0
<h-outK3>:        10
<h-outK4>:        20
<fanLow>:         39322
<fanMed>:         52429
<fanHi>:          65536
<maxCap>:         60000
$$>
```

When provisioning using the Eros functional simulator, the application generates an `eeprom.bin` file in the current working directory. This file should be copied over to the current working directory where the Ajax functional simulator will be run. This emulates the same EEPROM storage across the two simulators.

APPENDIX B   RUNNING THE EXAMPLE CODE

Functional Simulator

The functional simulator can run with or without a simulated display. The simulated display is provided by a C# Windows application, which is shown in Figure B-3. The simulated display emulates the physical display at the pixel data level. That is, the raw pixel data is transferred from the functional simulator via sockets to the C# Windows application. The C# Windows application also emulates the button inputs and the RGB LED output that is part of the physical display board. The mouse or keyboard can be used to "press the buttons." However, only the keyboard can be used to press multiple buttons simultaneously. For example, the B+Y key combination.

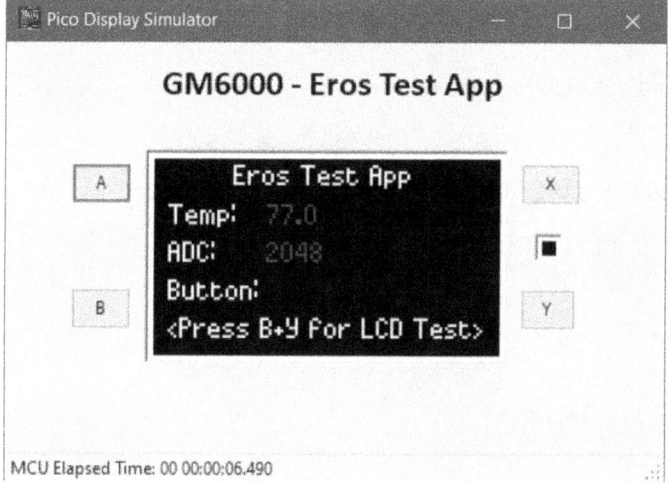

Figure B-3. Simulated display with Eros application

The epc repository contains a pre-built simulated display in the following directory:

projects\pico-display-simulator\simulator\bin\Release

APPENDIX B   RUNNING THE EXAMPLE CODE

The C# Visual Studio solution for the simulated display is located in following directory:

projects\pico-display-simulator

When running the functional simulator on a Windows host, there is a helper script named go.bat that launches both the simulated display and the functional simulator together. It is found in the Eros build directory.

Example output:

```
c:\work \epc\projects\GM6000\Eros\simulator\windows\vc12>go.bat
Launching display simulator...

Waiting for 1 seconds, press a key to continue ...

>> 00 00:00:00.122 (METRICS) METRICS:POWER_ON. Boot count = 2

--- Your friendly neighborhood TShell. ---

>> 00 00:00:02.161 (INFO) User Record size:         14 (30)
>> 00 00:00:02.161 (INFO) Metrics Record size:      39 (55)
>> 00 00:00:02.163 (INFO) Personality Record size: 193 (209)
>> 00 00:00:02.166 (INFO) Log Entry size:          159
$$>
```

Hardware Target

The Eros application can execute on the STM32 and Adafruit evaluation boards without any extra hardware such as the display board, EEPROM, temperature sensor, etc. However, depending on what the missing hardware is, the functionality of the application will be restricted.
Figure B-1 is a block diagram of the hardware for the GM6000's pancake control board.

Screen Test

The Eros application contains an LCD screen test to check for stuck and dead pixels. The screen test cycles through a series of screens with a single solid color (red, green, blue, black, and white). The LCD test is started by pressing the B+Y button simultaneously and then pressing any button to cycle through the different color screens.

Console Commands

This section covers the basic debug console commands used with the Eros application. The Eros application contains most of the console commands that the Ajax application supports, plus additional commands that directly exercise the electrical and physical components of the system. The commands and behavior are the same whether running on the target or the functional simulator. A full list of console commands (supported at runtime) can always be obtained by using the help command, for example, help, help *, or help <cmd>.

Example output:

```
$$> help
bye [app [<exitcode>]]
dm ls [<filter>]
dm write {<mp-json>}
dm read <mpname>
dm touch <mpname>
help [* | <cmd>]
hws
log [*|<max>]
log <nth> (*|<max>)
log clear
mapp
```

APPENDIX B   RUNNING THE EXAMPLE CODE

```
mapp start <mapp> [<args...>]
mapp stop <mapp>|ALL
mapp ls
nv ERASE
nv read <startOffSet> <len>
nv write <startOffset> <bytes...>
nv test (aa|55|blank)
prov <modelNumber> <serialNumber> <consolePwd> <h-outS>
<h-maxY> <h-errS> <h-dErrS> <h-outK0> <h-outK1> <h-outK2>
<h-outK3> <h-outK4> <fanLow> <fanMed> <fanHi> <maxCap>
pwm (heater|fan) <dutycycle%>
pwm backlight    <brightnes>
rgb off
rgb <red> <green> <blue>
rgb <brightness>
rnd <numBytes>
threads
tprint ["<text>"]
trace [on|off]
trace section (on|off) <sect1> [<sect2>]...
trace threadfilters [<threadname1> [<threadname2>]]...
trace level (none|brief|info|verbose|max)
trace here|revert
ui <event>
```

Hardware Outputs and Inputs

The following commands are used to directly drive the PWM output signals and to monitor the hardware high-temperature-safety circuit input to the MCU.

APPENDIX B RUNNING THE EXAMPLE CODE

```
pwm heater 33        // Set heater PWM duty cycle to 33%
pwm fan 80           // Set fan PWM duty cycle to 80%
pwm backlight 200    // Set LCD Backlight to 78% brightness level
rgb 0 255 0          // Sets the RGB LED to green
rgb 200              // Sets the RBB LED brigthness to 78% brightness level
hws                  // Display the high-temperature-safety input signal
```

Example output:

```
$$> pwm heater 33
$$> # On the simulator, read the mocked output value. 100%=65535
$$> dm read mockedHeaterPwmOut
{
  "name": "mockedHeaterPwmOut",
  "valid": true,
  "type": "Cpl::Dm::Mp::Uint32",
  "seqnum": 3,
  "locked": false,
  "val": 21626
}
$$> pwm fan 50
$$> # On the simulator, read the mocked output value.
100%=65535
$$> dm read mockedFanPwmOut
{
  "name": "mockedFanPwmOut",
  "valid": true,
  "type": "Cpl::Dm::Mp::Uint32",
  "seqnum": 4,
```

APPENDIX B   RUNNING THE EXAMPLE CODE

```
    "locked": false,
    "val": 32767
}
$$> rgb 0 255 0
RGB Color set to: 0 255 0
$$> rgb 200
Brightness set to: 200
$$> hws
HW Safety Limited Tripped: deasserted
$$>
```

Micro Applications

The Eros application contains a collection of micro applications. After a micro application is started, the micro application runs in the background until stopped. Meanwhile, other console commands can be issued while the micro application is running. The console command mapp is used to run and stop the micro applications. More than one micro application can be running at a time. The syntax for the mapp command is as follows:

```
$$> help mapp
mapp
mapp start <mapp> [<args...>]
mapp stop <mapp>|ALL
mapp ls
  Asynchronously starts/stops individual MApps (micro
  applications).  Issuing the command without arguments
  displays the list of running MApps

$$> mapp ls
AVAILABLE MApps:
cycle
Duty Cycles the Heating equipment.
```

APPENDIX B   RUNNING THE EXAMPLE CODE

```
args: [<heatpwm> <fanpwm> [<ontimems> <offtimems> [<repeat>]]]
  <heatpwm>    duty cycle % for the heater PWM. Default: 100
  <fanpwm>     duty cycle % for the fan PWM. Default: 100
  <ontimems>   duration (in msec) for the equipment
               on.  Default: 60000
  <offtimems>  duration (in msec) for the equipment off.
               Default: 60000
  <repeat>     Number of times to repeat the duty cycle.
               Default: 5

thermistor
Periodically Samples temperature and displays sample/
metric values.
args: [<displayms>]
  <displayms>  milliseconds between outputs. Default is 10000ms
$$>
```

The cycle micro application is used to exercise the heating element and fan by running *N* on/off cycles. For example, the following command runs ten on/off cycles where the on and off times are three minutes and one minute, respectively, and the heater and fan PWM signals (during an on cycle) are 90% and 85%.

```
$$> mapp start cycle 90 85 180000 60000 10
>> 00 00:55:04.570 (MApp) Starting: cycle
>> 00 00:55:04.570 (MApp) cycle: Configuration: hpwm=90
   fpwm=85, onTime=180000, offTime=60000, repeat=10
>> 00 00:55:04.570 (MApp) ON  Cycle#1. HPWM=90 , FPWM=85 ,
   OnTime=180000
>> 00 00:58:05.210 (MApp) OFF Cycle#1. OffTime=60000
>> 00 00:59:05.718 (MApp) ON  Cycle#2. HPWM=90 , FPWM=85 ,
   OnTime=180000
>> 00 01:02:06.400 (MApp) OFF Cycle#2. OffTime=60000
```

APPENDIX B RUNNING THE EXAMPLE CODE

```
$$> mapp stop cycle
>> 00 01:02:41.956 (MApp) Stopping: cycle
$$>
```

When running the `cycle` micro application on the Eros functional simulator, the temperature value is only displayed if it actually changes. This means that the developer must manually set the mocked ADC values for the temperature sensor using the `dm write` command to the `mockedADCBits` model point to see new temperature value displayed.

The `thermistor` micro application is used to monitor the temperature sensor inputs over time. For example, this command monitors the current values of the temperature inputs and outputs every three seconds until the micro application is stopped.

```
$$> mapp start thermistor 3000
>> 00 00:00:27.010 (MApp) Starting: thermistor
>> 00 00:00:27.010 (MApp) thermistor: Configuration:
   displayMs=3000 ms
>> 00 00:00:27.011 (MApp) thermistor: 'F= 77.5 (77.5 77.5
   -21474836.4), ADC= 2020 (2020 2020    0)
>> 00 00:00:30.434 (MApp) thermistor: 'F= 77.2 (77.2 77.1
   77.2), ADC= 2037 (2033 2020 2039)
>> 00 00:00:33.434 (MApp) thermistor: 'F= 77.1 (77.2 77.1
   77.2), ADC= 2041 (2035 2020 2041)
>> 00 00:00:36.434 (MApp) thermistor: 'F= 77.1 (77.2 77.1
   77.2), ADC= 2039 (2036 2020 2041)
```

```
>> 00 00:00:39.434 (MApp) thermistor: 'F= 77.1 (77.2 77.1
   77.2), ADC= 2039 (2037 2020 2042)
$$> mapp stop thermistor
>> 00 00:00:40.307 (MApp) Stopping: thermistor
$$>
```

EEPROM Testing

The nv console command is used to test and erase the nonvolatile storage in the off-board EEPROM. Here is the syntax for the nv command:

```
$$> help nv
nv ERASE
nv read <startOffSet> <len>
nv write <startOffset> <bytes...>
nv test (aa|55|blank)
  Exercises and tests the NV media.  The supported tests are:
    'aa'    - Writes (and verifies) 0xAA to all of the media
    '55'    - Writes (and verifies) 0x55 to all of the media
    'blank' - Verify if the media is 'erased'

# Example using the nv command to write and then read back 3
bytes to offset 640.
$$> nv write 640 1 2 3
wrote 3 bytes at offset 640
$$> nv read 640 3
01 02 03
$$>
```

APPENDIX B   RUNNING THE EXAMPLE CODE

Common Commands

The following console commands are also available in the Ajax application. See the "Ajax Application" section for example usage of the commands.

- bye—Exits or restarts the application
- dm—Operates on model point instances
- log—Views and clears the application's log entries
- threads—Displays the running threads
- trace—Controls and filters the printf tracing output
- ui—Triggers UI events

APPENDIX C

Introduction to the Data Model Architecture

The Data Model architecture is used to design highly decoupled code. It allows for the exchange of data between modules where neither module has dependencies on the other. For example, Figure C-1 illustrates a strongly coupled design.

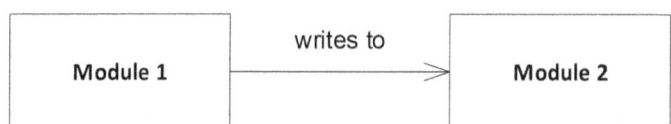

Figure C-1. *Strongly coupled design*

However, Figure C-2 illustrates how, by using the Data Model pattern, the design can be decoupled.

APPENDIX C   INTRODUCTION TO THE DATA MODEL ARCHITECTURE

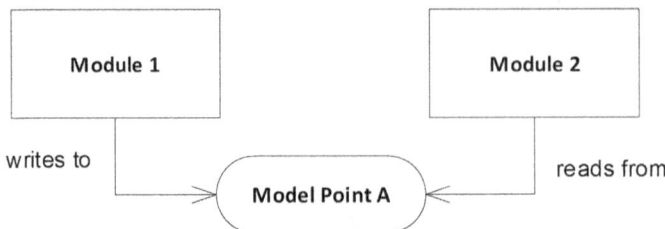

Figure C-2. Decoupled design using the Data Model pattern

In the decoupled design, both modules are passed a reference to Model Point A in their constructors or during initialization. While this may seem like you're introducing an unnecessary layer of abstraction, in reality, you're giving your design the following advantages:

- It makes it easier to extend existing functionality without modifying existing source code. For example, you could extend the preceding design by introducing a third module that takes the output of Module 1 and modifies it for input to Module 2. In this case, we would only need to create a new model point (Point AA). In Figure C-3, Module 3 is passed a reference to Model Point A and Model Point AA in its constructor or during initialization. The emphasis here is that even though there has been a feature change, the original Module 1 and Module 2 do not need to be rewritten. The only change would be to the code that constructs or initializes Module 2 so that it is passed a reference to Model Point AA (instead of Model Point A).

APPENDIX C   INTRODUCTION TO THE DATA MODEL ARCHITECTURE

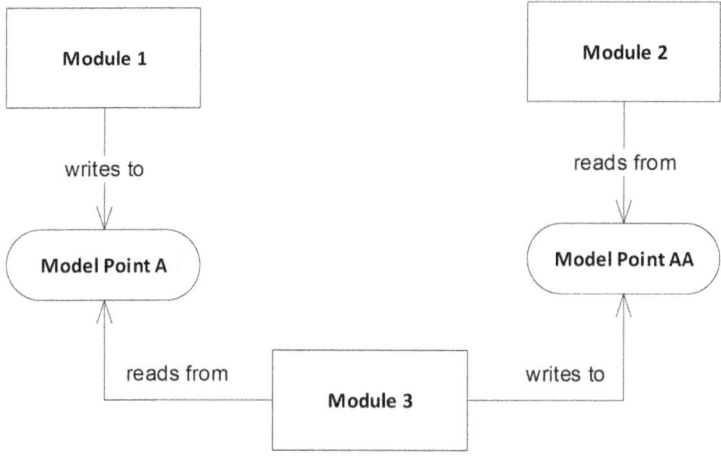

Figure C-3. Extending your design using the Data Model pattern

- It breaks up what might normally be a sequential bottom-up, or top-down, development process and facilitates parallel development, which is what allows you to add additional programmers to a project and have them actually contribute to shortening your development schedule.
- It simplifies the construction of unit tests.
- It simplifies writing platform-independent and compiler-independent source code.
- It simplifies the construction of a functional simulator.
- It creates a large number of reusable modules.

APPENDIX C INTRODUCTION TO THE DATA MODEL ARCHITECTURE

In the Data Model architecture, the modules or components interact with each other with no direct dependencies on each other. A well-defined model point will have the following features:

- Model points support any primitive data type or any data structure as their value. A model point's value should be strictly data and should not contain business rules or enforce policies (except for discrete, self-contained operations like value range checking).

- Individual model points are type specific with respect to their value. That is, all read/write operations are type safe.

- Model points have atomic operations that read or write their values. This means that accessing model point values is a thread-safe operation.

- Model points have valid or invalid states that are independent of their value.

- Model points provide a subscription mechanism for client entities to receive change notifications when the value of a model point changes or transitions to or from a valid state.

More Details

Additional resources for the Data Model architecture:

- Chapters 9 and 15 in *Patterns in the Machine: A Software Engineering Guide to Embedded Development*

- The following blog post details how change notifications are implemented:

    https://patternsinthemachine.net/2022/12/data-mode-change-notifications/.

APPENDIX D

LHeader and LConfig Patterns

The LHeader and LConfig patterns are two C/C++ patterns that leverage the preprocessor for compile-time binding of interface definitions. The patterns allow creating different flavors of your project based on compile-time settings. While it does add some additional complexity to the structure of your header files and build scripts, it also provides a reliable way to cleanly build multiple variants of your binary.

This appendix describes how to implement and use LHeader and LConfig patterns. A detailed discussion of why you would use these patterns is outside the scope of the book. For an in-depth discussion of the "why" and the importance of late binding times, I refer you to the companion book: *Patterns in the Machine: A Software Engineering Guide to Embedded Development*.[3]

LHeader

With the Late Header, or *LHeader*, pattern, you defer which header files are actually included until compile time. In this way, the name bindings don't occur until compile time. This decoupling makes the module more

---

[3] John Taylor and Wayne Taylor. *Patterns in the Machine: A Software Engineering Guide to Embedded Development*. Apress Publishers, 2021

APPENDIX D LHEADER AND LCONFIG PATTERNS

independent and reusable, and it simplifies the construction of unit tests. The original motivation for creating the LHeader pattern was to create compiler or platform-independent C code without using #ifdef/#else constructs in the source code files for each different platform that the source code is compiled for. The principal mechanism for this pattern is the C/C++ compiler's header search path options. That is, I deliberately remove path information from the header files and then wait until build time to supply it.

The LHeader pattern has four major components to it:

1. When creating a source code file, use a #include statement without any path information that references a header file that does not resolve to any header file in the baseline set of header search file paths. The file that is ultimately included at compile time is responsible for resolving the deferred name bindings in the source file. For example:

   ```
   #include "colony_map.h"     // Note: no path specified
   ```

2. Deferred name bindings are created by defining a preprocessor symbol that maps to another, yet to be resolved, symbol name. For example:

   ```
   /** Defer the definition of the a raw mutex type to the
       application's 'platform'
    */
   #define Cpl_System_Mutex_T       Cpl_System_Mutex_T_MAP
   ```

3. Then on a per-project basis—that is, in the build scripts for a specific project—a project-specific search path is added that allows the partial #include reference to be resolved to a project-specific instance of the header file name. For example, when

APPENDIX D LHEADER AND LCONFIG PATTERNS

building with the Visual Studio compiler, you can specify the compiler header search path using the -I command-line option.

Here are the compiler header search paths that are used for building the GM600 example application simulator. In this example, `project\GM600\Ajax\simulator\windows\vc12` is the build directory.

```
-I\_workspaces\zoe\epc\src
-I\_workspaces\zoe\epc\projects\GM6000\Ajax\simulator\windows\vc12
```

4. A per-project header file is created that resolves the deferred name bindings. This is illustrated in this snippet of the `colony_map.h` file located in the `projects\GM6000\Ajax\simulator\windows\vc12` directory.

```
// Platform mapping
#include "Cpl/Text/_mappings/_vc12/strapi.h"

// Cpl::System mappings
#include "Cpl/System/Win32/mappings_.h"
```

The `#include` statements in the `colony_map.h` header file pull in specific mappings that resolve the `Cpl::Text` and `Cpl::System` interfaces. This is illustrated in this snippet of the `Cpl/Text/strapi.h` file.

```
/** Same as strcasecmp, but only compares up to 'n' bytes. It
    has the same semantics as strncmp.

    Prototype:
        int strncasecmp(const char *s1, const char *s2,
        size_t n);
 */
#define strncasecmp             strncasecmp_MAP
```

355

APPENDIX D LHEADER AND LCONFIG PATTERNS

The `Cpl/Text/_mappings/_vc12/strapi.h` resolves the mapping when building with the Visual Studio compiler:

```
#define strcasecmp_MAP          _stricmp
```

Implementation Example

The CPL C++ library implements the LHeader pattern for deferring the concrete Mutex type. It relies on the *Patterns in the Machine* (PIM) best practices for file organization and `#include` best practices.

1. The header file name `colony_map.h` is a reserved header file name. No other module, class, interface, etc., can use this file name.

2. All `#include` statements (except for the LHeader `#include "colony_map.h"`) are relative to the `src/` directory. That is, path information is always part of `#include` statements. This means that there will not be an unintentional inclusion of the `colony_map.h` file.

3. The `colony.*` repositories use the NQBP build system. A feature of the NQBP build system is that all projects and unit test builds are performed in separate directory trees from the `src/` directory tree. Each project and unit test build script is customized by adding its build directory—the directory where the executable image is compiled and linked—to the compiler's header search path. This provides a unique per-project header search path. See Appendix F, "NQBP2 Build System," for additional details.

APPENDIX D LHEADER AND LCONFIG PATTERNS

4. An instance of the colony_map.h header file is placed in each of the aforementioned build directories. The content of each colony_map.h header is a collection of #include statements (which reference files under the src/ tree) that resolve the deferred name binding.

The src/Cpl/System/Mutex.h header file defines a concrete mutex that has deferred binding.

```
#ifndef Cpl_System_Mutex_h_
#define Cpl_System_Mutex_h_

#include "colony_map.h"

/** Defer the definition of the a raw mutex type to the
    application's 'platform'
 */
#define Cpl_System_Mutex_T          Cpl_System_Mutex_T_MAP

...
#endif // end Header latch
```

APPENDIX D   LHEADER AND LCONFIG PATTERNS

Figure D-1 illustrates how the deferred name binding is resolved.

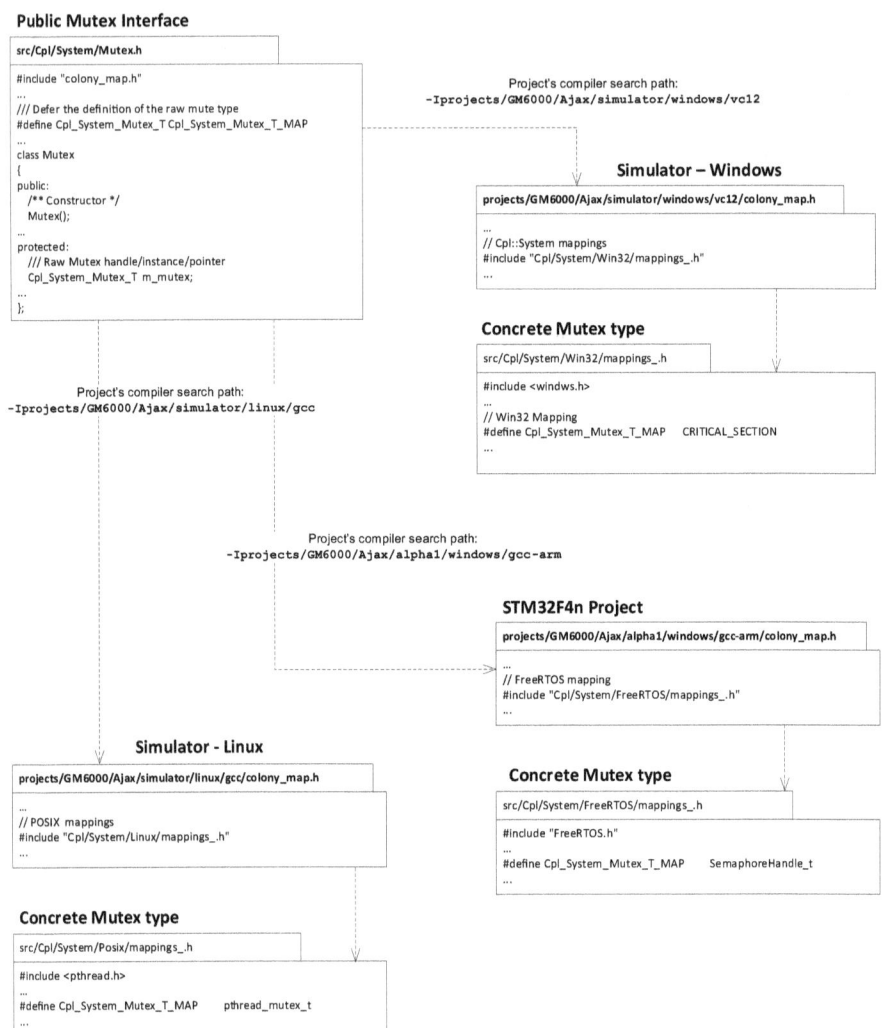

Figure D-1. *How deferred name bindings are resolved*

APPENDIX D   LHEADER AND LCONFIG PATTERNS

Caveat Implementor

The implementation described previously works well most of the time. Where it breaks down is when interface A defers a type definition using the LHeader pattern and interface B also defers a type definition using the LHeader pattern and interface B has a dependency on interface A. This use case results in a "cyclic header #include" scenario, and the compile will fail. If you are using C++, this use case typically does not occur. However, with C code, you will run into it, although it is not a frequent occurrence. When this use case is encountered in either C++ or C, the following constraints are imposed:

- The project-specific reserved header file (e.g., colony_map.h) shall only contain #include statements to other header files. Furthermore, this reserved header file (e.g., colony_map.h) shall not have a header latch (i.e., no #ifndef MY_HEADER_FILE construct at the top or bottom of the header file).

- The header files—which are included by the project-specific colony_map.h header file and which resolve the name bindings—shall have an additional symbol check in their header latch. The additional symbol check is for the header latch symbol of the module file that originally declared the name whose binding is being deferred. For example, the extra symbol check for the src/Cpl/System/Win32/mappings.h file would be

    ```
    // Header latch symbol from the Mutex interface
    #ifdef  Cpl_System_Mutex_h_

    // Traditional header latch for my file
    #ifndef Cpl_System_Win32_mappings_h_
    #define Cpl_System_Win32_mappings_h_
    ```

```
...
#endif // end header latch
#endif // end interface latch
```

The conventions described previously are only required when there are nested deferred typedefs. In the example code, the actual `Cpl/System/Win32/mappings.h` header file does not use the extra interface latch because none of the `Cpl::System` interfaces have nested deferred typedefs. Nevertheless, it is recommended that you always follow the "no header latch in the reserved header file" rule. It has minimal downside, and if you do find yourself with nested deferred typedefs, you won't get frustrated with failed compiles because you forgot to remove the header latch in the reserved header file. Diagnosing compile-time failures due to "cyclic header `#include`" statements is usually very frustrating. It is something you want to avoid.

LConfig

The Late Config, or *LConfig*, pattern is a specialized case of the LHeader pattern that is used exclusively for configuration. The LConfig pattern provides for project-specific header files that contain preprocessor directives or symbol definitions that customize the default behavior of the source code.

The LConfig pattern uses a globally unique header file name, and it relies on a per-project unique header search path to select a project-specific configuration. That is, it uses the same basic mechanisms as the LHeader pattern; however, LConfig is not used for resolving deferred function and type name bindings. Rather, LConfig is used to define, or configure, magic constants and preprocessor directives for conditionally compiled code. The CPL C++ library uses the reserved file name `colony_config.h` for the LConfig pattern. The following are examples of the LConfig pattern:

APPENDIX D LHEADER AND LCONFIG PATTERNS

Symbol definition in the src/ tree

```
#include "colony_config.h"          // LConfig pattern reserved header file

// Actual size value be overridden at compile using LConfig
#ifndef OPTION_FOO_BAR_MAX_BUFFER_SIZE
#define OPTION_FOO_BAR_MAX_BUFFER_SIZE      128
#endif
...
uint8_t my_buffer[OPTION_FOO_BAR_MAX_BUFFER_SIZE];
...
```

Configuration in the src/ tree

```
#include "colony_config.h"          // LConfig pattern reserved header file
...
// Defined in colony_config.h to enable tracing
#ifdef USE_CPL_SYSTEM_TRACE
...
#define CPL_SYSTEM_TRACE_MSG(sect, var_args)        do { ... } while(0)
...
#else
...
#define CPL_SYSTEM_TRACE_MSG(sect, var_args)
...
#endif // end USE_CPL_SYSTEM_TRACE
```

Example colony_config.h (in a project directory)

```
#ifndef COLONY_CONFIG_H
#define COLONY_CONFIG_H

// Make the buffer small to simply testing
#define OPTION_FOO_BAR_MAX_BUFFER_SIZE      5
```

APPENDIX D LHEADER AND LCONFIG PATTERNS

```
// Enable tracing (for debugging my unit test)
#define USE_CPL_SYSTEM_TRACE

#endif
```

Because the LConfig pattern is only used to define magic constants and preprocessor directives, it does not suffer from the potential circular header includes found in LHeader.

APPENDIX E

CPL C++ Framework

The CPL C++ framework is a class library where most of the code was developed for embedded software development. As such, it was designed to meet the constrained environment of embedded programming. The most obvious characteristic of the framework is its obsession with deterministic memory management and strict type checking. Another predominate theme in the CPL library is that it is completely decoupled from any specific target environment or compiler toolchains. The CPL library provides a small but robust Operating System Abstraction layer (OSAL) that is regularly built using multiple compilers.

The CPL framework, `colony.core`, is located on GitHub.[4] However, a snapshot of the CPL framework is integrated into this book's GM6000 example source code[5] using the Outcast[6] tool. The Outcast tool allows the `colony.core` repository to be overlaid into the root `src/` directory (thus reducing the complexity of the header paths).

The source code for the CPL framework is build system agnostic; it has no dependencies on a particular build engine. However, I only provide build scripts for the NQBP2 build system (see Appendix F, "NQBP2 Build System").

---

[4] https://github.com/johnttaylor/colony.core
[5] https://github.com/johnttaylor/epc/
[6] https://github.com/johnttaylor/Outcast

APPENDIX E   CPL C++ FRAMEWORK

Because the CPL framework is platform agnostic, many of the interfaces use the *LHeader* and *LConfig* patterns. Before diving too deeply into the CPL framework source code, I recommend reviewing these patterns in Appendix D, "LHeader and LConfig Patterns."

Running Doxygen[7] against the code base is part of the CI setup for the epc repository. The Doxygen output includes the CPL library as well as the example GM6000 application. The Doxygen output is available online here: https://johnttaylor.github.io/epc/namespaces.html.

The CPL C++ framework assumes UTF-8 byte encoding for strings. That is, it has not been internationalized for double-byte encodings per character.

Organization and Namespaces

The CPL source code is organized by component dependencies, or, said another way, organized by namespaces. By having the dependencies reflected in the directory structure, it provides a quick and visual sanity check to avoid undesired and cyclical dependencies. The principal directory structure maps directly to the namespace structure of code (along with some organizational, non-namespace directories that start with leading underscores).

---

[7] Doxygen is a documentation generator and static analysis tool for software source trees. The Doxygen output for the CPL framework is viewable online at https://johnttaylor.github.io/epc/namespaces.html

APPENDIX E   CPL C++ FRAMEWORK

About src/Cpl

Figure E-1 shows the directory structure of `src/Cpl`, and the following sections describe these directories and their associated namespaces for the CPL framework in the `colony.core` GitHub repository.

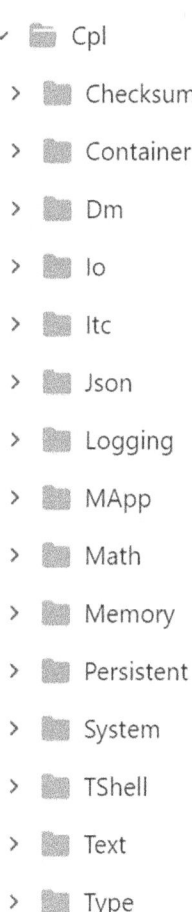

Figure E-1. Top-level directory structure of the CPL framework

APPENDIX E   CPL C++ FRAMEWORK

Checksum

The `Cpl::Checksum` namespace provides classes for various types of checksum, CRC, hashes, etc. The Checksum namespace does not contain an exhaustive collection of algorithms because these are only added in a just-in-time fashion. That is, new algorithms are only added when there is an explicit need for a new checksum or CRC algorithm.

Container

The `Cpl::Container` namespace provides various types of containers. What makes the CPL different from the C++ STL library or traditional containers is that the CPL containers use an intrusive listing mechanism. This means that every item that is put into a container has all the memory and fields that are necessary to be in the container. No memory is allocated when an item is inserted into a container, and all of the containers can contain an infinite number of items (RAM permitting). There are two major side effects of intrusive containers:

1. All items or classes that are put into containers must inherit from the base class `Cpl::Container::Item`.

2. A given item or instance can be in only one container at any given time.

The following are the currently supported types of containers. All of the containers are template classes so that the interfaces are type safe with respect to the items they contain.

- Singly linked list (`Cpl::Container::SList`)
- Stack with a fixed depth (`Cpl::Container::Stack`)
- Doubly linked list (`Cpl::Container::DList`)

- Hash table, or dictionary (`Cpl::Container::Dictionary`)
- AVL Binary tree, or sorted map (`Cpl::Container::Map`)
- Ring buffers (`Cpl::Container::RingBuffer`, `Cpl::Container::RingBufferMP`, `Cpl::Container::RingBufferMT`)

Data Model

The `Cpl::Dm` namespace provides a framework for the Data Model pattern. The Data Model software architecture pattern defines how modules interact with each other through data instances, or model points, with no direct dependencies between modules. See Appendix C, "Introduction to the Data Model Architecture," for an introduction to the Data Model pattern.

Model Point Types

The Data Model namespace currently provides the following model point types. **Note:** All model points are type safe. That is, each data type requires its own specific "data model point" type.

- `Cpl::Dm::Mp::Bool`
- `Cpl::Dm::Mp::Int32|64`
- `Cpl::Dm::Mp::Uint32|64`
- `Cpl::Dm::Mp::Float|Double`
- `Cpl::Dm::Mp::ElapsedPrecisionTime`
- `Cpl::Dm::Mp::RefCounter`
- `Cpl::Dm::Mp::Void`

- `Cpl::Dm::Mp::BitArray16`
- `Cpl::Dm::Mp::ArrayUint8|32|64`
- `Cpl::Dm::Mp::ArrayInt8|32|64`
- `Cpl::Dm::Mp::String<S>` where S is length of the string without the null terminator
- Base class for an enum that is defined as BETTER_ENUM[8] (`Cpl::Dm::Mp::Enum_`)

Persistent Storage

The Data Model namespace provides a mechanism for persistently storing model points (see `Cpl::Dm::Persistent`). One or more model points are grouped into a record, which is the atomic unit for reading and writing to nonvolatile storage. Persistently storing records relies on the `Cpl::Persistent` namespace. The `Cpl::Persistent` namespace implements a storage paradigm where data is only read from nonvolatile storage on startup and then written to nonvolatile storage at runtime.

TShell

The Data Model namespace provides a `Cpl::TShell` console command for interactively accessing model point instances at runtime (see `Cpl::Dm::TShell`). The dm command supports reading, writing, invalidating, and locking model points at runtime. The following snippet illustrates how to write and read a model point:

---

[8] BETTER ENUM is a single, lightweight header file that makes your compiler generate reflective enum types, that is, enums that can be serialized to and from text symbols.

```
$> dm write {name:"heatingMode",val:true}
$> dm read heatingMode
{
  "name": "heatingMode",
  "valid": true,
  "type": "Cpl::Dm::Mp::Bool",
  "seqnum": 2,
  "locked": false,
  "val": true
}
```

Io

The Cpl::Io namespace provides the base and common interfaces for reading and writing data from and to streams and files. Essentially the Cpl::Io namespaces provide platform-independent interfaces for operations that would typically be done using POSIX file descriptors or Windows file handles.

Serial Ports

The Cpl::Io::Serial namespace contains serial port drivers that conform to the Cpl::Io::InputOutput interface. Typically, the stream implementations have blocking/waiting semantics for reading and writing data.

While these serial port drivers are specific to serial port hardware, they are not specific to a particular board. For example, the Cpl::Io::Serial::ST::M32F4::InputOutput class is usable (without modifications) on any STM32 microcontroller that has a UART peripheral that is compatible with the UART peripheral on an STM32F4 microcontroller.

APPENDIX E   CPL C++ FRAMEWORK

Sockets

The `Cpl::Io::Socket` namespace contains support for creating and using target-operating-system-independent BSD socket connections. The `Socket` namespace provides a simple TCP listener using a dedicated listener thread as well as separate simple TCP connector.

Files

The `Cpl::Io::File` namespace contains basic support for creating, opening, reading, and writing files as well as file operations such as deleting and moving files, creating and deleting directories, traversing a directory's contents, etc. The `File` namespace is operating system independent and provides a standardized directory separator across platforms.

Itc

The `Cpl::Itc` namespace provides interfaces and implementation for message-based inter-thread communication (ITC). The ITC interfaces are built on top of the OSAL so they are platform independent. The message passing design has the following characteristics:

- The model is a client-server model, where clients send messages to servers.

  - Servers are required to execute in an event loop–based thread.

  - Clients sending messages asynchronously are required to execute in an event loop–based thread.

  - Clients sending messages synchronously can execute in any type of thread, but they must execute in a different thread than the server receiving the message.

APPENDIX E   CPL C++ FRAMEWORK

- Messages can be sent asynchronously or synchronously.

- Data flow between clients and server can be unidirectional or bidirectional as determined by the application. Because this is inter-thread communication, data can be shared via pointers since clients and servers share the same address space.

- Data is shared between clients and server using the concept of a "payload." In addition, a "convention of ownership" is used to provide thread-safe access to the payload.

    - A client initially owns the payload. That is, it can access the data in the payload without the use of critical sections.

    - When a client sends or posts a message, there is implicit transfer of the payload ownership. After sending the message, the client is obligated to not access the payload contents.

    - When a server receives a message, the server now owns the payload and can access the data in the payload without the use of critical sections.

    - When a server returns a message, there is implicit transfer of ownership of the payload back to the client. After returning the message, the server is obligated to not access the payload contents.

- No dynamic memory is used. Clients are responsible for providing all of the memory required for the individual messages. This means there are no hard limits to the number of messages a server can receive.

It also means that the application does not have to worry about overflowing message queues or mailboxes. Another side effect of this memory paradigm is that there are no broadcast messages.

- Data sent is 100% type safe. Messages and payloads are handled and dispatched with no typecasting required.

The CPL library also provides two other forms of inter-thread communications. One is the Data Model's change notifications, and the other is the OSAL event flags. All forms of ITC are compatible. That is, a single application can use all, none, or some of the ITC mechanisms as needed.

Json

The `Cpl::Json` namespace encapsulates the *ArduinoJson*[9] C++ JSON library. The ArduinoJson library was chosen because of the following:

- It has a fairly intuitive C++ interface for parsing and constructing JSON objects.

- While integrating seamlessly with the Arduino framework, it is not dependent on the Arduino framework.

- It has support for statically allocated JSON documents. That is, it does no dynamic memory allocation when parsing or constructing JSON objects. The CPL library uses version 6.x of the ArduinoJson library, as version 7.x deprecated statically allocated documents.

---

[9] https://github.com/bblanchon/ArduinoJson

Logging

The `Cpl::Logging` namespace provides a framework for logging events. While the bulk of code necessary for logging is part of the framework, the application is required to provide the definition of the logging categories and message identifiers and required to manage the persistent storage for the log messages. The framework provides the following features:

- The interface is thread safe.
- When an entry is logged, it is timestamped. The application is required to provide the implementation of the timestamp interface.
- Each entry logged has a Category and a Message identifier. The Category identifier is required to be globally unique across all logged items. Message identifiers are per Category and are only unique within a Category. The application is responsible for defining these identifiers.
- A log entry contains the following:
  - Timestamp
  - Category ID
  - Message ID
  - Text (interface uses `printf` semantics when creating a log entry)
- The logging framework supports selectively enabling/disabling logging by category. Log entries for disabled categories are silently discarded.

APPENDIX E CPL C++ FRAMEWORK

- When trace is enabled, log entries are echoed to the CPL trace engine. The category identifier text is used as the trace section identifier.

- The framework supports caching log entries before the application's persistent storage media are available.

- The application is responsible for storing log entries to persistent storage media. The logging framework dispatches each log entry to a thread-safe FIFO queue. It is the application's responsibility to consume the entries from the FIFO queue and to record them in persistent storage. The FIFO supports change notifications via a model point (see `Cpl::Containers::RingBufferMP`).

    - The log entry data structure inherits from the `Cpl::Persistent::Payload` interface. The Payload interface defines two methods to serialize and deserialize the log entry data structure. While this introduces a dependency on the `Cpl::Persistent` namespace, the Payload interface definition has no other dependencies. That is, the application is **not** required to use the `Cpl::Persistent` namespace for storing log entries to persistent media.

- The log entry FIFO queue can overflow if the application is not storing log entries faster than the application is generating entries. When this happens, the framework discards log entries until space frees up in the queue. The framework tracks how many log entries were discarded and generates a special log entry with the details once there is free space in the log queue.

MApp

The Cpl::MApp namespace provides framework for asynchronously running micro applications. A micro application can be anything. The original use case for the MApp framework was to support being able to selectively run, stop, pause, and resume a set of tests used for board checkout testing, end-of-line manufacturing testing, emissions testing, design validation testing, etc., from the TShell console.

A rough analog for a micro application would be launching a console command to execute in the background.

Math

The Cpl::Math namespace provides classes, utilities, etc., related to numeric operation. Most notably it provides almostEqual methods for comparing float and double values.[10]

Memory

The Cpl::Memory namespace provides a collection of interfaces that allow an application to manually manage dynamic memory independent of the actual heap. The memory allocated using the Memory namespace requires the application to use the C++ "placement new" operator when constructing C++ objects. For example, the Cpl::Memory::SPool template class statically allocates memory for *N* instances of an object of type *M*. The application calls the SPool class's allocate() and release() methods to request and free memory for dynamically creating objects of type *M* at runtime.

---

[10] For a discussion of why an almostEqual function is necessary, refer to https://randomascii.wordpress.com/2012/02/25/comparing-floating-point-numbers-2012-edition/

APPENDIX E   CPL C++ FRAMEWORK

Persistent

The `Cpl::Persistent` namespace provides a basic persistent storage mechanism for nonvolatile data. The persistent subsystem has the following features:

- The subsystem organizes persistent data into records. The Application is responsible for defining the data content of record, and it is the responsibility of the concrete record instances to initiate updates to the persistent media. A record is the unit of atomic read/write operations to persistent storage.
- On startup, the records are read, and the concrete record instances process the incoming data.
- All persistently stored data is CRC'd to detect data corruption. CRCs are only validated on startup.
- When the stored data has been detected as corrupt (i.e., a bad CRC), record instances are responsible for setting their data to defaults and subsequently initiating an update to the persistent media.
- The subsystem is independent of the physical persistent storage media.
- The record server can process an unlimited number of records. It is also okay to have more than one record server instance.
- The record server is a Runnable object and a Data Model mailbox. This means it executes in its own thread. All read/write operations to the persistent media are performed in this thread. It is assumed that the business logic for individual records is also performed in this thread and that each record instance is thread safe with respect to the rest of the system.

APPENDIX E   CPL C++ FRAMEWORK

System

The `Cpl::System` namespace provides the Operating System Abstraction Layer (OSAL) as well as basic system services. The CPL library provides an implementation of the OSAL for the following platforms:

- FreeRTOS
- Bare metal. That is, there is no operating system, just a single thread or super loop
- Windows operating system
- POSIX-compliant operating system, for example, Linux
- C++11 concurrency framework

Assert

The `src/Cpl/System/assert.h` file provides a replacement for the standard `assert()` macro where the fatal error handling of a non-true `assert()` call is routed through the `Cpl::System::FatalError` interface.

Elapsed Time

The `Cpl::System::ElapsedTime` interface provides the elapsed time from power-up or reset of the target platform. The interface provides time in three formats:

- Milliseconds (as an `unsigned long`)
- Seconds (as an `unsigned long`)
- `Precision_T`, which is a data structure that contains seconds and milliseconds

The interface also contains operations to manage delta times and to check for expired time durations. In addition, the interface supports simulated time.

Event Flags

The `Cpl::System::EventFlag` interface provides an inter-thread communication mechanism that is a collection of 32 Boolean event flags. An event loop-based thread can wait on zero or more event flags to be set. Event flags are set from other threads. Event flags have the following characteristics:

- An individual event flag can be viewed as binary semaphore with respect to being signaled or waiting (though waiting is done on a thread's entire set of event flags). The event loop provides an optional mechanism to call back into the application when the event loop is unblocked and is processing the set of event flags.

- An event loop-based thread waits for at least one event flag to be signaled. When the thread is waiting on event flags, and at least one flag is signaled, then all of the events that were in the signaled state when the thread was unblocked are processed and cleared.

- Each thread supports up to 32 unique event flags. Event flags are not unique across threads. That is, the semantics associated with EventFlag1 for Thread A is independent of any semantics associated with EventFlag1 for Thread B.

Event Loop

The Cpl::System::EventLoop class is a Cpl::System::Runnable object that forms the foundation of an event-driven application thread. Event loops are essentially threads that have a super-loop that contain blocking/waiting semantics on the following entities:

- Event flags—Setting an event flag unblocks an event loop.

- Software timers—Event loops periodically unblock and check the thread's active software timer list for expired timers.

- Semaphore—Each event loop has a semaphore that can signal to unblock a waiting event loop.

Event loops are implemented so that they can be extended. For example, the Cpl::Itc::MailboxServer and Cpl::Dm::MailboxServer classes extended the waiting semantics of event loops to include ITC Message processing and Model Point change notifications.

Fatal Error Interface

The Cpl::System::FatalError interface provides a functional interface for triggering fatal error handling. The interface supports various options for passing data or error messages when triggering fatal errors. This interface includes a method with printf semantics.

The application defines how fatal error data and messages are displayed or logged, as well as what actions to take (e.g., reboot the MCU, exit the application, etc.).

APPENDIX E   CPL C++ FRAMEWORK

Global Lock

The `Cpl::System::GlobalLock` interface provides lightweight mutual exclusion operations. The interface is intended to be an abstraction for disabling/enabling global interrupts when the target platform is running an RTOS. The `GlobalLock` has following constraints:

- Nonrecursive semantics—The calling thread cannot attempt to acquire the lock a second time after it has already acquired the lock.

- The code that is protected by this lock must be very short in terms of execution time and not call any operating system methods (e.g., any `Cpl::System` methods).

Initialization and Scheduling

The `Cpl::System::Api` interface provides methods for initializing the entire CPL library as well as methods for enabling, suspending, and resuming thread scheduling. When using the CPL library, the `Cpl::System::Api::initialize()` should be called as soon as possible after the application enters its `main()` function.

The implementation of the initialization of the CPL library provides a mechanism for registering callback functions that are executed when the CPL library is initialized. In addition, there are multiple levels to the callback functions where the level determines the execution order of the callbacks. While primarily intended for internal use by the CPL library, the application and unit tests can register their own initialization callback functions as needed.

Mutexes

The Cpl::System::Mutex class provides a platform-independent recursive mutex. The CPL library assumes that support for Priority Inheritance[11] in relation to mutexes is provided by the target's underlying operating system.

Periodic Scheduler

The Cpl::System::PeriodicScheduler interface is a "policy object" that is used to provide cooperative monotonic scheduling to a Runnable object or EventLoop. The interface can also be used in an application's defined super-loop. The Cpl::Dm::PeriodicScheduler class is an example of adding periodic scheduling to an event loop.

Scheduling is polled and cooperative, and it is the application's responsibility to not overrun or over-allocate the processing done during each interval. The periodic scheduler, then, makes its best attempt at being monotonic and deterministic, but the timing cannot be guaranteed. That said, the scheduler will detect and report when the interval timing slips.

Semaphores

The Cpl::System::Semaphore class provides a platform independent counting semaphore. The semaphore interface supports wait() and timedWait() methods. Semaphores can be signaled from other threads and from interrupt service routines.

---

[11] "In real-time computing, priority inheritance is a method for eliminating unbounded priority inversion. Using this programming method, a process scheduling algorithm increases the priority of a process (A) to the maximum priority of any other process waiting for any resource on which A has a resource lock (if it is higher than the original priority of A)." Priority Inheritance, Wikipedia.

Shell

The `Cpl::System::Shell` interface provides a platform-independent mechanism to execute native OS system commands. Support for this interface is optional. For example, there is no operating system shell available when running FreeRTOS on an MCU.

Sleep

The `Cpl::System::Api::sleep()` interface provides a blocking wait with one millisecond resolution.

Shutdown

The `Cpl::System::Shutdown` interface provides methods for gracefully shutting down an application. The interface provides a mechanism for registering callback functions that are executed when the application is requested to shut down. The application is responsible for registering a shutdown callback method that executes the graceful shutdown process.

Simulated Time

The CPL library has a concept of simulated time where the timing sources for all of the OSAL methods (i.e., the `Cpl::System` interfaces) are driven by a simulated tick. For the most part, enabling and using simulated time is transparent to the application code. The one exception is that for an application using simulated time, there must be at least one thread that executes in real time that generates the actual simulation ticks, which is done by using the `Cpl::System::SimTick` class.

The primary use cases for simulated time are as follows:

- Testing—A simulated system tick allows the test harness to have deterministic control of the application's time. In addition, time can be single-stepped, paused, or accelerated (e.g., run N days in M minutes).

- Model in the Loop (MIL)—An external application such as MATLAB/Simulink[12] can be used to provide the simulated tick input as well as to capture the application's output and provide the application inputs. However, connecting an MIL application to a simulation such as MATLAB/Simulink requires a communication layer that is not provided by the CPL library.

Software Timers

The Cpl::System::Timer interface provides software-based timers. Software timers execute a callback function when they expired. The timer-expired callback function executes in the same thread where the timer was started. Software timers can only be used with event-based threads, where the thread's Runnable object is an EventLoop.

The simplest usage pattern for an application to add a timer to the class is for the class to inherit from the Cpl::System::Timer class and then provide an implementation for the timer-expired method (i.e., void expired() noexcept). If a single class requires multiple timers, then the Cpl::System::TimerComposer object can be used. The TimerComposer takes a member function pointer in its constructor, and the member function pointer is the timer instance's timer-expired callback function.

---

[12] www.mathworks.com/products/simulink.html

APPENDIX E   CPL C++ FRAMEWORK

Software timers are inherently nondeterministic because they are thread based. This means that when the timer's expired-callback function is executed, it is not guaranteed to happen at any particular time, just sometime after the amount of time specified has elapsed.

Thread-Local Storage (TLS)

The Cpl::System::Tls interface provides a platform-independent "thread-local storage" (TLS). TLS is where each thread has its own instance of a variable. The canonical example of TLS is the C error code variable errno.

Threads and Runnable Objects

The Cpl::System::Thread and Cpl::System::Runnable interface provide support for platform-independent threads. The Cpl::System::Thread class is a wrapper for an actual thread, and the Cpl::System::Runnable class is the code that is executed when the thread runs. You can think of the Runnable class as the entry function for a thread.

The Cpl::System::Thread interface has the following features:

- Symbolic names for threads
- Thread priority—Platform-independent priority values are used.
- Configurable stack size—The application can optionally specify a thread's stack size or provide the stack memory itself.
- Simulated time—When a thread is created, the application can specify if the thread uses real time (default) or simulated time.

- Thread semaphore—Each thread contains a built-in counting semaphore that is usable by the application. This semaphore can be used to assist in implementing inter-thread communications and ISR-to-thread communications.

Tracing

The src/Cpl/System/Trace.h file provides an interface for printf-like debugging. The tracing interface consists of a collection of preprocessor macros. The macros can be conditionally "compiled out" for release builds of an application. By default, the trace output is routed to stdout. However, the application can optionally route the trace messages to any output stream (i.e., to any instance of Cpl::Io::Output). The trace engine has the following features:

- Trace messages can be globally enabled or disabled at run time.
- The application can configure different levels of verbosity for the messages.
- All trace messages have an associated *Section* text label. There is no limit to the number of section labels.
- Trace messages can be filtered at run time by section label. There is a limit, which is compile time configurable, to the number of concurrent section filters.
- Trace messages can be filtered at run time by thread name. Up to four different thread filters can be applied.
- The trace output can be redirected (and reverted) at run time to an alternate output stream.

APPENDIX E   CPL C++ FRAMEWORK

- The trace output can share the same output stream as the debug shell's (Cpl::TShell) output stream. In addition, the trace messages and the TShell outputs are atomic with respect to each other. Individual trace messages do not get intermingled with the TShell outputs.
- A debug shell command (Cpl::TShell::Cmd::Trace) is provided to access and manage the trace outputs at run time.

The Trace interface design and implementation pre-dates C++11. The age of the interface is visible when using its macros with printf semantics. That is, extra sets of parentheses are required to get the variable arguments semantics to work. It was not until the C++11 that direct support for variable arguments in macros was provided.

Text

The Cpl::Text interface is yet another string class with additional string and text processing utilities. What makes the Cpl::Text::String classes different from other string classes is that they support a ZERO dynamic memory allocation interface and implementation. There is also a dynamic memory implementation of the string interface for when strict memory management is not required. The String class only supports UTF-8 encodings.

Encoding

The `Cpl::Text::Encoding` namespace provides interfaces for encoding binary data as ASCII text (e.g., as a Base64 encoding).

Formatting and Parsing

The Text namespace contains interfaces for formatting text output (`src/Cpl/Text/format.h`) and the nondestructive parsing of text strings (`src/Cpl/Text/strip.h`).

Framing

The Cpl::Text::Frame namespace provides interfaces for encoding and decoding data within a frame that has a uniquely specified start and end of frame bytes. This is similar to character-based HDLC framing.

Standardized String Operations

There are several handy-dandy C string processing functions that are part of the POSIX and BSD standards but which are not part of the C language standard. This means that depending on your compiler or target platform, they may not be available to the application. One example of these functions is `strncasecmp()`. The `src/Cpl/Text/strapi.h` header file defines several of these non-C language standard functions so that they are always available regardless of the compiler or target platform. The `strapi.h` header file uses a variation of the LHeader pattern to support different compilers and platforms. The various compilers and platforms supported can be found in the `src/Cpl/Text/_mappings/` directory.

String Class

The Cpl::Text::String is an abstract class that defines the operations for UTF-8, null-terminated string. There are several concrete implementations of the string class:

- Cpl::Text::FString<N>—A template class that statically allocates memory for a string with a maximum length of *N* bytes not including the null terminator. Attempts to write more than *N* bytes will silently truncate the write to *N* bytes. However, the class maintains an internal "truncated flag" that can be queried by the application after write operations.

- Cpl::Text:DString—A concrete class that uses the dynamic memory from the heap to allocate memory for the string contents. The class will automatically increase the memory size as needed, but it does not attempt to reduce the amount of currently allocated string memory.

- Cpl::Text::DFString—A concrete class that uses the heap to allocate the initial amount of string memory. After the initial allocation, the class behaves like the Fstring class.

Text to/from Binary

The Text namespace contains interfaces for converting numeric text to binary values (src/Cpl/Text/atob.h) and for converting binary values to text (src/Cpl/Text/btoa.h) without using the sprintf() function.

Tokenizer

The `Cpl::Text::Tokenizer` namespace contains a collection of tokenizers that parse text strings into individual tokens. The `Tokenizer` namespace does not contain an exhaustive collection of algorithms. The namespace is only added in a just-in-time fashion. That is, new algorithms are only added when there is an explicit need for a new tokenizer algorithm.

TShell

The `Cpl::TShell` namespace provides a framework for a text-based shell that can be used at run time to interact with the application. Think of this as the debug or command console. The `TShell` uses the `Cpl::Io::Input` and `Cpl::Io::Output` streams for its command input and text output, respectively. Because the `Cpl::Io` stream abstractions are used, the `TShell` can be used with the C stdio, serial ports, sockets, etc.

The `TShell` optionally supports a basic user authentication mechanism (`Cpl::TShell::Security`) that enforces a user to log in before being able to execute any `TShell` commands. The application is responsible for providing the policies for authenticating users.

The `TShell` namespace supports blocking and nonblocking read semantics for reading its inputs. The use of the blocking semantics requires a dedicated reader thread. When using nonblocking semantics, the `TShell` can be used without a dedicated thread. That is, it can be implemented as part of super-loop or executed in a shared thread.

The `TShell` output can share the same output stream as the CPL Tracing interface. The `TShell` and trace outputs are atomic with respect to each other. Individual trace messages do not get intermingled with the TShell outputs and vice versa.

APPENDIX E CPL C++ FRAMEWORK

Commands

The Cpl::TShell::Cmd namespace provides a basic set of TShell commands. The design of the commands includes a self-registering mechanism. After adding the TShell framework code to the application, individual commands are added simply by creating an instance of the command. The command's constructor registers itself with the list of available commands.

The application can optionally include any of the following commands or create its own:

- Bye—Exits the TShell and the application.
- Help—Displays a list of available commands and optionally provides detailed help.
- Threads—Displays a list of active threads (which were created using the CPL library).
- Tick—Generates simulated time ticks (see Cpl::System::SimTick for more details).
- TPrint—Prints a message (including a timestamp) to the TShell output.
- Trace—Manages the CPL Trace engine runtime settings, filters, etc.
- User—Logs the user in and out when security has been enabled.
- Wait—Pauses the TShell engine for N milliseconds. This is useful when writing automated unit tests that interact with the application via the TShell.

Type

The `Cpl::Type` namespace provides a collection of typedefs and helper classes that function as general purpose types, generic callback mechanisms, etc.

One of the most notable types is the BETTER_ENUM[13] contained in the `src/Type/enum.h` header file. Better Enum is a single, lightweight header file that makes your compiler generate reflective enum types. The principal usage for Better Enums is the ability to serialize the symbolic enum names to and from text.

About src/Bsp

The `src/Bsp` directory tree contains one concrete Board Support Package (BSP) per target board. A BSP is a layer of software that allows applications and operating systems to run on the hardware platform. The contents of a BSP depend on the hardware platform, the targeted operating system (if one is being used), and potential third-party packages that may be available for the hardware (e.g., graphics libraries). The ideal BSP for a microcontroller encapsulates

- The compiler toolchain, as it relates to the specific MCU
- The MCU's datasheet
- The target board's schematic

---

[13] Better ENUM is not native to the CPL Library; it is a third-party package created and maintained by Anton Bachin. The canonical source for Better ENUM is at https://aantron.github.io/better-enums/

APPENDIX E   CPL C++ FRAMEWORK

The BSP directory tree is an exception to the namespace organization rule. The `Bsp/` directory does not map to a literal C++ namespace. This is for two reasons:

1. A given application only has one BSP; hence, there is no possibility of name collisions between different BSP implementations. Consequently, there is no need to have unique symbols and names across many BSPs.

2. The public BSP interfaces need to be C based so that they can be used with C-based SDKs provided by the MCU vendors.

The CPL framework uses the ST NUCLEO-F413ZH evaluation board, along with the GCC ARM-M/R cross compiler, as its principal hardware target. A user space BSP is provided as part of the CPL framework, which provides a mocked BSP when building for a simulated target (i.e., the functional simulators for Windows or Linux).

About src/Driver

The `Cpl::Driver` namespace contains a collection of reusable drivers. In this context, reusable means that the driver has no direct dependencies on an MCU or a compiler. However, the driver can be specific to hardware. For example, the `Driver::Nv::Onsemi::CAT24C512` driver is specific to OnSemi's 64KB I2C EEPROM chip but is independent of whatever MCU or I2C driver is being used.

The provided drivers are a mixed bag of functionality because drivers are only added when there is an explicit need for a new one. The core CPL framework has no dependencies on the `Driver` namespace. Or, said another way, there is no requirement to use the framework's drivers when using CPL framework.

APPENDIX E   CPL C++ FRAMEWORK

Porting

Porting the CPL library to run on a new target platform involves providing platform-specific implementations of the OSAL interfaces defined in the `Cpl::System` namespace as well as additional interfaces under the `Cpl::Io` namespace. The CPL OSAL is meant to provide an abstraction for, or a decoupling of, the underlying operating system. However, the CPL OSAL does not actually require an underlying operating system. For example, the CPL library contains a bare-metal port of the OSAL, and there is a port of the OSAL that runs on Raspberry PI Pico without an RTOS. It supports two threads, one for each of the PI Pico's ARM cores. In addition, the OSAL can be ported to run in non-RTOS environments such as Windows and Linux.

There are 15 different interfaces listed here that make up the OSAL. This may sound daunting, but it's straightforward to port the individual interfaces. The exception to this is the `Threading` interface, which is the most involved when it comes to the target implementation. The recommendation is to clone one of the existing target implementations and then modify that as needed.

- Assert
- Elapsed Time
- Fatal Error
- File and Directory Management
- File and Stream IO
- Global Lock
- Mutex
- Newline
- Semaphore
- Shell

APPENDIX E   CPL C++ FRAMEWORK

- Shutdown
- System API
- Threads
- Thread-Local Storage
- Tracing

Decoupling Techniques

For the most part, the decoupling of the OSAL from the target platform is done using link time binding and the LHeader pattern.

Basically, each target platform has it own implementation of the platform-specific implementations of the OSAL interfaces. As part of the LHeader pattern, there is a mappings_.h header file that provides the target-specific mappings and data types.

Caution   If your application contains C code that is developed in-house, you should avoid putting C++-specific types or constructs in the mappings_.h header file. Not having C++ code in the mappings_.h header file allows your C code to call non-C++-specific interfaces such as the CPL Assert interface. See the FreeRTOS mappings_.h, c_assert.h, and c_assert.cpp files as examples.

Runtime Initialization

The CPL library provides a mechanism that allows modules to register for callbacks when the framework is initialized (i.e., when Cpl::System ::Api::initialize() is called). In the context of porting the OSAL, this startup feature can be used to provide runtime initialization for statically allocated instances. For example, on the Raspberry PI Pico target, the SDK's mechanism for statically creating mutexes and semaphores does not "play well" with a C++ object design. This in turn leads to the OSAL implementation having to make explicit calls after main() is invoked in order to initialize mutex and semaphore structures. However, the OSAL semantics allow for mutexes and semaphores instances to be allocated statically as their constructors execute before main() is called. For the Raspberry PI Pico implementation, these classes use the CPL startup feature to initialize their underlying SDK mutex/semaphore structures after main() is called.

The CPL library also provides a mechanism that allows modules to register for callbacks when the library is being shut down.

Interfaces

This section discusses the 15 platform-specific implementations of the OSAL interface that need to be ported. I've used simplified pseudocode in place of the actual interfaces so you need to bring up the files in an editor to follow along. As the text in this appendix will become stale over time, you should always consider the header files to be the source of truth for the OSAL interfaces.

I recommend that you select one of the existing target implementations as a template to use when porting to a new target platform.

APPENDIX E   CPL C++ FRAMEWORK

Assert

The assert interface (src/Cpl/System/assert.h) only requires a platform-specific implementation of the CPL_SYSTEM_ASSERT() macro. Typically, this macro is mapped to the Cpl::System::FatalError interface. For example:

   LHeader mapping file for the Port: mappings_.h

```
#define CPL_SYSTEM_ASSERT_MAP(e) \
   do { if ( ! (e) ) Cpl::System::FatalError::logf( "ASSERT Failed at: file=%s, line=%d, func=%s\n", \
            __FILE__, __LINE__, CPL_SYSTEM_ASSERT_PRETTY_FUNCNAME ); \
   } while(0)
```

One case where this should not be done is if your application contains C files and you want to be able to call the CPL_SYSTEM_ASSERT macro from within these files. For this case, the assert macro must map to something that is legal C code. See the FreeRTOS mappings_.h, c_assert.h, and c_assert.cpp files as examples.

Elapsed Time

The Cpl::System::ElapsedTime interface has the following methods that require a platform-specific implementation:

```
unsigned long millisecondsInRealTime( void ) noexcept;
unsigned long secondsInRealTime( void ) noexcept;
Precision_T   precisionInRealTime( void ) noexcept;
unsigned long milliseconds( void ) noexcept;
unsigned long seconds( void ) noexcept;
Precision_T   precision( void ) noexcept;
```

However, there is a default implementation of the •••InRealTime() methods so that a new target only needs to supply a basic get-elapsed-time-in-milliseconds function and then have the milliseconds(),

seconds(), and precision() methods call the corresponding
...InRealTime methods.

If you do not want to use the default implementation for the
...InRealTime() methods, provide your own implementation and do not
build the ElapsedTime2.cpp file in the src/Cpl/System/ directory.

Why are there two methods—milliseconds() and
millisecondsInRealTime()—for getting elapsed time in milliseconds?
The reason is because the CPL library and the OSAL support simulated
time. If your target platform is a non-process-based RTOS, you typically
don't have a use case for supporting simulated time, so you simply
map milliseconds(), seconds(), and precision() methods to call
the corresponding ...InRealTime() methods. If you want to support
simulated time on your target platform, use the Win32 and POSIX
implementations as a template.

Fatal Error

The Cpl::System::FatalError interface has the following methods that
require a platform-specific implementation:

```
void log( const char* message );
void log( const char* message, size_t value );
void logf( const char* format, ... );
void logRaw( const char* message );
void logRaw( const char* message, size_t value );
```

It is fairly simple to implement these methods for a new target. In
addition, the target implementation has the freedom to interpret or ignore
the semantics of the log messaging. What matters is that

1. The functions are provided.

2. They are implemented in such a way that you can set breakpoints in the function bodies when running on the target.

APPENDIX E   CPL C++ FRAMEWORK

Another nuance to the `FatalError` interface is that while it is target specific, it can also be project specific. For example, I can be using FreeRTOS on boardA/ProjectA and boardB/ProjectB, but because of the differences between the boards and MCUs, the handling of the fatal errors needs to be done differently in the two projects. To solve this, just organize your code and build scripts so that each project can select or provide its own implementation of the `FatalError` interface.

File and Directory Management

Porting the `Cpl::Io::File::Api` interface is only required if you plan on using file system operations like delete file, create directory, etc., in addition to simply reading and writing files. Porting the `Cpl::Io::File::Api` interface requires the following:

1. Provide target-specific definitions for the following symbols in your OSAL LHeader mapping file:

   CPL_IO_FILE_NATIVE_DIR_SEP
   CPL_IO_FILE_MAX_NAME

   For example:
   LHeader mapping file for the Port: `mappings_.h`

   ```
   /// Win32 Mapping
   #define CPL_IO_NEW_LINE_NATIVE_MAP       "\015\012"

   /// Win32 Mapping
   #define CPL_IO_FILE_NATIVE_DIR_SEP_MAP   '\\'
   ```

2. Provide a concrete implementation using the target's file system for the following methods defined in the `Cpl::Io::File::Api` class:

   ```
   bool getInfo( const char* fsEntryName, Info& infoOut )
   bool canonicalPath( const char* relPath, Cpl::Text::String& absPath )
   ```

APPENDIX E   CPL C++ FRAMEWORK

```
bool getCwd( Cpl::Text::String& cwd )
bool exists( const char* fsEntryName )
bool createFile( const char* fileName )
bool createDirectory( const char* dirName )
bool renameInPlace( const char* oldName, const char* newName )
bool moveFile( const char* oldFileName, const char* newFileName )
bool remove( const char* fsEntryName )
bool walkDirectory( const char*     dirToList,
                    DirectoryWalker& callback,
                    int              depth,
                    bool             filesOnly,
                    bool             dirsOnly )
```

File and Stream IO

Porting of the `Cpl::Io::File` namespace for reading and writing files requires the following:

1. Provide a concrete implementation using the target's file system for the following methods in the `Cpl::Io::File::Common_` class.

```
static Cpl::Io::Descriptor open( const char* fileEntryName,
                 bool       readOnly=true,
                 bool       forceCreate=false,
                 bool       forceEmptyFile=false );
static bool length( Cpl::Io::Descriptor fd, unsigned long& length );
static bool currentPos( Cpl::Io::Descriptor fd, unsigned long& currentPos );
static bool setRelativePos( Cpl::Io::Descriptor fd, long deltaOffset );
static bool setAbsolutePos( Cpl::Io::Descriptor fd, unsigned long newoffset );
static bool setToEof( Cpl::Io::Descriptor fd );
```

2. The CPL library makes an assumption that the underlying operations for reading and writing to the target's stdio streams are the same operations for reading and writing files on the target. For example, the POSIX read() and write() methods using file descriptors can be used with the stdio stream, sockets, files, etc. This limits the porting activity for read and write operations to just porting the common stream operations. The following classes need to be implemented:

- Cpl::Io::Stdio::Input_
- Cpl::Io::Stdio::Output_

The Cpl::Io::File::Arduino namespace provides an example of how to port the File IO and Directory management interfaces using a third-party file system that is separate from the target's RTOS.

Global Lock

The Cpl::System::GlobalLock interface has the following methods that require a platform-specific implementation:

```
void begin( void );
void end( void );
```

These methods are essentially wrappers to enable/disable interrupts. For Windows or Linux targets, where the OSAL port is intended to run in user space in nonprivilege mode, this interface can be mapped or implemented using a mutex.

Mutex

The Cpl::System::Mutex interface consists of the following class. An instance of this class is created in each mutex instance. Here are the OSAL mutex semantics for a recursive mutex.

```
class Mutex
{
public:
    Mutex();
    ~Mutex();

    void lock( void );
    void unlock( void );

protected:
    Cpl_System_Mutex_T   m_mutex;
};
```

The definition of Cpl_System_Mutex_T is provided in the LHeader mappings_.h header file. For example:

```
#define Cpl_System_Mutex_T_MAP    pthread_mutex_t
```

The CPL library requires a set of mutex instances for its internal usage. While these mutexes are not directly exposed to the application, the OSAL port still needs to provide the mutexes. The following methods from the src/Cpl/System/Private_.h header file require a platform-specific implementation:

```
Mutex& system( void );
Mutex& sysLists( void );
Mutex& tracing( void );
Mutex& tracingOutput( void );
```

APPENDIX E   CPL C++ FRAMEWORK

Newline

The Cpl::Io::NewLine interface only requires a platform-specific implementation of the CPL_IO_NEW_LINE_NATIVE symbol. The definition of the newline string is provided in the LHeader mappings_.h header file. For example:

```
#define CPL_IO_NEW_LINE_NATIVE_MAP    "\n"
```

Semaphore

The Cpl::System::Semaphore interface consists of the following class. An instance of this class is created for each semaphore instance.

```
class Semaphore : public Signable
{
public:
    Semaphore( unsigned initialCount=0 );
    ~Semaphore();

    void wait( void ) noexcept;
    bool timedWait( unsigned long timeout ) noexcept;
    bool tryWait( void ) noexcept;

    int signal( void ) noexcept;
    int su_signal( void ) noexcept;

protected:
    Cpl_System_Sema_T  m_sema;

    void waitInRealTime( void ) noexcept;
    bool timedWaitInRealTime( unsigned long timeout ) noexcept;
};
```

The definition of Cpl_System_Sema_T is provided in the LHeader mappings_.h header file. For example:

```
#define Cpl_System_Sema_T_MAP    sem_t
```

The Semaphore interface is similar to the ElapsedTime interface in that is has a time aspect that is part of the CPL library's simulated time feature. If your target platform is a non-process-based RTOS, you typically don't have a use case for supporting simulated time. The implementations for the wait() and waitInRealTime() methods are identical, as are the implementations of the timedWait() and timedWaitInRealTime() methods. If you need to support simulated time on your target platform, use the Win32 and POSIX implementations as a template.

Shell

The Cpl::System::Shell interface has the following methods that require a platform-specific implementation for the following methods:

```
int execute( const char* cmdstring,
             bool        noEchoStdOut = true,
             bool        noEchoStdErr = true );
bool isAvailable();
```

Additionally, the platform-specific implementation of the following symbols is required in the LHeader mappings files:

CPL_SYSTEM_SHELL_NULL_DEVICE_
CPL_SYSTEM_SHELL_SUPPORTED_

For example, here is the LHeader mapping file for the Port: mappings_.h

```
/// Win32 Mapping
#define CPL_SYSTEM_SHELL_NULL_DEVICE_x_MAP    "NUL"

/// Win32 Mapping
#define CPL_SYSTEM_SHELL_SUPPORTED_x_MAP      1
```

APPENDIX E CPL C++ FRAMEWORK

Even if your projects do not use or require this interface, I recommend that you provide an "empty" implementation of this interface.

Shutdown

The `Cpl::System::Shutdown` interface has the following methods that require a platform-specific implementation:

```
int success( void );
int failure( int exit_code );
```

The shutdown logic is similar to the `FatalError` interface in that it can also be project specific. What this means for the porting exercise is that you should organize your code and build scripts in a way that each project can select or provide its own implementation of the Shutdown interface.

System API

The `Cpl::System::Api` interface has the following methods that require a platform-specific implementation:

```
void initialize( void );
void enableScheduling( void );
bool isSchedulingEnabled( void );
void sleep( unsigned long milliseconds ) noexcept;
void sleepInRealTime( unsigned long milliseconds ) noexcept;
void suspendScheduling(void);
void resumeScheduling(void);
```

The implementation of the `initialize()` method must always execute any registered startup callback functions. Typically, this is the only action required. For example:

APPENDIX E CPL C++ FRAMEWORK

```
#include "Cpl/System/Api.h"

namespace Cpl::System;

void Api::initialize( void )
{
    // Init the Colony.Core sub-systems
    StartupHook_::notifyStartupClients();
}
```

The implementation of enableScheduling() and isSchedulingEnabled() methods is very target specific. For example, for FreeRTOS, these methods make calls into the RTOS. On Windows and Linux, these methods are essentially NOPs (where isSchedulingEnabled() always returns true).

The two sleep methods are once again impacted by the CPL library's simulated time feature. If your target platform is a non-process-based RTOS, you typically don't have a use case for supporting simulated time, and the implementation for the sleep() and sleepInRealTime() methods is identical.

If you need to support simulated time on your target platform, use the Win32 and POSIX implementations as a template.

Threads

The Cpl::System::Thread interface is the most involved interface to port. This is because each target platform or OS or RTOS has its own interfaces, semantics, and nuances when it comes to creating threads, allocating stack space, prioritizing threads, etc.

In addition, on some platforms, the RTOS or OS will have created an initial thread before main(). This is problematic because many of the Cpl::System::Thread methods (e.g., getCurrent()) assume that an instance of the Thread class has been created and associated with the

APPENDIX E CPL C++ FRAMEWORK

current thread. A native target thread will not have the instance association because the thread was not created using the CPL createThread() method.

A final complication is that the CPL OSAL semantics for creating threads are "threads are created at run time" with the option for statically allocating the memory for the thread's stack.

The Thread interface is defined as an abstract class that also contains several static methods (see the following coded sample). The OSAL port requires a concrete child class as well as implementation for all of the thread's static methods.

```
class Thread : public Signable
{
public:
    virtual const char* getName() noexcept = 0;
    virtual size_t getId() noexcept = 0;
    virtual Cpl_System_Thread_NativeHdl_T getNativeHandle( void ) noexcept = 0;
    ...
    static Thread& getCurrent() noexcept;
    static void wait() noexcept;
    ...
    static Thread* create( Runnable&  runnable,
                           const char* name,
                           int         priority = CPL_SYSTEM_THREAD_PRIORITY_NORMAL,
                           int         stackSize = 0,
                           void*       stackPtr = 0,
                           bool        allowSimTicks = true );
    static void destroy( Thread& threadToDestroy );
};
```

The definition of Cpl_System_Thread_NativeHdl_T is provided in the LHeader mappings_.h header file. For example:

```
#define Cpl_System_Thread_NativeHdl_T    pthread_t
```

Create Thread

Because there is some much variation on how an RTOS or OS creates and manages threads, a given port of the OSAL may not be able to support all of the semantics of the preceding createThread() method. This is okay as long as the deviations are documented and are sufficiently functional for your needs on the target. The reason it is okay to deviate from the OSAL semantics is that the code that is creating threads is typically very platform-specific code. It is code that is not commonly reused across multiple target platforms.

> I strongly recommend that the developer porting the Threading interface be experienced and well versed in the target operating system's threading model.

Thread Priorities

It seems every OS and RTOS has a different scheme for thread priorities. The CPL OSAL handles thread priorities by defining a set of macro symbols that specify the highest, lowest, and nominal priorities values as well as two symbols to increase or decrease priority values. The port provides the target-specific values for these constants in the LHeader mappings_.h header file.

```
#define CPL_SYSTEM_THREAD_PRIORITY_HIGHEST_MAP    31
#define CPL_SYSTEM_THREAD_PRIORITY_NORMAL_MAP     15
#define CPL_SYSTEM_THREAD_PRIORITY_LOWEST_MAP     0

#define CPL_SYSTEM_THREAD_PRIORITY_RAISE_MAP      (1)
#define CPL_SYSTEM_THREAD_PRIORITY_LOWER_MAP      (-1)
```

APPENDIX E   CPL C++ FRAMEWORK

Native Thread vs. Cpl Thread

For the scenario where the target platform creates an initial thread for the entry main() function to execute in, the port needs to provide a mechanism for converting a native target thread to a CPL thread. The recommended approach for this is to use the CPL startup mechanism to register a callback that will convert the native thread to a CPL thread when Cpl::System::Api::initialize() is called. See the Win32, POSIX, and FreeRTOS ports for examples.

> **Caution**   There are other use cases where native threads, other than the initial main thread, can exist in your application. For example, if you are using a communication stack provided by your board vendor or third party, this stack creates a pool of worker threads from which callbacks into your application are made. This means that your code in these callbacks cannot directly or indirectly call any of the static class methods of the Cpl::System::Thread interface, except for the tryGetCurrent() method.

Thread-Local Storage

The Cpl::System::Tls interface consists of the Tls class. An instance of this class is created for each TLS instance.

```
class Tls
{
public:
    Tls();
    ~Tls();

    void* get( void );
    void set( void* newValue );
```

```
protected:
    Cpl_System_TlsKey_T  m_key;
};
```

The definition of `Cpl_System_TlsKey_T` is provided in the LHeader mappings_.h header file. For example:

```
#define Cpl_System_TlsKey_T_MAP    pthread_key_t
```

If the target platform does not natively support TLS, there are many possible options for implementing the TLS interface. For example, one option is to include the TLS storage as part of the concrete Thread class since there is an instance of the class in each thread. This is how the FreeRTOS port is done. Another example, which is very specific to the Raspberry PI Pico port, is to allocate the TLS storage per CPU core since threads map one to one with cores.

Tracing

The `Cpl::System::Trace` interface is another interface that, in addition to being target specific, can also be application specific. For this reason, I strongly recommend that the OSAL port provide a default implementation for the Tracing interface and allow for applications and build scripts to provide their own implementation.

For example, the CPL library provides a default implementation for the entire Tracing interface that relies on the `Cpl::Io::StdOut` interface. The default implementation is segregated into two directories: one for formatting the output and one for the target output stream. This allows an application to use part, all, or none of the default implementation.

The tracing interface has the following methods defined in the src/Cpl/System/Trace.h header file that require platform- and application-specific implementation:

APPENDIX E   CPL C++ FRAMEWORK

```
void redirect_( Cpl::Io::Output& newMedia );
void revert_( void );
Cpl::Io::Output* getDefaultOutputStream_( void ) noexcept;
```

The tracing interface defines the following methods from the src/Cpl/System/Private_.h header file that require platform- and application-specific implementation:

```
void appendInfo( Cpl::Text::String& dst,
                 Trace::InfoLevel_T info,
                 const char*        section,
                 const char*        filename,
                 int                linenum,
                 const char*        funcname );
void output( Cpl::Text::String& src );
```

APPENDIX F

NQBP2 Build System

For a variety of reasons, I built my own build system. It solves a lot of problems for me and allows me to build code and images in very useful ways without having to deal with the headache of makefiles. I realize that most of you either have a required build system or a build system that you prefer, but I'm describing the NQBP2 system in this appendix to illustrate the mechanisms that allow it to scale and address multiple hardware targets. Additionally, the code in the epc repository incorporates the NQBP2 build system so a few words seem to be in order. Nevertheless, feel free to skim or skip this appendix as your circumstances warrant.

NQBP2 is the latest generation of a Python-based build engine that I have used in some form or another over many years building projects. NQBP2 stands for *Not Quite Benv – Python*. The 2 indicates that it is the second generation of the tool that supports fast, incremental builds. The primary features of NQBP2 that I have come to rely on are as follows:

- Adding a new file in an existing directory requires zero effort.
- Adding a new source directory to a build is done by simply adding the new directory's name and path as single line entry to a single file.
- It supports both Windows and Linux host platforms.
- It frees me from having to deal with makefiles.

APPENDIX F   NQBP2 BUILD SYSTEM

Here is a more detailed list of NQBP2 features:

- Multi-host build engine for C, C++, and assembler builds
- Targeted specifically for embedded development
- Speed. It uses the Ninja[14] build tool to invoke the compiler toolchain.
- Command line based
- Supports many compiler toolchains
- Source code reusability. NQBP2 assumes that code will be shared across many projects.
- Reusability of compiler toolchains. After a particular compiler toolchain has been created or defined, it can be reused across an unlimited number of projects.
- Scalability. It is highly effective regardless of project size.

Installing NQBP2

NQBP2 is pre-installed in the epc repository. The only developer installation required is to install Python 3.6 or newer. See the Wiki page instructions on how to install Python. NQBP2 is managed as third-party package in the epc repository and is located in the xsrc/nqbp2/ directory. NQBP2 relies on specific environment variables being set with the env.bat and env.sh scripts. These variables are described in Table F-1.

---

[14] Ninja is a small build system from Google specifically built for speed (see https://ninja-build.org/).

APPENDIX F   NQBP2 BUILD SYSTEM

NQBP2 requires Python 3.6 or newer version. Be aware that Python 3.x is not always the default Python installation for Linux or Windows machines.

Table F-1. NQBP environment variables

Variable	Description
NQBP_BIN	The full path to the root directory where the NQBP2 package is located.
NQBP_PKG_ROOT	The full path to the package that is actively being worked on. Typically, this is the root directory of your local repository.
NQBP_WORK_ROOT	The full path of the directory containing one or more packages being developed. In practice, this is set to the parent directory of NQBP_PKG_ROOT.
NQBP_XPKGS_ROOT	The full path to external or third-party source code referenced by the build scripts. Typically this is set to the NQBP_PKG_ROOT/xsrc directory.

Usage

NQBP2 separates the build directories from the source code directories. It further separates the build directories into two buckets: unit tests (the tests/ directory) and applications (the projects/ directory). The NQBP2 build scripts will only work if they are executed under one of these two directories. It is up to you whether you have both or only one of these directories.

APPENDIX F   NQBP2 BUILD SYSTEM

```
<NQBP_WORK_ROOT>              ; Workspace root (i.e. collection of many repos)
└───<NQBP_PKG_ROOT>            ; Typically this is the root of your repo
    ├───<abc>
    ├───projects              ; Build applications/released images
    ├───<xyz>
    ├───src                   ; Source code directory
    ├───tests                 ; Build unit tests
    └───<NQBP_XPKGS_ROOT>      ; recommended name for this directory is 'xsrc'
```

Build Model

NQBP2 builds directories and, by default, builds all source code files found in each directory specified. The object files for each directory are then placed in an object library for that directory. main() is then linked against all of the object libraries created.

Incremental builds are supported so that NQBP2 only recompiles source code that has changed (directly or indirectly through header includes) since the last build. The incremental build feature is wholly managed by the Ninja build tool.

Object Files vs. Libraries

When NQBP2 compiles directories, it places all the object files into a library file for each directory built. The exception is NQBP2 does not create a library file for the objects in the build directory (i.e., the directory where you run nqbp.py script). During the link phase, it links your executable image against the object files in the build directory and the individual libraries it created during the compile phase. This has the positive effect of only including the code your application uses from a specific directory instead of including all the object files in an entire directory into your application. Once again, the exception to this rule is that all object files in the build directory are always linked into the application.

For example, if your application uses the `Cpl::Container::Dictionary` class but does not use any of the other classes from the `Cpl::Container` namespace, then, at compile time, the NQBP build scripts will compile the entire `Cpl/Container` directory. However, at link time, your application will only link in the `Cpl::Container::Dictionary` object code from the library. This is the C/C++ language defined behavior for linking against libraries.

There is one downside to this approach: if there are no references in your application code to a variable or function in an object file that is placed in a library, then it will not be linked. Oddly enough there can be required variables and functions that need to be linked that are not explicitly referenced. Here are some example cases:

- C/C++ run time code—This includes things like the code that executes when the reset interrupt occurs (i.e., the microcontroller's vector table). Your application does not have an explicit function call to any of the entries in the vector table. The vector table is typically placed into RAM at a very specific location by the linker script.

- C++ modules that are self-registered (with a container)—For this scenario, there is no calling module that references the self-registered instances directly by their names; the module only references the instances indirectly from the container. The "Catch-2" unit tests are an example of this. Each Catch2 test case self-registers with the test runner. At runtime, the test runner walks through its list of tests to execute the individual tests.

NQBP2 provides a mechanism—`firstobjs` and `lastobjs` parameters—to explicitly force linking against an arbitrary set of object files in addition to linking against directory libraries. See the *mytoolchain.py* section that follows for additional implementation details.

APPENDIX F   NQBP2 BUILD SYSTEM

Build Variants

NQBP2 supports the concepts of build variants. A build variant is where the same basic set of code is compiled and linked against different targets. For example, the automated unit test for the Cpl::Dm namespace using the MinGW compiler has three build variants: win32, win64, and cpp11. Here is a description of these variants.

- win32—A 32-bit application build using the native Win32 API for threading
- win64—A 64-bit application build using the native Win32 API for threading
- cpp11—A 64-bit application build using the C++11 threading interfaces

Each build variant can be built independently from the others. That is, if you build variant A, it does not delete any of the files for variant B.

NQBP2 does **not** consider a debug build a build variant. This means building with debug or without debug enabled will overwrite the previous build variant's files.

Build Scripts

Some of the Python scripts that NQBP2 uses are common across projects, and others are unique to individual projects. Table F-2 describes the primary components that make up a complete build script.

Table F-2. *Components of a complete build script with NQBP2*

Component	Description
`<compilerToolchain>.py`	This script contains the compiler and linker script commands, options, configurations, etc., that are needed to use a specific compiler to build a specific set of outputs. After a compiler toolchain has been created, it can be reused on an unlimited number of projects. These scripts are located under the `nqbp2/nqbplib/toolchains/` directory. If you are using a compiler that NQBP2 does not currently support, you will need to create a compiler toolchain script. See the `nqbp2/top/start_here.html` file for details on how to do this.
`nqbp.py`	This script is used to perform the builds. A copy of this script must be placed in each build directory. The content of this script is minimal; it basically calls scripts inside the `nqbp2/nqbplib` directory to perform the actual builds.
`mytoolchain.py`	This script is used to specify which compiler toolchain to use and to provide project-specific customization of the referenced compiler toolchain. Each build directory is required to have a `mytoolchain.py` file.
`libdirs.b`	This file is used to specify which directories to build. Each build directory is required to have a `libdirs.b` file.

(continued)

Table F-2. (*continued*)

Component	Description
sources.b	This file is optional. If used, this file specifies which .c|.cpp|.asm|.s files in a given directory to build. By default, NQBP2 builds all .c|.cpp|.asm|.s files found in directories specified by the libdirs.b file or in the build directory itself.

Selecting What to Build with NQBP

The principal mechanism for selecting which files to build is the libdirs.b file in the build directory and the optional sources.b files in source directories. The sources.b file simply contains file names that are listed singly on separate lines of the file. The libdirs.b file contains the directory names that are listed singly on separate lines of the file and specify which directories to compile and link. However, there are additional syntax and semantics for the libdirs.b file.

- Directories are referenced relative to the NQBP_PKG_ROOT directory.

- Entries in the file can reference another libdirs.b files within the repository. There are options for referencing a libdirs.b file:

    - Relative path—The syntax for this is to use a relative directory path qualifier to the reference included in your libdirs.b file, for example, ../../libdirs.b

- Package path—The syntax for this is to use a leading directory separator (/) to indicate the root of the package along with a "path" for referencing the libdirs.b file, for example, /top/libdirs/platform_win32_default_for_test_libdirs.b

- Blank lines, or lines starting with "#", are ignored.

- Environment variables can be referenced using leading and trailing $ characters to identify directories or partial directory paths.

- An entry that starts with *build-variant* enclosed within square brackets will only be compiled when *build-variant* matches the build variant specified when nqbp.py is invoked. For example:

  [cpp11] src/Cpl/System/_cpp11

- An optional pipe symbol (|) can be used to include multiple variants inside the square brackets. For example, you could specify [win32|win64].

- Entries with no variant prefix specified are compiled for all variants.

- Entries can specify two optional lists:

  - An optional trailing list of source files (in the specified directory) that will only be included if specified by the "less than character" (<)

  - Or an optional trailing list of source files (in the specified directory) that will be excluded if specified by the "greater than character" (>)

APPENDIX F   NQBP2 BUILD SYSTEM

Here are some examples of lines that can be included in a `libdirs.b` file:

```
# Build the src/foo directory in my package
src/foo

# Build the src/foo directory but do NOT build the hello.c
# and world.cpp files
src/foo > hello.c world.cpp

# Build the src/foo directory but ONLY build the hello.c
# and world.cpp files
src/foobar < hello.c world.cpp

# Build the third-party module Uncle under the xsrc/ directory
xsrc/Uncle/src

# Build using an absolute path that the base path is specified
# by an environment variable
# where ARDUINO_TOOLS=c:\Progra~2\Ardunio
$ARDUINO_TOOLS$/hardware/arduino/cores/arduino

# Directory specific to the 'cpp1' variant
[cpp11] src/Cpl/System/_cpp11

# Build all directories specified in the following file
# (relative to my build directory)
../../../libdirs.b

# Build a predefined list of directories
/top/libdirs/platform_win32_default_for_test_libdirs.b
```

Compiler Toolchains

The NQBP2 build engine is based on the concept of creating reusable compiler or target-specific toolchain scripts that individual projects and unit tests can then invoke. In addition, the toolchains can be customized per project and unit tested via the `mytoolchain.py` script in each build

APPENDIX F   NQBP2 BUILD SYSTEM

directory. The toolchain scripts are located under the nqbp2/nqbllib/toolchains directory. Table F-3 shows some example toolchains. As you can see, the toolchains can range from being fairly generic (Windows/Linux console applications) to very specific (the RP2040 toolchains).

Table F-3. *Example toolchains*

Description	Location under (nqbp/nqblib/toolchains/)
For a Windows host, this builds native 32-bit and 64-bit Windows console applications.	windows/vc12/console_exe.py
For a Linux host, this builds native 32-bit and 64-bit Linux console applications.	linux/gcc/console_exe.py
For a Windows host, this creates a cross-compiler build for the STM32F4 microcontrollers.	windows/arm_gcc_stm32/stm32f4.py
For a Windows host, this creates a cross-compiler build for the STM32F7 microcontrollers.	windows/arm_gcc_stm32/stm32f7.py
For a Windows host, this creates a cross-compiler build for the Raspberry PI RP2040 Microcontroller with USB for stdio.	windows/arm_gcc_rp2040/stdio_usb.py
For a Windows host, this creates a cross-compiler build for the Raspberry PI RP2040 Microcontroller with a UART for stdio.	windows/arm_gcc_rp2040/stdio_serial.py
For a Windows host, this creates a cross-compiler build for the Raspberry PI RP2040 Microcontroller with Wi-Fi (CYW43439) and a UART for stdio.	windows/arm_gcc_rp2040/w_stdio_serial.py

APPENDIX F   NQBP2 BUILD SYSTEM

Toolchain Details

Each toolchain script is a child class of the Toolchain Python class defined in the nqbp2/nqbplib/base.py. The Toolchain class is responsible for generating build rules for the Ninja build tool. Besides being fast, the Ninja tool handles the details of performing incremental builds.

The base Toolchain class defaults to building a command line executable using the native GCC compiler. The child classes can extend or customize any base class method as needed, but typically only the following methods need to be implemented by a child class:

- __init__()–The init method is the child class's constructor. This is where most of the compiler-specific details are specified. This includes

  - The executable names of the compiler, linker, librarian, etc.
  - The base or common set of header search paths
  - The base or common C/C++/Assembly flags
  - The base or common linker flags, library paths, and libraries

- link()–This method is responsible for providing the build rules for linking the image and generating the final build outputs.
- finalize()–This method is responsible for providing the default Ninja build rule. That is, it specifies which Ninja target to build with which rules.
- validate_cc()–This optional method can be called to validate that the proper compiler is available. That is it verifies that the compiler can be invoked by the script.

> **Note** There is a helper class, `Writer` (in the file `nqbp2/nqbblib/ninja_syntax.py`), that provides a wrapper for generating ninja rules.

mytoolchain.py

Each toolchain can be customized on a per-project and per-unit-test basis. The customization is done via the `mytoolchain.py` script that is located in each build directory. The `mytoolchain.py` script is responsible for

- Specifying which compiler toolchain to use
- Specifying the name of the final image or executable
- Defining build variants (e.g., 32-bit vs. 64-bit builds) by supplying customized compiler and linker options for each variant

Build Variant

A build variant is specified using a Python dictionary that contains three sets of customizable build options. These build options are OR-ed to the build options specified in the toolchain script. Each set of build options is an instance of the class `BuildValues`. The three sets of build options are

- `user_base`—Options that are common to both the debug and release builds.
- `user_optimized`—Options that are specific to building a release build. That is, the -g flag was **not** specified when invoking the `nqbp.py` script.
- `user_debug`—Options that are specific to building a debug build. That is, the -g flag was specified when invoking the `nqbp.py` script.

APPENDIX F   NQBP2 BUILD SYSTEM

The following is an example of defining the build options for a single build variant:

```
# Set project specific 'base' (i.e always used) options
base_release          = BuildValues() # Do NOT comment out this line
base_release.cflags   = '/W3 /WX /EHsc /D CATCH_CONFIG_FAST_COMPILE'
base_release.firstobjs = '_BUILT_DIR_.src/Cpl/Container/_0test'

# Set project specific 'optimized' options
optimzed_release      = BuildValues() # Do NOT comment out this line
optimzed_release.cflags = '/O2'

# Set project specific 'debug' options
debug_release         = BuildValues() # Do NOT comment out this line
debug_release.cflags  = '/D "_MY_APP_DEBUG_SWITCH_"'

# Dictionary for build variant
win32_opts = { 'user_base':base_release,
               'user_optimized':optimzed_release,
               'user_debug':debug_release
             }
```

Build Values

Table F-4 shows the settable data members that the `BuildValues` class contains. By default, all the data members are empty strings.

Table F-4. *Settable data members of the BuildValues class*

Option	Description
inc	This is a list of header search path directives. For example, -I xsrc/pimoroni/include.
asminc	This is a list of header search path directives that are only passed to the assembler.
cflags	This is a list of compiler options that are specified when compiling C and C++ code.
c_only_flags	This is a list of compiler options specified when compiling C code. This is used in addition to .cflags.
cppflags	This is a list of compiler options specified when compiling C++ code. This is used in addition to .cflags.
asmflags	This is a list of assembler options specified when compiling an assembly source file.
linkflags	This is a list of linker flags passed to the linker.
linklibs	This is a list of external libraries to link against. Do not include libraries generated per source directory.
firstobjs	This is a list of object files that will be the first object files to be specified to the linker. These files are unconditionally linked with the executable.
lastobjs	This is a list of object files that will be the last object files specified to the linker. These files are unconditionally linked with the executable.

Specifying Toolchain

To specify a compiler toolchain, at least one build variant must be created. Then all of the build variant's dictionaries are combined into yet another dictionary. The keyword values used in this dictionary are the values used when specifying the -b <variant> build option and in the `libdirs.b` files when specifying conditional builds (i.e., [cpp11] src/Cpl/System/_cpp11). For example:

```
# Win32 build variant
win32_opts = { 'user_base':base_release,
               'user_optimized':optimzed_release,
               'user_debug':debug_release
             }

# CPP11 variant
cpp11_opts = { 'user_base':base_cpp11,
               'user_optimized':optimzed_cpp11,
               'user_debug':debug_cpp11
             }

# Collection of all supported build variants
build_variants = { 'win32':win32_opts,   # 'win32' build
                     variant name
                   'cpp11':cpp11_opts,   # 'cpp11' build
                     variant name
                 }
```

The final step is to invoke the desired compiler toolchain. This is done by calling the toolchain's `create()` method. For example:

```
# Set the name for the final output item
FINAL_OUTPUT_NAME = 'a.exe'
...
```

APPENDIX F   NQBP2 BUILD SYSTEM

```
# Select Module that contains the desired toolchain
from nqbplib.toolchains.windows.vc12.console_exe import
ToolChain

# Function that instantiates an instance of the toolchain, with
# 'win32' as the default build variant
def create():
    tc = ToolChain( FINAL_OUTPUT_NAME, prjdir, build_variants,
    'win32' )
    return tc
```

In the preceding create() method, the arguments to the ToolChain () function are determined by the toolchain file imported.

Linking

As discussed earlier, the default linking paradigm for the NQBP2 is to link against libraries, not directly against object files. However, as this approach does not always work, there are ways to go about unconditionally linking object files:

1. Put the source code for the object files in the build directory. When these source code files are compiled their object files are always directly linked.

2. Use the firstobjs and lastobjs build options to explicitly link one or more object files. An object file is specified by its path to the object build directory, and this path needs to be *relative to the build-variant directory*—not the project directory. For example:

   ```
   base_release.lastobjs = \
       r'..\src\Bsp\Renesas\Rx\u62n\Yrdkr62n\Gnurx\vectors.o'
   ```

APPENDIX F   NQBP2 BUILD SYSTEM

Specifying an Entire Directory of Object Files

There is a shortcut to including all of the object files in a directory using the firstobjs and lastobjs variables. There is a special build-time symbol _BUILT_DIR_ that is translated in a pre-link step to generate a list of object modules by only specifying the directory. The directory to include is specified using the same syntax that directories were identified with in the libdirs.b file. For example:

base_release.firstobjs = '_BUILT_DIR_.src/Cpl/Dm/Mp/_0test'

> I recommend that you use the _BUILT_DIR_ approach instead of base_release.firstobjs = '../src/Cpl/Dm/Mp/_0test/*.o'. The reason is because the Windows command shell does not expand wildcards the same way a Linux/Unix shell does. For example, the preceding *.o notation does not work with the MinGW GCC compiler when running under Windows. However, it does work with the Visual Studio compiler because Microsoft compiler does the wildcard expansion itself.

Preprocessing Scripts

NQBP2 supports the ability to run preprocessing scripts prior to the compile stage. This allows NQBP2 to work with code bases and tools that auto-generate additional source code files from non-C/C++ source files or from files that were generated from the examination of other source files. An example of this is running QT's Moc compiler with each build.

APPENDIX F   NQBP2 BUILD SYSTEM

How Preprocessing Scripts Work

Place a preprocessing script in each source directory that requires one. Since the preprocessing script must be placed in every desired source directory, I recommend making the preprocessing script only be a simple wrapper that calls a single instance of the actual script.

The preprocessing script also has the following constraints:

- The name of any particular preprocessing scripts must be the same across a given project or test build.

- The name of a preprocessing script is specified in the project's `mytoolchain.py` script.

- When building a given source directory that contains the specified preprocessing script, the script is executed before any compiling occurs for that directory.

- The same sequence occurs when NQBP2 cleans a directory; it calls the preprocessing script with an argument to specify the clean operation.

Preprocessing Script Examples

This section provides an example of the two scripts that perform preprocessing. Additionally, it is an example of how to edit a project's `mytoolchain.py` file to enable the preprocessing.

Source Tree Script: `preprocess.py`

This script is placed in each source directory that needs preprocessing. This script is simply a wrapper that calls another (single instance) script that performs the actual work. The script must always accept six command-line arguments. In addition, depending on the project's requirements, it can take additional arguments.

APPENDIX F   NQBP2 BUILD SYSTEM

```
#!/usr/bin/python3
#----------------------------------------------------------------
# Usage: preprocess.py <arg1> ... <arg6> <compiler> where:
#               <arg1>: build|clean
#               <arg2>: verbose|terse
#               <arg3>: <workspace-dir>
#               <arg4>: <package-dir>
#               <arg5>: <project-dir>
#               <arg6>: <current-dir>
#               <compiler>: compiler being used, e.g. mingw|mingw_64|vc12|etc..
#----------------------------------------------------------------

import os
import sys

# MAIN
if __name__ == '__main__':
    # Create path to the 'real' script
    script = os.path.join(sys.argv[4], "scripts", "preprocess_base.py" )

    # Run the 'actual' pre-processing script
    sys.exit(os.system( script + " " + " ".join(sys.argv[1:])))
```

Preprocessing Script: scripts/preprocess_base.py

This script performs the actual preprocessing. There should only be a single instance of this script. It is responsible for preprocessing activities while building as well as cleaning up any artifacts if <arg1> is set to clean.

```
#!/usr/bin/python3
#----------------------------------------------------------------
# This is example of the 'single instance' NQBP pre-processing script
#       where <prjargs..>  are project specific arguments passed to the
#       <preprocess-script.py> script when it is executed.
#
# Usage:
#    preprocessing_base <a1> <a2> <a3> <a4> <a5> <a6> <prj1>
```

APPENDIX F   NQBP2 BUILD SYSTEM

```
#
#    where:
#       <a1>:    build|clean
#       <a2>:    verbose|terse
#       <a3>:    <workspace-dir>
#       <a4>:    <package-dir>
#       <a5>:    <project-dir>
#       <a6>:    <current-dir>
#       <prj1>: <compiler> // mingw|mingw_64|vc12|etc.
#-------------------------------------------------------------

# get definition of the Options structure
import sys

# Do stuff...
print( "--> Example Pre-Processing Script" )
if (sys.argv[2] == 'verbose'):
    print( "= ECHO: " + '  '.join(sys.argv) )
```

Enabling the Preprocessing Script

By default, preprocessing scripts are disabled. Enabling the preprocessing scripts is done on a per-build-project basis. The following edits to the project's mytoolchain.py are required. In this example, the compiler being used is for the Microsoft Visual Studio compiler (i.e., "vc12").

...

```
# Import methods to enable processing
from nqbplib.my_globals import NQBP_PRE_PROCESS_SCRIPT
from nqbplib.my_globals import NQBP_PRE_PROCESS_SCRIPT_ARGS
```

...

APPENDIX F   NQBP2 BUILD SYSTEM

```
#========================================================
# BEGIN EDITS/CUSTOMIZATIONS
#--------------------------------------------------------

# Set the name for the final output item
FINAL_OUTPUT_NAME = 'a.exe'

...

# Set the name of the pre-processing script to execute
NQBP_PRE_PROCESS_SCRIPT( "preprocess.py" )

# Specifiy 'extra' project specific argument(s)
NQBP_PRE_PROCESS_SCRIPT_ARGS( "vc12" )

...
```

Reverse-Engineering Compiler Options

Not everyone can or will want to use NQBP2 as their build system. The nqbp.py script has several command-line options to aid the developer when migrating NQBP2 build scripts to a different build system. Table F-5 enumerates the nqbp.py command-line options for reverse-engineering an NQBP2 build script.

Table F-5. NQBP script options

`--qry-dirs`	Displays the list of directories for the selected build variant referenced in the `libdirs.b` file.
`--qry-dirs2`	The same as `--qry-dirs`, except with the addition of any source files specifically included or excluded on a per-directory basis. The token ">>>" indicates excluded files. The token "<<<" indicates only included files.
`--qry-opt`	Displays all of the toolchain options, that is, compiler flags, header search paths, linker flags, etc.

APPENDIX F NQBP2 BUILD SYSTEM

Here are a few example outputs using these options:

```
c:\epc\tests\Driver\NV\_Otest\onsemi-cat24c512\NUCLEO-F413ZH-alpha1\windows\
gcc-arm>nqbp.py --qry-dirs2
===============================================================
= START of build for:  outtest
= Project Directory:   C:\epc\tests\Driver\NV\_Otest\onsemi-cat24c512\
                       NUCLEO-F413ZH-alpha1\windows\gcc-arm
= Toolchain:           GCC Arm-Cortex (none-eabi) Compiler
= Build Configuration: stm32
= Begin (UTC):         Sun, 08 Oct 2023 20:58:37
= Build Time:          1696798717 (652317fd)
===============================================================
local   src\Driver\NV\Onsemi\CAT24C512
local   src\Driver\NV\_Otest
local   src\Driver\I2C\STM32
local   src\Cpl\System\FreeRTOS\_fatalerror
local   src\Cpl\System\_trace
local   src\Cpl\Io\Stdio\_ansi
local   src\Cpl\Io\Serial\ST\M32F4
local   src\Cpl\Container
local   src\Cpl\Text
local   src\Cpl\Io\Stdio
local   src\Cpl\Io
local   src\Cpl\System
local   src\Cpl\System\FreeRTOS
local   src\Cpl\System\_assert
local   src\Bsp\ST\NUCLEO-F413ZH\alpha1\trace
local   src\Bsp\ST\NUCLEO-F413ZH\alpha1
local   src\Bsp\ST\NUCLEO-F413ZH\alpha1\MX
local   src\Bsp\ST\NUCLEO-F413ZH\alpha1\MX\Core\Src  >>> ['freertos.c']
local   src\Bsp\ST\NUCLEO-F413ZH\alpha1\console
local   src\Bsp\ST\NUCLEO-F413ZH\alpha1\SeggerSysView
xpkg    xsrc\stm32F4-SDK\Drivers\STM32F4xx_HAL_Driver\Src  >>>
    ['stm32f4xx_hal_timebase_rtc_alarm_template.c',
     'stm32f4xx_hal_timebase_rtc_wakeup_template.c',
     'stm32f4xx_hal_timebase_tim_template.c']
xpkg    xsrc\freertos
xpkg    xsrc\freertos\portable\GCC\ARM_CM4F
```

APPENDIX F NQBP2 BUILD SYSTEM

c:\epc\tests\Driver\NV_Otest\onsemi-cat24c512\NUCLEO-F413ZH-alpha1\windows\
gcc-arm>**nqbp.py --qry-opts**

\#   inc: -I. -I/epc/src -I/epc/xsrc -IC:/epc/tests/Driver/NV/_Otest/
   onsemi-Cat24c512/NUCLEO-F413ZH-alpha1/windows/gcc-arm
   -I/epc/xsrc/stm32F4-SDK/ Drivers/STM32F4xx_HAL_Driver/Inc
   -I/epc/xsrc/stm32F4-SDK/Drivers/STM32F4xx_HAL_Driver/Inc/Legacy
   -I/epc/xsrc/stm32F4-SDK/Drivers/CMSIS/Device/ST/STM32F4xx/Include
   -I/epc/xsrc/stm32F4-SDK/Drivers/CMSIS/Include
   -I/epc/xsrc/stm32F4-SDK/Middlewares/Third_Party/FreeRTOS/Source/CMSIS_RTOS
   -I/epc/xsrc/FreeRTOS/Include -I/epc/xsrc/FreeRTOS/portable/GCC/ARM_CM4F
   -I/epc/src/Bsp/ST/NUCLEO-F413ZH/alpha1/MX
   -I/epc/src/Bsp/ST/NUCLEO-F413ZH/alpha1/MX/Core/Inc

\#   asminc: --I. -I/epc/src -I/epc/xsrc -IC:/epc/tests/Driver/NV/_Otest/
   onsemi-Cat24c512/NUCLEO-F413ZH-alpha1/windows/gcc-arm
   -I/epc/xsrc/stm32F4-SDK/Drivers/STM32F4xx_HAL_Driver/Inc
   -I/epc/xsrc/stm32F4-SDK/Drivers/STM32F4xx_HAL_Driver/Inc/Legacy
   -I/epc/xsrc/stm32F4-SDK/Drivers/CMSIS/Device/ST/STM32F4xx/Include
   -I/epc/xsrc/stm32F4-SDK/Drivers/CMSIS/Include
   -I/epc/xsrc/stm32F4-SDK/Middlewares/Third_Party/FreeRTOS/Source/CMSIS_RTOS
   -I/epc/xsrc/FreeRTOS/Include
   -I/epc/xsrc/FreeRTOS/portable/GCC/ARM_CM4F
   -I/epc/src/Bsp/ST/NUCLEO-F413ZH/alpha1/MX
   -I/epc/src/Bsp/ST/NUCLEO-F413ZH/alpha1/MX/Core/Inc

\#   cflags: -Wall -DUSE_STM32F4XX_NUCLEO_144 -DSTM32F413xx -Werror
   -DENABLE_BSP_SEGGER_SYSVIEW -I/epc/src/Bsp/ST/NUCLEO-F413ZH/alpha1/SeggerSysView
   -c -mcpu=cortex-m4 -mfpu=fpv4-sp-d16 -mfloat-abi=hard -mthumb --specs=nano.specs
   --specs=nosys.specs -u _printf_float -ffunction-sections -fdata-sections
   -nostdlib --param max-inline-insns-single=500 -DUSE_HAL_DRIVER -Wno-array-bounds
   -Wno-stringop-truncation -Wno-stringop-overflow -g -DBUILD_VARIANT_STM32
   -DBUILD_NUMBER=0

\#   cppflags: -std=gnu++11 -Wno-int-in-bool-context   -Wno-restrict
   -Wno-address-of-packed-member -Wno-class-memaccess   -fno-rtti -fno-exceptions
   -fno-unwind-tables -fno-threadsafe-statics -fno-use-cxa-atexit

\#   asmflags: -DUSE_STM32F4XX_NUCLEO_144 -DSTM32F413xx -c -mcpu=cortex-m4
   -mfpu=fpv4-sp-d16 -mfloat-abi=hard -mthumb --specs=nano.specs --specs=nosys.specs
   -u _printf_float -ffunction-sections -fdata-sections -nostdlib

APPENDIX F NQBP2 BUILD SYSTEM

```
         --param max-inline-insns-single=500 -DUSE_HAL_DRIVER   -Wno-array-bounds
         -Wno-stringop-truncation -Wno-stringop-overflow -g -x assembler-with-cpp
         -DBUILD_VARIANT_STM32 -DBUILD_NUMBER=0

#        linkflags:     -mcpu=cortex-m4 -mfpu=fpv4-sp-d16 -mfloat-abi=hard -mthumb
         --specs=nano.specs –specs=nosys.specs -u _printf_float
         -T\epc\src\Bsp\ST\NUCLEO-F413ZH\alpha1\MX\STM32F413ZHTx_FLASH.ld
         -Wl,-Map=outtest.map -Wl,--gc-sections   -DNDEBUG

#        linklibs:      -Wl,--start-group -lc -lm -Wl,--end-group

#        firstobjs:     _BUILT_DIR_.src/Bsp/ST/NUCLEO-F413ZH/alpha1/MX/Core/Src
         src/Bsp/ST/NUCLEO-F413ZH/alpha1/MX/../stdio.o

#        lastobjs:      src/Bsp/ST/NUCLEO-F413ZH/alpha1/MX/../syscalls.o
```

Extras

NQBP2 also provides some additional scripts and features that are not directly used for building but are used to leverage, or support, the NQBP2 engine. Table F-6 lists a few of these supported scripts.

Table F-6. NQBP2 scripts that are used to leverage the NQBP2 engine

Script	Description
bob.py	The bob script is a tool that recursively builds multiple projects or tests. bob can only be run under the projects/ and tests/ directory trees. In addition, bob provides several options for filtering and specifying which projects or tests actually get built. For example, the following statement will build only tests that use the Visual Studio compiler. It also passes the -g option to the nqbp.py build scripts. For example: c:\work\pim\tests>bob.py vc12 -g

(continued)

Table F-6. (*continued*)

Script	Description
chuck.py	The chuck script is a tool that recursively runs executables or scripts. chuck can only be run under the projects/ and tests/ directories. Like bob, chuck provides several options for filtering and specifying which executables or scripts are run. For example, the following statement will execute all of the a.exe unit tests built using the Visual Studio compiler ten times each: c:\work\pim\tests>chuck.py --match a.exe --dir vc12 --loop 10
tca.py	The tca script is a wrapper script that is used to invoke the gcovr tool that generates code coverage reports and metrics. For example, the following statement generates coverage metrics for just the Cpl::Container module or namespace: tca.py rpt --filter .*Cpl/Container.* The tca script is run after the unit test executable has been run at least once. In the EPC repository, only the mingw_w64 32-bit builds are configured to be instrumented to generate code coverage metrics.

In the epc repository, the env.bat and env.sh scripts create macros, or aliases, for the bob.py and chuck.py scripts. This allows these scripts to be invoked without having to specify their path or add their path to the system's command path.

APPENDIX G

RATT

RATT is a Python-based automated test tool built on top of the pexpect[15] package. I specifically created it to perform automated testing with Units Under Test (UUTs). It supports a command-line interface, and it can be used with any application that supports interactive behavior with the parent process that launched the application (e.g., `stdio`). The following is a summary of RATT's features:

- It is a pure Python module that runs on Windows and Linux.
- It has an interactive mode, or it can run automated scripts. Interactive mode support includes listing all available scripts and displaying help for each script.
- Test scripts are written in Python.
- Test scripts can be located anywhere and can be placed in multiple locations in your build tree.

---

[15] A Python module for controlling interactive programs in a pseudoterminal. `https://github.com/pexpect/pexpect`

- It works with UUTs connected via
  - stdio
  - Serial port (using a command-line connection tool such as PuTTY's plink)
  - Telnet/SSH (using a command-line connection tool such as ssh)

Installing

RATT is pre-installed in the epc repository and is located in the xsrc/ratt/ directory.[16] It requires the following additional developer tools:

- Python 3.8 (or higher)
- pexpect library (4.8.0 or higher)

Detailed instructions for installing Python and pexpect can be found on the epc repository's Wiki page.

If you are connecting to a UUT via a serial port, telnet, TCP, or SSH, you will need to have a "command-line client application" that provides the connectivity. The following are some common utilities that can connect RATT to a UUT over a communication link:

- For Linux—cu, mincom, telnet, or ssh
- For Windows—plink from PuTTY

---

[16] RATT is managed as third-party package in the epc repository. The canonical repo for RATT is https://github.com/johnttaylor/ratt

> The native Windows `telent.exe` does not work with RATT because `pexpect` does not spawn applications in a terminal, and the Windows telnet application only supports interactive behavior when it detects it is running in a terminal.

Test Scripts

The basic execution model is that RATT scripts read and write data to the UUT's input and output streams, respectively. In addition, the read operations can optionally wait until a specific string or regular expression is detected in the output stream coming from the UUT.

The RATT package does not impose constraints or limits to the content of the test scripts that are written in Python. The exception is the entry script, which is expected to have the following semantics when it is launched from the command line:

- It contains a method named `main()` that takes no arguments and returns positive integers as follows:
  - Zero indicates pass.
  - Greater than zero indicates failure.

The entry script can be a stand-alone script, or it can load additional scripts. I recommend that the entry script be a test suite that in turn loads and executes one or more test case scripts.

APPENDIX G   RATT

Usage

Here is the usage for running a ratty.py script:

```
usage: ratt [options] --win <executable>...
       ratt [options] --linux <executable>...
       ratt [options] --nouut
```

To see the complete list of options, you can enter ratt.py -h on the command line. Here are some examples of running the ratt.py script.

- This command runs the mysuite.py script against a Windows console application:

    ratt.py --input mysuite.py --win mypath\my_utt.exe

- This command runs the mysuite.py script against a UUT connected to a Windows box via a serial port:

    ratt.py --input mysuite.py --win "C:\Program Files\PuTTY\plink.exe" -serial COM4 -sercfg 115200,8,1,N,N

- This command runs the mysuite.py script against a UUT running locally on the same Linux box connected via a raw TCP socket:

    ratt.py --input mysuite.py --linux telnet localhost 5002

- This command runs the RATT tool in an interactive Python shell against a Windows console application. Interactive mode is triggered when no entry script file is specified using the --input command-line option.

    ratt.py --win mypath\my_utt.exe

Script Locations

Test scripts can be located anywhere on your PC or on the network. When running a ratt.py script as a test suite—that is, as a script that calls other scripts—there are very specific semantics associated with searching for the entry script and for other scripts loaded by the entry script. The following hierarchical rules apply when loading test scripts:

1. Search the current working directory where the ratt.py script was launched.

2. If specified, search the directory identified by the --path1 command-line argument.

3. If specified, search the directory identified by the -path2 command-line argument.

4. If specified, search the directory identified by the -path3 command-line argument.

Example Scripts

Here are two example snippets of RATT test scripts used for the GM6000 project. One is a test suite, and the other is a test case. The std, uut, and output symbols in the following snippets are Python modules provided by the RATT engine that are available to your test scripts after the from rattlib import * statement executes. See the "rattlib" section that follows for a description of these modules.

Here is a test suite that verifies the GM6000 Heating algorithm:

src/Ajax/Heating/Simulated/_0test/test_suite.py

```
from rattlib import *
import config
import time
prompt_string = '$ '
```

APPENDIX G RATT

```python
def main():
    """ Entry point for the Test Suite
    """
    output.write_entry( __name__ )
    passcode = config.g_passed
    uut.setprompt( prompt_string )

    # Wait for the UUT to start
    r = uut.waitfor( 10, prompt_string )
    if ( r == None ):
        output.writeline("ERROR: The UUT is not responding")
        passcode = config.g_failed
    ...

    # Run tests...
    passcode = std.run("tc_basic_heating", passcode )
    # Load and run the test case file
    passcode = std.run("tc_heating_alerts", passcode )

    # Cleanly Exit the UUT
    uut.cli("bye app")

    output.write_exit( __name__ )
    return passcode
```

Here is the test case executed by the test suite script:

src/Ajax/Heating/Simulated/_Otest/tc_basic_heating.py

```python
from rattlib import *
import config

def run():
    """ Entry point for the Test Case
    """
```

```
output.write_entry(__name__)
helper = std.load( "tc_common" )
# load a RATT test script with a collection of common functions

passcode = config.g_passed

# Set up for heating
uut.cli( 'dm write {name:"heatingMode",val:true}' )
uut.cli( 'dm write {name:"heatSetpoint",val:7100}' )   # 71'F
uut.cli( 'dm write {name:"fanMode",val:"eHIGH"}' )
uut.cli( 'tick @60000') # Advance to a known time

# enable the house simulator
uut.cli( 'house enable 45')

# Advance 10 seconds
passcode = helper.advance_and_validate( passcode, 10000, "ON",
'eHIGH', 71, 0.52, 12, 100, "---", "---" )

# Advance 4 minutes
passcode = helper.advance_and_validate( passcode, 240000, "ON",
'eHIGH', 71, 0.37, 39, 100, "---", "---" )

# Advance 2 minutes
passcode = helper.advance_and_validate( passcode, 120000, "ON",
'eHIGH', 71, 0.0, 43, 100, "---", "---")

# Advance 4 minutes
passcode = helper.advance_and_validate( passcode, 240000, "ON",
'eHIGH', 71, -0.56, 26, 100, "---", "---")

# Advance 8 minutes
passcode = helper.advance_and_validate( passcode, 480000, "ON",
'eHIGH', 71, 0.47, 12, 100, "---", "---")

# end test case
uut.cli( 'dm write {name:"heatingMode",val:false}' )
uut.cli( 'house disable')
output.write_exit(__name__)
return passcode
```

APPENDIX G   RATT

Caveats

Be aware of the following caveats when using RATT:

- pexpect searches from the top of its UUT input buffer (i.e., oldest data first). Be careful not to match on a string that occurred previously, but which is not the one that the script is actually interested in.

- Searching the UUT's output for a match can take time. That is, there will be a delay between when RATT/pexpect recognizes a match and when it outputs the desired match content. To decrease the search time, I recommend that you call the uut.clear() command as late as possible before waiting on output. As the clear() command empties the UUT input buffer, there will be less data to search through. (Note that uut.cli() automatically issues a uut.clear() before it waits for a response or prompt, but only when called using waiting semantics.)

- The simpler the regular expression, the faster the search. Also be aware that with regular expressions, all matches are minimal (non-greedy), and that you will need to use \r\n to match for newline. For a detailed explanation of the newline regular expression, see the pexpect documentation.[17]

- The pexpect package was originally implemented on a Linux platform, and its support for Windows is good, but not as good as Linux. Under Windows, pexpect does not spawn applications in a terminal

---

[17] https://pexpect.readthedocs.io/en/stable/overview.html#find-the-end-of-line-cr-lf-conventions

window, and many Windows applications only support interactive behavior when they detect they are running in a terminal. In short, if you're running pexpect with a native Windows command-line tool like telnet, it doesn't work. You will need to find an alternative application (e.g., use PuTTY's plink as replacement for telnet).

Recommended Conventions

I recommend that you organize your RATT test scripts by test suites and test cases. Additionally, I recommend that you do the following things:

For all RATT test files:

- Include a Python docstring[18] in every script at the top of the file that describes the purpose of the script.

- Include a Python docstring in every function used in the test suite to document its semantics.

- Follow a naming convention for all your scripts that identifies the file as a test suite or a test script. The convention used for the epc repo is that all test case scripts file names are prefixed with "tc_" and test suite scripts files are named "test_suite.py" or are prefixed with "test_suite_".

---

[18] See https://peps.python.org/pep-0257

APPENDIX G   RATT

For test suite files:

- Meet the RATT entry script requirements for having a main() function that takes no arguments and that returns a positive integer where zero indicates pass and greater than zero indicates failure.

For test case files:

- Test case files should contain a method named run() that returns a positive integer where zero indicates pass and greater than zero indicates failure.
  - The run() method can have zero or more arguments.
  - I strongly recommend that the run() method has a single exit/return point.

The rattlib.man() module assumes you have followed these recommendations when it generates the help output for a test script file.

For the purposes of usability and debugging, here are the preferred output methods for scripts:

- For outputting instructions, general descriptions, or any other free-form text, use the rattlib.output.writeline() method.
- To record the entry and exit of the main() and run() methods in all of the script files, use the rattlib.output.write_entry() and rattlib.output.write_exit() methods.

- To output status or trace information, use the rattlib.output.writeline_verbose() and rattlib.output.write_verbose() methods. The output for these methods is turned off by default. That is, the ratt.py script must be executed with the "-v" command-line options to enable the outputs.

- To output detailed debugging information, use the rattlib.output.writeline_debug() and rattlib.output.write_debug() methods. The output for these methods is turned off by default. That is, the ratt.py script must be executed with the "-d" command-line options to enable the outputs.

The RATT tool contains an internal Python package named rattlib that provides a small set of Python functions to aid in writing test scripts. Individuals and organizations are welcome to add additional modules to the rattlib package, which is hosted on GitHub. The rattlib package is broken down into the following modules:

- **man**—Provides methods to get help on the available test scripts. This module is used primarily when running ratt.py scripts in interactive mode. Here is a snippet of the man module:

    ```
    >man.list()
    cplutils.py
    tc_basic_heating.py
    tc_common.py
    tc_heating_alerts.py
    tc_uut_alive.py
    test_suite.py
    >man.man('cplutils')
    ```

APPENDIX G RATT

```
MODULE NAME:
    cplutils
LOCATION:
    c:\_workspaces\zoe\epc\scripts\colony.core\ratt\
    cplutils.py
DESCRIPTION:
    Utilities, common functions, etc.
FUNCTIONS:
    get_uut_elapsed_time(display_time=False)
        Gets the current UUT elapsed time and returns
        it in milliseconds.
        When 'display_time' is True, the current time
        will be displayed on the console.
...
```

- **output**—Provides a collection of methods to output messages to the console and the log file. The developer has full control over where the output is written. The default behavior is that output is written to both stdout (i.e., the console) and the log file.

- **std**—Provides basic functionality for loading and executing test scripts (e.g., the std.load() and std.run() methods).

- **uut**—Provides a collection of methods to interact with the UUT. The primary methods are uut.cli() and uut.clear(). The cli() method writes data to the UUT's input stream. The clear() method is used to clear all previously received data from the UUT's output stream.

Interactive help is available for all modules in the rattlib when running ratt.py scripts in interactive mode.

APPENDIX H

GM6000 Requirements

This appendix provides examples of requirements documents that you can use as templates if your requirements process is informal, ad hoc, or inconsistent. In this case, the examples are the formal requirements for the GM6000 Digital Heater Controller project, and they are separated into several documents based on the principal document owner or discipline. That is, there are examples of

- Marketing Requirements (MRS)
- Product Requirements (PRS)
- Software Requirements (SRS)
- Hardware Requirements (HRS)

The document content is sparse, and the formatting is minimal, but the structure of the templates do address all the areas you should be paying attention to and thinking about.

APPENDIX H   GM6000 REQUIREMENTS

If you do not have a requirements database tool such as Doors, Jama, etc., I recommend using a spreadsheet to manage requirements because it allows you to dynamically sort and filter the requirements in real time. The `epc` repository contains an example GM6000 Software Requirements documents as spreadsheets. The spreadsheets are located in the `docs/GM6000 Example Docs/` directory.

Marketing Requirements

The sample document here is for the top-level requirements for a project. These requirements represent the customer and business needs.

Document Name and Number

MRS-1322: GM6000 Marketing Requirements Specification

Overview

The GM6000 product is a Digital Heater Controller (DHC) that can be used in many different physical form factors and heating capacities. The specifics of the final unit's physical attributes will be provisioned into the DHC during the manufacturing process.

It is acceptable for the initial release of the GM6000 to be a single form factor. Follow-up releases will include additional form factors as well as a wireless space temperature sensor.

APPENDIX H GM6000 REQUIREMENTS

Glossary

Term	Definition
DHC	Digital Heater Controller

Document References

Document #	Document name	Version
MRS-1322	GM6000 Marketing Requirements Specification	0.1

Requirements

The use of the words *shall, will,* and *must* indicates that the requirement must be implemented. The use of the words *should, may,* and *can* indicates that the requirement is desired but does not have to be implemented.

Req#	Name	Requirement	Rel
MR-100	Heating System	The DHC system shall provide indoor heating based on space temperature and a user-supplied heat setting.	1.0
MR-101	Heating Enclosures	The DHC shall support at least three different heater enclosures. The heating capacity of each heater enclosure can be different from the other enclosures.	1.0

(*continued*)

APPENDIX H   GM6000 REQUIREMENTS

Req#	Name	Requirement	Rel
MR-102	Control Board	DHC shall have a single control board that can be installed in many heater enclosures.	1.0
MR-103	Control Algorithm	The heater control algorithm in the control board shall accept parameters and configuration that customizes the algorithm for a specific heater enclosure.	1.0
MR-104	Provisioning	The DHC control board shall be provisioned to a specific heater enclosure during the manufacturing process. The provisioning shall include the heater control algorithm's parameters and configuration.	1.0
MR-105	Wireless	The control board shall support connecting to a wireless module for communicating with a wireless temperature input.	2.0
MR-106	Wireless	The DHC system shall support an external, wireless temperature sensor.	2.0
MR-107	User Interface	The DHC unit shall support a display, LEDs, and user inputs (e.g., physical buttons, keypad membrane, etc.). The arrangement of the display and user inputs can be different between heater enclosures.	1.0

(*continued*)

APPENDIX H GM6000 REQUIREMENTS

Req#	Name	Requirement	Rel
MR-108	User Actions	The DHC display, LEDs, and user inputs shall allow the user to do the following: • Turn the heater on/off • Set the maximum fan speed • Set the temperature setpoint	1.0
MR-109	User Information	The DHC display LEDs shall provide the user with the following information: • Current temperature • The DHC on/off state • Whether the DHC is actively heating • The fan on/off state • Alerts and failure conditions	1.0
MR-200	UI Languages	The User Interface text shall be in US English.	1.0
MR-201	Troubleshooting	The DHC shall support troubleshooting failures in the field and diagnostics for analyzing returned units.	1.0
MR-203	Lifetime	The DHC shall be designed for a lifetime of five years, with a minimum of 25,000 hours of active heating operations.	1.0

Change Log

Version	Date	Updated By	Changes
0.1	5/13/2023	D. Blake	Initial draft

APPENDIX H   GM6000 REQUIREMENTS

Product Requirements

The following sample document is for system-level or product-level requirements that identify a solution to the Marketing Requirements Specification (MRS).

Document Name and Number

PRS-1323: GM6000 Product Requirements Specification

Overview

The GM6000 product is a Digital Heater Controller (DHC) that can be used in many different physical form factors and heating capacities. The specifics of the final unit's physical attributes will be provisioned into the DHC during the manufacturing process. The following product requirements identify a solution for the GM6000.

Glossary

Term	Definition
DHC	Digital Heater Controller

Document References

Document #	Document Name	Version
MRS-1322	GM6000 Marketing Requirements Specification	0.1

Requirements

Req#	Name	Requirement	Rel
PR-100	Sub-assemblies	The DHC heater closure shall contain the following sub-assemblies: • Control Board (CB) • Heating Element (HE) • Display and User Inputs (DUI) • Blower Assembly (BA) • Power Supply (PS) • Temperature Sensor (TS)	1.0
PR-101	Wireless Module	The DHC heater closure shall contain the following sub-assemblies: • Wireless Module (WM)	2.0
PR-102	Temperature Sensor	The system shall support using an external wireless temperature as the primary space temperature with the onboard temperature sensor used as a back-up sensor in the case of no communications with the wireless sensor.	2.0
PR-103	Heater Safety	The Heating Element (HE) sub-assembly shall contain a hardware temperature protection circuit that forces the heating source off when it exceeds the designed safety limits.	1.0

(*continued*)

APPENDIX H GM6000 REQUIREMENTS

Req#	Name	Requirement	Rel
PR-105	Heater Element Interface	The Heating Element (HE) sub-assembly shall have a proportional heating output interface to the Control Board (CB).	1.0
PR-106	Blower Assembly Interface	The Blower Assembly (BA) sub-assembly shall have a proportional speed control interface to the Control Board (CB).	1.0
PR-107	Temperature Sensor	The Temperature Sensor (TS) sub-assembly shall use a thermistor for measuring space temperature.	1.0
PR-200	Console Debug	The Control Board (CB) console UART shall be used for debugging and troubleshooting the unit.	1.0
PR-201	Console Provisioning	Provisioning the Control Board (CB) at manufacturing shall be done through the CB console UART port.	1.0
PR-202	Console Security	The CB software shall require a password for console access. The password shall be unique for each DHC unit.	1.0
PR-203	Console Security	The Control Board (CB) console password shall be provisioned into the unit during the manufacturing process.	1.0

(*continued*)

APPENDIX H GM6000 REQUIREMENTS

Req#	Name	Requirement	Rel
PR-204	Console Security	The manufacturing provisioning process shall not require a console password.	1.0
PR-205	UI Display	The basic DUI board shall contain the following: • Approximately 1" (± 20%) Graphic LCD • Minimum color depth is eight colors • Minimum pixel resolution is 200 × 120 • Maximum pixel_resolution × color_depth shall require no more than 64KB of RAM for a full screen buffer • Four discrete momentary buttons • 1 RGB LED Note: In the future, there will be multiple DUI boards.	1.0
PR-206	Heater Safety	The Heating Element (HE) sub-assembly shall provide an indication to the Control Board (CB) when it has been shut off due to a safety limit.	1.0

(*continued*)

APPENDIX H   GM6000 REQUIREMENTS

Req#	Name	Requirement	Rel
PR-207	Temperature Control	The control algorithm shall maintain the sensed space temperature within ± one degree Celsius of the setpoint under a "steady-state" condition. The steady-state condition requires the following: • A constant thermal load on the space • At least five minutes has elapsed after the sensed space temperature reached the setpoint temperature. • The sensed space temperature is the measured value (after any SW/HW filtering). That is, it's not the actual, independently measured space temperature.	1.0

Change Log

Version	Date	Updated By	Changes
0.1	5/13/2023	S. Rogers	Initial draft

APPENDIX H   GM6000 REQUIREMENTS

Software Requirements

The following document is for detailed software-level requirements for the GM6000 project. With respect to software, this is the lowest, most-detailed level of requirements.

Document Name and Number

SRS-1324: GM6000 Software Requirements Specification

Overview

The GM6000 product is a Digital Heater Controller (DHC) that can be used in many different physical form factors and heating capacities. The specifics of the final unit's physical attributes will be provisioned into the DHC during the manufacturing process. The following software requirements identify the software specific requirements.

Glossary

Term	Definition
DHC	Digital Heater Controller

Document References

Document #	Document Name	Version
MRS-1322	GM6000 Marketing Requirements Specification	0.2
PRS-1323	GM6000 Product Requirements Specification	0.1

APPENDIX H   GM6000 REQUIREMENTS

Requirements

Req#	Name	Requirement	Rel
SWR-200	Console: Security	The CB's console UART shall be password protected to prevent unauthorized access.	1.0
SWR-201	Console: Security	The CB console password shall not be stored as plain text in nonvolatile storage.	1.0
SWR-202	UI Languages	Text displayed to the user shall be in English (United States) using only 7-bit ASCII character codes.	1.0
SWR-203	UI Splash Screen	On startup, the Unit shall display the model number and software version information for at least two seconds before displaying the home screen.	1.0
SWR-204	UI Home Status	The home screen shall display the following: • Selected unit mode (i.e., On/Off) • Selected fan speed • Current space temperature • Current temperature setpoint • Current heater control signal as a percentage • Current fan speed control signal as a percentage • Alert text—when present	1.0

(*continued*)

APPENDIX H   GM6000 REQUIREMENTS

Req#	Name	Requirement	Rel
SWR-205	UI Home Control	When on the home screen, the discrete button controls shall allow the user to	1.0
		• Toggle unit mode on/off • Cycle through the available fan speeds • Transition to the temperature Setpoint Edit screen • Cycle through the list of active alert messages	
SWR-206	UI Edit Setpoint	When on the Setpoint Edit screen, the discrete button controls shall allow the user to	1.0
		• Increase the setpoint value. The setpoint is limited to a max value • Decrease the setpoint value. The setpoint is limited to a min value. • Exit edit mode and return to the home screen.	

(*continued*)

APPENDIX H GM6000 REQUIREMENTS

Req#	Name	Requirement	Rel
SWR-207	UI LED Status	The RGB LED shall have the following behaviors: • Solid GREEN when the selected unit mode is ON and the heater element and fan motor are off. • ¼ Hz flashing BLUE when the selected unit mode is ON and the heater element is on. • 1 Hz flashing RED when there is one or more active alerts.	1.0
SWR-208	UI Home Control	When on the home screen, a two-button key combination shall be used to transition to the About screen.	1.0
SWR-209	UI About Status	The About screen shall display the following: • Model number • Software version information • Support phone number	1.0
SWR-210	UI About Control	Pressing any discrete button control transitions the home screen.	1.0

(*continued*)

APPENDIX H   GM6000 REQUIREMENTS

Req#	Name	Requirement	Rel
SWR-211	UI Error	When an unrecoverable error has been detected, the software shall	1.0

		• Generate a 2 Hz "red flash" pattern on the RGB LED
		• Disable all UI controls (e.g., ignore button presses)
		• Display an error screen with the following information:
		  • Error code
		  • Model number
		  • Software version information
		  • Support phone number	

Change Log

Version	Date	Updated By	Changes
0.1	5/15/2023	V. Dinkley	Initial draft
0.2	2/25/2024	V. Dinkley	Update LED behaviors for better usability (i.e., not solely rely on colors)

Hardware Requirements

The following document is for detailed (electrical) hardware-level requirements for the GM6000 project. With respect to hardware, this is the lowest, most-detailed level of requirements.

APPENDIX H   GM6000 REQUIREMENTS

Document Name and Number

HRS-1325: GM6000 Electrical Hardware Requirements Specification

Overview

The GM6000 product is a Digital Heater Controller (DHC) that can be used in many different physical form factors and heating capacities. The specifics of the final unit's physical attributes will be provisioned into the DHC during the manufacturing process. The following hardware requirements identify the hardware specific requirements.

Glossary

Term	Definition
DHC	Digital Heater Controller

Document References

Document #	Document name	Version
MRS-1322	GM6000 Marketing Requirements Specification	0.1
PRS-1323	GM6000 Product Requirements Specification	0.1

Requirements

Req#	Name	Requirement	Rel
HWR-200	MCU: Peripherals	The microcontroller shall support at least two UART peripherals, one SPI master peripheral, and one I2C master peripheral.	1.0
HWR-201	Display Interface	The LCD display controller shall have a serial interface.	1.0
HWR-202	Heater PWM	The proportional control of the heater shall be a Pulse Width Modulation (PWM) signal. The PWM frequency is **TBD** Hz. The duty cycle is modulated from 0% (off), 50% (50% capacity), or 100% (100% capacity).	1.0
HWR-203	Fan PWM	The proportional control of the fan speed shall be a PWM signal. The PWM frequency is **TBD** Hz. The duty cycle is modulated from 0% (off), 50% (50% speed), to 100% (full speed).	1.0
HWR-204	UI Display	The graphic LCD assembly shall contain an LCD controller (with graphics RAM) that has an 8-bit SPI interface to the MCU.	1.0

APPENDIX H GM6000 REQUIREMENTS

Change Log

Version	Date	Updated By	Changes
0.1	5/16/2023	F. Jones	Initial draft

APPENDIX I

GM6000 System Architecture

This appendix provides an example of a system architecture document that you can use as template. It is the system architecture document for the GM6000 Digital Heater Controller project. The document's example content is sparse, and it omits almost all non-software-related content.

> The `epc` repository contains the example GM6000 System Architecture document as a Microsoft Word document. The document is located in the `docs/GM6000 Example Docs/` directory.

Document Name and Number

SYSA-1326: GM6000 System Architecture

Overview

Build a Digital Heater Controller (DHC) that can be used in many different physical form factors and heating capacities. The specifics of the final unit's physical attributes will be provisioned into the DHC during the manufacturing process.

APPENDIX I   GM6000 SYSTEM ARCHITECTURE

Glossary

Term	Definition
DHC	Digital Heater Controller

Document References

Document #	Document Name	Version
MRS-1322	GM6000 DHC Marketing Requirements Specification	0.1
PRS-1323	GM6000 Product Requirements Specification	0.1

Block Diagram

To meet the marketing needs of multiple form factors and capacities, the decision was made to break down the DHC unit into six major sub-assemblies (see Figure I-1). The individual sub-assemblies can be specific to physical enclosures with the exception of a single Control Board sub-assembly that is common to all enclosures.

The DHC system consists of the following components that will be physically located within the primary physical enclosure. There can be many different physical enclosures.

APPENDIX I   GM6000 SYSTEM ARCHITECTURE

Digital Heater Controller (DHC)

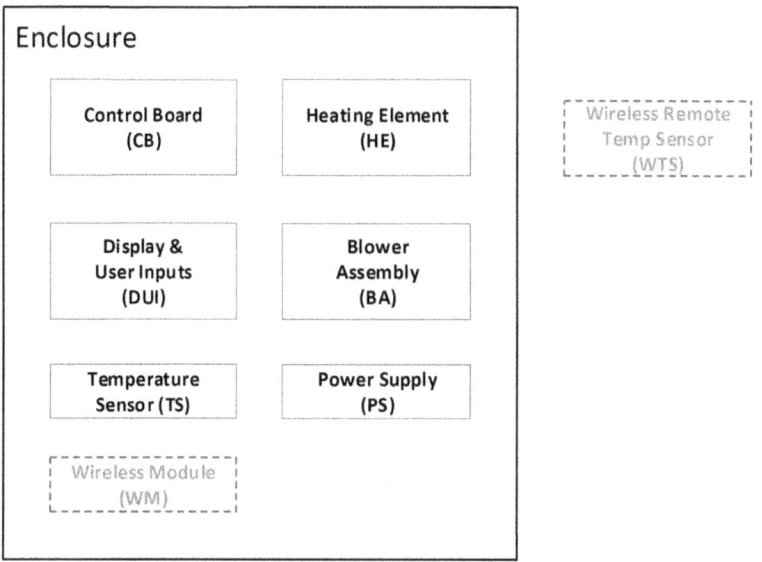

Figure I-1. System architecture block diagram

Component	Description
Control Board (CB)	This contains the microcontroller that runs the heater controller. The CB contains circuits and other chips as needed to support the MCU and software.
Display and User Inputs (DUI)	A separate board that contains the display, buttons, and LEDs used for interaction with the customer. This DUI can be located anywhere within the enclosure and is connected to the CB via a wire harness or cable.

(*continued*)

APPENDIX I   GM6000 SYSTEM ARCHITECTURE

Component	Description
Temperature Sensor (TS)	A thermistor is used to measure the unit's temperature. The TS can be located anywhere within the enclosure and is connected to the CB via a wire harness or cable. **Note:** Physical placement of the TS is important to the overall performance of the unit. That is, it must be thermally isolated and located such that it can accurately measure the space temperature.
Heating Element (HE)	This is the heat source for the unit. The HE must support a Pulse Width Modulation (PWM) input signal that is used to control its variable heating capacity. The HE shall contain a temperature protection circuit that prevents the HE from exceeding the safe design limits. The details of the HE heating capacity are provisioned into the CB when the unit is manufactured. The HE can be located anywhere within the enclosure and is connected to the CB via a wire harness or cable.
Blower Assembly (BA)	The Blower Assembly delivers the HE's heat output to the space. The primary components of the BA are the following: • Fan • Fan housing • Fan motor The BA must support a PWM input signal that is used to control the speed of the fan motor. The details of the BA capabilities are provisioned into the CB when the unit is manufactured. The BA can be located anywhere within the enclosure and is connected to the CB via a wire harness or cable.

(*continued*)

APPENDIX I   GM6000 SYSTEM ARCHITECTURE

Component	Description
Power Supply (PS)	The power supply accepts line power in and is responsible for providing the appropriate voltage inputs and current ratings to the CB, HE, and BA. The PS is connected to the CB, HE, and BA via wire harnesses or cables. **Note:** The DUI and the optional WM board are powered via their connection with the CB.

The following components are optional depending on the configuration of the final end product.

Component	Description
Wireless Module (WM)	This board can be attached to the unit (when manufactured) to provide a wireless connection to a remote temperature sensor. The presence or absence of the WM is provisioned into the CB when the unit is manufactured. The WM can be located anywhere within the enclosure and is connected to the CB via a wire harness or cable.
Wireless Remote Temperature Sensor (WTS)	This is a fully stand-alone component that measures space temperature and reports the temperature to the main unit via the WM.

Change Log

Version	Date	Updated By	Changes
0.1	5/13/2023	S. Rogers	Initial draft

APPENDIX J

GM6000 Software Architecture

This appendix provides an example of a software architecture (SWA) document that you can use as template. It is the software architecture document for the GM6000 Digital Heater Controller project. The document's example content is not exhaustive, but the structure of the template does address all the areas you should be paying attention to and thinking about.

> The epc repository contains the example GM6000 Software Architecture document as a Microsoft Word document. The document is located in the docs/GM6000 Example Docs/ directory.

Document Name and Number

SWA-1327: GM6000 Software Architecture

APPENDIX J   GM6000 SOFTWARE ARCHITECTURE

Scope

This document captures the software architecture for the GM6000 software. The software architecture identifies a high-level solution and defines the rules of engagement for the subsequent design and implementation steps of the GM6000 software.

The target audience for this document is software developers, system engineers, and test engineers. In addition, authors are required to view the audience as not only being the original development team but also future team members on future development efforts.

Requirements Tracing

For requirements tracing purposes, the *[SWA-nnn]* identifiers are used to label traceable architectural items. The SWA identifiers, once assigned, shall not be reused or reassigned to a different item. The *nnn* portion of the identifier is simply a free running counter to ensure unique identifiers within the document.

Overview

The GM6000 is a Digital Heater Controller (DHC) that can be used in many different form factors and heating capacities. The specifics of the unit's physical attributes will be provisioned into the DHC when the final assembly of the DHC is performed. The GM6000's software executes on a microcontroller that is part of the unit's Control Board (CB). The Control Board is physically located within the unit's enclosure. The software interacts with other sub-assemblies—Heating Element, Blower Assembly, Display and User Inputs, and Temperature Sensor—within the enclosure. In the future, the software will interact with an external wireless temperature sensor. Figure J-1 summarizes the system architecture.

APPENDIX J   GM6000 SOFTWARE ARCHITECTURE

Digital Heater Controller (DHC)

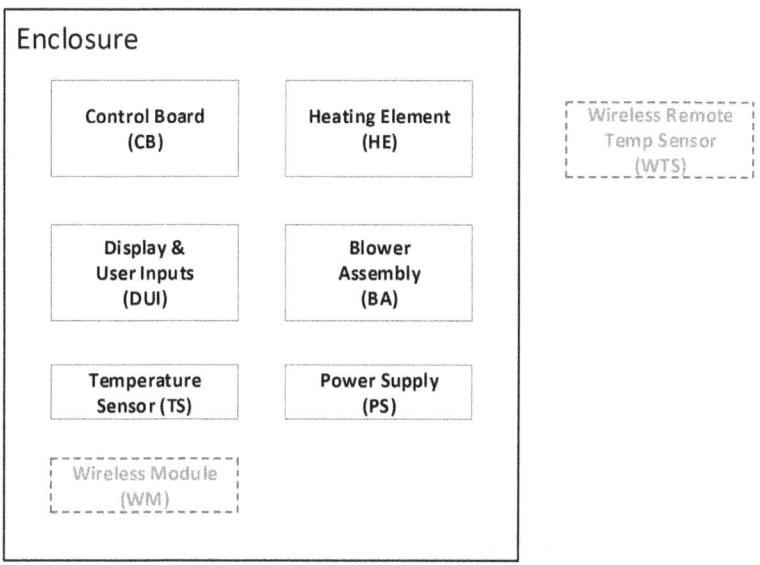

Figure J-1. System architecture block diagram

Glossary

Term	Definition
BSP	Board Support Package
DHC	Digital Heater Controller
ITC	Inter-thread communication
MCU	Microcontroller
PII	Personally identifiable information
UART	Universal asynchronous receiver-transmitter

475

APPENDIX J   GM6000 SOFTWARE ARCHITECTURE

Document References

Document #	Document Name	Version
MRS-1322	GM6000 Marketing Requirements Specification	0.1
PRS-1323	GM6000 Product Requirements Specification	0.1
SRS-1324	GM6000 Software Requirements Specification	0.2
QMS-018	Cyber Security Work Instructions	
SYSA-1326	GM6000 System Architecture	0.1

Hardware Interfaces

Figure J-2 illustrates the input and output signals to the Control Board's microcontroller. It defines what the MCU's inputs and outputs are.

APPENDIX J   GM6000 SOFTWARE ARCHITECTURE

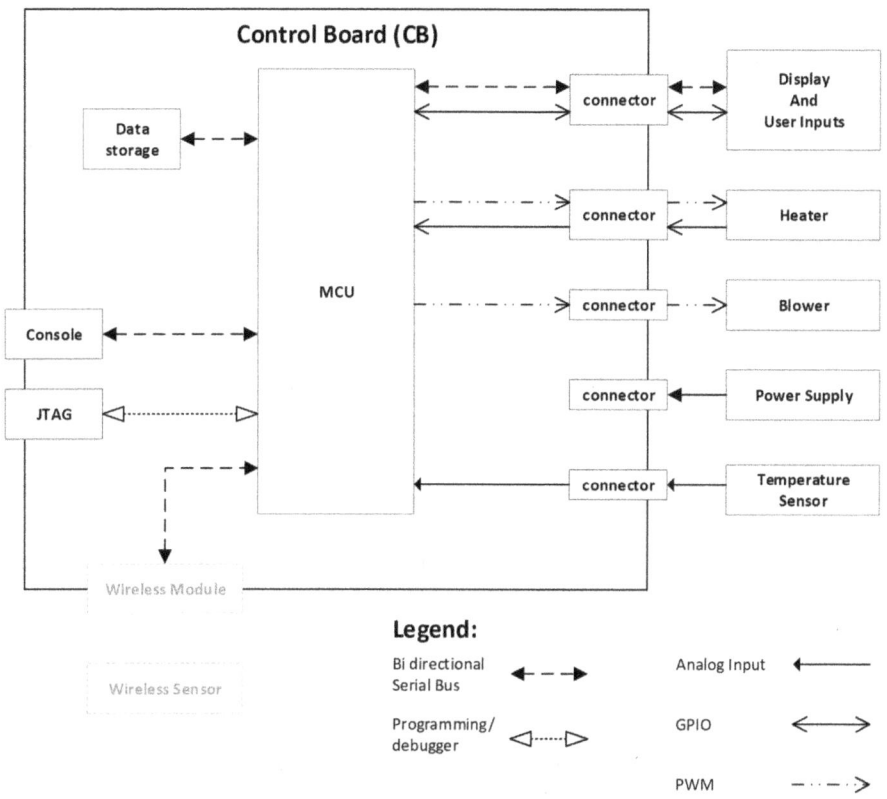

Figure J-2. Hardware block diagram

Component	Description
Control Board (CB)	A single PCBA that contains the microcontroller that operates the heater controller. The board has numerous connectors for off-board connections to the other sub-assemblies.
Data Storage	Serial persistent data storage for configuration, user settings, etc.

(*continued*)

Component	Description
Console	A UART interface that will be used for provisioning (and testing) the CB during manufacturing. The Console will also be used during development as a debug console.
Wireless Module (WM)	An optional (future release) module for wireless communications
Wireless Sensor (WS)	An optional (future release) wireless temperature sensor that communicates to the CB via the WM
Display and User Inputs	A sub-assembly that contains the following: • A physical display with a display controller and backlight LEDs. The interface to the controller is via a serial bus. • One or more LEDs for the indications and status • Discrete buttons
Heater	The heating element or heating source. The heater is proportionally controlled using a Pulse Width Modulation (PWM) signal. The heater contains a hardware safety circuit to prevent unsafe heater operation. When the safety circuit has disabled the heater, it asserts a signal to the MCU.
Power Supply	The power supply module generates and distributes multiple power buses or voltages to the various sub-assemblies.
Temperature Sensor	A thermistor for measuring space temperature

Performance Constraints

This section summarizes the analysis performed—and documents the decisions made—with respect to real-time performance.

Data Storage

The off-board data storage is used for storing configuration, user settings, device logs, etc. All of this data can be written and retrieved in the background. However, on orderly shutdown, all pending write actions must be completed before the Control is powered off or the MCU is put to sleep. The assessment and recommendations are as follows:

- No real-time constraints
- The shutdown sequence of the application is required to ensure all pending writes are completed before the MCU is powered off or put to sleep.

Display

The MCU communicates with the display controller via a serial bus (e.g., SPI or I2C). There is a time constraint in that the physical transfer time for an entire screen's worth of pixel data (including color data) must be fast enough to ensure a good user experience. There is also a RAM constraint with respect to the display in that the MCU will need at least one off-screen frame buffer that can hold an entire screen's worth of pixel data. The size of the pixel data is a function of the display's resolution times the color depth. The assessment and recommendations are as follows:

- The maximum size of the pixel data is limited to 64K to meet the timing and RAM constraints.
- Assuming a 16 MHz serial bus, the wire transfer time for a full screen is 41 msec without accounting for protocol overhead, ISR jitter, thread context switches, etc.

APPENDIX J   GM6000 SOFTWARE ARCHITECTURE

Display Backlight

The control of the display's backlighting is assumed to be either a discrete GPIO enable signal or a PWM signal that proportionally controls brightness. For the PWM use case, the MCU hardware will generate the PWM signal, and it is assumed that changes in the brightness do not have to occur immediately (i.e., there is no requirement for faster than 1 Hz). The assessment and recommendations are as follows:

- No real time constraints
- PWM control (if needed) requires a MCU timer or PWM peripheral.

User Inputs

The application must respond to user button presses in a timely manner. The time for sampling and debouncing the input signals and then providing feedback to the user (updated display, LED change state, etc.) must also be taken into consideration. A button press (and release) must be detected and debounced in approximately 50 msec. The assessment and recommendations are as follows:

- Button input signals are required to be interrupt driven to detect the initial edges.[19]
- A high-priority driver thread is required to debounce the button input signals.

---

[19] This architectural constraint of "interrupt driven" will be changed in the Software Detailed Design. It is left in its original form here to illustrate that original ideas can change in the course of the development process and that when changes occur, it's simply a matter of documenting the change and, as necessary, documenting the agreement for the change.

LEDs

In general, the LEDs only change state based on the application changing state, so LED changes should be slower than 1 Hz. The exception is if there are requirements to flash one or more LEDs. However, since flashing LEDs will be in the context of conveying a particular state or fault condition to the user, it is not critical to have precise and 100% consistent flash intervals. The assessment and recommendations are as follows:

- No real-time constraints for LEDS that are not flashing.
- For flashing LEDS, a medium to high-priority thread can be used to generate the flash rate.

Heater Control

The heating capacity of the heater element is controlled by a PWM signal. Controlling space temperature is a relatively slow system (i.e., much slower than 1 Hz), and the heater element has its own safety protection. The assessment and recommendations are as follows:

- PWM control requires an MCU timer or PWM peripheral.

Heater Safety Indication

The heater element has self-contained safety protection circuits that override the MCU's PWM signal when there is an unsafe condition. When the safety circuits are active, the heater element generates an input signal to the MCU to notify it that a heating element has been forced off. The assessment and recommendations are as follows:

- No real-time constraints since the software is not responsible for the safe operation of the heating element.

APPENDIX J   GM6000 SOFTWARE ARCHITECTURE

Blower Control

The fan speed of the Blower Assembly is controlled by a PWM signal. Controlling space temperature is a relatively slow system (i.e., much slower than 1 Hz). The assessment and recommendations are as follows:

- PWM control requires an MCU timer or PWM peripheral.

Temperature Sensor

The space temperature must be sampled and potentially filtered before being input into the control algorithm. However, controlling space temperature is a relatively slow system (i.e., much slower than 1 Hz). The assessment and recommendations are as follows:

- No real-time constraints on sample or filtering.

Console

The console port is used during manufacturing for provisioning and testing. It can also be used for live troubleshooting. In either case, it is a text-based command/response interface that has no critical timing requirements. The assessment and recommendations are as follows:

- No real-time constraints, except that the UART driver must be interrupt driven and use hardware FIFOs or DMA when possible.

Wireless Module

The MCU will interface with the wireless module via a serial bus. The assumption is that the wireless module itself handles all of the real-time aspects of the wireless protocol. In addition, since only space temperature is being reported (and not at a high frequency), there is not much data to be transferred.

- No real-time constraints

Control Algorithm

Controlling space temperature is a relatively slow system. The control algorithm will execute periodically at a rate slower than 1 Hz. The assessment and recommendations are as follows:

- No real-time constraints

Password Hashing

The console is password protected. The password is not stored in plain text in persistent storage; rather, a hash of the password is stored. Depending on the type of hash and number of iterations, the hashing process can take a considerable amount of time and CPU usage. However, this is a one-time-per-console-session event, and it is okay for the user to wait for authorization. The assessment and recommendations are as follows:

- The hashing of passwords must be performed in a low-priority thread.

APPENDIX J   GM6000 SOFTWARE ARCHITECTURE

Threading

A Real-Time Operating System (RTOS) with many threads will be used. Switching between threads (a context switch) requires a measurable amount of time. This becomes important when there are sub-10-millisecond timing requirements and when looking at overall CPU usage. The RTOS also adds timing overhead for maintaining its system tick timer, which is typically interrupt based. The assessment and recommendations are as follows:

- The RTOS context switching time and tick counter overhead only needs to be considered when there are requirements for response or detection times that are less than 1 millisecond.

Summary

There are no real-time and performance constraints that require microsecond or sub-10-millisecond processing. The most impactful constraints are for the display driver and the user buttons with processing times in the tens of milliseconds, which can be accommodated using high-priority interrupts and threads. There is a hardware requirement that the MCU has at least two to three PWM outputs (depending on how the backlight is controlled).

Programming Languages

The software shall be a C/C++ application—predominantly C++. The Software Development Plan will specify the specific ISO language and coding standards to follow.

APPENDIX J GM6000 SOFTWARE ARCHITECTURE

Subsystems

Figure J-3 illustrates the subsystems that the control board software is broken down into.

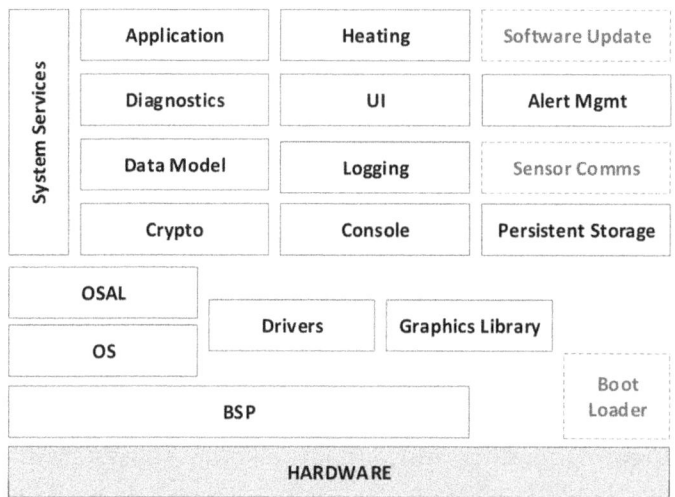

Figure J-3. Subsystems

[SWA-10] Alert Management

The alarm management subsystem is responsible for summarizing and managing the user's interaction with active alerts. This includes functionality such as the following:

- Summarizing the superset of internal alerts into the subset of alerts that are presented to the user
- Prioritizing which alert is indicated first when there is more than one active alert

- Presenting alert indications that are not done via the main display, for example, LEDs, audio tones, etc.

- Managing the semantics of user-acknowledged, but still active, alerts

The subsystem is not responsible for raising or clearing individual alerts. Alert detection logic is spread throughout the entire system. That is, each individual subsystem is responsible for declaring its own alerts.

[SWA-11] Application

The application subsystem contains the top-level business logic for the entire application. This includes functionality such as the following:

- The top-level state of the entire device

- Creating, starting, and stopping all other subsystems

[SWA-12] Bootloader

The bootloader subsystem consists of the nonmutable bootloader that is responsible for

- Determining the validity of the application software

- Launching the application software

- Reprogramming application software in persistent storage

At this time, the bootloader is not a required subsystem. That is, there is no requirement for field upgradable software.

[SWA-13] BSP

The Board Support Package (BSP) subsystem is responsible for abstracting the details of the MCU's datasheet. For example, it is responsible for the following:

- The low-level code that directly configures the MCUs hardware registers
- The encapsulation of the MCU vendor's supplied SDK, including any modifications or extensions needed
- Compiler-dependent constructs (e.g., setting up the MCU's vector table)

The BSP is specific to a target PCBA. That is, each board spin will have its own BSP. The BSP may or may not contain driver code. Driver code that is contained within the BSP is by definition dependent on a specific target. Whether or not a specific driver is generic—that is, it has no direct dependency on the BSP—will be determined on a case-by-case basis. The preference is for generic drivers.

[SWA-14] Console

The console subsystem provides a command-line interface (CLI) for the application. The CLI is used to provision the unit during manufacturing. The console will be secured so that only authorized users have access to it after the unit is shipped. The CLI is also used for

- Live unit troubleshooting
- White box testing
- Development debugging

APPENDIX J   GM6000 SOFTWARE ARCHITECTURE

[SWA-15] Crypto

The Crypto subsystem provides application-specific cryptography services as well as abstract APIs to low-level crypto services provided by the MCU, SDK, and third-party software.

[SWA-16] Data Model

The Data Model is a data-oriented architectural pattern where modules interact with each other via data instances with no direct dependencies between modules. The Data Model is the primary mechanism for sharing data between subsystems. The following Data Model best practices shall be followed:

- Model points contain data, not objects. In addition, model points do not contain business rules or enforce policies other than potential basic value range checking rules.

- Model points shall be uniquely typed by their contained data values and their usage semantics. For example, it provides the definition of what constitutes a change for change notifications.

- There is no synchronization between model points. Operations on a single model point instance are atomic. When synchronization across model points is required, it must be provided by the application.

- Never cache a model point value across function calls. It is okay to read a model point value in a method and then use a local value (i.e., model point value stored in an automatic variable of the method) for the rest of the

APPENDIX J GM6000 SOFTWARE ARCHITECTURE

method call. But never read a model point value and then store it in a class member or global variable for later use.

- Always check the valid state of a model point before operating on the read value. The application cannot assume that a model point always has a valid value, and any module interacting with the model point needs to include logic for dealing with the invalid data.

- A model point's change notification semantics guarantee that a client will get a notification when there is a change to the model point's value or state. However, it does not guarantee notifications for all changes, just the last change.

- All model point instances will be statically allocated. The static allocation is to facilitate debugging (i.e., all of the MPs are always in scope for the debugger) and unit testing (i.e., individual tests can use or leverage the existing allocation code).

- All model point instances shall be encapsulated in the mp namespace.

- All model point instances should be instantiated in their invalid state. This ensures that there are no false valid-to-invalid transitions for model points that have their true initial values set from external interfaces. It also reinforces the behavior of first checking the model's state.

- For non-application-specific or nondomain-specific classes and modules (i.e., generic middleware, drivers, etc.), always provide references or pointers to model point instances. That is, for nonspecific classes and modules, avoid hard-coded model point instance names.

- For application-specific and domain-specific classes, it is okay to use hard-coded model point instance names. This reduces the constructor and initialization overhead of passing around references and pointers to model point instances.

[SWA-17] Diagnostics

The Diagnostics subsystem is responsible for monitoring the software's health, diagnostics logic, and self-testing the system. This includes features such as power-on self-tests and metrics capture.

[SWA-18] Drivers

The Driver subsystem is the collection of driver code that does not reside in the BSP subsystem. Drivers that directly interact with hardware are required to be separated into layers. There should be at least three layers:

- A hardware-specific layer that is specific to a target platform.
- A platform-independent layer. Ideally the majority of the business logic is contained in this layer.
- A Hardware Abstraction Layer (HAL) that separates the other two layers. That is, the hardware-specific layer implements the HAL, and the platform-independent layer calls the HAL.

How drivers interact with the application-level code will be done on a case-by-case basis, with preference for using model points to share data.

[SWA-19] Graphics Library

The Graphics library subsystem is responsible for providing graphic primitives, fonts, window management, widgets, etc. The expectation is that the Graphics library will be third-party software. The minimum requirements for the graphics library are as follows:

- It is platform independent. That is, there are no direct dependencies on the MCU or physical display.

- It supports a bare-metal runtime environment. That is, it can be used with or without an RTOS. This constraint is so that System Services OSAL's event-based threads can be used directly for events, timers, ITC messages, etc., in the thread where the UI executes. This eliminates the need for an adapter layer to translate the System Services events into Graphics library specific events.

[SWA-20] Heating

The heating subsystem is responsible for the closed-loop space temperature control (in other words, the algorithm code).

[SWA-21] Logging

The logging subsystem is responsible for creating and managing a device log. The device log is a persistent collection of timestamped events and data that is used for profiling the device's behavior, algorithm performance, etc., and for troubleshooting returned units. Individual entries in the device log are generated throughout the system and subsystems as interesting events and data occur. In other words, the logging subsystem is not the source of the log entries. At a minimum, the contents of the device log are retrievable via the console.

[SWA-22] OS

The Operating System subsystem will be a third-party software package. The OS for the hardware target's platform must be an RTOS with priority-based thread preemption and priority inheritance features (for mutexes).

[SWA-23] OSAL

The Operating System Abstraction Layer (OSAL) subsystem decouples the application and driver code from a specific operating system executing on the target platform.

[SWA-24] Persistent Storage

The persistent storage subsystem provides interfaces, framework, data integrity checks, etc., for storing and retrieving data that is stored in local persistent storage. The persistent storage paradigm is a RAM-cached model. The RAM-cached model is as follows:

1. On startup, persistent record entries are read from nonvolatile storage, validated, and loaded into RAM.

    a. If the data is invalid, then the associated RAM values are set to factory default values, and the nonvolatile storage is updated with the new defaulted values.

2. The application updates the entries stored in RAM via an API. When an update request is made, the RAM value is updated, and then a background task is initiated to update the values stored in nonvolatile storage.

The definition of a persistent record—its content, default values, etc.—is outside the scope of the persistent storage subsystems. This is done by individual subsystems and components that require persistent storage.

[SWA-25] Sensor Comms

The sensor communications subsystem is responsible for managing the wireless protocol used to communicate space temperature from a wireless temperature sensor. This includes items such as

- Discovering sensors
- Connecting to and disconnecting from a sensor
- Transferring sensor data into the application
- Issuing "sensor offline" alerts

Note The sensor communication subsystem is not required for the initial release.

[SWA-26] Software Update

As part of the application, the software update subsystem contains the business logic that downloads new firmware to the board. In addition, the subsystem is responsible for triggering the physical upgrade process as well as any migration or update to the persistent storage application data as part of the upgrade process.

At this time, the software update subsystem is not required. There is no requirement for field upgradable software.

[SWA-27] System Services

The System Services subsystem provides various services such as containers, checksums, string handling, software timers, inter-thread communication (ITC), stream handling, parsers and formatters, memory pools, etc.

[SWA-28] UI

The user interface (UI) subsystem is responsible for the business logic and interaction with end users of the unit. This includes displaying the LCD screens, screen navigation, processing button inputs, LED outputs, etc. The UI subsystem has a hard dependency on the Graphics library subsystem. This hard dependency is acceptable because the Graphics library is platform independent.

[SWA-31] Interfaces

The preferred, and primary, interface for sharing data between subsystems will be done via the Data Model pattern. The secondary interface will be message-based inter-thread communications (ITC). Which mechanism is used to share data will be determined on a case-by-case basis with the preference being to use the data model. However, the decision can be "both" because both approaches can co-exist within a subsystem.

The Data Model pattern supports publish-subscribe semantics as well as a polling approach to sharing data. The net effect of this approach is that subsystems are decoupled. That is, there are no direct dependencies on other subsystems. In Figure J-4, the arrows represent dependencies between the subsystems. Note that model point data is bidirectional between the subsystems.

A third option for a subsystem interface is a functional API. This should be used for subsystems (e.g., System Services) that have no external dependencies on other subsystems and typically only execute when their APIs are called by other subsystems.

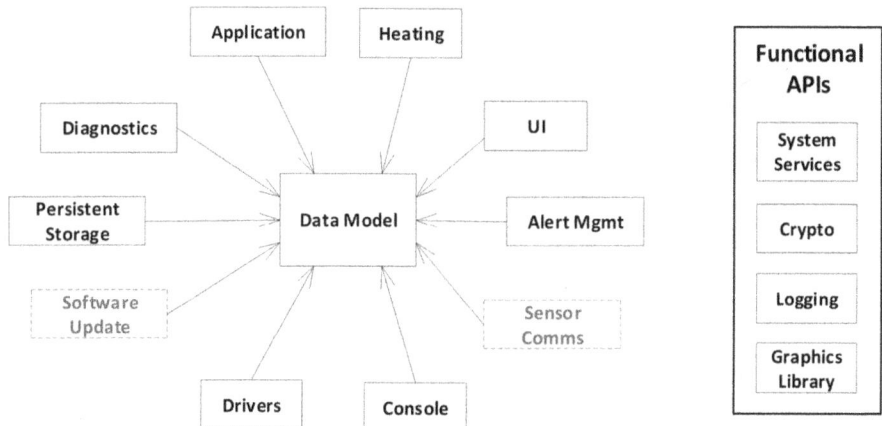

Figure J-4. Subsystem interdependencies using the Data Model

[SWA-32] Process Model

The software will be implemented as a multithreaded application using real-time preemptive scheduling. The preemptive scheduling provides for the following:

- Decoupling the UI from the rest of the application (with respect to timing and sequencing). This allows the UI to be highly responsive to the user actions without delaying or blocking time-critical business logic.

- Using deferred interrupt handlers. A deferred interrupt handler is where the time-consuming portion of the interrupt service routine is deferred to a high-priority thread in order to make the interrupt service routine as short as possible.

- Simplifying sequential designs that utilize nonbusy blocking wait semantics.

[SWA-33] Thread Priorities

The application shall be designed such that the relative thread priorities between individual threads do not matter with respect to correctness. Correctness in this context means the application would still function, albeit sluggishly, and not crash if all the threads had the same priority. The exception to this rule is for threads that are used exclusively as deferred interrupt handlers.

[SWA-39] Data Integrity

Any data that is shared between threads must be implemented in a manner that ensures the integrity of the data. That is, read, write, and read-modify-write operations are atomic with respect to other threads accessing the data. The following is a list of allowed mechanisms for sharing data across threads:

- Data is shared using data model point instances. This is the preferred mechanism.

- Data is shared using the System Services inter-thread-communication (ITC) message passing interfaces. ITC messaging is recommended for when the interface semantics have a many-to-one relationship between the clients and servers and the clients that are sending data to the server.

- Synchronous ITC messaging—where the client is blocked while the server processes the message—is only allowed when the server actions are well bounded in time and are of short duration. For example, invoking an HTTPS request to an off-board website is considered an unbounded transaction because there are too many variables associated with determining when a request will complete or fail (e.g., TCP retry timing, routing, website availability, etc.).
- Asynchronous ITC messaging can always be used.

- Encapsulated API—That is, the API implementation uses an internal mutex, which is not exposed to the API's clients, to provide atomic data access. In addition, the internal implementation must guarantee that there are no nested mutex calls when it locks its internal mutex. This approach should only be used as a last resort option and must be clearly documented in the detailed design.

When sharing data shared between a thread and an interrupt service routine (ISR), the critical section mechanism shall be disabling or enabling the ISR's specific interrupt. Relying on the MCU's instruction set for atomic read, write, and read-modify-write operations to a memory location is strongly discouraged and must be clearly documented in the detailed design. The following guidelines shall be followed for sharing data between a thread and ISRs:

- Only disable/enable a specific interrupt. Do not globally disable/enable interrupts.

- Keep the period of time that the interrupt is disabled as short as possible. You should only be moving data and clearing hardware registers—and nothing else—while the interrupt is disabled.

- Temporarily suspend thread scheduling before disabling the interrupt and then resume scheduling after enabling the interrupt. This ensures that there will not be a thread context switch while the thread has disabled the interrupt.

[SWA-34] Simulator

The software architecture and software design include the concept of a functional simulator. A functional simulator executes the production source code on a platform that is not the target platform. The simulator provides the majority of the functionality, but not necessarily the real-time performance. Or, more simply, functional simulation enables developers to develop, execute, and test production code without target hardware. Figure J-5 illustrates what is common, and different, between the software built for the target platform and that built for the functional simulator.

APPENDIX J GM6000 SOFTWARE ARCHITECTURE

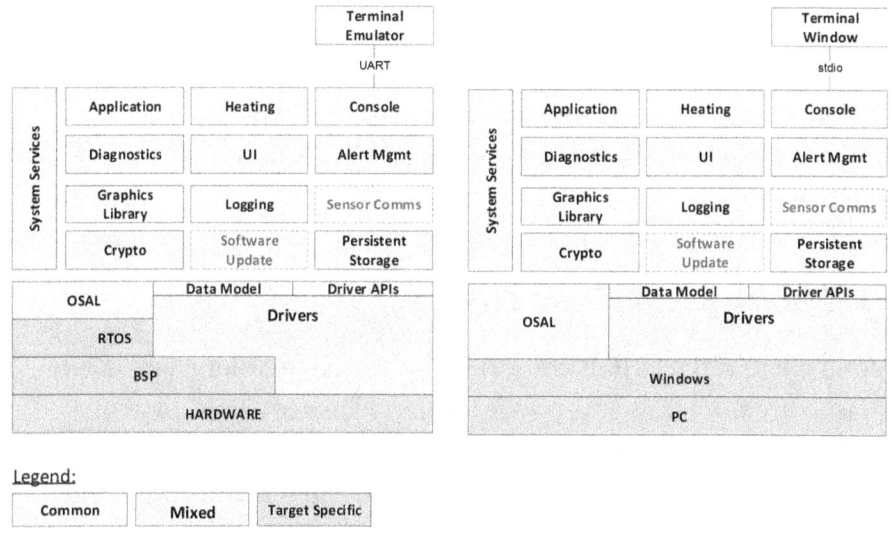

Figure J-5. *Functional simulator*

The functional simulator has the following features, attributes, and limitations:

- The functional simulator shall be a Windows or Linux console executable.

- The executable's `stdio` is the stream interface for the application's console.

- The host's operating system file system will be used to mock the nonvolatile storage.

- The bootloader is not simulated.

During detailed design of the various drivers, the decision about how that driver will be simulated will be made. The following options are allowed when simulating hardware:

- Mocked—A mocked simulation is where you provide a minimal implementation of the device's HAL interface so that the application compiles, links, and does not cause aberrant behavior at runtime.

APPENDIX J   GM6000 SOFTWARE ARCHITECTURE

- Simulated—A simulated device is where only the core functionality of the device is implemented.
- Emulated—An emulated device is where you replicate a device's behaviors at its lowest, most basic level.

[SWA-35] Cybersecurity

The software in the DHC is considered to be a low-risk target in that it is easier to compromise the physical components of a DHC than the software. Assuming that the software is compromised, there are no safety issues because the Heating Element has hardware safety circuits. The worst-case scenarios for compromised software are along the lines of a denial-of-service (DOS) attack in that the DHC may be unable to heat the space, resulting in uncomfortable temperature control and possibly a high energy bill.

No PII is stored in persistent storage. There are no privacy issues associated with the purchase or use of the GM6000.

Another possible security risk is the theft of intellectual property, for example, a malicious actor stealing and reverse-engineering the software in the Control Board. This is considered low risk as well because there are no patented algorithms or trade secrets contained within the software and because the software only has value with the company's hardware.

The considered attack vectors are as follows:

- Console—The console's command-line interface provides essentially super admin access to the software. To mitigate this, the console logic shall require a user to authenticate before being given access. In addition, each DHC unit shall have a unique key/password for the authentication. Programming the key/password into the device will be done during the manufacturing

APPENDIX J   GM6000 SOFTWARE ARCHITECTURE

provisioning process. The key/password shall not be stored in plain text in the unit's nonvolatile storage. Note that the manufacturing process will require a certain level of physical and electronic security measures to ensure that the database of the console key/passwords is secure.

- Off-board storage—The risk is a malicious actor could read or write plain text data stored in off-board nonvolatile storage. The reading scenario would be an intellectual property concern. The writing scenario could cause improper operation of the DHC. Both of these outcomes have already been determined to be low risk (i.e., acceptable), and therefore, no mitigation is required.

- Wireless (future)—The risk is that the DHC might connect to the wrong sensor or otherwise receive incorrect temperature data. These two scenarios are not unique to a cyber-attack. For example, poor placement of wireless sensor can have the same impact as a hacked wireless sensor. Both of these scenarios have already been determined to be low risk (i.e., acceptable), and therefore, no mitigation is required.

- Software update (future feature)—The concern is that unauthorized or malicious software could be loaded on the DHC during the software update process. The mitigation for this is to have cryptographically signed software images, and the nonmutable bootloader will only accept or load signed images. The software image itself is not required to be encrypted.

[SWA-36] Memory Allocation

To prevent memory leaks and fragmentation, no dynamic memory allocation is allowed. The application may allocate memory from the heap at startup but not after the system is up and running. This practice guarantees the system will not fail over time due to lack of memory.

For objects or structures that must be dynamically created or deleted after startup, the design is required to pre-allocate a memory pool (on a per-type basis) that will be used to construct the objects or structures at runtime.

[SWA-37] Message Passing (ITC)

Data between threads can be shared using message passing. However, there shall be only one message passing framework. The framework has the following requirements and constraints.

- The message passing model is a client-server model, where clients send messages to servers. Messages can be sent asynchronously or synchronously.

- Data flow between clients and servers can be unidirectional or bidirectional as determined by the application. Because this is an inter-thread communication, data can be shared via pointers since clients and servers share the same address space.

- Data is shared between clients and servers using the concept of a payload. In addition, the following convention of ownership is used to provide thread-safe access to the payload:

    - A client initially owns the payload. That is, the client can access the data in the payload without the use of critical sections.

- When a client sends or posts a message, there is an implicit transfer of ownership of the payload. After sending the message, the client is obligated to not access the payload contents.

- When a server receives a message, the server now owns the payload and can access the data in the payload without the use of critical sections.

- When a server returns a message, there is an implicit return of ownership of the payload back to the client. After returning the message, the server is obligated to not access the payload contents.

- No dynamic memory is used. Clients are responsible for providing all required memory for the individual messages. This translates to no hard limits to the number of messages a server can receive. It also means that the application does not have to worry about overflowing message queues or mailboxes. Another side effect of the memory paradigm is that there are no broadcast messages.

- The messages and payloads must be type safe. That is, they are handled and dispatched with no type casting required.

[SWA-38] File and Directory Organization

Source code files shall be organized by dependencies, not by project. Or said another way, the code will be organized by C++ namespaces where namespaces map one to one with directory names. The exceptions

APPENDIX J   GM6000 SOFTWARE ARCHITECTURE

to the namespace rule are for the BSP subsystem and third-party packages. In addition to namespaces, the following conventions shall be followed:

- All in-house developed source code shall be under the top-level src/ directory.

- #include statements in header files shall contain path information relative to the src/ directory.

- There shall not be separate include/ directories to contain header files. That is, do **not** separate header files and .c|.cpp files into different directories based solely on file type.

- Non-namespace directories can be created for organizational purposes. Non-namespace directory names shall be prefixed with a leading underscore.

- The build directories shall not be under the top-level src/ directory.

- The top-level build directory for non-unit test images shall be the projects/ directory.

- The top-level build directory for unit test images shall be the tests/ directory.

For example:

```
workspace_root/             // Reposiotry root directory
+-- projects/               // Build directories for applications
+-- src/                    // Inhouse Source code
|   +-- Cpl/                // Namespace directory (Cpl)
|       +-- Checksum        // Namespace directory (Cpl::Checksum)
|       |   + -- _Otest/    // Directory for unit test code
```

```
|    |       +-- flecher16.cpp    // Unit test application
|    +-- Flecther16.cpp           // Implementaiton file
|    +-- Flecther16.h             // Interface file
+- tests/                         // Build directories for unit tests
```

[SWA-40] Localization and Internationalization

The product is targeted to the North American, US English-speaking market only (as determined by the Product Manager). In the context of the software, the 7-bit ASCII character code is sufficient for all text presented to an end user.

[SWA-42] Unit Testing

The internally developed software shall have unit tests per the Software Development Plan. The design of individual components, modules, etc., should consider how the entity will be unit tested. That is, they should be "designed for testability" (DFT). Particularly, there is an emphasis for having automated unit tests wherever possible.

[SWA-41] Engineering and Manufacturing Testing

Various product testing—for example, EMC, HALT, end-of-line manufacturing, etc.—on the physical product will be performed. Specialized software for the Control Board will be required to support these tests. Support for these test scenarios shall be one of the following:

1. Test modules or test logic incorporated into the final, released software image that can be executed as needed. These modules will be part of the diagnostic subsystem.
2. Or a stand-alone application that is built separately and whose use and availability are strictly controlled by engineering or manufacturing. The application shall be built on the top of the framework used for the final released image and share common code (e.g., drivers, console, etc.).

Change Log

Version	Date	Updated By	Changes
0.1	5/21/2023	V. Dinkley	Initial draft

APPENDIX K

GM6000 Software Development Plan

This appendix provides an example of a Software Development Plan (SDP) document that you can use as template. It is the SDP for the GM6000 Digital Heater Controller project. Several tools such as JIRA, Git, Jenkins, etc., are called out in this document. Consider these tool names to be placeholders or labels for the functionality they provide. That is, you can replace these names with the names of the tools you use.

The contents of this SDP are verbose in some areas in that they describe work instructions for certain processes. If your organization has existing documentation for a particular process, simply reference that documentation instead of providing details. Ideally, your SDP should not be the source of details for process work instructions.

The epc repository contains the example GM6000 Software Development Plan document as a Microsoft Word document. The document is located in the `docs/GM6000 Example Docs/` directory.

APPENDIX K   GM6000 SOFTWARE DEVELOPMENT PLAN

Document Name and Number

SWA-1328: GM6000 Software Development Plan

Overview

This document captures the software development decisions, activities, and logistics for developing all of the software that executes on the GM6000 Digital Heater Controller's Control Board. This includes all the software that is needed to formally test, validate, manufacture, and release a GM6000.

Glossary

Term	Definition
Candidate Release	A candidate release is a formal build that has a human-friendly version identifier assigned to it. It is submitted for final verification before being declared a gold release.
CCB	The Change Control Board is responsible for assigning priorities to software tasks and bugs as well as determining which bugs must be resolved in order to ship the software. The CCB is composed of the principal stakeholders for the project, and, by definition, they are empowered to make final and binding decisions with respect to the software's quality and content.
CI	Continuous integration is the practice of validating code (by compiling it and running automated tests against it) that has been checked in before merging the code to a stable repository branch.

(continued)

APPENDIX K GM6000 SOFTWARE DEVELOPMENT PLAN

Term	Definition
Confluence	A web-based corporate wiki tool from Atlassian
DHC	Digital Heater Controller
Doxygen	Doxygen is the de facto standard tool for generating documentation from annotated C/C++ sources (www.doxygen.nl/).
Formal build	A formal build is a software image that was • Built from a stable branch of source code that was tagged and labeled in the Git repositories • Built by the build server • Labeled with a canonical version identifier
GitHub	An SCM Git server is where the source code repositories are hosted as private repositories.
Gold Release	A gold release is a candidate release that has passed all of the verification testing and is publicly released to customers.
Jenkins	An open source automation server that helps automate the building, testing, and deployment of software. It also facilitates continuous integration and continuous delivery.
JIRA	An issue tracking tool from Atlassian
MCU	Microcontroller
MRS	Marketing Requirements Specification
PLM	Product Lifecycle Management manages all of the information and processes at every step of the product life cycle across globalized supply chains. Windchill and SAP are examples of PLM tools.
PRS	Production Requirements Specification

(*continued*)

APPENDIX K   GM6000 SOFTWARE DEVELOPMENT PLAN

Term	Definition
Pull Request	A pull request (PR) informs others about changes that developers have pushed to a branch in a GIT repository.
QMS	Quality Management System
SCM	Software Configuration Management is the process and tools used to store, track, and control changes to the source code. For example, git is an SCM tool.
Software BOM (SBOM)	Software Bill of Materials is a list of all third-party packages and their version information that were included in the released software. The Software BOM can contain existing internal packages that are being used with the released software.
SRS	Software Requirements Specification
SWA	Software Architecture Document
SWD	Software Detailed Design document
Ticket	A ticket represents a unit of work with respect to the source code that is atomically merged to a stable branch in the SCM repository. Tickets are required to be formally identified and tracked by JIRA.
Validation	Validation is the process of checking whether the specification captures the customer's requirements, that is, "are we building the right thing." Examples of validation might be collecting voice-of-the-customer inputs, running focus groups with users using mock-ups or prototypes, etc.
Verification	Verification is the process of checking that the software fulfills requirements, for example, functional software testing.

APPENDIX K GM6000 SOFTWARE DEVELOPMENT PLAN

Document References

Document #	Document Name	Version
QMS-001	Quality Manual	1.16
QMS-004	Requirements Management	1.2
QMS-010	Software Development Life Cycle Process	1.13
QMS-011	Software Defect Tracking Workflow	1.6
QMS-018	Cyber Security Work Instructions	1.0
SW-1002	Software C/C++ Embedded Coding Standard	1.1
PM-402	GM6000 Project Plan	1.0
SWQA-1401	Software Test Plan	1.0

Roles and Responsibilities

The following roles need to be defined for the project. Which engineers are assigned to these roles is captured in the top-level project plan.

APPENDIX K   GM6000 SOFTWARE DEVELOPMENT PLAN

Role	Responsibility
Software Lead	The Software Lead is the technical lead for all software contained within the GM6000 control board. This role is responsible for the following: • Software architecture • Software Detailed Design • SRS requirements • Resolving (software) technical issues • Ensuring the software-specific processes are followed (especially reviews) • Signing off on the final releases • All the responsibilities of a Software Developer
Software Developer	The Software Developer writes and tests code. This role is responsible for the following: • Assisting with software architecture • Assisting with Software Detailed Design • Assisting with SRS requirements • Implementing code and unit tests • Participating in design and code reviews • Following the defined SDLC processes
Software Test Lead	The Software Test Lead is responsible for all things related to software verification: • Creating the formal test plan and test matrix • Creating test reports • Resolving (software testing) technical issues • Ensuring that the software test-specific processes are followed • Signing off on the final releases • All the responsibilities of a Software Tester

(*continued*)

APPENDIX K GM6000 SOFTWARE DEVELOPMENT PLAN

Role	Responsibility
System Engineer	The System Engineer is responsible for the system-level design, algorithms, etc., across all disciplines. This role is responsible for the following: • Creating the PRS requirements and system architecture • Resolving system technical issues • As needed, participating in design and code reviews • Signing off on the software test plan • Signing off on the final releases
Software Tester	The Software Tester formally tests the software. This role is responsible for the following: • Assisting with the test plan and test matrix • Assisting with test reports • Developing and executing test cases • Authoring bug tickets • Following defined software development life cycle (SDLC) processes
Hardware Lead	The Hardware Lead is the technical lead for all things hardware. This role is responsible for the following: • Creating the electrical hardware architecture • HWR requirements • Resolving EE hardware technical issues • Ensuring that hardware development processes are followed • Signing off on the final releases • As needed, participating in design and code reviews

APPENDIX K   GM6000 SOFTWARE DEVELOPMENT PLAN

Software Items

The software items covered under this development plan are as follows:

1. Software that executes on the GM6000 control board when it is shipped to a customer

    a. This software item requires formal testing and verification before being released.

    b. The software shall be programmed in C/C++ and conform to *SW-1002 Software C/C++ Embedded Coding Standard*.

2. Manufacturing test software (which executes on the GM6000 control board) that is used when manufacturing the GM6000

    a. This software item will be informally verified by engineering before being released to manufacturing.

    b. The software shall be programmed in C/C++ and conform to *SW-1002 Software C/C++ Embedded Coding Standard*.

3. Engineering test software used for external testing (e.g., UL, FCC, etc.) and internal formal testing (e.g., HALT, etc.)

    a. This software item will be informally verified by engineering before being used in external or internal testing.

    b. The software shall be programmed in C/C++ and conform to *SW-1002 Software C/C++ Embedded Coding Standard*.

    c. This software is not for public release.

All of the aforementioned software items—even those not formally verified—are required to go through the formal process with respect to software builds.

Documentation Outputs

1. The supporting documentation shall be created in accordance with the processes defined in the *QMS-010 Software Development Life Cycle Process* document.

2. A software architecture document shall be created and assigned a formal document number. The Software Lead is responsible for this document.

3. A Software Detailed Design document shall be created and assigned a formal document number. The Software Lead is responsible for this document.

4. The Doxygen tool shall be used to document the code level details. A formal document number will be assigned to the Doxygen output and must be included on the home page of the Doxygen output. The Doxygen output shall be created as part of the CI build process.

5. Code reviews are performed as part of the pull request process. The review comments and actions are available by accessing the GitHub repositories for the project. Later, the review comments and artifacts can be retrieved using GitHub REST APIs for consolidation into a stand-alone document.

6. Design reviews are done iteratively as part of the ticket workflow process.

   a. Review comments are captured as "comments" in the documents under review section. After the updates or actions have been satisfactorily completed, the comments are marked as resolved. (But the comments are not deleted.)

   b. The review comments can only be deleted after a snapshot of the document has been archived.

7. The following documentation artifacts are captured in Confluence as wiki pages. The Software Lead is responsible for these items:

   a. Instructions on how to set up a developer's local build environment

   b. Instructions on how to manage the tools on the build server

   c. Instructions on how to set up the CI platform

   d. The list of all development tools (and their version information) that were used for development

8. Internal release notes shall be created for each formal build that is provided to the software test team for verification testing. These notes can be captured in an email or on wiki pages. The Software Lead is responsible for these artifacts.

9. For candidate releases, a single release notes document shall be created and assigned a formal document number. The Software Lead is responsible for this document.

APPENDIX K   GM6000 SOFTWARE DEVELOPMENT PLAN

10. A Software Bill of Materials (SBOM) document shall be created and assigned a formal document number. The SBOM shall be updated every time there is a new gold release. The Software Lead is responsible for this document.

    a. The SBOM shall identify and reference open source and proprietary licensing requirements and agreements.

11. A release cover page shall be created when releasing the software into the PLM system. The Software Lead is responsible for supplying the content for this document. The specifics of the cover page are dedicated by the PLM system.

Requirements

1. The supporting documentation shall be created in accordance with the processes defined in the *QMS-004 Requirements Management* document.

2. The MRS is a formal document with an assigned number that captures all of the top-level user and business needs. The Product Manager is responsible for this document.

3. The PRS is a formal document with an assigned number that captures the system-level requirements that are derived from the MRS. The System Engineer is responsible for this document.

APPENDIX K   GM6000 SOFTWARE DEVELOPMENT PLAN

4. The HRS is a formal document with an assigned number that captures the hardware-level requirements that are derived from the MRS and PRS. The Hardware Lead is responsible for this document.

5. The SRS is a formal document with an assigned number that captures the software-level requirements that are derived from the MRS and PRS. The Software Lead is responsible for this document.

6. Traceability. The project has the following traceability requirements:

    a. All requirements will have a globally unique requirement number assigned to them.

    b. The SRS requirements shall be traceable to at least one parent requirement in the MRS or PRS.

    c. All SRS requirements shall be traceable to at least one or more software architecture output items.

    d. Software architecture:

        i. All output items identified shall be assigned a unique identifier. An output item is a documentation section that contains design outputs.

        ii. The output items identified shall be traceable to at least one MRS, PRS, or SRS requirement.

APPENDIX K   GM6000 SOFTWARE DEVELOPMENT PLAN

    e. Software Detailed Design:

        i. All output items identified shall be assigned a unique identifier. An output item is a documentation section that contains design outputs.

        ii. All output items shall be traceable to an output item in the software architecture document.

        iii. All output items shall specify the source code (by directory) that implements the design.

    f. A trace matrix document shall be created (with an assigned number) that enumerates this traceability process. The System Engineer is responsible for the trace matrix.

Software Development Life Cycle Process (SDLC)

1. All project-specific SDLC processes shall be developed in accordance with the processes defined in the *QMS-010 Software Development Life Cycle Process* document.

2. There are four phases: planning, construction, verification, and release.

APPENDIX K   GM6000 SOFTWARE DEVELOPMENT PLAN

3. The Planning phase shall consist of planning, gathering requirements, creating the software architecture, and preparing the tools and infrastructure needed for the construction phase.

    a. This process will generally follow an iterative, Agile Kanban process with tasks captured in JIRA.

    b. All code checked into GitHub during this phase requires a ticket. The ticket workflow shall be the same as the workflow described under the Construction phase.

    c. With respect to software development, the Planning phase is considered waterfall in that the Construction phase shall not begin until the Planning phase has completed.

    d. The Planning phase is exited after the following deliverables have been completed:

        i. The first draft of the *SWA-1327 GM6000 Software Architecture* document has been reviewed.

        ii. The foundational skeleton application can be successfully built by the CI server (including skeleton automated unit tests).

4. The Construction phase shall consist of detailed design, implementation, testing, and bug fixing.

    a. This process will generally follow an iterative, Agile Kanban process with tasks captured in JIRA.

APPENDIX K   GM6000 SOFTWARE DEVELOPMENT PLAN

b. All code checked into GitHub during this phase requires a ticket. The following steps are associated with each ticket during this phase. Some of the steps (except for Pull Request and Merge) can be waived with verbal approval from the Software Lead.

   i. Requirements—The requirements for the work to be performed are identified. Generally, the requirements are listed or captured in the JIRA card.

   ii. Detailed design—The developer is responsible for documenting the detailed design associated with the work to be performed in the SDD.

   iii. Design review—This is a peer review of the detailed design.

   iv. Coding and unit testing—The code is written and verified using unit tests.

   v. Pull request and code review—The completed and tested code is submitted for peer review by creating a pull request. The pull request cannot be merged until after the changes are approved by the reviewer or reviewers, until there are no build errors, and until all automated tests pass. It also assumes the merge is a trivial merge; that is, there are no merge conflicts that need to be resolved.

   vi. Merge—The pull request is merged to a stable branch.

APPENDIX K   GM6000 SOFTWARE DEVELOPMENT PLAN

   c. The software team is responsible for additional system level and integration testing. The testing activities will be tracked as cards in JIRA. For each integration test cycle, the following steps are performed:

      i. A test plan has been created. The test plan includes the goal or purpose of each test case and specifies how each test case will be executed and what the pass/fail criteria are.

      ii. The test plan has been executed.

      iii. A summary report of the testing has been created.

   d. The Construction phase is only exited when the Release phase ends.

5. Verification shall consist of the formal verification of the software. The Verification phase runs in parallel with the Construction phase; that is, the first pass through the test plan shall begin as soon as features and functionality are realized in code.

   a. The Software Test Lead is responsible for the formal verification of the software. The SWQA-1401 Software Test Plan documents how the testing will be conducted.

   b. The management of reported bugs shall be done in accordance with the processes defined in the *QMS-011 Software Defect Tracking Workflow* document.

APPENDIX K   GM6000 SOFTWARE DEVELOPMENT PLAN

    c. All bugs found will be logged as bug cards in JIRA.

    d. The Verification phase is only exited when the Release phase ends.

6. The Release phase starts before the end of the Verification phase, and it ends with the release of the software into the PLM system.

    a. During the release phase, the CCB is responsible for approving all code changes and fixes.

    b. The CCB is responsible for determining when the software can be released into the PLM system.

    c. The CCB is responsible for approving the scope of regression testing after merging bug fixes into the upcoming release branch.

7. The Release phase (as well as the Construction and Verification phases) can be restarted—as determined by the CCB—to address issues found in the software released to the PLM prior to physically shipping units.

Cybersecurity

1. The cybersecurity needs of the project shall follow the processes defined in *QMS-018 Cyber Security Work Instructions*.

2. The cybersecurity analysis and control measures shall be documented in the software architecture document. The Software Lead is responsible for the cybersecurity content.

APPENDIX K   GM6000 SOFTWARE DEVELOPMENT PLAN

Tools

1. The software that executes on the DHC's Control Board hardware shall be compiled with the GCC cross compiler for the specific microcontroller.

    a. The version of the compiler shall not be changed during the Construction and Release phases unless there is a documented compiler bug that impacts the software.

    b. The compiler toolchain shall be archived along with the source code in the GitHub.

    c. The compiler toolchain shall be tagged and labelled when a formal build is performed.

2. The GCC MinGW compiler shall be used for building automated unit tests. The GCC compiler is used because of its capability to instrument the test executables for the collection of code coverage data. Any compiler version 9.2 or higher can be used.

3. The Python gcovr library shall be used to generate the raw code coverage metrics. Any version 5.2 or higher can be used.

4. The Catch2 test framework shall be used for automated unit tests.

    a. Version 2.x of the framework shall be used.

    b. The Catch2 framework shall be archived along with the source code in the GitHub.

    c. The framework shall be tagged and labelled when a formal build is performed.

APPENDIX K   GM6000 SOFTWARE DEVELOPMENT PLAN

5. Doxygen shall be used to generate code-level documentation.

   a. The Doxygen output pages shall be converted into a Windows Help File (.chm).

   b. The Doxygen installer, the Graphviz installer, and the Microsoft Help Compiler shall be archived in a long-term storage location.

6. No static code analyzer will be used on this project.

7. Python shall be used for all internal script development.

   a. All developers, testers, and the build servers shall use the same version of Python.

   b. The Python installer for the version of Python being used shall be archived in a long-term storage location.

8. JIRA shall be used to track tickets and bug cards.

9. Confluence shall be used for project-specific software wiki pages.

10. GitHub shall be used to host the Git repositories.

11. Jenkins shall be used for automating continuous integration tasks.

    a. All formal builds are performed using Jenkins and its build agents.

    b. Jenkins will be installed on a VM, and the VM will be archived in long-term storage for each gold release.

APPENDIX K   GM6000 SOFTWARE DEVELOPMENT PLAN

Software Configuration Management (SCM)

1. GitHub private repositories shall be used to version control all of the source code for the project.

   a. A single repository shall be used. The repository URL is https://github.com/xxxxx/gm6000.

   b. The repository will also contain all third-party packages and the cross-compiler toolchain used when building for the target hardware.

2. The branching strategy shall be a modified trunk-based development model.

   a. The main branch shall be used for all candidate releases.

   b. A child branch of main—develop—will be used as the stable branch for day-to-day development and pull requests. The develop branch will be merged to main for candidate releases.

   c. Each ticket will be used to create a short-lived branch off of the develop branch. The ticket number shall be part of the branch name.

3. A project unique build number, generated by the Jenkins CI tool, shall provide the canonical build identifier for all formal releases.

   a. The build number shall be included as part of the SCM tag or label that is applied to each formal build. This is the canonical version identifier.

b. The source code shall contain compile-time, human-readable version identifiers, which are set before the code is merged to the develop branch. The human-readable version identifier is **not** to be used as the canonical identifier since there will be many formal builds with the same human-readable version identifier.

Testing

1. The software team is responsible for unit testing and integration testing.
2. The source code is organized by namespaces (per *SW-1002 Coding Standard*). Each namespace is required to have at least one unit test for the code it contains.

    a. If the namespace has a direct target platform dependency, the unit test shall be a manual test that executes on the target platform.

    b. The BSP directories are exempt from the unit test requirements.

    c. If the namespace contains implementation for the UI, the unit test shall be a manual test that executes either on the target platform or the simulator. The automated unit test requirement is relaxed with respect to the UI because the test infrastructure does not include tools for automated verification of the UI's visual presentation.

d. All other namespaces shall have an automated unit that is a stand-alone application that returns pass/fail. Automated unit tests are executed as part of the CI process for all builds. All automated unit tests are required to meet the following code coverage metrics:

   i. Line coverage >= 80%

   ii. Branch coverage >= 60%.

   Because of the tools being used (gcc and gcovr), the branch coverage metrics are not always correct for C++ code. Consequently, the branch coverage threshold is intentionally lower to compensate.

3. The Software Lead is responsible for defining development milestones where integration testing shall be done.

   a. At least one integration test milestone shall be an automated sanity check (using the functional simulator) that will be executed as part of the CI build process.

4. Third-party packages will be verified as part of the overall software function during formal verification.

   a. Unit tests are not required for third-party packages.

5. It is permissible—under certain circumstances—for integration and formal software verification testing to use the software functional simulator instead of a physical hardware target.

APPENDIX K   GM6000 SOFTWARE DEVELOPMENT PLAN

a. The Software Test and Software Leads must approve, on a per-test-case or per-test-suite basis, when the functional simulator can be used in integration and formal testing.

Deliverables

This section provides a summarized list of deliverables that the software team is responsible for on the project. There are numerous other deliverables (e.g., the GM6000 Software Test Plan) that are not summarized here because the software team in not responsible for the deliverables.

Deliverable	Phase(s)	Notes
SDP-1328 GM6000 Software Development Plan	Planning Construction	A reviewed first draft is required to exit the planning phase.
SRS-1324 GM6000 Software Requirement Specification	Planning Construction	A reviewed first draft is required to exit the planning phase.
SWA-1327 GM6000 Software Architecture	Planning Construction	A reviewed first draft is required to exit the planning phase.
SDD-1329 GM6000 Software Detailed Design	Planning Construction	
SDX-1330 GM6000 Software Doxygen Output	Planning Construction	
SW-1002 Software C/C++ Embedded Coding Standard	Planning	

(*continued*)

APPENDIX K GM6000 SOFTWARE DEVELOPMENT PLAN

Deliverable	Phase(s)	Notes
Code Review Artifacts	Construction	This is captured in GitHub as part of the pull requests.
Design Review Artifacts	Construction	These are point-in-time versions of the documents with review comments that have been archived.
Developer and Build Server Setup Instructions	Construction	Wiki pages
CI Platform Setup and Maintenance Instructions	Construction	Wiki pages
Software Development Tools List	Construction	Wiki pages
SWT-1331 GM6000 Software Requirements Trace Matrix	Construction Release	These are iterative drafts created during the Construction phase.
SWB-1332 GM6000 Software Bill of Material	Construction Release	These are iterative drafts created during the Construction phase.
Engineer Test Software	Construction	This is a formal build of the Engineering test software images.
Manufacturing Test Software	Construction	This is a formal build of the Manufacturing test software images.
Integration Testing Artifacts	Construction	Per each test milestone, the test plan, procedure, and report documents will be archived.

(continued)

APPENDIX K GM6000 SOFTWARE DEVELOPMENT PLAN

Deliverable	Phase(s)	Notes
Internal Release Notes	Construction	These are provided per each formal release that is deployed for internal testing.
SWR-1333 GM6000 Release Notes	Release	These are updated for each Candidate Release.
<plm-id> GM6000 Software Release Cover Page	Release	This is updated for each gold release, and it includes references or links to the released software images.

Change Log

Version	Date	Updated By	Changes
0.1	5/27/2023	V. Dinkley	Initial draft

APPENDIX L

GM6000 Software Detailed Design (Initial Draft)

This appendix is a point-in-time snapshot of the GM6000 Software Detailed Design document that should be in place before exiting the planning stage. It is meant to illustrate the minimum amount of up-front detailed design that is necessary before starting the construction stage.

But I don't want you to read this appendix. What I want you to do is scan it and look at the empty headings. That is, the point of this appendix is to illustrate structure, not content. This is why throughout this particular document, at this particular stage in its development, you'll see a lot of headings with no content; they are just placeholders for content that is coming in the next stage. During the construction stage, content will be added to these empty sections at the same time the functionality is developed.

For examples or models for what to write in an SDD, read Appendix M, "GM6000 Software Detailed Design (Final Draft)," which is the full-fledged version of the SDD. In this appendix, though, just note the kinds of things that need to be done and the kinds of things that can be left undone.

APPENDIX L   GM6000 SOFTWARE DETAILED DESIGN (INITIAL DRAFT)

Document Name and Number

SWA-1329: GM6000 Software Detailed Design

Scope

This document captures the design of the individual Software Items (e.g., subsystems, features) and Software Units (e.g., modules) contained within the GM6000 software. Each of the Software Items and Units is designed in accordance with the GM6000 Software Architecture and can be designed in an Agile just-in-time manner. This document is supplemented by the Doxygen output file that provides header file–level details.

The target audience for this document are software developers, system engineers, and test engineers. In addition, authors are required to view the audience as not only being the original development team, but also future team members on future development efforts.

Requirements Tracing

For requirements tracing purposes, the *[SDD-nnn]* identifiers are used to label traceable design items. The SDD identifiers, once assigned, shall not be reused or reassigned to a different item. The *nnn* portion of the identifier is simply a free running counter to ensure unique identifiers within the document.

Overview

The GM6000 is a Digital Heater Controller (DHC) that can be used in many different form factors and heating capacities. The specifics of the unit's physical attributes will be provisioned into the DHC when the final

APPENDIX L   GM6000 SOFTWARE DETAILED DESIGN (INITIAL DRAFT)

assembly of the DHC is performed. The GM6000's software executes on a microcontroller that is part of the unit's Control Board (CB). The Control Board is physically located within the unit's enclosure. The software interacts with other sub-assemblies that are within the unit's enclosure:

- Heating Element
- Blower Assembly
- Display and User Inputs
- Temperature Sensor

In the future, the software will interact with an external wireless temperature sensor. Figure L-1 summarizes the system architecture.

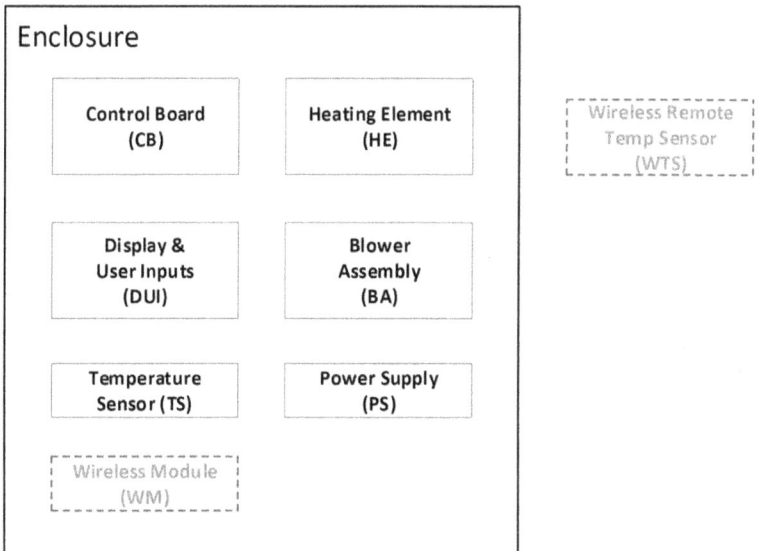

Figure L-1. System architecture block diagram

APPENDIX L   GM6000 SOFTWARE DETAILED DESIGN (INITIAL DRAFT)

The software for the GM6000 product includes two applications. The first application, codenamed *Ajax*, is the application that is shipped with the physical hardware. The second application, codenamed *Eros*, is an engineering-only test application used for environmental, emissions, and end-of-line manufacturing testing.

Glossary

Term	Definition
BSP	Board Support Package
DHC	Digital Heater Controller
ITC	Inter-thread communication
MCU	Microcontroller
UART	Universal asynchronous receiver-transmitter

Document References

Document #	Document Name	Version
MRS-1322	GM6000 Marketing Requirements Specification	0.1
PRS-1323	GM6000 Product Requirements Specification	0.1
SRS-1324	GM6000 Software Requirements Specification	0.1
SYSA-1326	GM6000 System Architecture	0.1
SWA-1327	GM6000 Software Architecture	0.1
SW-1002	Software C/C++ Embedded Coding Standard	1.1

APPENDIX L   GM6000 SOFTWARE DETAILED DESIGN (INITIAL DRAFT)

Software Architecture Overview

The control board software is broken down into subsystems. In addition, the software architecture supports a functional simulator with the majority of the code being common between the target and simulator images (see Figure L-2).

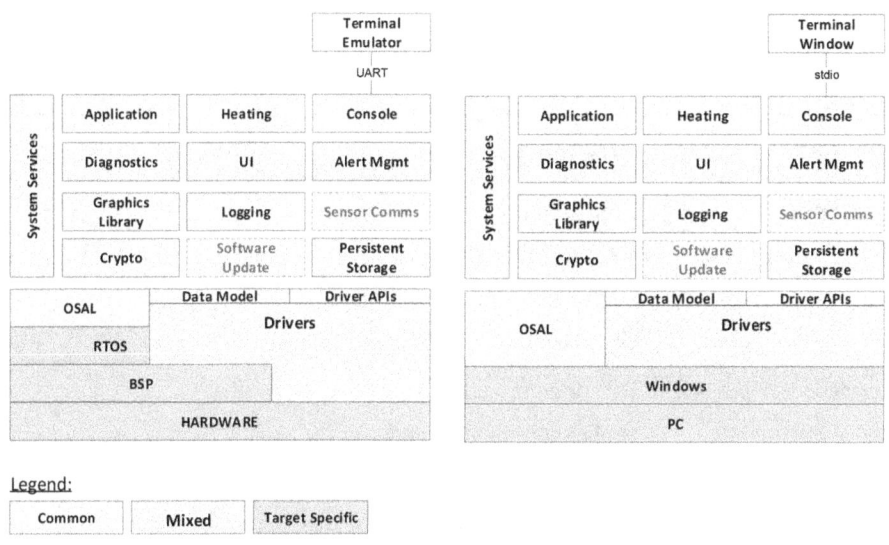

Figure L-2. Subsystems and simulator

[SDD-35] Source Code

A single GitHub repository will be used to store all of the source code used to build the GM6000 source code. This means that all third-party code will be copied into the single repository. This "my project first" approach has the benefits of reusing and consuming packages from other repositories with no impact to the day-to-day workflow of the developers. In addition, this approach allows edits to the third-party packages without worrying about compatibility with other projects or waiting on updates from the original repository. The open source tool Outcast[20] will be used to manage the incorporation of third-party repositories.

Per the *SW-1002 Software C/C++ Embedded Coding Standard*, the source code files are organized by component dependencies (e.g., by C++ namespaces) and not by project. As a naming convention, those directories that do not map one to one with a namespace should be prefaced with a leading underscore (e.g., _0test/). The following table identifies the top-level source code directories.

Directory	Description	Notes
arduino/	This directory contains Arduino libraries that are used by Adafruit's Grand Central M4 Express board.	
src/Ajax	This directory contains all application-specific code for the GM6000 software.	
src/Bsp/Initech	This directory contains in-house developed source code for the various GM6000 BSPs.	Board-specific code that is auto-generated by the STM32 Cube MX application is located in this tree.
src/Catch	This directory contains the Catch2 Unit Test framework.	

(*continued*)

---

[20] https://github.com/johnttaylor/Outcast

Directory	Description	Notes
src/Cpl	This directory contains the source code for the generic System Services. It also contains any non-application-specific middleware code developed during the GM6000 project.	There is no requirement to make generic middleware or components in the GM6000 project.
src/Driver	This directory contains driver source code that is not specific to a particular BSP or board.	There is no requirement to make generic drivers in the GM6000 project.
src/Eros	This directory contains all of the application-specific code for the engineering-only test application used for environmental, emissions, and manufacturing testing of the GM6000 product.	
xsrc/	This directory tree contains (almost all) the third-party source code that is used in the GM6000 product.	This tree contains the ST SDKs and the Windows GCC ARM7 cross compiler.

[SDD-62] Unit Testing

Per the Software Development Plan, all namespaces shall have at least one unit test. While the unit tests can be manual or automated, the preference is for automated unit tests. To simplify the CI build process, the following naming conventions are imposed for the unit text executables.

APPENDIX L   GM6000 SOFTWARE DETAILED DESIGN (INITIAL DRAFT)

Name	Description
a.exe, a.out	Used for all automated units that can be run in parallel with other units.
aa.exe, aa.out	Same as a.exe, a.out except the executables cannot be run in parallel. For example, this could be a test that uses a hard-wired TCP port number.
b.exe, b.out	Used for all automated units that can be run in parallel and that require an external Python script to run the test executable. For example, this could be a test that pipes a golden input file to stdin of the test executable.
bb.exe, bb.out	Same as b.exe, b.out except that executables cannot be run in parallel.
a.py	Used to execute the b.exe and b.out executables
aa.py	Used to execute the bb.exe and bb.out executables
<all others>	Manual units can use any name for the executable except for the ones listed previously.

[SDD-31] Subsystems
[SDD-10] Alert Management
[SDD-11] Application

The application subsystem contains the top-level business logic for the entire application.

APPENDIX L   GM6000 SOFTWARE DETAILED DESIGN (INITIAL DRAFT)

[SDD-32] Creation and Startup (Application)

The GM6000 uses the Main pattern for creating, starting, and stopping all of the other subsystems at run time. The Main pattern states that an application is built by wiring together independent components and modules. The Main pattern consists of the following:

- The resolution of interface references with concrete implementations
- The initialization and shutdown sequencing

The implementation of the Main pattern uses internal interfaces so that the core creation and sequencing logic can be common across platform and application variants. There are at least two platforms:

- The initial NUCLEO-F413ZH board
- The functional simulator

And there are at least two application variants:

- The Ajax application for the production release of the GM6000
- The Eros engineering-only test software application

The design decision to share the startup code across the different variants was made to avoid maintaining *N*-number of separate startup sequences.

Per the coding standard, the use of `#ifdef` within functions is not allowed. The different permutations are done by defining functions (i.e., internal interfaces) and then statically linking the appropriate implementations for each variant.

APPENDIX L GM6000 SOFTWARE DETAILED DESIGN (INITIAL DRAFT)

The following directory structure and header files (for the internal interfaces) shall be used. The directory structure assumes that the build scripts for the different variants build different directories, as opposed to cherry-picking files within a directory.

```
src/Ajax/Main/          // Platform/Application independent implementation
+--- platform.h         // Interface for Platform dependencies
+--- application.h      // Interface for App dependencies
+--- _app/              // Ajax specific startup implementation
+--- _plat_xxxx/        // Platform variant 1 start-up implementation
|    +--- app_platform.h    // Interface for Platform specific App dependencies
|    +--- _app_platform/    // Ajax-Platform specific startup implementation
+--- _plat_yyyy/        // Platform variant 2 start-up implementation
|    +--- app_platform.h    // Interface for Platform specific App dependencies
|    +--- _app_platform/    // Ajax-Platform specific startup implementation
```

The base implementation for the Main pattern is located at the `src/Ajax/Main/` directory tree. The base implementation is for the Ajax application.

The Eros Main pattern implementation is built on top of the Ajax implementation. The Eros customizations are located at `src/Eros/Main`.

[SDD-12] Bootloader
[SDD-13] BSP
[SDD-14] Console
[SDD-15] Crypto
[SDD-16] Data Model
[SDD-17] Diagnostics
[SDD-18] Drivers

[SDD-36] Button Driver

[SDD-37] GPIO Output Driver

[SDD-39] Pico Display Driver

[SDD-40] PWM Driver

[SDD-42] SPI Driver

[SDD-19] Graphics Library

[SDD-20] Heating

[SDD-21] Logging

[SDD-22] OS

[SDD-23] OSAL

[SDD-24] Persistent Storage

[SDD-25] Sensor Communications

[SDD-26] Software Update

[SDD-27] System Services

[SDD-28] UI

[SDD-29] Functional Simulator

[SDD-30] Engineer Test Application

[SDD-33] Creation and Startup (Test Application)

APPENDIX L   GM6000 SOFTWARE DETAILED DESIGN (INITIAL DRAFT)

The Eros application shares or extends the Ajax Main pattern (see [SDD-32] Creation and Startup (Application)). The following directory structure shall be used for the Eros-specific code and for extensions to the Ajax startup and shutdown logic.

```
src/Eros/Main/              // Platform/Application Specific implementation
+--- app.cpp                // Eros Application (non-platform) implementation
+--- _plat_xxxx/            // Platform variant 1 start-up implementation
|    +--- app_platform.cpp  // Eros app + specific startup implementation
+--- _plat_yyyy/            // Platform variant 2 start-up implementation
|    +--- app_platform.cpp  // Eros app + specific startup implementation
```

Change Log

Version	Date	Updated By	Changes
0.1	6/14/2023	V. Dinkley	Initial draft—Outline and Source code organization

APPENDIX M

GM6000 Software Detailed Design (Final Draft)

This appendix provides an example of a detailed design document that you can use as template. It is the detailed design document for the GM6000 Digital Heater Controller project. The formatting is minimal, but the structure of the template does address all the areas you should be paying attention to and thinking about.

The first part of this appendix is the same as it was in Appendix L, "GM6000 Software Detailed Design (Initial Draft)." There are a few changes here and there, but mostly this appendix fills out the empty table of contents that I outlined in the initial draft. If for any reason you see something in Appendix L that is different or contradicts what's in this appendix, consider this appendix the canonical SDD for the GM6000 project.

And, for the record, I'd like to state that I did this "by the book." I didn't write a single section of code for the GM6000 project before I had written up the detailed design in this document.

APPENDIX M   GM6000 SOFTWARE DETAILED DESIGN (FINAL DRAFT)

The epc repository contains the example GM6000 Software Detailed Design document as a Microsoft Word document. The document is located in the docs/GM6000 Example Docs/ directory.

Document Name and Number

SWA-1329: GM6000 Software Detailed Design

Scope

This document captures the design of the individual Software Items (e.g., subsystems, features) and Software Units (e.g., modules) contained within the GM6000 software. Each of the Software Items and Units is designed in accordance with the GM6000 Software Architecture and can be designed in an Agile just-in-time manner. This document is supplemented by the Doxygen output file that provides header file–level details.

The target audience for this document are software developers, system engineers, and test engineers. In addition, authors are required to view the audience as not only being the original development team but also future team members on future development efforts.

Requirements Tracing

For requirements tracing purposes, the *[SDD-nnn]* identifiers are used to label traceable design items. The SDD identifiers, once assigned, shall not be reused or reassigned to a different item. The *nnn* portion of the identifier is simply a free running counter to ensure unique identifiers within the document.

APPENDIX M   GM6000 SOFTWARE DETAILED DESIGN (FINAL DRAFT)

Overview

The GM6000 is a Digital Heater Controller (DHC) that can be used in many different form factors and heating capacities. The specifics of the unit's physical attributes will be provisioned into the DHC when the final assembly of the DHC is performed. The GM6000's software executes on a microcontroller that is part of the unit's Control Board (CB). The Control Board is physically located within the unit's enclosure. The software interacts with other sub-assemblies that are within the unit's enclosure:

- Heating Element
- Blower Assembly
- Display and User Inputs
- Temperature Sensor

In the future, the software will interact with an external wireless temperature sensor.

Figure M-1 summarizes the system architecture.

APPENDIX M   GM6000 SOFTWARE DETAILED DESIGN (FINAL DRAFT)

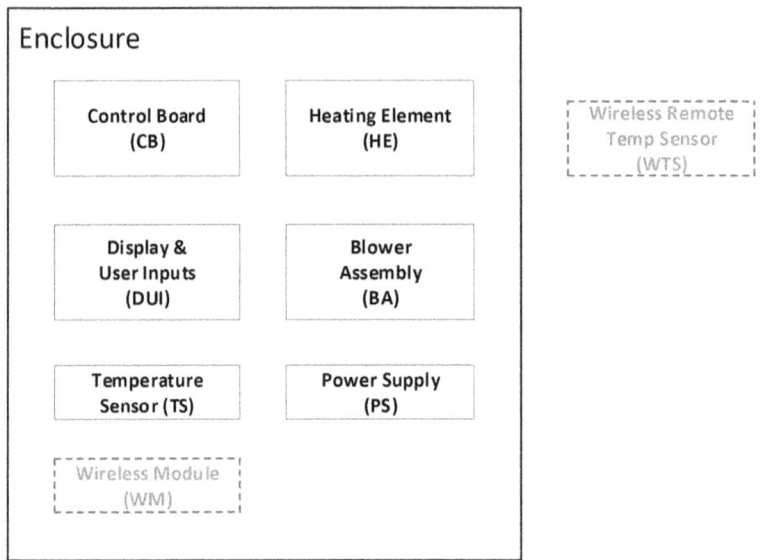

Figure M-1. System architecture block diagram

The software for the GM6000 product includes two applications. The first application, codenamed *Ajax*, is the application that is shipped with the physical hardware. The second application, codenamed *Eros*, is an engineering-only test application used for environmental, emissions, and end-of-line manufacturing testing.

Glossary

Term	Definition
BSP	Board Support Package
DHC	Digital Heater Controller

(*continued*)

APPENDIX M   GM6000 SOFTWARE DETAILED DESIGN (FINAL DRAFT)

Term	Definition
ITC	Inter-thread communication
MCU	Microcontroller
UART	Universal asynchronous receiver-transmitter

Document References

Document #	Document Name	Version
MRS-1322	GM6000 Marketing Requirements Specification	0.1
PRS-1323	GM6000 Product Requirements Specification	0.1
SRS-1324	GM6000 Software Requirements Specification	0.1
SYSA-1326	GM6000 System Architecture	0.1
SWA-1327	GM6000 Software Architecture	0.1
SW-1002	Software C/C++ Embedded Coding Standard	1.1

Software Architecture Overview

The control board software is broken down into subsystems. In addition, the software architecture supports a functional simulator with the majority of the code being common between the target and simulator images (see Figure M-2).

APPENDIX M   GM6000 SOFTWARE DETAILED DESIGN (FINAL DRAFT)

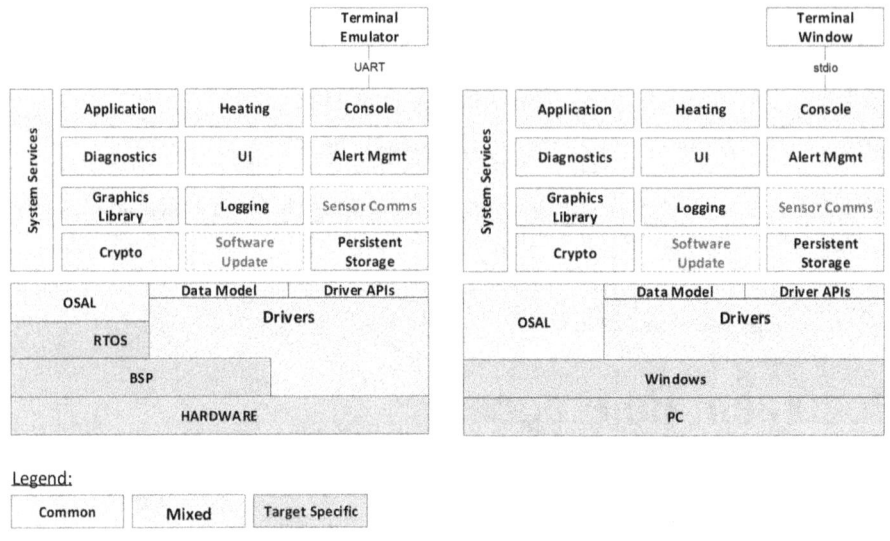

Figure M-2. Subsystems and simulator

[SDD-35] Source Code

A single GitHub repository will be used to store all of the source code used to build the GM6000 source code. This means that all third-party code will be copied into the single repository. This "my project first" approach has the benefits of reusing and consuming packages from other repositories with no impact to the day-to-day workflow of the developers. In addition, this approach allows edits to the third-party packages without worrying about compatibility with other projects or waiting on updates from the original repository. The open source tool Outcast[21] will be used to manage the incorporation of third-party repositories.

---

[21] https://github.com/johnttaylor/Outcast

APPENDIX M   GM6000 SOFTWARE DETAILED DESIGN (FINAL DRAFT)

Per the *SW-1002 Software C/C++ Embedded Coding Standard*, the source code files are organized by component dependencies (e.g., by C++ namespaces) and not by project. As a naming convention, those directories that do not map one to one with a namespace should be prefaced with a leading underscore (e.g., _0test/). The following table identifies the top-level source code directories.

Directory	Description	Notes
arduino/	This directory contains Arduino libraries that are used by Adafruit's Grand Central M4 Express board.	
src/Ajax	This directory contains all application-specific code for the GM6000 software.	
src/Bsp/Initech	This directory contains in-house developed source code for the various GM6000 BSPs.	Board-specific code that is auto-generated by the STM32 Cube MX application is located in this tree.
src/Catch	This directory contains the Catch2 Unit Test framework.	
src/Cpl	This directory contains the source code for the generic System Services. It also contains any non-application-specific middleware code developed during the GM6000 project.	There is no requirement to make generic middleware or components in the GM6000 project.

(*continued*)

APPENDIX M   GM6000 SOFTWARE DETAILED DESIGN (FINAL DRAFT)

Directory	Description	Notes
src/Driver	This directory contains driver source code that is not specific to a particular BSP or board.	There is no requirement to make generic drivers in the GM6000 project.
src/Eros	This directory contains all of the application-specific code for the engineering-only test application used for environmental, emissions, and manufacturing testing of the GM6000 product.	
xsrc/	This directory tree contains (almost all) the third-party source code that is used in the GM6000 product.	This tree contains the ST SDKs and the Windows GCC ARM7 cross compiler.

[SDD-62] Unit Testing

Per the Software Development Plan, all namespaces shall have at least one unit test. The unit tests can be manual or automated, but the preference is for automated unit tests. To simplify the continuous integration (CI) build process, the following naming conventions are imposed for the unit text executables.

APPENDIX M   GM6000 SOFTWARE DETAILED DESIGN (FINAL DRAFT)

Name	Description
a.exe, a.out	Used for all automated units that can be run in parallel with other units.
aa.exe, aa.out	Same as a.exe, a.out except that executables cannot be run in parallel. For example, this could be a test that uses a hard-wired TCP port number.
b.exe, b.out	Used for all automated units that can be run in parallel and that require an external Python script to run the test executable. For example, this could be a test that pipes a golden input file to stdin of the test executable.
bb.exe, bb.out	Same as b.exe, b.out except that executables cannot be run in parallel.
a.py	Used to execute the b.exe and b.out executables.
aa.py	Used to execute the bb.exe and bb.out executables.
<all others>	Manual units can use any name for the executable except for the ones listed previously.

[SDD-31] Subsystems

The following sections describe the individual subsystems in detail.

[SDD-10] Alert Management

Individual alerts are raised, and lowered, throughout the application at their source—not by the alert management subsystem. The alert management subsystem is only responsible for summarizing the active alerts. This includes the following:

APPENDIX M   GM6000 SOFTWARE DETAILED DESIGN (FINAL DRAFT)

- Maintaining a count of active alerts.

- Managing a list of currently active alerts. The list is a prioritized list where index 0 is the highest priority, index 1 is the next highest priority, etc. The list is implemented as an array of pointers to alert model points: Ajax::Dm::MpAlert* (which are sorted by priority).

- Encapsulating the aforementioned information into a single model point of type: Ajax::Dm::MpAlertSummary.

For the Alerts themselves, a model point instance is created for each possible alert instance. A raised alert is indicated by the model point instance having a valid value. When the alert is lowered or is inactive, the model point instance is set to invalid.

The alert data structure for Ajax::Dm::MpAlert includes the following fields:

- name—Enum that identifies the individual alert instances

- priority—Alert priority, where 0 is the highest priority and 255 is the lowest priority

The source code for the alert management is located at src/Ajax/Alerts.

[SDD-11] Application

The application subsystem contains the top-level business logic for the entire application.

[SDD-32] Creation and Startup (Application)

The GM6000 uses the Main pattern for creating, starting, and stopping all of the other subsystems at run time. The Main pattern states that an application is built by wiring together independent components and modules. The Main pattern consists of the following:

- The resolution of interface references with concrete implementations
- The initialization and shutdown sequencing

The implementation of the Main pattern uses internal interfaces so that the core creation and sequencing logic can be common across platform and application variants. There are at least two platforms:

- The initial NUCLEO-F413ZH board
- The functional simulator

And there are at least two application variants:

- The Ajax application for the production release of the GM6000
- The Eros engineering-only test software application

The design decision to share the startup code across the different variants was made to avoid maintaining *N*-number of separate startup sequences.

Per the coding standard, the use of #ifdef within functions is not allowed. The different permutations are done by defining functions (i.e., internal interfaces) and then statically linking the appropriate implementations for each variant.

APPENDIX M   GM6000 SOFTWARE DETAILED DESIGN (FINAL DRAFT)

The following directory structure and header files (for the internal interfaces) shall be used. The directory structure assumes that the build scripts for the different variants build different directories, as opposed to cherry-picking files within a directory.

```
src/Ajax/Main/            // Platform/Application independent implementation
+--- platform.h           // Interface for Platform dependencies
+--- application.h        // Interface for App dependencies
+--- _app/                // Ajax specific startup implementation
+--- _plat_xxxx/          // Platform variant 1 start-up implementation
|   +--- app_platform.h   // Interface for Platform specific App dependencies
|   +--- _app_platform/   // Ajax-Platform specific startup implementation
+--- _plat_yyyy/          // Platform variant 2 start-up implementation
|   +--- app_platform.h   // Interface for Platform specific App dependencies
|   +--- _app_platform/   // Ajax-Platform specific startup implementation
```

The base implementation for the Main pattern is located at the src/Ajax/Main/ directory tree. The base implementation is for the Ajax application.

The Eros Main pattern implementation is built on top of the Ajax implementation. The Eros customizations are located at src/Eros/Main.

[SDD-12] Bootloader

This remains a placeholder for now since there is not currently a requirement for upgradable firmware in the initial release. However, it is fully expected in the future.

[SDD-13] BSP

There will be a Board Support Package (BSP) for each hardware platform used in the development process from prototypes to final platform. The first hardware platform BSP is for the ST NUCLEO-F413ZH evaluation

APPENDIX M GM6000 SOFTWARE DETAILED DESIGN (FINAL DRAFT)

board. This board will be used for the "pancake"[22] hardware platform. In addition, the BSP software will be developed incrementally. That is, support for the SPI driver will not be implemented until there is an LCD controller it can communicate with.

The general structure of a BSP is

- Dependent on a specific compiler

- The source code or SDK provided by the board's MCU supplier. This code may be referenced or copied directly into the src/Bsp tree (or both).

- Any in-house developed source code that has direct dependencies on the source code for the second bullet shown previously. This source code will be located under the src/Bsp tree and will provide a Cpl::Io stream for the debug console.

[SDD-69] alpha1

The alpha1 BSP supports the initial firmware development using the ST NUCLEO-F413ZH evaluation board.

The BSP relies on the ST Cube MX application to generate the low-level initialization of the board, peripherals, and IO. The ST Cube MX project file for the BSP is located in the following directory: src/Bsp/Initech/alpha1/MX.

The BSP is dependent on FreeRTOS, and the configuration of FreeRTOS is done via the ST Cube MX tool.

---

[22] A "pancake board" is where a collection of individual off-the-shelf hardware boards—spread across a workbench—are wired together to provide the functionality of the final customized PCBA.

APPENDIX M   GM6000 SOFTWARE DETAILED DESIGN (FINAL DRAFT)

All of the IO required for the initial release is supported. See the STM32-Alpha board Pin Out wiki page for the board's pin out.

The BSP also includes support for running the Segger SystemView tool. To include the SystemView tool, the build script must define the ENABLE_BSP_SEGGER_SYSVIEW symbol and build the `src/Bsp/Initech/alpha1/SeggerSysView` directory.

The BSP is located at `src/Bsp/Initech/alpha1`.

[SDD-70] alpha1-atmel

The `alpha1-atmel` BSP is an alternate platform that uses the Atmel SAMD51 microcontroller. The platform is Adafruit's Grand Central M4 Express evaluation board. Adafruit supplies Arduino support for the board.

The BSP relies on the Arduino framework for the bulk of the MCU startup and peripheral initialization and usage.

The BSP is dependent on FreeRTOS and supports the Arduino framework design of creating an initial thread that calls the Arduino `setup()` and `loop()` methods. The BSP contains a header file for the FreeRTOS Configuration. However, each project or test build directory is required to contain a `FreeRTOSConfig.h` header file that references this file:

`src/Bsp/Initech/alpha1-atmel/FreeRTOSConfig_bsp.h`

All of the IO required for the initial release is supported. See the Adafruit-Grand-Central-Alpha board Pin Out wiki page for the board's pin out.

The BSP is located at `src/Bsp/Initech/alpha1-atmel`.

APPENDIX M   GM6000 SOFTWARE DETAILED DESIGN (FINAL DRAFT)

[SDD-14] Console

The debug console subsystem provides a command-line interface (CLI) into the firmware application. The CLI provides commands for debugging and white box testing as well as a text-based scriptable interface to exercise the unit's functionality.

The debug console is implemented using the CPL library's TShell framework. For target builds, a UART is used for the stream IO. For simulation builds, stdio is used for the stream IO.

The TShell framework has the following features:

- A single, dedicated thread is used for reading the input stream and then executing the command. All commands are executed sequentially and atomically with respect to other commands.

- The TShell relies on Cpl::Io::Input and Cpl::Io::Output stream references for reading commands and outputting text messages. By default, the output of text messages is synchronized with the Cpl::System::Trace engine so that TShell and Tracing messages are atomic with respect to each other.

- The TShell processor has a list of supported commands, and each command is its own C++ child class of Cpl::TShell::Command.

- The TShell processor is responsible for reading and performing the initial parsing of the input stream. After a valid, supported command has been found, the command is executed by invoking the matched command instance's execute() method. Commands have the following features:

- Each instantiated TShell command self-registers with the TShell processor. There is no limit to the number of commands that can register.

- Each command provides its own terse and verbose help text.

- The TShell processor supports each command that has a permission level. There are four supported levels. When this feature is enabled, a user is required to log in before being allowed to execute commands. The TShell processor will not allow a logged-in user to execute a command if they have insufficient permissions.

[SDD-61] Console Security

The debug console is enabled in the production firmware. The console will be used during verification and validation (V&V) testing and for engineering root cause analysis on production units.

In order to prevent unauthorized access to the console, a user is required to log in before having access to the console's command set. The security features are as follows:

- The console password is unique per unit. The password is generated during the manufacturing process.

- The console password is stored as a hashed value in the external EEPROM. If no password has been stored, console access is not allowed.

- The console password has the following complexity requirements:
  - The minimum length is 12 characters.
  - The maximum length is 32 characters.

- It must contain at least one
  - Numeric character
  - Uppercase letter
  - Lowercase letter
  - Special character: !@#$%^&*();:.?<>,[]{}
- No prompts or error responses are displayed during the login process.

The Eros build is used for provisioning and executing end-of-line manufacturing tests. Consequently, Eros will be used to set a unit's console password. The Eros firmware will not have the console password feature; no password is required to access its console. In addition, the debug builds of the Ajax application will disable the console password feature to make day-to-day development simpler.

[SDD-15] Crypto

The cryptography functions needed are as follows:

- A hash function for storing the console password. The hash shall be SHA512 since it's required by the ED25519 key generation.
- A random number generator, which is needed to generate a salt value when hashing the console password.
- The ED25519 asymmetric key generator for digitally signing firmware images (see RFC-8032) along with a function for validating a signed firmware image.

An abstraction layer is defined for all of the crypto functions to decouple the application from the underlying implementation. The interface definitions are located at `src/Driver/Crypto/`.

[SDD-58] ED25519

An open source implementation of the ED25519 is used to provide a software-only implementation of the algorithm. The algorithm is implemented using standard C, and it has, no platform dependencies. The source code is located at `xsrc/orlp/ed25519/`.

The "adapter" for the `Driver::Crypto` interfaces to the aforementioned implementation is located at `src/Driver/Crypto/Orlp`.

[SDD-59] Password Hashing

Since the ED25519 algorithm uses a SHA512 hash function as part of key generation, the decision was made to use the SHA512 hash function for hashing the console password. The following is the complete algorithm for hashing the console password.

H = FUNC(HF, plaintext, salt, c)

where

- H is the output of FUNC, the final result of the hashing process. The size, in bytes, of H is 32 bytes, which is the size of the HF function's digest.
- FUNC is the top-level function.
- HF is the cryptographic hashing function, which is the SHA512 algorithm.
- `salt` is a random 16-byte array that is stored along with the hash password.
- `plaintext` is the password in ASCII. This is the password that is being hashed.

- c the number of iterations to run the HF hashing algorithm. The first iteration is performed on plaintext + salt; subsequent iterations use plaintext + <previous-iteration-output> as their input. The output of each iteration is XOR'd to produce the final result. Here is the algorithm:

```
F(plaintext, salt, c) = U1 ^ U2 ... ^ Uc
```

   where

```
U1 = HF(plaintext + salt)
U2 = HF(plaintext + U1)
Uc = HF(plaintext + Uc-1)
```

   The value of c is TBD.

The password hashing algorithm implementation is located at src/Driver/Crypto/PasswordHash.

[SDD-60] Random Number

The implementation for the Random Number interface is platform dependent.

- STM32—The STM32 HAL's true random number generator is used, although how "true" is dependent on the specific MCU. The implementation is located in the BSP directory for the target hardware (e.g., src/Bsp/Initech/alpha1/Random.cpp).

- Atmel SAMD51–The Atmel SAMD51's true random number is used. The implementation is located in the BSP directory for the target hardware (e.g., src/Bsp/Initech/alpha1-atmel/Random.cpp).

- Win32—The Win32 `CryptGenRandom()` method is used. The implementation is located at `src/Driver/Crypto/Win32`.

- Posix—The source of random numbers is `/dev/random`. The implementation is located at `src/Driver/Crypto/Posix`.

[SDD-16] Data Model

The Data Model software architecture pattern is a data-oriented pattern where modules interact with each other via data instances with no direct dependencies between modules. See the *GM6000 Software Architecture* document for a more detailed discussion of the Data Model pattern.

The Data Model framework and basic model point types are located at `src/Cpl/Dm`.

The GM6000 application adds additional Model Point types for application-specific data. The new model point types are defined in the `src/Ajax/Dm` directory.

[SDD-71] Model Point Change Notification

The data model's change notification semantics guarantee that a client will get a notification when there is a change to a model point's value or state. However, there are some nuances to using change notification:

- A client is not guaranteed to be notified for every change—just a notification for the last one. For example, consider a system that is configured for the following behavior:

  - A Sensor Driver is updating model point A every millisecond with a different analog value.

- Module B subscribes for change notification from model point A.
- The Sensor Driver and Module B execute in different threads.

  Depending on thread priorities, CPU performance, and other activities in the system, Module B is unlikely to be able to process a change notification every millisecond. If, let's say, Module B's thread is delayed by 5 ms before the change notification can be executed, Module B will receive a single change notification (not five), and the value of model point A will be the last value written by the Sensor Driver.
- A client may receive multiple change notifications where the model point appears to have not changed. The change notification mechanism uses sequence numbers to determine when a change notification is required. Each observer instance has a sequence number that is compared against the model point sequence number every time the model point value or state is changed. If the two sequence numbers are different after the change, then a change notification is generated. When the change notification callback occurs, the observer's sequence number is set to the model point's sequence number. However, there is a potential race condition between when the observer's sequence number is updated and when a potential second update to the model point when the client's callback method executes, resulting in a double notification. The good news is this race condition can

be eliminated by using the readAndSync(...) and isNotValidAndSync(...) model point methods when sampling the model point in the change notification callback. The use of the readAndSync(...) and isNotValidAndSync(...) methods is required to be used for all change notification callbacks.

[SDD-17] Diagnostics

The Diagnostics subsystem is responsible for monitoring and self-testing the system. This includes features such as power-on self-tests and metrics.

[SDD-72] POST

During startup, the system performs one or more power-on self-tests (POST). If any of the self-tests fail, then

- The ePOST_FAILURE alert is raised
- The heating mode is set to OFF
- The UI Error screen is triggered

The system still attempts to start up and run when there is a POST error; however, the UI will be locked on the error screen. The POST performs the following tests:

- Verifying communications with the off-board EEPROM
- Verifying that the on-board temperature sensor is functioning

APPENDIX M GM6000 SOFTWARE DETAILED DESIGN (FINAL DRAFT)

The POST tests are platform specific. They are located under the following directory trees: src/Ajax/Main/_plat_xxxx.

Be aware that the simulator has command-line arguments that can be used to simulate a POST failure.

[SDD-73] Metrics

The metrics module does the following:

- It monitors the state of the system via model points.
- It updates the metrics model points.
- It periodically flushes the model points to persistent storage.

The metrics module executes in the application thread.

On an orderly shutdown of the system, the application, or the application's shutdown sequence, is required to flush the Metrics Storage record (Ajax::Main::MetricsRecord) to persistent storage.

The following metrics are tracked and stored in persistent storage.

MP Name	Type	Description	Update Freq
metricBootCounter	Uint32	Free running counter that is incremented on every reset-cycle. The counter is set to zero during the provisioning process. This model point is managed as part of the startup sequence (not part of the metrics module).	The counter is updated to persistent storage every time the application starts up.

(*continued*)

APPENDIX M GM6000 SOFTWARE DETAILED DESIGN (FINAL DRAFT)

MP Name	Type	Description	Update Freq
metricRunningTime	Uint64	Number of seconds that the unit has been powered on.	The counter is updated to persistent storage every 15 minutes and on an orderly shutdown.
metricHeaterOnTime	Uint64	Number of seconds that the heater PWM value is greater than zero.	The counter is updated to persistent storage: - Every 15 minutes - on heater off transitions - on an orderly shutdown
metricFanOnTime	Uint64	Number of seconds that the fan PWM value is greater than zero.	The counter is updated to persistent storage: - Every 15 minutes - On fan off transitions - On an orderly shutdown

(*continued*)

APPENDIX M   GM6000 SOFTWARE DETAILED DESIGN (FINAL DRAFT)

MP Name	Type	Description	Update Freq
metricFaultHeaterSafety	Uint32	Free running counter that is incremented every time the eHITEMP_HEATER_FAILSAFE alert is raised.	The counter is updated to persistent storage on every change.

The metrics module is located at src\Ajax\Metrics.

[SDD-18] Drivers

There is a single driver thread. The driver thread shall have higher priority than the UI thread and the control algorithm thread. Drivers that have strict time constraints shall execute in the driver thread.

[SDD-74] Onboard Analog Driver

The onboard temperature sensor is a 10K NTC thermistor that is sampled using the MCU's ADC peripheral. Since the space temperature is consumed at a very low rate (i.e., less than 1 Hz), the ADC is polled.

The driver uses 12-bit ADC resolution.

To filter out noise on the input, the driver averages *N* physical consecutive samples per logical reading. The averaging is performed on the raw ADC bit values.

The driver takes a logical ADC sample at 1 Hz and updates the mp::onBoardIdt model point with the result. Because of the low 1 Hz sampling rate and the busy-wait semantics when reading the ADC registers, the analog driver runs in the *application* thread and **not** in the high-priority *driver* thread.

APPENDIX M GM6000 SOFTWARE DETAILED DESIGN (FINAL DRAFT)

The driver relies on an HAL interface defined in the header file `src/Driver/AIO/HalSingle.h`. A platform-specific implementation of the HAL interface is located at `src/Driver/AIO`.

A mocked HAL driver—using a model point for the ADC bit values—is provided in the analog driver with the functional simulator. The mocked HAL driver is located at `src/Driver/AIO/Simulated`. The source code for the driver is located at `src/Driver/AIO/Ajax`.

[SDD-36] Button Driver

The `Driver::Button::PolledDebounced` driver supplied by the CPL C++ class library will be used for the display board's discrete input buttons. The driver will execute in the driver thread.

The debounce sampling time is 100 Hz and requires that two consecutive samples match in order to declare a new button state.

The existing button driver only requires the low-level HAL interface to be implemented for the target platform.

For the functional simulator, the buttons on the display board are simulated using the `TPipe` implementation of the `Driver::PicoDisplay` driver. The driver is located at `src/Driver/Button`. The target-specific implementation is located at `src/Driver/Button/STM32`.

The driver deviates from the SWA recommended implementation in that it does not use interrupts to detect the initial button edge. The proposed design meets the SWA requirements of debouncing a button within 50 msec (worst case for the current design is 30 msec), and the continually polling is not overly burdensome for the application. The tradeoff was deemed acceptable. That is, the simplicity of leveraging existing code was prioritized over writing a more complex driver from scratch.

[SDD-84] GPIO In Driver

The Driver::DIO::In driver supplied by the CPL C++ class library will be used for simple Digital Input signals.

The existing driver uses the LHeader pattern for decoupling the interface from the hardware platform.

The CPL driver has an existing simulated implementation that uses model points to mock the driver interface.

The driver is located at

- src/Driver/DIO

The target-specific implementations are located at

- src/Driver/DIO/STM32
- src/Driver/DIO/Arduino

The simulated implementation is located at

- src/Driver/DIO/Simulated

[SDD-37] GPIO Out Driver

The Driver::DIO::Out driver supplied by the CPL C++ class library will be used for simple Digital Output signals.

The existing driver uses the LHeader pattern for decoupling the interface from the hardware platform.

The CPL driver has an existing simulated implementation that uses model points to mock the driver interface.

The driver is located at

- src/Driver/DIO

The target-specific implementations are located at

- src/Driver/DIO/STM32
- src/Driver/DIO/Arduino

APPENDIX M   GM6000 SOFTWARE DETAILED DESIGN (FINAL DRAFT)

The simulated implementation is located at

- src/Driver/DIO/Simulated

[SDD-53] I2C Driver

The Driver::I2C abstract interface supplied by the CPL C++ class library will be used for the I2C bus driver. The I2C driver is used to communicate with the following device:

- I2C EEPROM, using address 0x50

The concrete driver for the STM32 microcontroller family uses the ST HAL I2C interfaces for the underlying I2C bus implementation, specifically using the ST Cube MX generated code for configuration and initialization.

The concrete driver for the Adafruit Grand Central board uses the Arduino framework's I2C driver.

For the functional simulator, the EEPROM functionality is simulated at a higher layer (i.e., the Cpl::Persistent::RegionMedia layer).

The abstract I2C driver interface is located at

- src/Driver/I2C

The target-specific I2C implementations are located at

- src/Driver/I2C/STM32
- src/Driver/I2C/Arduino

[SDD-38] LCD Controller

The LCD screen on the display board is a 1.14" IPS LCD screen. The physical screen is controlled by a Sitronix ST7789 LCD controller with frame memory.

The LCD controller's 4-line, 8-bit serial interface is used. Data is only written to the LCD controller. The following signals are used:

- CSX—SPI chip select
- SDA—SPI input data (the MCU's MOSI signal)
- DCX—SPI clock signal (the MCU's SPI CLK signal)
- WRX—The data/command flag, where "low" is command and "high" is data

The platform-independent port of the Pimoroni Pico library's `pimoroni::ST7789` driver is used. The driver requires a `Driver::SPI` driver instance and two instances of the `Driver::DIO::Out` drivers for the CSX and DCX signals.

The Pimoroni platform-independent ST7789 driver is located at `xsrc/pimoroni/drivers/st7789`.

[SDD-39] PicoDisplay Driver

The display board has the same basic hardware (240x135 LCD, LCD controller, discrete buttons, etc.) as the Pico Display sold by Pimoroni. The `Driver::PicoDisplay` driver supplied by the CPL C++ class library is used to decouple the display board hardware from the hardware.

The PicoDisplay driver requires the following:

- Two GPIO output signals for the CS and DC signals used with the LCD controller's SPI interface
- An ST7789 driver LCD controller. The LCD controller's SPI Bus interface is used. (The ST7789 driver requires an SPI driver)
- A PWM output signal to control LCD backlight brightness

APPENDIX M GM6000 SOFTWARE DETAILED DESIGN (FINAL DRAFT)

- Four GPIO input signals for the momentary buttons
- An RGB LED driver

The concrete driver for the STM32 and Atmel SAM51x microcontroller families uses the STM32 and Arduino framework implementations of the following drivers:

- `Driver::DIO::Out`
- `pimoroni::ST7789` (LCD controller driver)
- `Driver::SPI`
- `Driver::DIO::Pwm`
- `Driver::Button::PolledDebounced`
- `Driver::LED::RedGreenBlue`

For the functional simulator, the `Driver::PicoDisplay::TPipe` implementation is used.

The PicoDisplay driver is located at

- `src/Driver/PicoDisplay`

The target-specific PicoDisplay implementations are located at

- `src/Driver/PicoDisplay/STM32`
- `src/Driver/PicoDisplay/Arduino`

The simulated TPipe implementation is located at

- `src/Driver/PicoDisplay/TPipe`

[SDD-40] PWM Driver

The `Driver::DIO::Pwm` driver supplied by the CPL C++ class library will be used for simple PWM Output signals.

574

APPENDIX M   GM6000 SOFTWARE DETAILED DESIGN (FINAL DRAFT)

The existing driver uses the LHeader pattern for decoupling the interface from the hardware platform.

For the functional simulator, the PWM outputs to the display board are simulated using the TPipe implementation of the Driver::PicoDisplay driver.

For the functional simulator, the CPL driver's existing simulated implementation, which incorporates model points to mock the driver interface, will be used.

The driver is located at

- src/Driver/DIO

The target-specific implementations are located at

- src/Driver/DIO/STM32
- src/Driver/DIO/Arduino

The simulated implementation is located at

- src/Driver/DIO/Simulated

[SDD-41] RGB LED Driver

The Driver::LED::RedGreenBlue abstract interface supplied by the CPL C++ class library will be used for the display board's RGB LED.

The concrete driver for the target hardware is a thin wrapper on top of the platform-independent port of the Pimoroni Pico library's pimoroni::RGBLED driver. The pimoroni::RGBLED driver in turn uses the CPL's Driver::DIO::Pwm interface for the PWM output signals.

The abstract driver interface is located at

- src/Driver/LED/RedGreenBlue.h

The concrete driver of the interface is located at

- src/Driver/LED/Pimoroni/RedGreenBlue.h

The Pimoroni platform-independent port of the RGB LED driver is located at

- `xsrc/pimoroni/drivers/rgbled`

For the functional simulator, the `Driver::PicoDisplay::TPipe` implementation is used.

[SDD-42] SPI Driver

The `Driver::SPI` abstract interface supplied by the CPL C++ class library will be used for the SPI bus driver.

The concrete driver for the STM32 microcontroller family uses the ST HAL SPI interfaces for the underlying SPI bus implementation, specifically using the ST Cube MX generated code for configuration and initialization.

The concrete driver for the Adafruit Grand Central board uses the Arduino framework's SPI driver.

For the functional simulator, the SPI bus to the display board is simulated using the TPipe implementation of the `Driver::PicoDisplay` driver.

The abstract SPI driver interface is located at

- `src/Driver/SPI`

The target-specific SPI implementations are located at

- `src/Driver/SPI/STM32`
- `src/Driver/SPI/Arduino`

[SDD-43] TPipe Driver

The TPipe driver provides a point-to-point full duplex pipe that is used to pass text-based commands between two end points. Each command is encapsulated in an HDLC-like frame (i.e., prefaced by Start-of-Frame characters and terminating with End-of-Frame characters). The first token

APPENDIX M   GM6000 SOFTWARE DETAILED DESIGN (FINAL DRAFT)

in the frame is a command verb. The command verb and any additional frame data are application specific. The command verb must start immediately after the SOF character (with no leading whitespace).

A separate C# Windows application, simulator.exe, is used to simulate the physical display. The simulator.exe application uses bit maps to emulate the LCD display and the RGB LED. Dialog buttons in the application are used to emulate the four physical momentary buttons. The buttons can be pressed using the mouse or the keyboard. The keyboard option supports multi-button pressed combinations. The GM6000 functional simulator connects to the simulator.exe application via TCP sockets using the TPipe protocol to transfer data and button events. Note that the backlight brightness is not simulated.

The TPipe driver is located at

- src/Driver/TPipe

The TPipe command set for the RGB LED is defined in

- src/Driver/LED/TPipe/RedGreenBlue.h

The TPipe command set for the momentary buttons is defined in

- src/Driver/Button/TPipe/Hal.h

The TPipe command set for the LCD data is defined in

- src/Driver/PicoDisplay/TPipe/Api.h

The C# simulator.exe application is located at projects/pico-display-simulator.

APPENDIX M   GM6000 SOFTWARE DETAILED DESIGN (FINAL DRAFT)

[SDD-19] Graphics Library

The SWA requires that the Graphics library be platform independent and that it can run without an RTOS. There are several commercial libraries for embedded systems that meet these requirements. The decision was made to use the Pimoroni Graphics Library for the following reasons:

- No cost—The library is open source with an MIT license.
- The CPL C++ class library provides a platform-independent port for the Pimoroni graphics library.
- The Pimoroni library comes with drivers for the ST7789 LCD controller and an RGB LED.

Note: This decision should be revisited for future GM6000 derivatives that have a different display or a more sophisticated UI. The Pimoroni library has the following limitations that do not recommend it as a foundational component:

- It has no support for Window management.
- It requires C++14 (or newer) and uses C++ features or STL that use dynamic memory.
- It is larger than the desired footprint (because it pulls in the entire standard C++ library code).

The library is located at `xsrc/pimoroni`.

[SDD-20] Heating

The heating subsystem is a collection of several components. The core algorithm for heating is a fuzzy logic controller.

APPENDIX M GM6000 SOFTWARE DETAILED DESIGN (FINAL DRAFT)

[SDD-63] Supervisor

The heating supervisor is responsible for the top-level control of the heating algorithm. Specifically, the heating supervisor does the following:

- It runs the fuzzy logic controller on a periodic basis.

- It determines which temperature input source to use. This feature is mostly a placeholder until a wireless temperature sensor is available.

- It generates the command output value for the heating and fan PWM signals. It writes to the PWM output signal model points.

- It raises and lowers the following alerts:

    - No temperature sensor is available.

    - Hardware high-temperature safety has been tripped.

- It keeps the Fan running when there is a high-temperature safety condition.

Note that the tuning and selection of the fuzzy logic controller parameters are TBD while waiting for a representative sample unit to be built and for room and temperature testing to be done.

The following state machine is used to manage the heating algorithm at run time. Figure M-3 is a diagram of the state machine. The canonical state diagram for it is located at src/Ajax/Heating/Supervisor/Fsm.cdd.

APPENDIX M   GM6000 SOFTWARE DETAILED DESIGN (FINAL DRAFT)

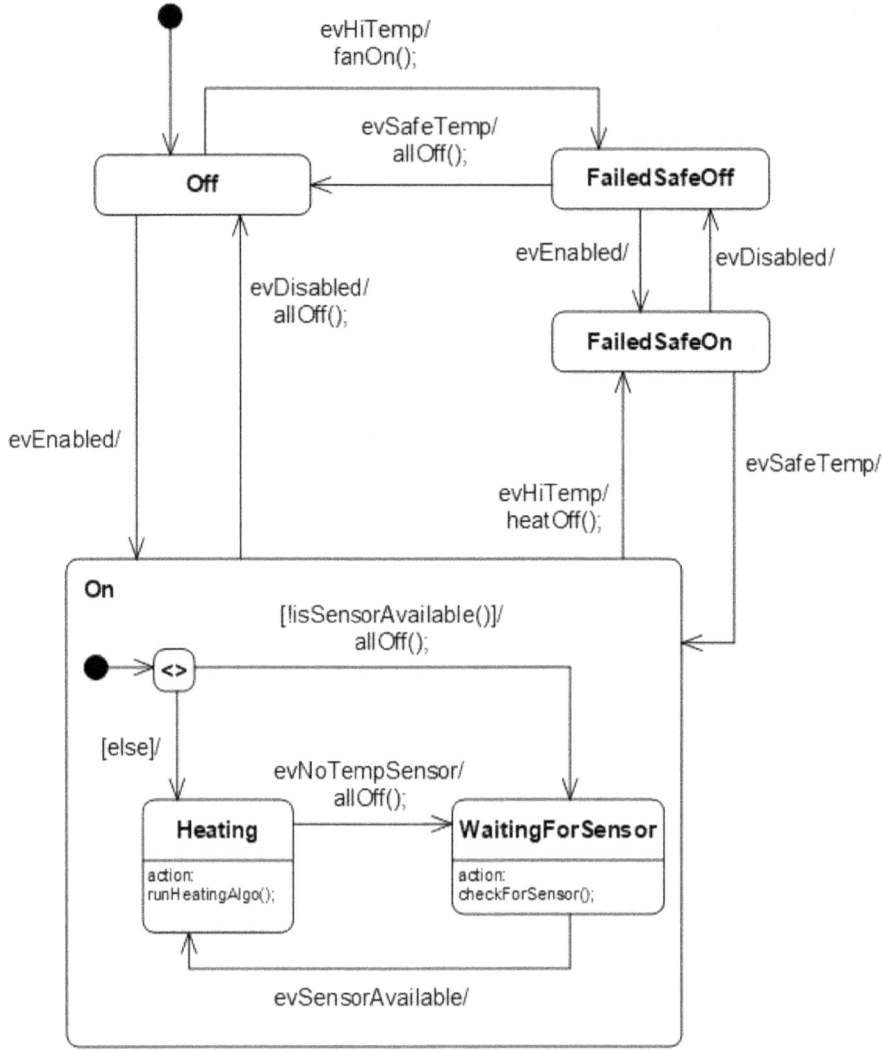

Figure M-3. Heating supervisor finite state machine

The source code files are located at src/Ajax/Heating/Supervisor.

[SDD-64] Model Points

All inputs and outputs are passed using model points. The following table enumerates the model points.

Name	Type	Description/Comments
heatingMode	Cpl::Dm::Mp::Bool	User input. When true, the user has turned on heating mode.
fanMode	Ajax::Dm::MpFanMode	User input
heatSetpoint	Cpl::Dm::Mp::Int32	User input. Units are hundredths of a degree Fahrenheit.
onBoardIdt	Cpl::Dm::Mp::Int32	The built-in temperature sensor. Units are hundredths of a degree Fahrenheit. When the value is invalid, then the sensor is not operational or is missing.
remoteIdt	Cpl::Dm::Mp::Int32	Wireless remote temperature sensor. Units are hundredths of a degree Fahrenheit. When the value is invalid, then the sensor is not operational or missing. Note: This is future functionality.
hwSafetyLimit	Cpl::Dm::Mp::Bool	Is set to true when the hardware temperature safety circuit has tripped as a result of an asserted input signal to the MCU.

(*continued*)

APPENDIX M   GM6000 SOFTWARE DETAILED DESIGN (FINAL DRAFT)

Name	Type	Description/Comments
cmdHeaterPWM	Cpl::Dm::Mp::Uint32	The commanded value for the Heater output PWM signal.
cmdFanPWM	Cpl::Dm::Mp::Uint32	The commanded value for the Fan motor output PWM signal.
sensorFailAlert	Ajax::Dm::MpAlert	Alert for "no working sensor available." When the MP is in the valid state, the Alert is present. When the MP is in the invalid state, there is no alert.
failedSafeAlert	Ajax::Dm::MpAlert	Alert for the high-temperature safety limit tripped. When the MP is in the valid state, the Alert is present. When the MP is in the invalid state, there is no alert.
flcConfig	Ajax::Dm::FlcConfig	Configuration and custom parameters for the fuzzy logic control algorithm.
fanLowPercentage	Cpl:Dm::Mp::Uint32	PWM percentage for the fan low speed
fanMedPercentage	Cpl::Dm:Mp::Uint32	PWM percentage for the fan medium speed
fanHighPercentage	Cpl::Dm:Mp::Uint32	PWM percentage for the fan high speed

APPENDIX M   GM6000 SOFTWARE DETAILED DESIGN (FINAL DRAFT)

[SDD-85] IO

The heating supervisor operates on logical hardware inputs and outputs via model points. The heating IO component is responsible for converting the model point values to and from hardware signals. This includes the following:

- The heater and fan PWM model points (cmdHeaterPWM, cmdFanPWM) are monitored for change, and the hardware outputs are updated on a value change.

- The hardware-safety-limit-tripped input signal is sampled periodically and is used to update the hardware safety limit model point (hwSafetyLimit). The hardware input is sampled or updated at four times the rate that the heating supervisor executes at.

- The heating IO component executes in the same thread as the heating supervisor.

The heating IO implementation is located in the directory src/Ajax/Heating/Io.

[SDD-34] Fuzzy Logic Controller

A fuzzy logic controller (FLC) is used to calculate updates to the requested output capacity. It is the responsibility of the control algorithm to call the FLC on a periodic basis. The FLC takes the current temperature and the temperature setpoint as inputs and generates a delta-change-to-capacity output value every time it is called.

The FLC is implemented per the *SWA-1330 GM6000 Fuzzy Logic Temperature Control* specification in the software architecture document. The implementation has the following features and characteristics:

- An algorithm supervisor is required to call the FLC on a fixed periodic basis and pass it the current temperature and heating setpoint. The FLC does not assume any particular unit of measure for temperature and setpoints. It is the responsibility of the algorithm supervisor to ensure the consistency of input values with respect to units of measure.

- The geometry of the membership functions cannot be changed. However, there is a runtime configurable Y-axis scaling parameter.

- All math operations are performed using integer math. Clients provide a scaling factor that is used during the defuzzification process to compensate for the lack of floating arithmetic.

- Supports a single input membership function, where the sets are defined by triangles.

- Math operations support a single centroid output membership function whose output sets have configurable weights.

- Math operations have fixed, predefined inference rules.

- Configurable algorithm parameters are provided through model points.

The source code files are located at src/Ajax/Heating/Flc.

[SDD-65] House Simulation

A primitive house simulation has been created to provide real-time feedback to the heating algorithm. The goal of simulation is simply to provide run-time feedback to the heating algorithm, not to actually model the thermodynamics of a house and heating system.

Typically, the house simulation is only incorporated into the simulator or test builds to provide closed loop operation of the heating algorithm. However, the house simulation can be included in a target build if desired in lieu of having actual heating and temperature sensor hardware.

The house simulation is done by using electrical theory for charging and discharging a capacitor through a resistance. The external temperature environment load is the discharge path, and active heating is the charging path.

The house simulation implementation is located in the following directories:

```
src/Ajax/SimHouse/
src/Ajax/Heating/Simulated/
```

[SDD-21] Logging

The CPL C++ logging framework (Cpl::Logging) was selected for the logging interface. The CPL logging framework just provides the framework, and it defers the definition of logging categories and message identifiers to the application. In addition, the application is responsible for storing (or subsequently retrieving) the log entries to and from persistent storage.

The CPL logging framework identifies each log entry by categories with a sub-message ID, where category identifiers are unique and message IDs are only unique within a category. Table M-1 shows the top-level logging categories.

APPENDIX M   GM6000 SOFTWARE DETAILED DESIGN (FINAL DRAFT)

Table M-1. *Top-level logging categories*

Category	Description
CRITICAL	A nonrecoverable error condition was encountered.
WARNING	An undesirable or unexpected state or condition occurred, but the device can still operate, albeit with possible degraded performance. Note: Internal errors encountered by the logging framework are logged to this category.
EVENT	Something interesting or noteworthy occurred.
ALERT	An alert condition or state was encountered, where alert is defined as a UX alert.
INFO	Current activity (informational). Typically used for detailed troubleshooting and is not recommended to be enabled by default.
METRICS	Usage information. This is used to capture metrics to the device's log file. Expected usage metrics are periodically written in the log file.

The message IDs per category will be defined on an as-needed basis. See the Doxygen output for latest defined message IDs. The category and message IDs are common to the Ajax and Eros applications.

A Log entry has the following content.

Field	Length (bytes)	Description
timestamp	8	The elapsed time in milliseconds since boot-up when the log entry was generated
category	4	Category identifier (see Table M-1)
msgId	2	Message identifier (see Doxygen output)
msgText	129	Free-form text. The logging API uses `printf` semantics. The maximum text length is 128 bytes, and the null terminator is stored in persistence storage
Total Len	**143**	

The application-specific extensions to the logging framework are located at `src/Ajax/Logging`.

[SDD-52] Persistent Storage

The CPL C++ persistent storage framework is used to store log entries to the external EEPROM. Specifically the `Cpl::Persistent::IndexedEntry Record` class is used to store *N* log entries. The following is a summary of features and limitations of the `IndexedEntryRecord` implementation:

- A single instance of `IndexedEntryRecord` is used to store *N* log entries.

- The `Cpl::Logging::EntryData_T` class is the payload for `IndexedEntryRecord`. All log entries have the same fixed length.

- The individual entries are logically stored in a ring buffer. This means that once the ring buffer is full (i.e., all of the space available in the `RegionMedia` has been written to), older entries are overwritten when there is a request to write a new entry.

- Only a pointer to the head of the logical ring buffer is persistently stored. This means that all traversals or searching for log entries always begins by retrieving the newest log entry.

- An additional secondary record with its own chunk handler is used to persistently store the pointer to the head of the logical ring buffer. The chunk handler for the secondary record is a `MirrorChunk` instance to guard against corrupting the head pointer when it is being updated should a power failure occur.

- Each individual log entry has a unique key assigned to it, which persists across reboots. The larger the key value, the newer the log entry. The key is a free running 64-bit counter.
- An individual corrupt log entry does not invalidate any other existing log entries. Corrupt entries are skipped when reading out log entries.

[SDD-22] OS

The operating system for the target hardware is the open source FreeRTOS. Only the basic kernel (i.e., the task scheduler) is used. For the functional simulator (and automated testing), the operating system is Windows and Linux.

[SDD-23] OSAL

The Operating System Abstraction Layer is provided by the System Services subsystem.

[SDD-24] Persistent Storage

The Persistent Storage subsystem provides the interfaces, framework, data integrity checks, etc., for storing and retrieving data that is stored in persistent storage. The persistent storage paradigm is a RAM-cached model. The RAM-cached model has the following behaviors:

APPENDIX M GM6000 SOFTWARE DETAILED DESIGN (FINAL DRAFT)

1. On startup, persistent record entries are read from NVRAM, validated, and loaded into RAM.

    a. If the loaded data is invalid, then the associated RAM values are set to default or factory values, and the NVRAM storage is updated with new defaulted values.

2. The application updates the entries stored in RAM via an API. When an update request is made, the RAM value is updated, and then a background task is initiated to update the values stored in NVRAM.

3. Each subsystem and component is responsible for defining the data to be stored, as well as providing the initial or factory default values for the data.

[SDD-54] Frequency of Updates

The GM6000 uses an off-board EEPROM for its persistent storage. The EEPROM is specified as having at least 1,000,000 write cycles of endurance. The DHC is required to operate for at least five years. This translates to at most 22.8 EEPROM write cycles per hour for the life of the product.

The highest frequency of application data updates to EEPROM is the metrics data, which occur every 15 minutes, or four writes per hour. Since four writes per hour is significantly less than the 22.8 writes per hour endurance limit, no wear leveling of the EEPROM will be implemented.

[SDD-55] Records

The application data is persistently stored using records. A record is the unit of atomic read/write operations to and from persistent storage. The CPL C++ class library's persistent storage framework is used. In addition, the library's model point records are used, where each record contains one or more model points.

APPENDIX M   GM6000 SOFTWARE DETAILED DESIGN (FINAL DRAFT)

All records are mirrored. That is, two copies of the data are stored to ensure that no data is lost when there is power failure during a write operation.

All the records use a 32-bit CRC for detecting data corruption.

Separate records—instead of a single record—are used to insulate the data against data corruption. For example, the metrics record is updated multiple times per hour, and, consequently, has the highest probability of data corruption when compared with the personality record that is written once. The application data is broken down into the following records:

- User settings
- Personality, which contains customizations to the algorithms, model and serial number, unique console password, etc.
- Metrics

Figure M-4 illustrates the CPL framework and delineates what components the application provides. Only the classes with bolded outlines need to be implemented, as all other classes are provided by the CPL library.

APPENDIX M GM6000 SOFTWARE DETAILED DESIGN (FINAL DRAFT)

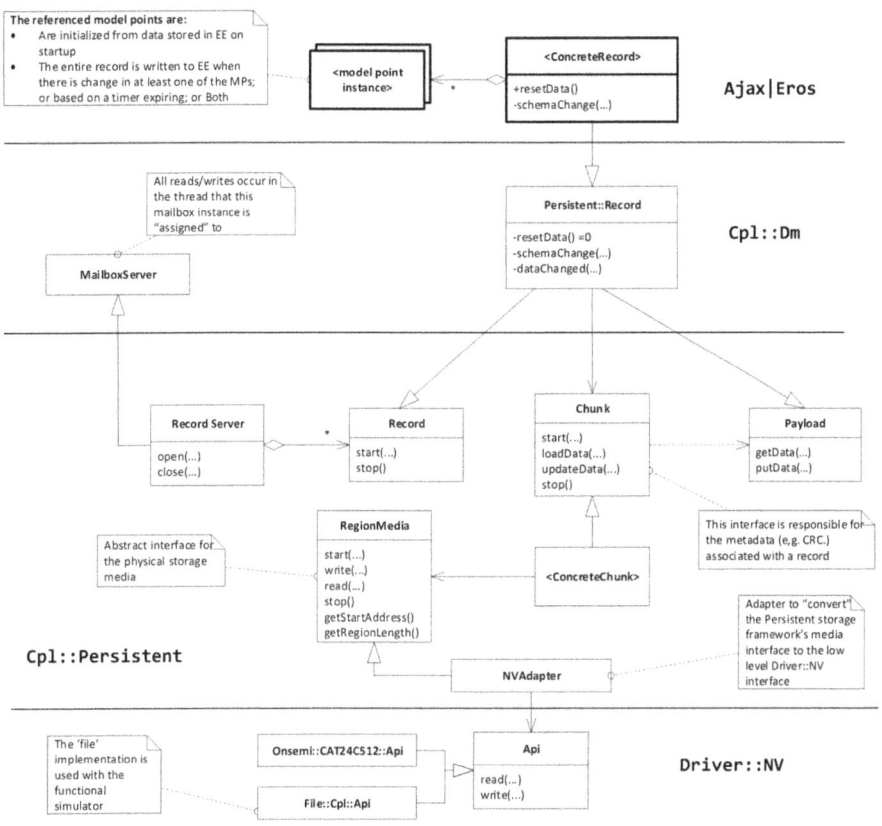

Figure M-4. Data model persistent storage class diagram

The concrete record instances are defined per project variant (e.g., Ajax vs. Eros), and the source code files are located at

src/Ajax/Main
src/Eros/Main

The hardware targets have an off-board I2C-based EEPROM IC. The CPL library Driver::NV::Onsemi::CAT24C512::Api class is used to read/write to the EEPROM.

APPENDIX M   GM6000 SOFTWARE DETAILED DESIGN (FINAL DRAFT)

The functional simulator uses the provided CPL library `Driver::NV::File::Cpl::Api` class, which uses the host's file system as the physical persistent storage.

[SDD-56] Memory Map

The following table details the offset locations in the EEPROM of the various persistently stored records and data.

Record/Data	Region Start	Region Length	Data Length	Chunk Overhead	Reserved/ Expansion
Personality-A	0	273	193	16	64
Personality-B	273	273	193	16	64
UserSettings-B	546	94	14	16	64
UserSettings-B	640	94	14	16	64
Metrics-A	734	124	44	16	64
Metrics-A	858	124	44	16	64
Log Entries[23]	982	40704	40704	0	0
LogIndex-A	41686	60	12	16	32
LogIndex-B	41746	60	12	16	32
Allocated		41806	40.8K		
Capacity		65536	64.0K		
Available		23730	23.2K		

---

[23] A single entry with the per-entry metadata is 159 bytes.

[SDD-25] Sensor Communications

This is a placeholder for the remote temperature. It is not a feature for the initial release.

[SDD-26] Software Update

This is a placeholder. There is currently no requirement for upgradable firmware in the initial release. However, it is fully expected to be required in the future.

[SDD-27] System Services

The System Services subsystem provides various services such as containers, checksums, string handling, software timers, inter-thread communications (ITC), data model infrastructure, OSAL, etc. The system services are provided by the CPL C++ class library (i.e., the open source colony.core repository). The Outcast2 tool is used to create a clone of the CPL repository into the GM6000's single repository. Any fixes, updates, enhancements, etc., to the CPL code are made in the GM6000 repository. There is no requirement to push these changes back to the original CPL repository.

The source code for the system services is located at src/Cpl.

The CPL C++ class library also provides a collection of drivers and framework for an abstract BSP. These items are located at the src/Driver and src/Bsp directories.

APPENDIX M   GM6000 SOFTWARE DETAILED DESIGN (FINAL DRAFT)

[SDD-28] UI

The UI is event driven. Events sources are as follows:

- Model point change notifications
- Software timers
- CPL event flags
- Internal UI subsystem events

The UI subsystem assumes a single thread model, and it is not thread safe. All data flowing in and out of the UI subsystem is required to be done via model points.

[SDD-44] Screen Manager

The GUI consists of a set of screens. At any given time, only one screen is active. Each screen is responsible for the display content and is expected to react to UI events (e.g., button presses) as well as model point change notifications from the application.

Navigation between screens uses a home-screen stack model. That is, transitioning to a new screen pushes the current screen onto the navigation stack and then makes the new screen the active screen. Navigating back is done by popping one or more screens from the navigation stack or clearing the entire navigation stack and making the home screen the active screen.

Which screen instance is the home screen is determined by the contents of a model point instance. This allows the application to change what the home screen is based on the overall state of the application.

There are three special screens that do not follow the aforementioned paradigm. They are as follows:

- Splash screen—Displayed when the system is starting up

APPENDIX M GM6000 SOFTWARE DETAILED DESIGN (FINAL DRAFT)

- Shutdown screen—Displayed when the system is shutting down
- UI Halted screen—Displayed when an error occurs that prevents continued operation

Figure M-5 is the state machine diagram that shows the life cycle of the screen manager. It describes the behavior; it is not intended to be an implementation.

The screen manager should be opened as soon as possible during the startup sequence, so the splash screen is displayed (instead of a blank screen).

During an orderly shutdown, the application should trigger the UI-shutdown request as the first step in the shutdown sequence and then close the screen manager as late as possible in the shutdown sequence.

APPENDIX M   GM6000 SOFTWARE DETAILED DESIGN (FINAL DRAFT)

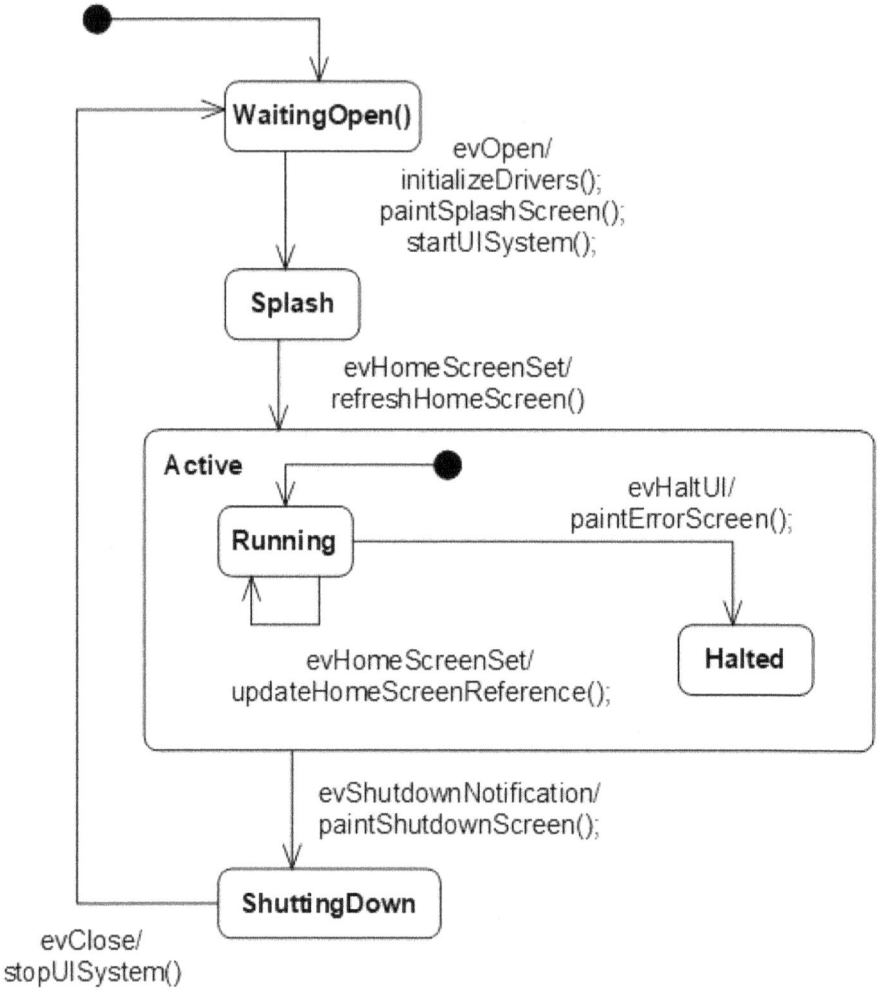

Figure M-5. Screen management finite state machine

Figure M-6 identifies the classes and functionality of the screen manager. The classes in ***italics*** are the public interfaces exposed to the application. Classes in gray (i.e., "Splash shutting down error," "main," and "about") are not part of the screen manager namespace.

APPENDIX M GM6000 SOFTWARE DETAILED DESIGN (FINAL DRAFT)

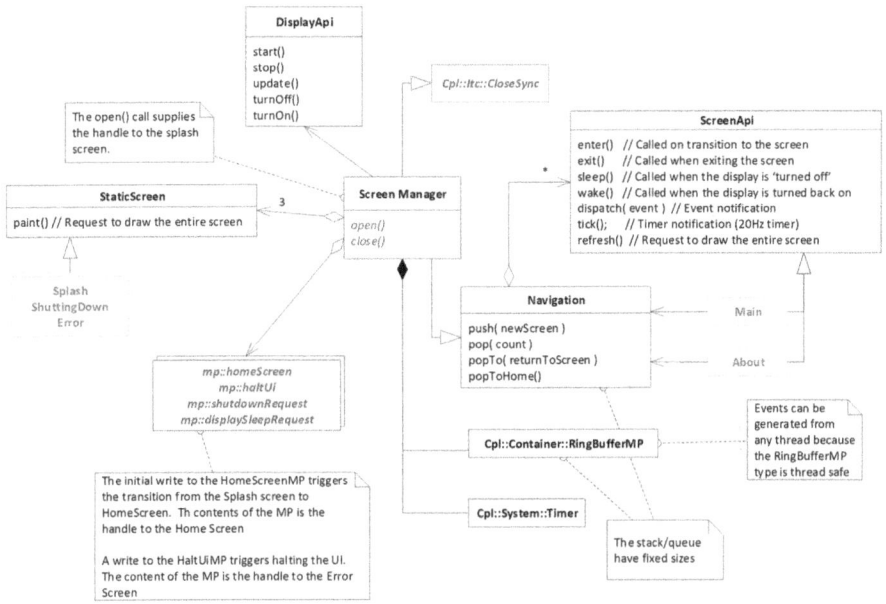

Figure M-6. *Screen manager class diagram*

The screen manager is independent of the Graphics library that is used to draw or update the physical display.

The UI events are application specific. The screen manager uses the LHeader pattern for the event type to decouple itself from the application.

The screen manager namespace is Ajax::ScreenMgr. The source code is located at src/Ajax/ScreenMgr.

[SDD-45] Events

The UI events are limited to discrete button events. From the GUI wireframes, there are five different button events: one per discrete button (x4) and one logical button, which is two keys (B and Y) pressed together.

The UI events are defined as a C-compatible enumeration. This is because the event type is mapped to the screen manager's AjaxScreenMgrEvent_T using the LHeader pattern. The implementation of the LHeader pattern—the `colony_map.h` header file—is included by C modules as well as C++ modules, so all of the mapped code needs to be valid C code.

The header file for the UI events is `src/Ajax/Ui/Events.h`.

[SDD-51] Button Events

A `LogicalButton` class will be responsible for polling the physical buttons and then converting the physical key press/release actions into UI button events. The `LogicalButton` class uses the Pico display driver for polling the physical buttons. The Pico display driver itself is responsible for the actual button debouncing.

The `LogicalButton` driver executes in the UI thread and uses a software timer to generate the polling frequency. The polling rate is 100 Hz to meet the timing requirements.

Because the `LogicalButton` driver is polling the physical button, it already has dependency on the Pico display driver. The `LogicalButton` driver calls the Pico display driver's `nop()` method. This method does nothing on the target, but when running on the simulator, it is used to update time on the simulated display. The `nop()` function is called at 10 Hz.

The source code for the `LogicalButton` class is located at `src/Ajax/Ui`.

[SDD-46] Screens

The following sections detail the individual screens. The screens directly access the Pimoroni graphics library. That is, they have a dependency on the library (see section [SDD-19]).

The `Driver::PicoDriver` is used to implement the screen manager's `DisplayApi`.

All temperatures are displayed in degrees Fahrenheit.

Individual screens use hard-coded model point names when consuming data from or updating data in the application. This is to simplify the construction and implementation of the screen instances.

For screens that have dynamic data sourced from model points, the screens subscribe for change notifications and refresh themselves on change.

None of the individual screens have unit test projects. The screens are manually tested as they are integrated into the Ajax or Eros projects.

[SDD-47] About Screen

The About screen shall have a white background with black text. The model number, serial number, firmware version, and the technical support contact information (e.g., telephone number, email, URL) are displayed on the screen.

The source code for the screen is located at `src/Ajax/Ui/About`.

[SDD-67] Edit Screen

The Edit screen shall have a black background with static white text. The editable fields are displayed with a blue background with white text. The following information is displayed:

- Current temperature setpoint
- Text labels for what actions the buttons perform

The following controls are available:

- Button (X) to increment the setpoint. The screen is responsible for clamping the setpoint at the "max allowed" value.
- Button (Y) to decrement the setpoint. The screen is responsible for clamping the setpoint at the "min allowed" value.
- Button (B) returns the UI to the home screen.

The source code for the screen is located at `src/Ajax/Ui/EditSetpt`.

APPENDIX M   GM6000 SOFTWARE DETAILED DESIGN (FINAL DRAFT)

[SDD-50] Error Screen

The error screen shall have a red background with white text. The firmware version, model number, error code, and error title are displayed on the screen.

The error condition, code, or alert that is displayed is the highest-priority active alert.

The implementation is responsible for converting the individual alert conditions into user facing text and error codes. The user facing error text and codes are located in the header file src/Ajax/Ui/Error/error_.h.

The source code for the screen is located at src/Ajax/Ui/Error.

[SDD-66] Home Screen

The home screen shall have a white background with static black text, dynamic yellow text, and red alert text. The following information is displayed:

- Current space temperature—The home screen's constructor takes a reference to the space temperature model point. This allows adding a secondary or remote temperature sensor in the future without impacting the home screen. Because temperature is an analog value, and because it triggers notification constantly, the model point change notification is not used. Instead, the temperature model point is polled once every two seconds.

- Current temperature setpoint

- Equipment status—This is the specified PWM values for the heater and fan. Because they are analog-ish values, the PWM values are polled (at the same rate as space temperature) instead of being change-driven notifications.

- Alerts when present. An "n of m" indicator is displayed along with the current alert.

The following controls are available:

- Button (A) to toggle the operation mode
- Button (X) to cycle through the fan modes
- Button (B) to cycle through the active alert list (does nothing when there are no active alerts)
- Button (Y) to allow for changing the setpoint. Editing is done by transitioning to the editing screen.
- Button (B+Y) transitions to the About screen.

The source code for the screen is located at src/Ajax/Ui/Home.

[SDD-49] Shut-Down Screen

The shut-down screen shall have a black background with green text. The following text is displayed: "Restarting. Please wait".

The source code for the screen is located at src/Ajax/Ui/Shutdown.

[SDD-48] Splash Screen

The splash screen shall have a blue background with green text. The firmware version, model number, and company name are displayed on the screen.

The source code for the screen is located at src/Ajax/Ui/Splash.

[SDD-68] Status Indicator

The display board's RGB LED has three possible states:

- Green—When the board is powered and the heater element is off and there are no active alerts

- Blue—When the heater element is on and there are no active alerts
- Red—When there is at least one active alert

The aforementioned logic is implemented by monitoring the `mp::cmdHeaterPWM` and `mp::alertSummary` model points. The status indicator logic executes in the UI thread.

If the software is unable to determine the LED state (e.g., because there are one or more invalid MPs), then the LED is set to white.

There is no automated unit test for this module. As with the screen module, the verification is done via manual testing using the Ajax projects.

The source code for the status indicator is located at `src/Ajax/Ui/StatusIndicator`.

[SDD-29] Functional Simulator

The functional simulator supports running the entire Ajax and Eros applications as console applications on Windows or Linux host machines. All the non-platform-dependent source code is used for both the simulator and the target builds. That is, functional simulators execute the production code whenever possible. See the individual driver sections for how each driver is simulated (or is not simulated).

The LCD is emulated using a separate stand-alone C# Windows application. The functional simulator communicates with the LCD application via TCP sockets. See the *[SDD-43] TPipe Driver* for additional details.

The functional simulator does not require the LCD emulation in order to execute. The simulator will attempt to connect the LCD emulation and, on a connection-failure, will pass a null IO stream for the socket descriptor to the TPipe driver. There is also a *TShell* command that will generate UI events from the debug console.

See the "[SDD-32] Creation and Startup (Application)" section on how the platform and hardware differences are managed between the target and simulator builds.

[SDD-30] Engineer Test Application

The Eros application is an engineering test application used to perform various tests to verify or characterize the GM6000 hardware platform. The Eros application is also used during manufacturing to provision and functionally test individual heaters.

Because the Eros application is an "engineering-only" tool, it does not require that Eros-specific code have unit tests. Verification of the Eros-specific code will be done by verifying that the tool meets the testing needs.

The majority of the Eros-specific code is located under the src/Eros/ directory. Other Eros-specific source code will be identified by having Eros in its namespace.

[SDD-33] Creation and Startup

The Eros application shares or extends the Ajax Main pattern (see [SDD-32] Creation and Startup (Application)). The following directory structure shall be used for the Eros-specific code and for extensions to the Ajax startup and shutdown logic.

```
src/Eros/Main/              // Platform/Application Specific implementation
+--- app.cpp                // Eros Application (non-platform) implementation
+--- _plat_xxxx/            // Platform variant 1 start-up implementation
|   +--- app_platform.cpp   // Eros app + specific startup implementation
+--- _plat_yyyy/            // Platform variant 2 start-up implementation
|   +--- app_platform.cpp   // Eros app + specific startup implementation
```

[SDD-81] Provisioning

The Eros application provides a `TShell` debug console command to provision each heater unit. All the provisioning parameters are stored in the personality record using model points. The following table enumerates the data that is required to be provisioned.

Parameter	Model Point	Notes
Serial number	`mp::serialNumber`	Must be less than 16 characters
Model number	`mp::modelNumber`	Must be less than 16 characters
Password	`mp::consolePwdHash` `mp::consolePwdSalt`	The plain text password is hashed, and the random salt is generated during the hashing process and then stored in NVRAM.
Fuzzy logic controller configuration	`mp::flcConfig`	The configuration for the heating algorithm. Engineering is responsible for supplying these values to manufacturing per model type.

The provisioning TShell command is located at src/Ajax/TShell/ Provision.h|.cpp.

Usage:

```
prov <modelNumber> <serialNumber> <consolePwd>
  <h-outS> <h-maxY> <h-errS> <h-dErrS>
  <h-outK0> <h-outK1> <h-outK2> <h-outK3> <h-outK4>
  <fanLow> <fanMed> <fanHi> <maxCap>
```

Example:

```
$$> prov T-101 SN800 123456789Ab$ 1000 1000 5 5 -20 -10 0 10 20
39322 52429 65536 60000
```

The canonical command usage is defined in the Provision.h header file.

[SDD-75] Tests

The following sections provide brief descriptions of the individual tests that the Eros application can perform. The Eros application supports the following types of tests:

- Synchronous—A synchronous test is one that can execute wholly in the context of single invocation of a TShell command. For example, this could be a test to erase all of NVRAM. Synchronous tests execute in the context of the TShell thread.

- Asynchronous—An asynchronous test is one that continues to execute after the initiating TShell command completes. For example, this could be a test to monitor the temperature sensor over a period of time. Asynchronous tests execute in the context of the application thread. The CPL C++ library's micro-application (MApp) framework is used for executing asynchronous tests.

- UI—A UI test is one that only involves the UI. For example, this could be an LCD test for manually inspecting for dead pixels. UI tests execute in the context of the UI thread.

For the asynchronous tests, the MApp framework and the TShell command to start and stop tests are located under the src/Cpl/MApp/ directory. The TShell command to manage asynchronous tests is mapp.

Usage:

```
mapp
mapp start <mapp> [<args...>]
mapp stop <mapp>|ALL
mapp ls
```

Example:

```
$$> mapp start thermistor 5000
```

The canonical command usage is defined in the src/Cpl/Mapp/Cmd.h header file.

Multiple asynchronous tests can be executed at the same time. For example, the cycling and thermistor test can be run concurrently.

[SDD-76] Button

The button test is a UI test. The Eros home screen displays which button was pressed last for buttons A, B, X, and Y. The button state is also output to the debug console. The logical key combination B+Y is used to transition to the LCD test screen.

The Eros home screen code is located at src/Eros/Ui/Home.

[SDD-77] Cycling

The cycling test is an asynchronous test that is used to exercise the heating element and fan. The test allows the engineer to specify heater and fan on/off times as well as PWM values.

The mapp TShell is used to start/stop the cycling test. The command usage is

```
$$> mapp start cycle [<heatpwm> <fanpwm> [<ontimems> <offtimems> [<repeat>]]]
```

The Cycling Monitor test is located at src/Eros/Test/Cycle.

[SDD-78] EEPROM

The EEPROM test is a synchronous test that is used to verify the operation of the off-board EEPROM chip. The command can also be used to erase the entire EEPROM contents. The TShell command for the test is nv. The source code is located at src/Driver/NV/_tshell/Cmd.h|.cpp.

Usage:

```
nv ERASE\n
nv read <startOffSet> <len>
nv write <startOffset> <bytes...>
nv test (aa|55|blank)
```

Example:

```
$$> nv read 0 10
```

The canonical command usage is defined in the Cmd.h header file.

[SDD-86] Hardware Safety Limit Input

The hardware safety limit input test is a synchronous test that is used to sample the hardware safety limit signal. The TShell command for the test is hws. The source code is located at src/Ajax/TShell/HwSafety.h|.cpp.

Usage:

hws

The canonical command usage is defined in the HwSafety.h header file.

[SDD-79] LCD

The LCD test is a UI test that is used to visually inspect the LCD for dead pixels. The test is launched by pressing the B+Y buttons on the Eros home screen. The user is walked through a series of solid color screens by pressing any button. After all colors have been displayed, the next button press returns the user to the home screen.

[SDD-83] PWM

The PWM test is a synchronous test that is used to directly command the heater, fan, and backlight. The TShell command for the test is pwm. The source code is located at src/Ajax/TShell/Pwm.h|.cpp.

Usage:

```
pwm (heater|fan) <dutycycle%>
pwm backlight <brightness>
```

Example:

```
$$> pwm heater 50
```

The canonical command usage is defined in the Pwm.h header file.

APPENDIX M GM6000 SOFTWARE DETAILED DESIGN (FINAL DRAFT)

[SDD-82] RGB LED

The RGB LED test is a synchronous test that is used to verify the operation of the RGB LED on the display board. The TShell command for the test is rgb. The source code is located at src/Ajax/TShell/Rgb.h|.cpp.

Usage:

```
rgb off
rgb <red> <green> <blue>
rgb <brightness>
```

Example:

```
$$> rgb 240 240 0
```

The canonical command usage is defined in the Rgb.h header file.

[SDD-80] Temperature Monitor

The temperature monitor test is an asynchronous test that polls the onboard thermistor sensor every N seconds and outputs the ADC samples and the converted temperature value to the console output.

A specialized ADC driver is used to expose ADC bits to the Eros application (via specific model points). The analog driver is located at src/Driver/AIO/Eros.

The TShell command mapp is used to start/stop the temperature monitor test. The command usage is

```
$$> mapp start thermistor [<displayms>]
```

The temperature monitor test is located at src/Eros/Test/Thermistor.

Independent of the temperature monitor test, the onboard thermistor temperature value and the ADC bit value are displayed on the home screen.

APPENDIX M   GM6000 SOFTWARE DETAILED DESIGN (FINAL DRAFT)

Change Log

Version	Date	Updated By	Changes
0.1	6/14/2023	V. Dinkley	Initial draft—Outline and source code organization
0.2	7/30/2023	V. Dinkley	Updated with drivers for the display board
0.3	10/9/2023	V. Dinkley	Updated with UI screens and alert management
0.4	11/4/2023	V. Dinkley	Update/add engineering test app (Eros) sections

APPENDIX N

GM6000 Fuzzy Logic Temperature Control

This appendix provides an example of a control algorithm design statement. It is the design statement for the fuzzy logic temperature control.

This is another appendix I don't want you to read. That is, it is not here to explain fuzzy control logic to you. Rather, it is here as a specific example of a design statement where an algorithm is provided by a subject matter expert who is not part of your team.

Document Name and Number

SDX-1330: GM6000 Fuzzy Logic Temperature Control

Overview

The GM6000 is a Digital Heater Controller (DHC) that can be used in many different form factors and heating capacities. The specifics of the unit's physical attributes will be provisioned into the DHC when the final assembly of the DHC is performed. The GM6000's software executes on microcontroller that is part of the unit's Control Board (CB). Figure N-1 summarizes the system architecture.

APPENDIX N GM6000 FUZZY LOGIC TEMPERATURE CONTROL

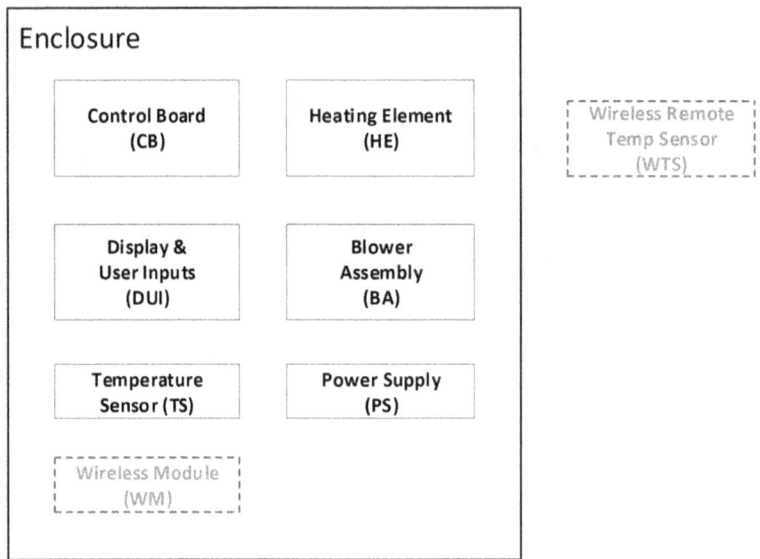

Figure N-1. System architecture block diagram

Because the software has to support numerous physical configurations and heating capacities, a fuzzy logic temperature controller was chosen over a proportional-integral-derivative (PID) control scheme because of complexity involved in tuning a PID to numerous physical permutations. The algorithm has been optimized to be performed with integer math.

The document assumes that the reader is familiar with fuzzy logic control theory.

Glossary

Term	Definition
DHC	Digital Heater Controller

APPENDIX N GM6000 FUZZY LOGIC TEMPERATURE CONTROL

Document References

Document #	Document name	Version

Fuzzification

There are two input membership functions: one for absolute temperature error and one for differential temperature error. Both membership functions use triangle membership sets as shown in Figure N-2.

Absolute error is calculated as

```
error  = temperatureSetpoint - currentSpaceTemperature
```
$error_s$ = error * J_{error}

Differential error is calculated as

```
dError = error - lastError
```
$dError_s$ = dError * J_{derror}

APPENDIX N   GM6000 FUZZY LOGIC TEMPERATURE CONTROL

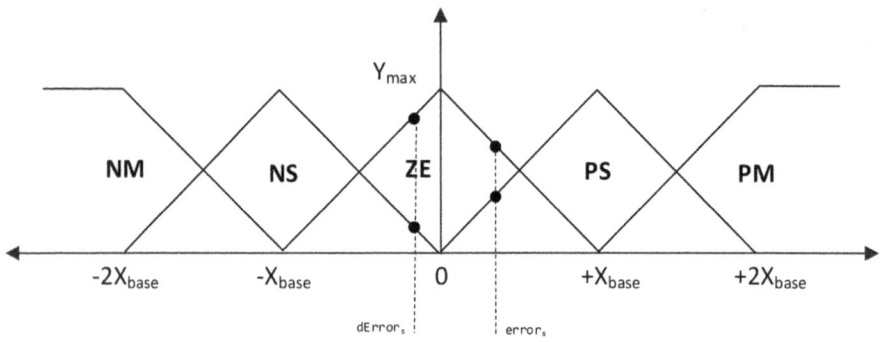

Membership sets:
NM: Negative medium
NS: Negative small
ZE: zero equal (i.e. at setpoint)
PS: Positive small
PM: Positive medium

$X_{base} = Y_{max}$

Figure N-2. Membership function

The values for `Ymax`, `Jerror`, and `Jderror` are configurable.

The units for the X axis are hundredths degrees Celsius.

The Y axis is unitless. It represents a logical 0.0 to 1.0 weighted membership value.

An input (e.g., `error` or `dError`) is fuzzified by determining its weighted membership in each of the membership sets. For example, given

```
Ymax            = 1000
Jerror          = 4
Jderror         = 16
error           = 0.8°C = 80    ; Below setpoint
errors          = 320
dError          = -0.04C = -4   ; Moving towards the setpoint
dErrors         = -64
Set mid points = [-2000, -1000, 0, 1000, 2000]
```

APPENDIX N GM6000 FUZZY LOGIC TEMPERATURE CONTROL

then

```
m1[] = membership(error_s)  = [0, 0, 680, 320, 0]
m2[] = membership(dError_s) = [0, 64, 936, 0, 0]
```

Fuzzy Inference

Fuzzy inference is the process of mapping fuzzified inputs to an output using fuzzy logic. Table N-1 is used with Zadeh MAX-MIN relations to generate the fuzzy output vector. The inference sequence is as follows:

1. Initialize the output vector "out" to all zeros.
2. Take the first element of the "m1" vector.
3. Compare it to every element in the "m2" vector. The minimum value between the two vectors is recorded in the temporary vector.
4. Find the maximum value in the temporary minimum vector from step 3. Record the position "maxidx" in the temporary minimum vector of where the maximum value is found.
5. Add the maximum value found to the "out" vector. The position that the maximum value is added to is determined by the inference rules (see Table N-1). The current element position (in m1) is used to select the row, and the maxidx position is used to select the column. The indexed cell value is used as the position where the maximum value is added to the "out" vector.
6. Repeat steps 3–5 for the remaining elements in m1.

APPENDIX N   GM6000 FUZZY LOGIC TEMPERATURE CONTROL

Table N-1. Inference rule table

		m2[] (dError)				
		NM	**NS**	**ZE**	**PS**	**PM**
m1 [] (error)	**NM**	PM	PM	PM	PS	ZE
	NS	PM	PM	PS	ZE	NS
	ZE	PM	PS	ZE	NS	NM
	PS	PS	ZE	NS	NM	NM
	PM	ZE	NS	NM	NM	NM

For example, given

```
out[] = [0, 0, 0, 0, 0]
m1[]  = membership(errors) = [0, 0, 680, 320, 0]
m2[]  = membership(dErrors) = [0, 64, 936, 0, 0]
```

For m1[0]:

```
min[]  = [0, 0, 0, 0, 0]
max    = 0
maxidx = 0
rules[0][maxidx] = NM = 0
out[] = [0, 0, 0, 0, 0]
```

For m1[1]:

```
min[]  = [0, 0, 0, 0, 0]
max    = 0
maxidx = 0
rules[1][maxidx] = NM = 0
out[] = [0, 0, 0, 0, 0]
```

For m1[2]:

```
min[]  = [0, 64, 680, 0, 0]
max    = 680
maxidx = 2
rules[2][maxidx] = ZE = 2
out[] = [0, 0, 680, 0, 0]
```

For m1[3]:

```
min[]  = [0, 64, 320, 0, 0]
max    = 320
maxidx = 2
rules[3][maxidx] = NS = 1
out[] = [0, 320, 680, 0, 0]
```

For m1[4]:

```
min[]  = [0, 0, 0, 0, 0]
max    = 0
maxidx = 0
rules[4][maxidx] = ZE = 2
out[] = [0, 320, 680, 0, 0]
```

Defuzzification

The output of the control algorithm is a change to the proportional output value that represents the heater output capacity.

The defuzzied output value is obtained by finding the centroid point of the function that is the result of the multiplication of the output membership function and the output vector from the fuzzy inference phase (see Figure N-3).

APPENDIX N   GM6000 FUZZY LOGIC TEMPERATURE CONTROL

A positive *defuz* value indicates that there is too much heating capacity, so the value needs to be multiplied by -1 to invert the polarity so that the final result represents the needed change to the requested capacity. out_{final} represents a delta change that should be applied to the actual output signal, where a positive value indicates that more capacity is needed.

$$\frac{\sum_{i=0}^{4} out[i] \times K[i]}{\sum_{i=0}^{4} out[i]}$$

where K[ ] is the relative output strengths for the membership sets:

K[ ] = [K_{nm}, K_{ns}, K_{ze}, K_{ps}, K_{pm}]

Note: The range of *defuz* determines the granularity of the change to output capacity per execution cycle of the algorithm.

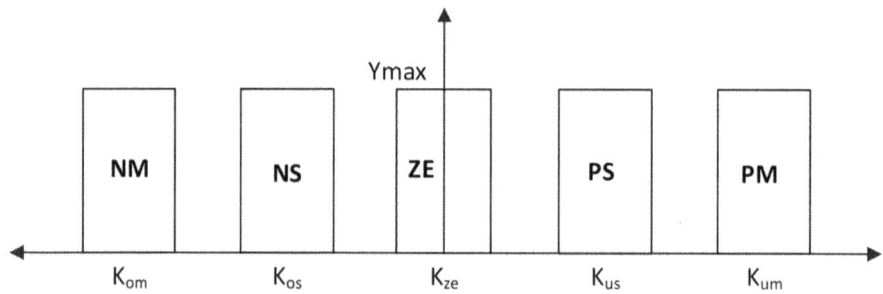

Figure N-3. *Output membership function*

The Y axis is the same as the input membership functions.
The X axis is unitless. It represents the relative strengths between the memberships.
The absolute values for the K constants are configurable.
For example, given

```
K[] = [-20, -10, 0, 10, 20]
out[] = [0, 320, 680, 0, 0]
```

then
$$defuz = \frac{0\times(-20)+320\times(-10)+680\times(0)+0\times(10)+0\times(20)}{0+320+680+0+0}$$

$$defuz = \frac{-3200}{1000} = -3.2; \text{ less than zero} \rightarrow \text{ not enough capacity}$$

out_{final} = 3.2; add the value to the controller's commanded capacity output

Change Log

Version	Date	Updated By	Changes
0.1	6/14/2023	S. Rodgers	Initial draft

APPENDIX O

Software C/C++ Embedded Coding Standard

This appendix is the C/C++ embedded coding standard document used on the GM6000 Digital Heater Controller project. It provides an example of a coding standard document that you can use as template. The document content is sparse, and the formatting is minimal, but the structure of the template does address all the areas you should be paying attention to and thinking about.

> The epc repository contains the example coding standard document as a Microsoft Word document. The document is located in the `docs/ GM6000 Example Docs/` directory.

Document Name and Number

SW-1002: Software C and C++ Embedded Coding Standard

APPENDIX O SOFTWARE C/C++ EMBEDDED CODING STANDARD

Overview

This document defines the C++ coding standards and style for developing embedded software. Coding standards and coding style are often mixed together, which is unfortunate.

Coding standards should be reserved for coding practices that bear directly on the reliability of code. This means that violating a coding standard puts your code at risk for errors. Because it is unacceptable, for example, for embedded software to periodically reboot because of exhausted or squandered resources (e.g., no memory available), adhering to coding standards specifically tailored to working in an embedded environment supports the robustness and reliability of the software.

Coding style guidelines, on the other hand, address issues like formatting and naming conventions. Deviating from the style guidelines doesn't necessarily introduce errors, but it does affect the readability and maintainability of your code, and the establishment of a common coding style can facilitate

- Understanding and maintaining code developed by more than one programmer
- Team cooperation in the development of the same program
- Someone other than the code's author understanding and being able to maintain the code

The document defines a minimum set of standard and style guidelines for embedded development that are practical to implement. The goal here is to maximize "bang for the buck." The more onerous an organization's standards and styles are, the less likely it is that the developers will faithfully follow them. So these guidelines focus on things that really make a difference.

Scope

This standard applies to source code that is developed for new in-house projects (i.e., "greenfield code"). Code development for legacy code bases shall follow the coding standards of the legacy code's existing coding standards. This standard does not apply to third-party code bases.

Deviation from the Standard

The standards documented here are targeted at reducing errors while developing code. This includes both compile-time and run-time errors. For the standards to be effective, strict enforcement is required. This is usually accomplished through code reviews, which are a requirement for merging code branches.

Whenever a standard is not followed, it must be clearly documented in the source code. This documentation serves two purposes: first, it provides crucial information to other developers who may end up maintaining the code, and, second, it forces the original programmer to think through the justification for why the standards did not apply.

When commenting on a deviation in the source code, the comment block should start with the `C-STD-EXCEPTION` marker.

While deviations in style are frowned upon, they are not required to be documented.

APPENDIX O   SOFTWARE C/C++ EMBEDDED CODING STANDARD

Glossary

Term	Definition
Camel Case	Camel case is used to eliminate white space in symbol names by using mixed case to separate words. The first word starts with a lowercase letter, for example, `camelCase`.
Pascal Case	Pascal case is used to eliminate white space in symbol names by using mixed case to separate words. The first word starts with an uppercase letter, for example, `PascalCase`.
Snake Case	Snake case is used to eliminate white space in symbol names by using an underscore to separate words. Snake case is all lowercase, for example, `snake_case`.
Namespace Case	Namespace case is a variant of snake case that is used when prefixing a C symbol with its logical namespace. Namespace case uses an underscore to separate words like snake_case, but the first letter of each namespace is uppercase, for example, `Foo_Bar_hello_world`, where `Foo::Bar` is the logical namespace.

Document References

Document #	Document name	Version

Coding Standards

Standards tagged with an REQ label must always be followed, and any deviations must be documented in the source code. Standards without the REQ label are strongly recommended, but deviation is allowed (without documenting the deviation). Some required standards explicitly call out exceptions. For these cases, no deviation documentation is required.

Language (REQ)

All C++ code shall be compliant with the C++11 standard (ISO/IEC 14882:2011). All C code shall be compliant with C11 standard (ISO/IEC 9899:2011). Language features defined in a newer language standard shall not be used. Note that older standards are intentionally used to facilitate a broader range of tools and legacy platforms.

No Dynamic Memory Allocation (REQ)

To prevent memory leaks and fragmentation, no dynamic memory allocation is allowed. The application may allocate memory from the heap at startup. But after the system is "up and running," the application shall not allocate memory from the heap. This practice guarantees the system will not fail over time due to lack of memory.

For objects that must be dynamically created or deleted, the application programmer is required to pre-allocate a memory pool (on a per-object-type basis) that will be used to construct objects at run-time. This requires the developer to use the "placement new" operator to create an object. To delete an object, the developer must explicitly call the object's destructor and then return the memory back to its associated memory pool.

The use of `malloc()`, `calloc()`, `realloc()`, `reallocarray()`, and `free()` functions shall be restricted in the same way as the `new` and `delete` operators.

No Recursion (REQ)

Recursion shall not be used. Recursion is simply dynamic memory allocation in disguise. That is, it uses the stack instead of the heap as the memory source. Recursion is also more dangerous because instead of a failure indication when memory is exhausted, a stack overrun simply overwrites other memory. A stack overrun is even more likely on embedded systems since the range of stack sizes on embedded platforms is typically small (e.g., 0.5K to 4K).

Note that in some cases, the recursion is bounded. That is, maximum stack usage can be statically determined. Nevertheless, these scenarios are not allowed because it opens up the potential of future failures as the code is maintained and extended.

Use const Wherever Possible

Every possible modification of data should occur according to explicit relaxation of the default read-only policy. In this context, think `const`. Member functions should be `const` by default. Only when you have a clear, explicit reason should you omit the `const` modifier on member functions.

No Type Casting (REQ)

Take every possible measure to avoid type casting. Errors caused by casts are among the most pernicious, particularly because they are so hard to recognize. Strict type checking is your friend; take full advantage of it! Here are the exceptions that are allowed:

- The use of void* pointers in C code in interfaces (in lieu of abstract classes).

- Casting within a class or module is allowed (though strongly discouraged) as long as casting is not exposed to consumers of the class or module.

No Compiler Warnings (REQ)

Code that compiles with warnings will not be accepted for integration. While developing code, eliminate the warnings as soon as possible as the warnings tend to be the source of logic and run-time errors. Build scripts are required to enable the compiler options to treat warnings as errors.

No Explicit Constants (REQ)

Do not write explicit constants into code, except to establish identifiers to represent them. The exception to the rule is the constant "0". Always use the keywords true and false for Boolean values. For C code, this means you must include <stdbool.h>.

No goto Statements (REQ)

The use of the goto statement is not allowed.

APPENDIX O   SOFTWARE C/C++ EMBEDDED CODING STANDARD

Use nullptr (REQ)

C++ code must use the `nullptr` keyword instead of zero or the `NULL` macro when assigning a null value to a pointer.

Conditionally Compiled Code Is Not Allowed Within a Function Body (REQ)

Do not use the preprocessor `#ifdef`/`#ifndef` constructs to support platform-, hardware-, or system-dependent code within a function body. All platform-, hardware-, and system-dependent code must be isolated into individual files that are specific to the dependencies. This means the developer, at the design stage, must identify and plan for handling these dependencies.

Virtual Destructors (REQ)

If a class has at least one virtual function, you must also declare the destructor as virtual.

```
class Foo
{
public:
  /// Constructor
  Foo( .... );

  /// Destructor
  virtual ~Foo();

public:
  /// A virtual do something function
  virtual void doSomething( .... );
  ...
};
```

Rule of Five (REQ)

This standard only applies to situations where a deviation from the "No Dynamic Memory Allocation" standard has been approved. It requires that classes that utilize dynamic storage implement the following five methods to ensure proper and efficient data handling when copying and moving the class's dynamic data:[24]

- Destructor
- Copy constructor
- Copy assignment operator
- Move constructor
- Move assignment operator

Here are examples:

```
class Foo
{
private:
  char* m_string;

public:
  /// Constructor
  Foo(const char* src = "")
  : m_string(nullptr) {
    if (src) {
      m_string = new char[strlen(src) + 1];
      strcpy(m_string, src );
    }
  }
```

---

[24] See "The rule of three/five/zero" at https://en.cppreference.com/w/cpp/language/rule_of_three

```cpp
/// Destructor
~Foo() {
  delete[] m_string;
}

/// Copy Constructor
Foo(const Foo& other)
: Foo(other.m_string) {
}

/// Copy assignment
Foo& operator=(const Foo& other) {
  if ( this != &other ) {
    delete[] m_string;
    m_string = new char[strlen(other.m_string) + 1];
    strcpy(m_string, other.m_string);
  }
  return *this;
}

/// Move constructor
Foo(Foo&& other) noexcept
  : m_string(other.m_string) {
  other.m_string = nullptr;
}

/// Move assignment
Foo& operator=(Foo&& other) noexcept {
  if ( this != &other ) {
    delete[] m_string;
    m_string = other.m_string;
    other.m_string = nullptr;
  }
```

```
    return *this;
  }
};
```

Pass and Return Objects by Reference

References provide stricter semantics than raw pointers. That is, a reference requires that the object it points to exists while a raw pointer does not. If the interface semantics are such that the object must always exist, use references in the interface even if the internal implementation is using pointers. By using references in interfaces whenever possible, the compiler can enforce more of the semantics of the interface.

Protect Header Files with the #ifndef Read-Once Latch (REQ)

Use the following templates when implementing the read-once latch. In this example, `Namespace` maps to the directory path (relative to the root `src/` directory), and `ClassName` maps to the file name.

```
#ifndef Namespace_ClassName_h_
#define Namespace_ClassName_h_

...
#endif

#ifndef Cpl_System_Win32_Thread_h_
#define Cpl_System_Win32_Thread_h_

...
#endif
```

APPENDIX O   SOFTWARE C/C++ EMBEDDED CODING STANDARD

Minimize the #include Statements in Your Header Files (REQ)

Headers files should only include those (additional header) files that are required for the header file to compile. Do not include files that are only used by the associated `.cpp|.c` file. The `#include` statements in your header files define the dependencies of the file. And the fewer dependencies, the better.

Avoid the Global Namespace Unless Absolutely Necessary

It should be obvious why you want to avoid polluting the global namespace. If you ever "import" code from a developer, department, third-party vendor, etc., there is potential for collision in the global namespace. If a collision occurs, someone's code must change—and in most cases, it will be yours. As modifying proven code is always a bad thing, the two common options to avoiding polluting the global namespace are as follows:

- Nest enumerations, constants, helper classes, etc., inside of existing classes.
- Use the C++ namespace feature.

Use Standard Integer Types (REQ)

When using types that need to be a specific number of bits, use the language standard integer types, for example, `int8_t, uint32_t`.

Do Not Use Nonportable Constructs

Avoid any of the following constructs, types, pragmas, etc., since they are not guaranteed by the language standards to be portable across all standard compliant compilers:

- Data structures, or typedefs for defining data structures, that are exchanged between processors since the use and/or inclusion of packed bytes within a data structure is not guaranteed by the language standard.

- Situations where data-alignment requirements for addressing multibyte words are different between MCUs or CPUs.

- Situations that assume endian-ness of multiple byte integers when moving data across MCUs, CPUs, or platforms.

- Bit fields because the ordering of the bit is not a language standard field (e.g., MSB 0 is bit field 0 vs. MSB 7 is bit field 0 in an octet).

- Nonstandard pragmas and preprocessor symbols. For example, #pack and __PRETTY_FUNCTION__ are not language-standardized pragmas and preprocessor symbols. Only use C/C++ language–defined pragmas and preprocessor symbols.

Array Indices (REQ)

Array indices must be guaranteed or explicitly checked to be within the array size prior to use.

APPENDIX O SOFTWARE C/C++ EMBEDDED CODING STANDARD

Pointer Check (REQ)

All functions and methods shall validate that all pointer arguments are non-null before dereferencing the point arguments. The use of the ASSERT() macro or its equivalent is sufficient to meet this requirement.

Coding Style

The intent of the style guide is to establish a style baseline that all developers are required to follow. This baseline provides consistency across source code files and aids in reading and maintaining the code. In addition, following a common programming style will enable the construction of tools that leverage a knowledge of these standards to assist in the development and maintenance of the code.

This guide specifies only basic requirements; the individual programmer is allowed to impose their own style preferences on top of these requirements. There are only two absolute rules to observe when it comes to creating your own coding style. The first rule is consistency. Establish a style and stick to it. The second is tolerance. When you must modify code written by others that has a different style, adopt their style, and do not convert the code to your style.

Style rules tagged with an REQ label should always be followed, and any deviations will need to be justified during the code review process. Style rules without the REQ label are strongly recommended, but deviation is allowed (without any justification). Some required style rules explicitly call out exceptions. For these cases, no deviation document in the source is required.

Comments

Header Files (REQ)

Header files must be completely documented. This means every class, method, and data member must have comments. Header files describe the interfaces of the system and, as such, should contain all the information a developer needs to use and understand the interface.

Header file comments shall not be duplicated in or copied to the .c|.cpp files.

Use Doxygen Comments in Header Files (REQ)

Document your code so that the Doxygen tool can extract the information stored in your header file comments. Detailed information about Doxygen can be found at www.doxygen.nl. Here are examples of a Doxygen comment.

```
/** This abstract class ...
 */
class FooBar {
public:
   /// Enables the Widget to begin sending data
   virtual void enableWidget() =0;
};
```

C|CPP Files

The quantity and quality of the comments in a CPP file are left to the individual developers to decide. Comments in the C|CPP files should be limited to implementation detail, not the semantics and usage of the functions, methods, classes, etc. (as these are commented in header files).

Add comments whenever you feel that the code is complex, nonstandard, or clever. Remember if you want the luxury of having other people maintaining your code, they must be able to understand it.

File Organization
Organize by Namespace (REQ)

Organize your files by component dependencies, not by project. That is, do not create your directory structure to reflect a top-down project decomposition. Rather, organize your code by namespaces where nested namespaces are reflected as subdirectories in their parent namespace directory. By having the dependencies reflected in the directory structure, it is a quick and visual sanity check to avoid undesired and cyclical dependencies.

File names (.h|.c|.cpp files) do not have to be globally unique. The file names only need to be unique within a given directory and namespace. Directories and namespaces are your friends when it comes to naming because they provide a simple mechanism for avoiding future naming collisions.

The C programming language standard does support namespaces. However, the concept of namespace can still be implemented with C by applying the following convention:

- For all functions, types, enums, variable names, preprocessor symbols, etc., that appear in header files, prefix the namespace to the symbol name. For example, for a hypothetical function hello_world() in the Foo::Bar namespace, the function name would be Foo_Bar_hello_world(). The hello_world() function definition would be in a header file in the directory Foo/Bar/. The prefixing rule does not apply to symbols that are exclusive to a .c file (e.g., static functions and variables).

README.txt (REQ)

Each namespace directory shall contain a README.txt file that describes the purpose or content of the namespace. The file should provide descriptions, comments, usage semantics, etc., that span multiple files and classes in the namespace.

The file is required to include a Doxygen-readable comment that describes the namespace. For example:

```
/** @namespace Cpl::System

The System namespace contains platform independent foundation
abstractions and classes related to program execution. The
interfaces and abstractions are designed to support multi-
threaded application.

*/
```

Non-namespace Directories (REQ)

Non-namespace directories can be created for organizational purposes. Non-namespace directories shall start with leading underscores. For example, given the directory path of Cpl/Container/_0test, the _0test/ directory would be a non-namespace directory.

Namespace Directories (REQ)

Namespace directories names shall match—including case—the namespace they represent or contain.

Files (REQ)

The file names .h and .cpp files that define a C++ class shall match the contained class (including case). If multiple classes are contained in a single file, the recommendation is to name the file after the primary class in the file.

Single Module or Class in a Namespace

Often you will have a case where the natural naming of module of class within a namespace is the same name as the namespace. For example, consider a scenario where the namespace is Foo and the logical class module would also be Foo. To avoid 'stuttering' (e.g. Foo::Foo) in the naming, the recommendation would be that the module or class be named api.h|.c (for C) or Api.h|.cpp (for C++). In turn, the module or class name is also api and Api (e.g. Foo::Api), respectively.

Keep Header and Source Files Together (REQ)

Place header files (.h) and their corresponding .c|.cpp files in the same directory. Do **not** create separate source/ and include/ directories. This rule does not apply to header files that declare an interface (e.g., a pure abstract class) where there are, or where there will be, multiple implementations of the interface.

Fully Qualified Header include Statements (REQ)

Reference header files with a full path relative to the root of the source tree. This means that your #include for header files will contain the relative directory path for each header file. Here is an example of #includes with full paths:

APPENDIX O   SOFTWARE C/C++ EMBEDDED CODING STANDARD

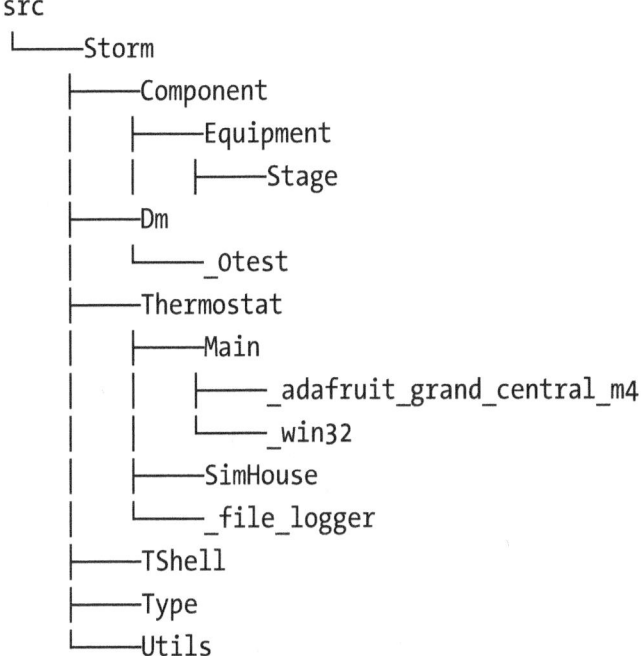

```
src
└───Storm
    ├───Component
    │   ├───Equipment
    │   │   ├───Stage
    ├───Dm
    │   └───_0test
    ├───Thermostat
    │   ├───Main
    │   │   ├───_adafruit_grand_central_m4
    │   │   └───_win32
    │   ├───SimHouse
    │   └───_file_logger
    ├───TShell
    ├───Type
    └───Utils
```

File: Storm/Component/AirFilterMonitor.h

#include "Storm/Component/Base.h"
#include "Storm/Dm/MpSimpleAlarm.h"
#include "Storm/Dm/MpVirtualOutputs.h"

File: Storm/Component/Equipment/Cooling.h

#include "Storm/Component/Control.h"
#include "Storm/Component/Equipment/StageApi.h"

This rule only applies to #include statements in header files. #include statements in .c|.cpp files are not required to use directory paths for files in the same directory.

APPENDIX O SOFTWARE C/C++ EMBEDDED CODING STANDARD

Naming

In general, C++ names use camel and Pascal case, while C names use snake and namespace case. Refer to the glossary for definitions of the case terminology.

C++ Namespaces, Classes, Methods, and Variables (REQ)

- Namespace names are nouns, should be single words, and shall use Pascal case.
  - Namespace names should be singular; for example, use `Jcl::Container` instead of `Jcl::Containers`.
- Class names are nouns and use Pascal case.
- Class methods shall contain a verb and use camel case.
- Class data member names start with a leading "m_" followed by a camel case, for example, `int m_myCount;`.
- Static class data member names start with a leading "g_" followed by camel case, for example, `static int g_instanceCounts;`.
- Typedefs and structs use Pascal case.
- Do not abbreviate names or words; long names are preferred over cryptic abbreviations.

C Functions, Variables, Typedefs, and Structs (REQ)

- Snake case or namespace case shall be used for all C functions, variables, typedefs, and structs.
- Function names shall contain a verb.

Preprocessor and Macros (REQ)

Preprocessor symbols and macros shall be all uppercase with underscores to separate words.

Statically Scoped Variables (REQ)

Statically scoped variables in .cpp files use camel case. Statically scoped variables in .c files use snake case. In addition, all statically scoped variables shall have a trailing underscore appended to their name to indicate that they are statically scoped (e.g., static int foo_;).

Global Variables (REQ)

Globally scoped C++ variables use camel case with a leading "g_" prefixed to the name, for example, int g_fooBar;. Globally scoped C variables use Snake Case with a leading "g_" prefixed to the name, for example, int g_foo_bar;. The exception to this rule is when the variable instance is encapsulated inside a namespace (which is not the standard namespace).

Reserved Function and Method Names (REQ)

- Functions or methods that perform in-thread initialization of an object shall be named start(...).

- Functions or methods that perform in-thread shutdown of an object shall be named stop(...).

- Functions or methods that invoke ITC (inter-thread communication) initialization (e.g., invoke initialization across thread boundaries) shall be named open(...).

- Functions or methods that perform ITC shutdown (e.g., reclaiming resources across thread bounders) shall be named `close(...)`.

Formatting

Indenting Spacing (REQ)

Tab stops will be set to 4, and spaces shall be used for indenting. It is recommended that developers configure their editor and IDE to insert spaces for tabs.

Braces (REQ)

The Allman brace style and indenting shall be used.[25] For example:

```
while (x == y)
{
    something();
    somethingElse();
}
finalThing();
```

Flow Control Statements (REQ)

The flow control primitives `if`, `else`, `while`, `for`, and `do` should be followed by a block, even if it is an empty block or a single statement. For example:

---

[25] See https://en.wikipedia.org/wiki/Indentation_style

```
while( /* do something */ )    // NOT Allowed
    ;
while( /* do something */ )    // Good
{
}
if( isOpened() )               // NOT Allowed
    foobar();
if( isOpened() )               // Good
{
    foobar();
}
```

Elimination of Dead Code

All dead code shall be eliminated from the source code. In addition, no blocks of commented-out code shall be in a source file when the file is merged to a stable branch in the repository.

Change Log

Version	Date	Updated By	Changes
1.0	11/26/2022	V. Dinkley	Initial draft
1.1	5/1/2023	V. Dinkley	Updated to restrict the use of recursion and nonportable constructs

APPENDIX P

GM6000 Software Requirements Trace Matrix

This appendix illustrates how to trace GM6000 Digital Heater Controller project software requirements to software design artifacts. The tracing includes forward tracing (i.e., from requirements down into software architecture, design, etc.) as well as backward tracing (i.e., from software design and architecture up to requirements). The document does not include tracing requirements to test protocols or test cases.

Requirements tracing can be done manually, or it can be done using a requirements management tool (e.g., Doors or Jama). The advantage of using requirements management tools is that they are good at handling the many-to-many relationships that occur when tracing requirements and provide both forward and backward traces.

In the absence of something better, use this document as a template for tracing your requirements to software design artifacts. The formatting is minimal, but the structure of the template addresses all the areas you should be paying attention to and thinking about.

APPENDIX P   GM6000 SOFTWARE REQUIREMENTS TRACE MATRIX

The recommendation when not using a requirement management tool is to use spreadsheets for capturing and tracing requirements. The epc repository contains an example GM6000 Software Requirements Trace Matrix document as spreadsheet. The spreadsheet uses Excel's database functionality and pivot tables to provide forward and backward tracing. The spreadsheet is located in the docs/GM6000 Example Docs/ directory.

Document Name and Number

SWT-1331: GM6000 Software Requirements Trace Matrix

Overview

This document captures the forward and backward tracing of software requirements for the GM6000 Digital Heater Controller to and from software architecture and design.

Glossary

Term	Definition
DHC	Digital Heater Controller
NFR	Nonfunctional requirement. Functional requirements are those that define what a product or system is supposed to do; nonfunctional requirements define how the product or system should do it.

APPENDIX P   GM6000 SOFTWARE REQUIREMENTS TRACE MATRIX

Document References

Document #	Document name	Version
MRS-1322	GM6000 Marketing Requirements Specification	
PRS-1323	GM6000 Product Requirements Specification	
SRS-1324	GM6000 Software Requirements Specification	
SWA-1327	GM6000 Software Architecture	
SDD-1329	GM6000 Software Detailed Design	

Software Requirements Traced to PRS and MRS

Backward tracing of Software Requirements (SRS) to System (PRD) and Marketing (MRS) requirements.

SRS #	Name	PRS	MRS	Notes
SWR-200	Console: Security	PR-200, PR-201, PR-202, PR-203, PR-204	MR-201	
SWR-201	Console: Security	PR-200, PR-201, PR-202, PR-203, PR-204	MR-201	
SWR-202	UI Languages		MR-200	
SWR-203	UI Splash Screen		MR-107, MR-109	
SWR-204	UI Home Status		MR-107, MR-109	

(*continued*)

APPENDIX P   GM6000 SOFTWARE REQUIREMENTS TRACE MATRIX

SRS #	Name	PRS	MRS	Notes
SWR-205	UI Home Control		MR-107, MR-108	
SWR-206	UI Edit Setpoint		MR-107, MR-108, MR-109	
SWR-207	UI LED Status		MR-107, MR-109	
SWR-208	UI Home Control		MR-107, MR-108	
SWR-209	UI About Status		MR-107, MR-109	
SWR-210	UI About Control		MR-107, MR-108	

Software Requirements Traced to Software Architecture

Forward tracing of Software Requirements (SRS) to software architecture.

SRS #	Name	SWA Section	Notes
SWR-200	Console: Security	SWA-14, SWA-15	
SWR-201	Console: Security	SWA-14, SWA-15, SWA-24	
SWR-202	UI Languages	SWA-28, SWA-18, SWA-19	
SWR-203	UI Splash Screen	SWA-28	
SWR-204	UI Home Status	SWA-28	
SWR-205	UI Home Control	SWA-28	
SWR-206	UI Edit Setpoint	SWA-28	
SWR-207	UI LED Status	SWA-28	
SWR-208	UI Home Control	SWA-28	
SWR-209	UI About Status	SWA-28	
SWR-210	UI About Control	SWA-28	

APPENDIX P   GM6000 SOFTWARE REQUIREMENTS TRACE MATRIX

Software Architecture Traced to Requirements

Backward tracing of the software architecture to formal requirements (SRS, PRS, MRS).

SWA Section	Section Name	SRS #	PRS #	MRS #	Notes
SWA-10	Alert Management		PR-102, PR-206	MR-109	
SWA-11	Application		PR-100	MR-102	
SWA-12	Bootloader				No parent requirement
SWA-13	BSP		PR-100	MR-102	
SWA-14	Console	SWR-200, SWR-201	PR-200, PR-201, PR-203, PR-204	MR-104	
SWA-15	Crypto	SWR-200, SWR-201	PR-202	MR-104	
SWA-16	Data Model		PR-100	MR-102	
SWA-17	Diagnostics			MR-201	
SWA-18	Drivers		PR-100	MR-102	
SWA-19	Graphics Library		PR-205	MR-107, MR-108, MR-109, MR-200	

(*continued*)

APPENDIX P GM6000 SOFTWARE REQUIREMENTS TRACE MATRIX

SWA Section	Section Name	SRS #	PRS #	MRS #	Notes
SWA-20	Heating		PR-100, PR-102, PR-103, PR-104, PR-105, PR-106, PR-107, PR-206, PR-207	MR-100, MR-101, MR-103, MR-106	
SWA-21	Logging			MR-201	
SWA-22	OS		PR-100	MR-102	
SWA-23	OSAL		PR-100	MR-102	
SWA-24	Persistent Storage	SWR-201	PR-201, PR-203	MR-103, MR-104	
SWA-25	Sensor Comms		PR-101, PR-102	MR-105, MR-106	
SWA-26	Software Updated				No parent requirement
SWA-27	System Services		PR-100	MR-102	

(*continued*)

APPENDIX P   GM6000 SOFTWARE REQUIREMENTS TRACE MATRIX

SWA Section	Section Name	SRS #	PRS #	MRS #	Notes
SWA-28	UI	SWR-202, SWR-203, SWR-204, SWR-205, SWR-206, SWR-207, SWR-208, SWR-209, SWR-210		MR-107, MR-108, MR-109, MR-200	
SWA-29	Programming Languages	NFR			Project decision
SWA-30	Subsystems	n/a			Organization heading
SWA-31	Interfaces	NFR			Implicit from the QMS/SDLC processes
SWA-32	Process Model	NFR			Implicit from the QMS/SDLC processes
SWA-33	Thread Priorities	NFR			Implicit from the QMS/SDLC processes

(*continued*)

APPENDIX P   GM6000 SOFTWARE REQUIREMENTS TRACE MATRIX

SWA Section	Section Name	SRS #	PRS #	MRS #	Notes
SWA-34	Simulator	NFR			Project decision (i.e., work smarter, not harder)
SWA-35	Cybersecurity	NFR			Implicit from the QMS/SDLC processes
SWA-36	Memory Allocation	NFR			Implicit from the QMS/SDLC processes
SWA-37	Message Passing (ITC)	NFR			Implicit from the QMS/SDLC processes
SWA-38	File and Directory Organization	NFR			Implicit from the QMS/SDLC processes
SWA-39	Data Integrity	NFR			Implicit from the QMS/SDLC processes
SWA-40	Localization and Internationalization	MR-200			

(*continued*)

APPENDIX P   GM6000 SOFTWARE REQUIREMENTS TRACE MATRIX

SWA Section	Section Name	SRS #	PRS #	MRS #	Notes
SWA-41	Engineering and Manufacturing Testing	Other			Functional requirements for software needed to support the project that will not be released to the public
SWA-42	Unit Testing	NFR			Implicit from the QMS/SDLC processes

Software Architecture Traced to Detailed Software Design

Forward tracing of the software architecture to Detailed Software Design.

SWA Section	SWA Section Name	SDD Section	Notes
SWA-10	Alert Management	SDD-10	
SWA-11	Application	SDD-11	
SWA-12	Bootloader	SDD-12	
SWA-13	BSP	SDD-13	

(*continued*)

APPENDIX P GM6000 SOFTWARE REQUIREMENTS TRACE MATRIX

SWA Section	SWA Section Name	SDD Section	Notes
SWA-14	Console	SDD-14	
SWA-15	Crypto	SDD-15	
SWA-16	Data Model	SDD-16	
SWA-17	Diagnostics	SDD-17	
SWA-18	Drivers	SDD-18	
SWA-19	Graphics Library	SDD-19	
SWA-20	Heating	SDD-20	
SWA-21	Logging	SDD-21	
SWA-22	OS	SDD-22	
SWA-23	OSAL	SDD-23	
SWA-24	Persistent Storage	SDD-24	
SWA-25	Sensor Comms	SDD-25	
SWA-26	Software Updated	SDD-26	
SWA-27	System Services	SDD-27	
SWA-28	UI	SDD-28	
SWA-29	Programming Languages	SDD-35	
SWA-30	Subsystems	n/a	Organizational section heading
SWA-31	Interfaces	SDD-16, SDD-27	
SWA-32	Process Model	NFR	SDLC, best practice
SWA-33	Thread Priorities	SDD-11	
SWA-34	Simulator	SDD-29	
SWA-35	Cybersecurity	SDD-12, SDD-15	

(*continued*)

APPENDIX P GM6000 SOFTWARE REQUIREMENTS TRACE MATRIX

SWA Section	SWA Section Name	SDD Section	Notes
SWA-36	Memory Allocation	NFR	SDLC, best practice
SWA-37	Message Passing (ITC)	SDD-27	
SWA-38	File and Directory Organization	SDD-34	
SWA-39	Data Integrity	SDD-16, SDD-18, SDD-27	
SWA-40	Localization and Internationalization	SDD-28	
SWA-41	Engineering and Manufacturing Testing	SDD-30	
SWA-42	Unit Testing	SDD-62	

Detailed Software Design Traced to Software Architecture

Backward tracing of the Detailed Software Design to software architecture. Note that only the top-level or parent sections are traced (because sections trace if their parent section traces).

SDD Section	SDD Section Name	SWA Section	Notes
SDD-10	Alert Management	SWA-10	
SDD-11	Application	SWA-11, SWA-35	
SDD-12	Bootloader	SWA-12	
SDD-13	BSP	SWA-13	

(*continued*)

APPENDIX P   GM6000 SOFTWARE REQUIREMENTS TRACE MATRIX

SDD Section	SDD Section Name	SWA Section	Notes
SDD-14	Console	SWA-14	
SDD-15	Crypto	SWA-15, SWA-35	
SDD-16	Data Model	SWA-16, SWA-39	
SDD-17	Diagnostics	SWA-17	
SDD-18	Drivers	SWA-18, SWA-39	
SDD-19	Graphics Library	SWA-19	
SDD-20	Heating	SWA-20	
SDD-21	Logging	SWA-21	
SDD-22	OS	SWA-22	
SDD-23	OSAL	SWA-23	
SDD-24	Persistent Storage	SWA-24	
SDD-25	Sensor Comms	SWA-25	
SDD-26	Software Updated	SWA-26	
SDD-27	System Services	SWA-27, SWA-37, SWA-39	
SDD-28	UI	SWA-28, SWA-40	
SDD-29	Functional Simulator	SWA-34	
SDD-30	Engineering Test Application	SWA-41	
SDD-31	Subsystems	SWA-30	
SDD-34	Source Code	SWA-38	

APPENDIX P GM6000 SOFTWARE REQUIREMENTS TRACE MATRIX

Change Log

Version	Date	Updated By	Changes
0.1	6/1/2023	S. Rogers	Initial draft
0.2	10/2/2023	V. Dinkley	Add SDD backward tracings
0.3	12/1/2023	V. Dinkley	Update tracing for being feature complete

APPENDIX Q

GM6000 Software Bill of Materials

This appendix is the Software Bill of Materials document for the GM6000 Digital Heater Controller project. In the absence of something better, this document can be used as a starting point for your Software Bill of Materials document.

> The epc repository contains the example Software Bill of Materials document as a Microsoft Excel document. The document is located in the `docs/GM6000 Example Docs/` directory.

Document Name and Number

SWB-1332: GM6000 Software Bill of Materials

Overview

This document enumerates all the third-party packages and source code that are contained in the publicly released software for the GM6000 Digital Heater Controller.

APPENDIX Q   GM6000 SOFTWARE BILL OF MATERIALS

Glossary

Term	Definition
DHC	Digital Heater Controller

Document References

Document #	Document Name	Version
SDD-1329	GM6000 Software Detailed Design	

Packages

The following table lists all the third-party software and packages that get compiled into the release executables for the GM6000 project. The license column should be considered a required column in this table.

Item	Description	License	Notes
FreeRTOS	Real-Time Operating System for Microcontrollers	MIT	The official LTS version has been locally patched to support integration with the Segger SystemView tool.
colony.core	CPL C++ class library	BSD 3-Clause	

(*continued*)

APPENDIX Q GM6000 SOFTWARE BILL OF MATERIALS

Item	Description	License	Notes
ArduinoJson	JSON parser and formatter that does not require dynamic memory allocation	MIT	
STM32F4-SDK	STMicroelectronics SDK for the STM32F4 microcontroller family	BSD 3-Clause	There are many licenses under the xsrc/stm32F4-SDK repo. However, the project only uses code that falls under the BSD 3-Clause license.
docopt-cpp	C++ command-line argument parser	MIT	This code is only used for Windows and Linux executables.
BetterENUM	Reflective compile-time enum library with clean syntax, in a single header file, and without dependencies.	BSD 2-Clause license	
pimoroni-pico	Graphics Libraries and supporting drivers	MIT	The library has been ported to be platform independent.
Arduino core for SAMD21/51	Adafruit's Arduino Core for the Atmel SAMD21/51 MCUs)	GNU Lesser GPL v2.1	Only used with Atmel SAMD51-based boards
ED25519 public-key signature	Orson Peter's portable implementation of ED25519 algorithm	ZLib License	

APPENDIX Q   GM6000 SOFTWARE BILL OF MATERIALS

Versions

The following table lists the versions (and their location in the repositories) of packages listed in the previous section.

Item	Version	Source Location	Notes
FreeRTOS	10.4.3-LTS-Patch1	xsrc/freertos	
colony.core	4.4.1	Under the src/ tree	The Outcast tool is used to overlay the package into the src/ tree.
ArduinoJson	6.10.0	src/Cpl/Json/Ardunio.h	This is included as part of the colony.core package.
STM32F4-SDK	1.27.1	xsrc/stm32F4-sdk/Drivers/	
docopt-cpp	0.6.3	xsrc/docopt-cpp	
BetterENUM	0.11.3	src/Cpl/Type/enum.h	This is included as part of the colony.core package.
pimoroni-pico	1.19.7-1	xsrc/pimoroni	
Arduino core for SAMD21/51	1.6.0	ardunio/hardware/samd	
ED25519 public-key signature	n/a	xsrc/orlp/ed25519	Commit Hash: b1f19fab4aebe607805620d25a5e42566ce46a0e

APPENDIX Q GM6000 SOFTWARE BILL OF MATERIALS

Change Log

Version	Date	Updated By	Changes
0.1	5/13/2023	V. Dinkley	Initial draft
0.2	8/12/2023	V. Dinkley	Updated version info

APPENDIX R

GM6000 Software Release Notes

This appendix provides an example of a release notes document for formal releases (e.g., candidate and gold releases) for the GM6000 Digital Heater Controller project. In the absence of something better, this document can be used as a starting point for your release notes documentation.

> The epc repository contains the example Software Release Notes as a Microsoft Word document. The document is located in the `docs/ GM6000 Example Docs/` directory.

Document Name and Number

SWR-1333: GM6000 Release Notes

Overview

The GM6000 product is a Digital Heater Controller (DHC) that can be used in many different physical form factors and heating capacities. The specifics of the final unit's physical attributes will be provisioned into the DHC during the manufacturing process.

APPENDIX R GM6000 SOFTWARE RELEASE NOTES

The document contains the release notes for all candidate releases. The intended audience is for internal stakeholders only. The individual candidate releases are listed latest first.

Glossary

Term	Definition
DHC	Digital Heater Controller
Candidate Release	A candidate release is a formal build that has a human-friendly version identifier assigned to it. It is submitted for final verification before being declared a gold release.
Gold Release	A gold release is a candidate release that has passed all of the verification testing and that has been publicly released to customers.

Document References

Document #	Document Name	Version
MRS-1322	GM6000 DHC Marketing Requirements Specifications	0.1
PRS-1323	GM6000 Product Requirements Specification	0.1
SRS-1324	GM6000 Software Requirements Specification	0.2

APPENDIX R   GM6000 SOFTWARE RELEASE NOTES

RC2

Date:	2/27/2024
Summary:	Bug fixes and usability improvements
Build Number:	20000013
Versions:	Ajax: 1.0.0
	Eros: 0.0.1
Git Label:	MAIN-2000013
	957d1e33d57abdc97cefbd91e3b839d98bdff4bb
Artifacts:	ajax-alpha.bin|elf
	ajax-simulator.exe
	eros-alpha.bin|elf
	eros-simulator.exe

Changes

- #125—Added code to flash LED indicators. This is a usability enhancement so users do not need to rely solely on LED colors to determine state.

Bug Fixes

- #123—Fixed a problem where LED does not flash when there is a hard error

APPENDIX R   GM6000 SOFTWARE RELEASE NOTES

Known Issues

- The heating algorithm configuration (provisioned during manufacturing) still needs to be tuned to the final physical components (e.g., heater elements) and mechanical layout.

RC1

Date:	1/27/2024
Summary:	First candidate release
Build Number:	2000008
Versions:	Ajax: 1.0.0
	Eros: 0.0.1
Git Label:	MAIN-2000008
	0a33083bcc57592e9d3d06c10277f8b3750580ec
Artifacts:	ajax-alpha.bin|elf
	ajax-simulator.exe
	eros-alpha.bin|elf
	eros-simulator.exe

Changes

- n/a

Bug Fixes

- n/a

Known Issues

- The heating algorithm configuration (provisioned during manufacturing) still needs to be tuned to the final physical components (e.g., heater elements) and mechanical layout.

Change Log

Version	Date	Updated By	Changes
0.1	1/27/2024	V. Dinkley	RC1
0.2	2/27/2024	V. Dinkley	RC2

Index

A

Adafruit, 10, 217, 218, 285, 302, 321, 322, 340, 538, 551, 558, 572, 576, 661
Agile, 5, 6, 62, 69, 158, 160, 162, 267, 520, 534, 546
Ajax application, 113, 114, 291, 298, 308, 313
    console password, 316–318
    debug version, 318, 323
    functional simulator, 291, 316
        command-line options, 320, 321
        epc repository, 319
        go.bat directory, 319, 320
        provisioning, 319
        simulated display, 318, 319, 321
    hardware, 321, 322
    provisioning, 314–316, 337, 604, 605
Arduino, 227
    Arduino framework, 9, 217, 236, 249, 256, 261, 548, 574
Asynchronous test, 605–607

B

BA, 21, 22, 30, 455, 456, 470, 535
Blower Assembly (BA). *See* BA
Board Support Package (BSP). *See* BSP
Bootloader, 55, 222–223, 486, 556
BSP, 36, 37, 45, 228, 391, 475, 487, 536, 548, 556
    board schematic, encapsulate, 216
    bootloader, 55, 222–223, 486, 556
    C/C++ runtime code, 107, 214, 221
    compiler toolchain, 214
    creation, 220
    microcontroller hardware, 213
Build-all scripts
    characteristics, 124
    CI server, 125, 135
    directories, 125, 126
    GM6000, 125
    Linux build_all script, 133–134
    naming convention, 126, 127
    Windows build_all script, 129–132

INDEX

Build directory, 116, 119, 296, 300, 427, 504
BuildValues class, 424, 425
build variant, 423, 424
Button test, 606
bye command, 336

C

Cadifra, 310
Candidate release, 272, 273, 278, 508, 666
CCB, 273, 283, 508
C/C++ embedded coding standard
   array indices, 633
   coding practices, 622
   coding style, 622
   const modifier, 626
   deviation, 623
   document name/number, 621
   document references, 624
   epc repository, 621
   global namespace, avoid, 632
   no goto statement, 627
   headers files, 632
   integer types, 632
   language, 625
   no compiler warnings, 627
   no dynamic memory allocation, 625
   no explicit constants, 627
   nonportable constructs, avoid, 633
   no recursion, 626
   no type casting, 627
   NULL, 628
   pass/return objects, reference, 631
   pointer check, 634
   preprocessor, 628
   read-once latch, 631
   rule of five, 629–631
   virtual destructor, 628
C/C++ runtime code, 107, 214, 221
Change Control Board (CCB). *See* CCB
chunk.py script, 126
CI, 77, 78, 82–84, 87, 123, 508, 552
CI build scripts, 89, 135
CLI, 49, 487, 559
Code coverage metrics, 304–307
Coding style
   basic requirements, 634
   change log, 643
   comments, 635, 636
   formatting, 642, 643
   naming, 640–642
   rules, 634
Command-line interface (CLI). *See* CLI
Common vulnerabilities and exposures (CVEs). *See* CVEs
Confluence, 77, 87, 509
Console commands
   heating modes and setpoint, 324, 326, 327
   help commands, 323, 324, 341

INDEX

indoor temperature, 327–329
model points, 329
PWM outputs, 330
text file, 324
ui command, 331, 332
Continuous integration
(CI). *See* CI
CPL C++ framework, 363
colony.core, 363, 365
Cpl:Driver, 392
decoupling, 394
Doxygen, 66, 167, 304, 364, 509, 515, 525, 635
interfaces, 393, 395
assert, 396
Cpl, 396–397, 408–410
namespaces, 364
organization, 364
patterns, 364
porting, 393
runtime initialization, 395
src/Bsp directory, 391, 392
threads, , 405, 407
creation, 407
native thread *vs.* Cpl thread, 408
priorities, 407
CPL C++ persistent storage framework, 587–588
createThread() method, 406, 407
CVEs, 268, 274
Cycling test, 607
Cybersecurity, 48, 49, 70, 500, 501, 523

D

Database tools, 450
Data model architecture
advantages, 350, 351
coupled design, 349
decoupled design, 349, 350
features, 352
resources, 352
Data storage, 477, 479
Decoupling, 264, 353, 394
Defuzzification, 617–618
Denial-of-service (DOS). *See* DOS
Designed for testability (DFT). *See* DFT
Design statement, 139, 140, 142, 144, 149, 611
Development environment, 270, 286
DFT, 505
DHC, 6, 450, 451, 454, 459, 464, 467, 468, 474, 475, 509, 534, 536, 547, 548, 611, 612, 646, 660, 665, 666
Digital Heater Controller (DHC). *See* DHC
Display and User Inputs (DUI). *See* DUI
dm console command, 327
DOS, 49
Doxygen, 66, 167, 304, 364, 509, 515, 525, 635
Drivers
binding times, 226, 227
business logic, 225

673

INDEX

Drivers (*cont.*)
    Hardware Abstraction Layer, 231
    public interface, 227–229
DUI, 455, 469, 478

E

EEPROM, 156, 157, 169, 172, 174, 191, 340, 392, 589, 592
eeprom.bin file, 316, 319, 338
EEPROM test, 347, 607, 608
Encoding, 387
epc repository, 142, 285, 286, 288, 291, 297, 298, 308, 312, 319, 322, 339, 411, 412, 436, 438
Eros application, 336
    console commands, 348
    creation/startup, 603
    eeprom.bin file, 338
    functional simulator, 339, 340
    hardware, 340
    provisioning, 314, 337, 338, 604, 605
    screen test, 341
    tests, 605–606
Event flags, 378, 379
Event loops, 378, 379

F

Failure Mode and Effects Analysis (FMEA). *See* FMEA
finalize() method, 422

File organization
    file names, 638
    header/source files, 638
    #include statements, 52, 223, 228, 233, 256, 257, 356, 357, 359, 360, 504, 632, 639
    namespace directories, 636, 637
    non-namespace directories, 637
    README.txt file, 637
    single module/class, 638
FLC, 176, 583, 584
FMEA, 137, 138
Formal build, 83, 207, 270–272, 509
Forward traceability, 54
Foundation
    build system/scripts, 92–94
    CI build all script, 94
    performing tasks, 89
    SCM tool, 90
    skeleton projects, 94
    source code organization, 90
Framing, 387
Functional simulator, 45–47, 51, 93, 94, 97, 101, 102, 109, 120, 145, 167, 172, 208, 291, 318–321, 339, 498, 499, 592, 602
Fuzzification, 141, 613–614
Fuzzy logic controller (FLC). *See* FLC
Fuzzy logic temperature control
    block diagram, 611, 612
    change log, 618
    defuzzification, 617–618
    fuzzification, 141, 613–614
    fuzzy inference, 614–616

INDEX

G

GCC compiler, 116, 133, 297, 299, 300, 304, 305, 524
genfsm.py script, 311
GitHub, 509
    projects, 78–79
    Wiki, 79–82
GitHub repository, 110, 135, 286, 365, 537, 550
Git server, 77
GM6000 control board software, 36
GM6000 digital heater controller, 29, 64, 449, 467, 473, 507, 508, 545, 621, 645, 646, 665
GM6000 project, 205
    Ajax application, 291
    C/C++ embedded coding standard, 621
    fuzzy logic temperature control, 611
    Hardware Requirements Specifications, 464–466
    Marketing Requirements Specifications, 450–453
    NQBP2, 285
    Product Requirements Specifications, 454–458
    simulator, 285
    Software Requirements Specifications, 459–463
GM6000 SDD (final draft)
    alert management, 553
    application, 548, 554–556
    block diagram, 547, 548
    bootloader, 55, 222–223, 486, 556
    change log, 610
    console, 559–560
    cryptography, 488, 561–564
    data model, 41, 349–352, 367, 376, 488–491, 494–496, 564
    diagnostics, 566–568
    document name/number, 546
    document references, 549
    Eros application, 603
    functional simulator, 549, 550, 602
    graphics library, 38, 177, 196, 491, 494, 578, 597
    logging framework, 585–588
    operating system (OS), 588
    operating system abstraction layer, 1, 36, 38, 103–104, 120, 363, 370, 372, 377, 382, 393–395, 397, 398, 400, 401, 406, 407, 409, 492, 588, 593
    requirements tracing, 546
    sensor communications, 593
    software update, 593
    source code, 550–552
    system services, 593
    unit testing, 552, 553
GM6000 SDD (initial draft)
    change log, 544
    creation/startup, 541, 543, 555, 556
    document name/number, 534
    document references, 536

INDEX

GM6000 SDD (initial draft) (*cont.*)
    drivers, 552
    functional simulator, 537, 543
    requirements, 534
    scope, 534
    source code, 537, 539
    subsystems, 537, 540, 546
    unit testing, 539
GM6000 system architecture, 26, 27
    block diagram, 468, 469
    change log, 471
    components, 469–471
    Digital Heater Controller, 6, 450, 451, 454, 459, 464, 467, 468, 474, 475, 509, 534, 536, 547, 548, 611, 612, 646, 660, 665, 666
    document name/number, 467
    document references, 468
    epc repository, 467
go.bat directory, 319, 340
Graphics Library, 38, 177, 196, 491, 494, 578, 597

H

HAL, 103, 225, 490
    facade driver, 231, 232
    polymorphism, 256–262
    PWM driver, 233–237
    separation of concerns approach
        button driver, 241–245, 247–249, 251–254
        interface, 238

LHeader pattern, 181, 218, 219, 226, 228–230, 233, 239–241, 243, 245–250, 252–255, 259, 261, 353–356, 359, 360, 362, 387, 394, 396, 398, 401–403, 571, 575, 597, 598
    unit testing, 255
Hardware Abstraction Layer (HAL). *See* HAL
Hardware safety limit input test, 608
HE, 22, 30, 138, 139, 330, 456, 470, 474, 500
Heating element (HE). *See* HE
Heating subsystem
    fuzzy logic controller, 176, 583, 584
    house simulation, 585
    IO component, 583
    model points, 581, 582
    supervisor, 579, 580

I

init method, 422
Integration testing
    GM6000 project, 205, 209
    RF, 206, 207
    SDLC process, 204
    smoke tests, 208, 210
    test reports, 211
Intellectual property (IP). *See* IP
Inter-process communication (IPC). *See* IPC

INDEX

Interrupt service routine (ISR). *See* ISR
Inter-thread communication (ITC). *See* ITC
IP, 48, 49, 500, 501
IPC, 20, 48, 50
ISR, 43, 44, 106, 496, 497
ITC, 28, 38, 40, 44, 50, 370, 372, 379, 475, 491, 494, 496, 497, 536, 549, 593, 641, 642
   asynchronous ITC messaging, 44, 497
   synchronous ITC messaging, 44, 497

J, K

Jenkins, 77, 78, 84, 85, 129, 509, 525, 526
JIRA, 77, 161, 509, 525
Just-in-time detailed design
   button driver, 174
   coding, 184
   components, 166, 167
   design artifacts, 182–184
   design reviews, 182
   fuzzy logic controller, 175, 176, 583, 584
   Graphics Library, 177
   purpose, 165, 166
   screen manager, 178–181
   subsystems, 168–170, 172
   I2C driver, 173

L

LCD test, 341, 606, 608
LConfig, 119, 218, 226, 228, 353, 360–362, 364
LHeader, 181, 218, 219, 226, 228–230, 233, 239–241, 243, 245–250, 252–255, 259, 261, 353–356, 359, 360, 362, 387, 394, 396, 398, 401–403, 571, 575, 597, 598
Linux
   application development, 298–300
   build directories, 300
   compiler configuration, 298
   epc repository, 297, 298
   source code, 298
   tools, 297
Localization and internationalization, 52–53, 505
log command, 334, 335

M

Main pattern, 113
   Ajax/Eros, 113–116
   application, 106
   application dependencies, 102, 103
   application variant, 110, 111
   architectural pattern, 121
   build scripts, 115–117

INDEX

Main pattern (*cont.*)
    Hardware Abstraction Layer, 103, 104, 225, 490
    implementation, 106–110
    marketing abstraction layer, 112
    operating system abstraction layer, 1, 36, 38, 103–104, 120, 363, 370, 372, 377, 382, 393–395, 397, 398, 400, 401, 406, 407, 409, 492, 588, 593
    planning, 101
    preprocessor, 119
    simulator, 119, 120
    target application, 105
mapp command, 344, 345
Marketing Requirements Specification (MRS). *See* MRS
MCU, 33, 37, 38, 44, 156, 157, 214–216, 218, 219, 221–223, 227, 239, 322, 382, 392, 398, 475, 478–484, 487, 509, 536, 549, 557, 558, 563, 569, 573, 633
Micro applications, 344–346
Microcontroller unit (MCU). *See* MCU
MIL, 383
Model in the Loop (MIL). *See* MIL
MRS, 17, 19, 35, 68, 138, 142, 148, 454, 509, 517, 518, 647
Mutexes, 381, 401
mytoolchain.py script, 198, 415, 417, 423, 429, 431

N

NFR, 16, 145, 146, 646
Nonfunctional requirement (NFR). *See* NFR
Nonrecursive semantics, 380
NQBP2 system, 285, 411
    build scripts, 416–418
    builds directories, 414
    build variants, 416
    _BUILT_DIR_approach, 428
    command-line options, 432–435
    environment variables, 413
    features, 411, 412
    installation, 412
    libdirs.b file, 418–420
    linking, 427
    methods, 422
    mytoolchain.py, 198, 415, 417, 423, 429, 431
    object files, 428
    object files *vs.* libraries, 414, 415
    preprocessing scripts, 428–432
    scripts, 435, 436
    specification, toolchain, 426, 427
    toolchains, 421
    usage, 413, 414

O

Operating system abstraction layer (OSAL). *See* OSAL
Orphan subsystems, 55

OSAL, 1, 36, 38, 103–104, 120, 363, 370, 372, 377, 382, 393–395, 397, 398, 400, 401, 406, 407, 409, 492, 588, 593
Outcast, 286, 312, 363, 538, 550

P

Patterns in the machine (PIM). *See* PIM
Periodic scheduler, 381
Persistent storage subsystem
    frequency of updates, 589
    memory map, 592
    RAM-cached model, 588
    records, 589, 591
Personally identifiable information (PII). *See* PII
PID, 140, 612
PII, 48, 475, 500
PIM, 34, 356
Pimoroni graphics library, 177, 578, 598
POST, 490, 566–567
Power-on self-tests (POST). *See* POST
Preemptive scheduling, 43
Process model, 43
Product Requirements Specifications (PRS). *See* PRS
Product Lifecycle Management (PLM) tool, 67, 277, 509
Programming languages, 9, 28, 34, 484, 636

Proportional-integral-derivative (PID). *See* PID
prov console command, 314, 323
Provisioning, 314, 337, 604, 605
PRS, 17, 19, 35, 55, 68, 138, 148, 149, 509, 517, 518, 649
Pull requests (PRs), 189, 510
Pulse Width Modulation (PWM). *See* PWM
PuTTY, 303
PWM, 32, 227, 465, 470, 478
Python 3.8.5, 287, 297

Q

QMS, 145, 204, 280, 510
Quality Management System (QMS). *See* QMS

R

RATT library, 209, 437
    caveats, 444
    features, 437
    installation, 438
    modules, 447, 448
    output methods, 446
    ratty.py script, 440
    script locations, 441
    set up and run, 308, 309
    smoke test, 308
    test case, 442–443, 446
    test files, 455
    test scripts, 439

INDEX

RATT library (cont.)
    test suite, 441, 442, 446
    user interactions, 308
README.txt file, 637
Real-Time Operating System (RTOS). See RTOS
Release stage
    anomalies list, 284
    archived artifacts, 284
    archived documentation, 284
    archived software, 284
    archived source code, 284
    release notes, 283
    Software Bill of Materials, 283
Requirements
    analysis, 138
    collection challenges, 18
    formal, 14, 15
    functional *vs.* nonfunctional, 16
    fuzzification, 141, 142, 144
    GM6000, 19, 20
    missing formal requirement, 144, 145
    problem statement, 22
    product, 13
    requirement tracing, 146–150
    risk control measurement, 138
    sources, 16, 17, 137
    statements, 13
Requirement traceability, 54–56
RGB LED, 609
RTOS, 34, 38, 177, 380, 393, 397, 405, 407, 484, 496, 578

S

SBOM, 268, 274–275, 283, 517
SCM, 60, 63, 71, 72, 82, 83, 510, 526, 527
SCM repository strategy, 61
scripts/preprocess_base.py, 430–431
SDD, 89, 95, 147, 162, 183, 223, 266
    check-in strategies, 189
    coding, 188
    granularity, 191
    I2C driver, 191–193, 195
    pull requests, 189, 190, 200
    screen manager, 196, 197, 200
    unit tests, 200
SDD drivers
    button, 570
    GPIO in driver, 571
    GPIO out driver, 571
    LCD controller, 573
    onboard analog, 569, 570
    PicoDisplay, 573, 574
    PWM, 575
    RGB LED, 575, 576
    SPI, 576
    TPipe, 576, 577
SDLC, 145, 513, 519, 520, 522, 523
    activities, 6
    advantages, 8
    counterarguments, 5
    development stages, 5
    outputs/artifacts, 7
    regulated industries, 10

INDEX

SDP, 86, 223, 266
   additional guidelines, 62
   change log, 531
   cybersecurity, 48, 49, 70, 500, 501, 523
   deliverables, 74, 529, 530
   development processes and standards, 60
   documentation outputs, 66, 67, 515–517
   document name/number, 508
   document references, 511
   epc repository, 507
   GM6000's SDP, 63
   housekeeping, 64
   project-specific processes/standards, 61
   requirements, 68, 517–519
   requirements documents, 59
   roles/responsibilities, 64, 511–513
   software development phases, 69
   software items, 65, 514
   testing, 73, 74, 527–529
   tools, 71, 524, 525
Segger J-Link tools, 302
Segger Ozone debugger, 303
Segger SystemView, 303
Semaphore, 379, 381, 402
Simulated display, 318, 319, 339, 340
Simulated time, 382–383
SinelaboreRT, 311
Smoke/sanity tests, 208
Software architecture (SWA). *See* SWA
Software Bill of Materials (SBOM). *See* SBOM
Software Configuration Management (SCM). *See* SCM
Software Detailed Design (SDD). *See* SDD
Software Detailed Design document (SWD). *See* SWD
Software development life cycle (SDLC). *See* SDLC
Software Development Plan (SDP). *See* SDP
Software development processes, 2–4
Software release notes
   change log, 669
   document name/number, 665
   document references, 666
   epc repository, 665
   RC1, 668, 669
   RC2, 667
Software Requirements Specifications (SRS). *See* SRS
Software requirements trace matrix
   change log, 657
   document name/number, 646
   document references, 647
   epc repository, 646
   Marketing Requirements Specifications, 647, 648
   Product Requirements Specifications, 647, 648
   requirements, 649–653

INDEX

Software requirements trace
　matrix (*cont.*)
　requirements management
　　tool, 645
　Software Detailed Design,
　　654, 655
　Software architecture, 648,
　　655, 656
Software tasks
　code review, 156
　detailed design, 155
　elements, 153, 154
　granularity, 158
　requirements, 154
　source code/unit test, 155
　tickets/agile, 160, 161
　types, 159
Software timers, 379, 383–384
src/Cpl
　Checksum namespace, 366
　Cpl::Container
　　namespace, 366
　Cpl::Io, 369
　Cpl::Itc, 370, 371
　Cpl::Json, 372
　Cpl::Logging, 373, 374
　Cpl::MApp, 375
　Cpl::Math, 375
　Cpl::Memory, 375
　Cpl::Persistent, 376
　Cpl::System, 377–385
　Cpl::Text, 386–391
　data model, 367–368
　directory structure, 365

SRS, 17, 55, 68, 138, 142, 148, 149,
　449, 510, 518, 647–648
State machine tools, 310–312
ST HAL library, 235, 259
STM32 Cube IDE, 301
STM32 Cube MX, 301
STM32 setDutyCycle()
　method, 235–237
ST NUCLEO, 217, 285, 288, 322,
　392, 556, 557
Subsystems, SWA
　alert management, 485, 486
　application, 486
　Board Support Package, 36, 37,
　　45, 228, 391, 475, 487, 536,
　　548, 556
　bootloader, 55, 222–223, 486, 556
　console, 487
　crypto, 488
　cybersecurity, 48, 49, 70, 500,
　　501, 523
　data integrity, 496–498
　data model, 488–490
　diagnostics, 490
　drivers, 490
　engineering testing, 505, 506
　file/directory organization,
　　503, 504
　functional simulator, 498–500
　graphics library, 491
　interdependencies, 41
　interfaces, 494, 495
　internationalization, 505
　localization, 505

logging, 491, 492
manufacturing testing, 505, 506
memory allocation, 502
message passing, 502, 503
operating system (OS), 492
OSAL, 492
persistent storage, 492, 493
process model, 495, 496
sensor communications, 493
software update, 493, 494
system services, 494
thread priorities, 496
UI, 494
unit testing, 505
SWA
 cybersecurity, 48, 49
 definition, 28
 design decision, 28
 file/directory
  organization, 51-52
 functional simulator, 45-48
 hardware interfaces, 29, 31, 32
 memory allocation, 49-50
 performance
  assessments, 32, 33
 process model, 42-45
 programming language, 34
 subsystems, 37-40
SWA document, 25, 162, 223,
  266, 510
 block diagram, 474, 475
 change log, 506
 components, 477, 478
 document name/number, 473
 document references, 476
 epc repository, 473
 hardware interfaces, 476, 477
 performance
  constraints, 479-483
 programming languages, 484
 requirements tracing, 474
System architecture (SA), 25-27,
  266, 467, 469, 475, 535,
  548, 612

T

TDD, 155, 188
Temperature monitor test, 609
Temperature Sensor (TS). *See* TS
Terminal emulator, 303
 PuTTY, 303
 Tera term, 304
Test-Driven Development
  (TDD). *See* TDD
Thread interface, 406
Thread-local storage (TLS). *See* TLS
Threads command, 332, 333
Ticket, 160, 510
TLS, 384, 394, 408-409
Tokenizers, 389
Toolchain class, 422
trace command, 333, 334
Traceability, 518
TS, 33, 321, 328, 340, 455, 456, 470,
  474, 478
TShell, 368, 375, 386, 389, 390, 559,
  560, 602, 604, 605, 607-609

INDEX

U

UART, 11, 32, 214–216, 221, 263, 271, 369, 475, 478, 482, 536, 549, 559
UI, 39, 494
   events, 594, 597, 598
   screen manager, 595–597
   screens
      about screen, 599
      dynamic data, 599
      edit screen, 599
      error screen, 600
      hard-coded model, 598
      home screen, 600, 601
      navigation, 594
      Pimoroni graphics library, 598
      shut-down screen, 601
      splash screen, 601
      state machine diagram, 595, 596
      types, 594, 595
   status indicator, 601, 602
Units Under Test (UUTs). *See* UUTs
Unit testing, 73, 97, 160, 187, 198, 255, 505, 539
Universal asynchronous receiver-transmitter (UART). *See* UART
User interface (UI). *See* UI
UUTs, 437–439, 444, 448

V

validate_cc() method, 422
Validation, 510
Verification, 510, 522
Visual Studio compiler, 129, 287, 291, 292, 355, 356, 428, 431

W, X, Y, Z

Waterfall, 5, 17, 29, 62, 70, 75, 162, 165, 520
Windows
   application builds, 290
   build directories, 296
   compiler
      configuration, 288–290
   functional simulator, 291–293
   hardware
      targets, 293, 294, 296
   source code, 288
   tools, 287, 288
Windows build_all
   script, 129–132
Wireless module (WM). *See* WM
Wireless Remote Temperature Sensor (WTS). *See* WTS
Wireless sensor (WS). *See* WS
WM, 22, 452, 455, 471, 478, 483
WS, 20, 205, 478, 501
WTS, 205, 471

GPSR Compliance
The European Union's (EU) General Product Safety Regulation (GPSR) is a set of rules that requires consumer products to be safe and our obligations to ensure this.

If you have any concerns about our products, you can contact us on

ProductSafety@springernature.com

In case Publisher is established outside the EU, the EU authorized representative is:

Springer Nature Customer Service Center GmbH
Europaplatz 3
69115 Heidelberg, Germany